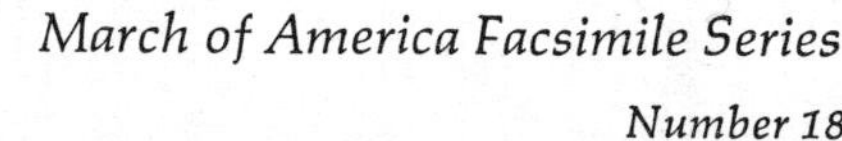

March of America Facsimile Series

Number 18

The Generall Historie of Virginia

John Smith

The Generall Historie of Virginia, New-England, and the Summer Isles

by John Smith

ANN ARBOR

UNIVERSITY MICROFILMS, INC.

A Subsidiary of Xerox Corporation

LIBRARY OF CONGRESS CATALOG CARD NO. 66-26303

MANUFACTURED IN THE UNITED STATES OF AMERICA

Foreword

The Generall Historie of Virginia, New England & The Summer Isles . . . By Captaine John Smith, Sometymes Governour in those Countryes and Admirall of New England, printed in London in 1624 is the first publication to claim specifically to be a history of English territory in the New World. Smith planned the work to serve as propaganda for the colonial enterprise—and as an apology and defense of his own activities in Virginia.

While the book was in preparation the Virginia Company of London, which had jurisdiction over the colony at Jamestown, became virtually bankrupt and in 1624 King James declared Virginia a royal colony. At this juncture Smith's book was rushed through the press in order that it might take advantage of the renewed interest in Virginia and might also help to advertise the potential assets of the royal colony. Smith himself took pains to emphasize the value of his book as propaganda. A copy of *The Generall Historie,* preserved in the Huntington Library, has a letter, written in Smith's own hand, presenting the volume to the Society of Cordwainers. In it Smith reminds this organization of shoe manufacturers that the shores of the New World are rough and the oyster shells on the beaches are certain to cut up many shoes. It behooves the Cordwainers to encourage colonies where, in time to come, many thousands of shoes will be required.

Smith's *Generall Historie* is a compilation, a sort of anthology, of writings about Virginia, New England, and Bermuda. With scissors and paste, Smith put together his account, usually without giving the original writers credit for their work, a literary practice common in this period. But here and there Smith inserted his own comments, criticisms, and explanations, particularly in the portions dealing with his career in Virginia. The work was equipped with six engravngs, including a title page and three maps, a portrait of Pocahontas, and a portrait of Frances, Duchess of Richmond and Lennox, who had provided money to see the work through the press. Vignettes around the maps, adapted from DeBry's engravings, add scenes showing Captain John Smith's deeds of daring. Modern scholarship has demonstrated that Smith's work, once condemned as a piece of vanity on the compiler's part, contains much valuable information on the early history of the English colonial efforts. A useful account of the work is contained in *The Three Worlds of Captain John Smith* by Philip L. Barbour (Boston, 1964), pp. 350-369.

The Generall Historie of Virginia

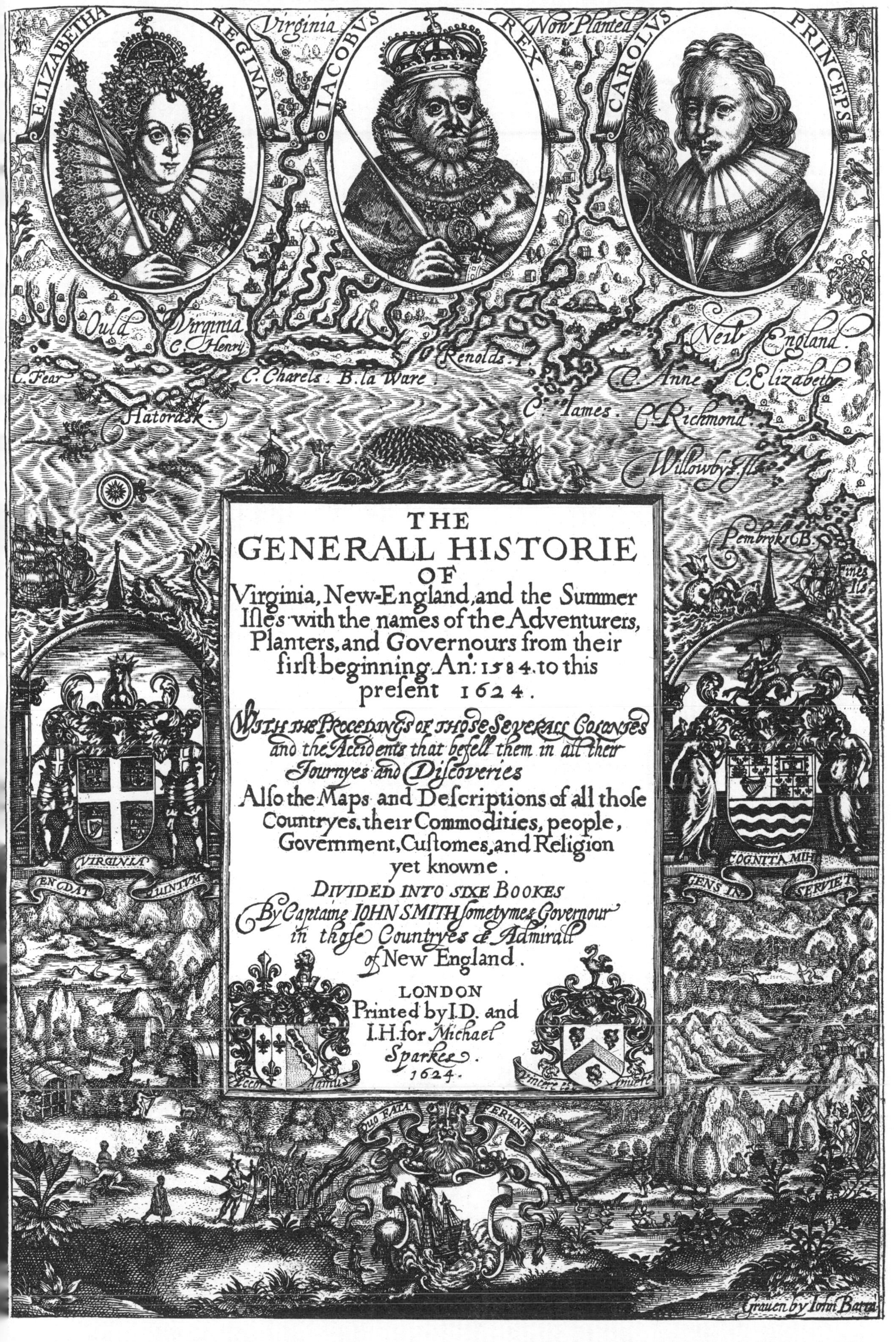

THE GENERALL HISTORIE OF Virginia, New-England, and the Summer Isles with the names of the Adventurers, Planters, and Governours from their first beginning An: 1584. to this present 1624.

WITH THE PROCEDINGS OF THOSE SEVERALL COLONIES and the Accidents that befell them in all their Journyes and Discoveries

Also the Maps and Descriptions of all those Countryes, their Commodities, people, Government, Customes, and Religion yet knowne.

DIVIDED INTO SIXE BOOKES

By Captaine IOHN SMITH *sometymes Governour in those Countryes & Admirall of* New England.

LONDON
Printed by I.D. and I.H. for *Michael Sparkes*.
1624.

The portraiture of the illustreous **Princeße Frances Duchess** *of* **Richmond** *and* **Lenox** *daugter of* **Thomas Lo. Howard** *of* **Bindon** *sonne of* **Thomas Duke** *of* **Norfok.** *Whose mother was* **Elisabeth** *daughter of* **Edward Duke** *of* **Buckingham.**

Anno 1623 insculptum a Guilh: Passeo Londinum.

TO THE ILLVSTRIOVS AND MOST NOBLE PRINCESSE, the Lady FRANCIS, Duchesse of RICHMOND and LENOX.

Ay it please your Grace,

This History, as for the raritie and varietie of the subiect, so much more for the iudicious *Eyes* it is like to vndergoe, and most of all for that great *Name*, whereof it dareth implore Protection, might and ought to haue beene clad in better robes then my rude military hand can cut out in Paper Ornaments. But because, of the most things therein, I am no Compiler by hearsay; but haue beene a reall Actor; I take my selfe to haue a propertie in them: and therefore haue beene bold to challenge them to come vnder the reach of my owne rough Pen. That, which hath beene indured and passed through with hardship and danger, is thereby sweetned to the *Actor*, when he becometh the *Relator*. I haue deeply hazarded my selfe in doing and suffering, and why should I sticke to hazard my reputation in Recording? He that acteth two parts is the more borne withall if he come short, or fayle in one of them. Where shall we looke to finde a *Iulius Cæsar*, whose atchieuments shine as cleare in his owne Commentaries, as they did in the field? I confesse, my hand, though able to weild a weapon among the Barbarous, yet well may tremble

ble in handling a Pen among ſo many *Iudicious* : eſpecially when I am ſo bold as to call ſo piercing, and ſo glorious an *Eye*, as your *Grace*, to view theſe poore ragged lines.

Yet my comfort is, that heretofore honorable and vertuous *Ladies*, and comparable but amongſt themſelues, haue offred me reſcue and protection in my greateſt dangers: even in forraine parts, I haue felt reliefe from that ſex. The beauteous Lady *Tragabigzanda*, when I was a ſlaue to the *Turkes*, did all ſhe could to ſecure me. When I overcame the *Baſhaw* of *Nalbrits* in *Tartaria*, the charitable Lady *Callamata* ſupplyed my neceſſities. In the vtmoſt of many extremities, that bleſſed *Pokahontas*, the great Kings daughter of *Virginia*, oft ſaved my life. When I eſcaped the crueltie of Pirats and moſt furious ſtormes, a long time alone in a ſmall Boat at Sea, and driven aſhore in *France*, the good Lady *Madam Chanoyes*, bountifully aſſiſted me.

And ſo verily theſe my adventures haue taſted the ſame *influence* from your *Gratious hand*, which hath given birth to the publication of this *Narration*. If therefore your *Grace* ſhall daigne to caſt your eye on this poore Booke, view I pray you rather your owne *Bountie* (without which it had dyed in the wombe) then my *imperfections*, which haue no helpe but the ſhrine of your *glorious Name* to be ſheltered from cenſorious condemnation. Vouchſafe ſome glimpſe of your honorable *aſpect*, to accept theſe my labours; to protect them vnder the ſhadow of your excellent *Name*: which will inable them to be preſented to the *Kings royall Maieſtie*, the moſt admired Prince *Charles*, and the *Queene of Bohemia*: your ſweet Recommendations will make it the worthier of their good countenances. And as all my endevours are their due tribute: ſo this Page ſhall record to poſteritie, that my ſervice ſhall be to pray to *God*, that you may ſtill continue the renowned of your ſexe, the moſt honored of men, and the highly bleſſed of *God*.

Your Graces *faithfull*

and devoted ſervant,

IOHN SMITH.

To my worthy friend Captaine *Iohn Smith.*

HOw great a part of knowledge had wee lost,
Both of Virginia and the Summer Isles,
Had not thy carefull diligence and cost
Inform'd vs thus, with thy industrious stile!
Like Cæsar now thou writ'st what thou hast done,
These acts, this Booke will liue while ther's a Sunne.

Edw: Worseley.

To his much respected Friend Captaine *Iohn Smith.*

ENvie avant. For Smith, whose Anvill was Experience,
Could take his heat, knew how and when to Strike,
Wrought well this Peece; till After-negligence
Mistaking temper, Cold, or Scorch'd; or like
Vnskilfull workmen, that can never Fyle
Nor Pollish it, that takes in Forge such toyle:
Heere Noble Smith, thou shewest the Temper true,
Which other Tampring-Tempres never knew.

Ro: Norton.

To his loving friend Captaine *Iohn Smith.*

WHere actions speake the praises of a man,
There, Pennes that vse to flatter silent be,
Or if they speake, it is to scorne or scanne;
For such with vertue seldome doe agree.

When I looke backe on all thy labours past,
Thy travels, perils, losses oft sustaind
By Sea and Land; and (which is worst and last)
Neglect or small reward, so dearely gaind.

I doe admire thy still vndanted spirit;
vnwearied yet to worke thy Countries good.
This be thy praise then, due vnto thy merit;
For it th' hast venter'd life; and lost thy blood.

1. 2. 3. 1. 2. 3.
Truth, travayle, and Neglect, pure, painefull, most vnkinde,
1. 2. 3. 1. 2. 3.
Doth proue, consume, dismay, the soule, the corps, the minde.

Edw: Ingham.

To my deare friend by true Vertue ennobled Captaine *Iohn Smith.*

MOre then enough I cannot thee commend:
Whose both abilities and Loue doe tend
So to advance the good of that Estate,
By English charge, and Planters propagate
Through heapes of painfull hazards; in the first
Of which, that Colony thy Care hath nurst.
And often that effected but with ten
That after thee, and now, three hundred men

Haue faild in, 'mong the Salvages; *who shake*
At bruit of Thee, as Spaine *at Name of* Drake.
Which well appeares; considering the while
Thou governedst, nor force of theirs, ne guile
Lessend a man of thine; but since (I rue)
In Brittish *blood they deeply did imbrue*
Their Heathen hands. And (truth to say) we see,
Our selues wee lost, vntimely leaving Thee.
Nor yet perceiue I any got betweene
Thee and thy merit; which hath better beene
In prayse; or profit much; if counted iust;
Free from the Weales abuse, or wronged trust.
Some few particulars *perhaps haue sped;*
But wherein hath the publicke *prospered?*
Or is there more of those Vast Countries knowne,
Then by thy Labours and Relations showne
First, best? And shall wee loue Thee now the lesse?
Farre be it! fit condignely to expresse
Thankes, by new Charge, or recompence; by whom,
Such past good hath, such future good may come.

David Wiffin.

Noble Captaine *Smith*, my worthy Friend

NOt like the Age wherein thou liu'st, to lie
Buried in basenesse, sloth, or Ribaldrie
(For most doe thus) hast thou thy selfe applide;
But, in faire Actions, Merits height descride:
Which (like foure Theaters to set thee forth)
The worlds foure Quarters testifie thy worth.
The last whereof (America *) best showes*
Thy paines, and prayse; and what to thee shee owes,
(Although thy Sommer shone on th' Elder Three,
In as great Deeds as great varietie)
For opening to Her Selfe Her Selfe, in Two *
Of Her *large Members; Now* Ours, *to our view.*
Thereby endearing vs to thy desart,
That doubly dost them to our hands impart;
There *by thy* Worke, Heere *by thy* Workes; *By each*
Maist thou Fames lasting Wreath (for guerdon) reach.
And so become, in after Times t' ensue,
A President for others, So *to doe.*

William Grent.

* *Virginia* now inhabited, and *New-England.*

To his worthily affected Friend, Captaine *Iohn Smith.*

AMongst so many that by learned skill,
Haue given iust prayse to thee, and to thy Booke,
Deare friend receiue this pledge of my good will,
Whereon, if thou with acceptation looke,
And thinke it worthie, ranke amongst the rest:
Vse thy discretion, I haue done my best.

Ἀνώνυμος.

The

The Contents of the generall History, divided into six Books.

The first Booke.

The second Booke.

Of *Virginia* now planted, discovered by Captaine SMITH.

The third Booke.

Of the Accidents and Proceedings of the *English.*

The fourth Booke.

With their Proceedings after the alteration of the Government.

The fift Booke.

The sixt Booke.

Its not his part that is the best Translator,
To render word for word to every Author.

Samuel Purchas of his friend Captaine *Iohn Smith*, and his *Virginia*.

LOe here SMITHS *Forge, where Forgery's Roague-branded,*
True Pegasus *is shoo'd, fetters are forged.*
For Silke-sotts, Milk-sops, base Sloth, farre hence landed;
*(Soile-chang'd,*Soule-soil'd still)* Englands *dregs, discharged,*
To plant (supplant!) Virginia, *home-disgorged:*
Where vertues praise frames good men Stories armour
'Gainst Time, Achilles-*like, with best Arts charged;*
Pallas, *all-arm'd, all-learn'd, can teach Sword-Grammer,*
Can Pens of Pikes; Armes t' Arts; to Scholar, Souldier, hammer:

Can Pilgrim *make a* Maker; *all so well*
Hath taught Smith *scoure my rustie out-worne* Muse,
And so coniur'd her in Virginian *Cell,*
That things vnlearned long by want of vse,
Shee fresh areeds me read, without abuse
By fabling. Arthurs *great Acts little made*
By greater lies she saith; seales Faith excuse
[a]*T'* Island, Groonland, Estotiland *to wade*
After lie-legends; Malgo, Brandon, *are wares braide.*

The Fryer of Linne [b] *frights her with his black Art;*
Nor Brittish Bards *can tell where* Madoc [c] *planted.*
Cabots, Thorns, Elyots *truth haue wonne her heart,*
Eldest discov'rers of New Worlds Cont'nent (granted
So had iust Fates.) Colon *and* Vespuce *panted;*
This got the name [d]*, last, least of Three; the Other*
New Worlds Isles found first: Cabot *is most chanted*
In Three-Mens-song; did more New World discover
Then both, then any; an hundred degrees coasted over.

Haile S[ir] Sebastian, Englands *Northern Pole,*
Virginia's *finder; Virgin* Eliza *nam'd it,*
Gaue't Raleigh. (Rut, Prat, Hore, *I not enrole)*
Amadas *rites to* English *right first fram'd it.*
Lane *planted, return'd, nor had* English *tam'd it:*
Greenviles *and* Whites *men all slaine; New Plantation*
IAMES *founds, Sloth confounds, feare, pride, faction sham'd it:*
Smiths *Forge mends all, makes chaines for* Savage *Nation,*
Frees, feeds the rest; the rest reade in his Bookes Relation.

* *Cælum non animum mutant*

[a] These are said a thousãd yeares agoe to haue beene in the North parts of *America*.

[b] He is said to discover the Pole 1360.

[c] *Madoc ap Owen* Planted some remote Westernparts. 1170.

[d] *America* named of *Americus Vesputius*, which discovered les then *Colon* or S[ir] *Sebastian Cabot*, and the Continent later. *Colõ* first found the Isles 1492. the Continent 1498. Aboue a yeare after *Cabot* had don it. He was set forth by *Henry* 7 and after by *Hen*. 8. Knighted, and made grand Pilot of *Englãd* by *Ed*. 6 Vnder whõ he procured the sending of S[ir] *Hugh Willoughby*, & discovery of *Greenland* and *Russia*: having by himself discovered on *America* frõ 67 North lat. to neere 40 South.

A Thomas

Thomas Macarnesse to his worthy friend and Countryman, Captaine *Iohn Smith.*

VVHo loues *to* liue *at home, yet* looke *abroad,*
And know *both* passen *and* vnpassen *road,*
The prime Plantation of an vnknowne shore,
The men, *the* manners, fruitfulnesse, *and* store:
Read but this little Booke, and then confesse,
The lesse *thou* lik'st *and* lou'st, *thou* liu'st *the* lesse.

He writ it with great labour, for thy good,
Twice over, now in paper, *'fore in* blood;
It cost him deare, both paines, without an ayme
Of private *profit, for thy* publicke *gaine.*
That thou mightst read *and* know *and safely* see,
What he by practice, *thou by* Theoree.

Commend *him for his loyall loving heart,*
Or else come mend *him, and take thou his part.*

To his friend Captaine *Iohn Smith*, and his Worke.

IKnow not how Desert more great can rise,
Then out of Danger t'ane for good mens Good;
*Nor who doth better winne th'*Olympian *prize,*
Than he whose Countryes Honor stirres his bloud;
Private respects haue private expectation,
Publicke designes, should publish reputation.

This Gentleman whose Volumne heere is stoard
With strange discoverie of GODS strangest Creatures,
Giues vs full view, how he hath Sayl'd, and Oar'd,
And Marcht, full many myles, whose rough defeatures,
Hath beene as bold, as puissant, vp to binde
Their barbarous strength's, to follow him dog-linde.

But wit, nor valour, now adayes payes scores
For estimation; all goes now by wealth,
Or friends; tush! thrust the beggar out of dores
That is not Purse-lyn'd; those which liue by stealth
Shall haue their haunts; no matter what's the guest
In many places; monies well come best.

But those who well discerne, esteeme not so:
Nor I of thee braue Smith, *that hast beat out*
Thy Iron thus; though I but little know
To what t'hast seene; yet I in this am stout:
My thoughts, maps to my minde some accidents,
That makes mee see thy greater presidents.

Io: Done.

¶ A Preface of foure Poynts.

I. THis plaine History humbly sheweth the truth; that our most royall King Iames hath place and opportunitie to inlarge his ancient Dominions without wronging any; (which is a condition most agreeable to his most iust & pious resolutions:) and the Prince his Highnes may see where to plant new Colonies. The gaining Prouinces addeth to the Kings Crown: but the reducing Heathen people to ciuilitie and true Religion, bringeth honour to the King of Heauen. If his Princely wisedome and powerfull hand, renowned through the world for admirable government, please but to set these new Estates into order; their composure will be singular: the counsell of divers is confused; the generall Stocke is consumed; nothing but the touch of the Kings sacred hand can erect a Monarchy.

II. Most noble Lords and worthy Gentlemen, it is your Honors that haue imployed great paines and large expence in laying the foundation of this State, wherein much hath beene buried vnder ground, yet some thing hath sprung vp, and giuen you a taste of your adventures. Let no difficulties alter your noble intentions. The action is an honour to your Country: and the issue may well reimburse you your summes expended. Our practices haue hitherto beene but assayes, and are still to be amended. Let your bountie supply the necessities of weake beginnings, and your excellent iudgements rectifie the proceedings; the returne cannot choose in the end but bring you good Commodities, and good contentments, by your aduancing shipping and fishing so vsefull vnto our Nation.

III. Yee valiant and generous spirits, personall possessors of these new-found Territories, banish from among you Cowardise, covetousnes, iealousies, and idlenes, enemies to the raising your honours and fortunes; vertue, industry, and amitie, will make you good and great, and your merits liue to ensuing Ages. You that in contempt of necessities, hazard your liues and estates, imploying your studies & labours in these faire endevours, liue and prosper as I desire my soule should prosper.

IIII. For my selfe let emulation and enuie cease, I ever intended my actions should be vpright: now my care hath beene that my Relations should giue every man they concerne, their due. But had I not discovered and liued in the most of those parts, I could not possibly haue collected the substantiall truth from such a number of variable Relations, that would haue made a Volume at least of a thousand sheets. Though the beginning may seeme harsh in regard of the Antiquities, breuitie, and names; a pleasanter Discourse ensues. The stile of a Souldier is not eloquent, but honest and iustifiable; so I desire all my friends and well-wishers to excuse and accept it, and if any be so noble as to respect it, he that brought New England to light, though long since brought in obscuritie, he is againe to be found a true servant to all good designes.

So I ever rest yours to command,

IOHN SMITH.

A Gentleman desirous to be vnknowne, yet a great Benefactor to *Virginia*, his loue to the Author, the Company, and History.

S*Tay, reade, behold, skill, courage, knowledge, Arts;*
Wonder of Nature: Mirror *of our Clime.*
Mars, Vulcan, Neptune *striue to haue their parts,*
Rare Ornaments, rich honours of our time.

From far fetcht Indies, *and* Virginia's *soyle,*
Here Smith *is come to shew his Art and skill:*
He was the Smith *that hammered famins foyle,*
And on Powhatan's *Emperour had his will.*

Though first Colũbus, Indies *true* Christofer;
Cabots, *braue* Florida, *much admirer;*
Meta Incognita, *rare* Martin Frobisher; *(rer;*
Gilberts *braue* Humphery, Neptunes *deuou-*

Captaine Amadis, Raleighs *discouerer;*
Sir Richard Grenvill, Zealands *braue coaster:*
Drake, *doomes, drowne, death,* Spaines *scorner;*
Gosnolds *Relates,* Pring *prime obseruer.*

Though these be gone, and left behinde a name,
Yet Smith *is here to Anvile out a peece*
To after Ages, and eternall Fame,
That we may haue the golden Iasons *fleece.*

He Vulcan-*like did forge a true Plantation,*
And chain'd their Kings, to his immortall glory;
Restoring peace and plentie to the Nation,
Regaining honour to this worthy Story.

By him the Infidels *had due correction,*
He blew the bellowes still of peace and plentie:
He made the Indians *bow vnto subiection,*
And Planters ne're return'd to Albion *empty.*

The Colonies pin'd, staru'd, staring, bones so feeble,
By his braue proiects, proued strong againe:
The Souldiers' lowance he did seeke to treble,
And made the Salvage *in vncouth place remaine.*

He left the Countrey in prosperous happie state,
And plenty stood with peace at each mans doore:
Regarding not the Salvage *loue nor hate:*
Themselues grew well, the Indiãs *wondrous poore.*

This there he did and now is home return'd,
To shew vs all that neuer thither goe:
That in his heart, he deepely oft hath mourn'd,
Because the Action goeth on so slow.

Braue, graue, Wise, Rich, prize Benefactors,
Replant, want, continue still good Actors.

Be kinde, and finde, bring eyes to blind;
By Gods great might, giue Indians *light.*

Spend money, Bloud, to doe that good,
That may giue Indians *heau'nly food.*

And God no lesse, you still shall blesse;
Both you and yours the Lands possesse.

S. M.

See here behold as in a Glasse,
All that is, or is and was.

T. T. 1624.

HOW ANCIENT AVTHORS REPORT, THE NEVV-VVORLD, Now called *America*, was discovered: and part thereof first Planted by the ENGLISH, called VIRGINIA, *with the Accidents and Proceedings of the same.*

The first Booke.

FOR the Stories of *Arthur*, *Malgo*, and *Brandon*, that say a thousand yeares agoe they were in the North of *America*; or the Fryer of *Linn* that by his blacke Art went to the North pole in the yeare 1360. in that I know them not. Let this suffice.

The Chronicles of *Wales* report, that *Madock*, sonne to *Owen Quineth*, Prince of *Wales* seeing his two brethren at debate who should inherit, prepared certaine Ships, with men and munition, and left his Country to seeke aduentures by Sea: leauing *Ireland* North he sayled west till he came to a Land vnknowne. Returning home and relating what pleasant and fruitfull Countries he had seene without Inhabitants, and for what barren ground his brethren and kindred did murther one another, he provided a number of Ships, and got with him such men and women as were desirous to liue in quietnesse, that arriued with him in this new Land in the yeare 1170: Left many of his people there and returned for more. But where this place was no History can show. 1170.

The *Spanyards* say *Hanno* a Prince of *Carthage* was the first: and the next *Christopher Cullumbus*, a Genoesian, whom they sent to discover those vnknowne parts. 1492. 1492.

But we finde by Records, *Cullumbus* offered his seruice in the yeare 1488. to King *Henry* the seauenth; and by accident vndertooke it for the *Spanyards*. In the Interim King *Henry* gaue a Commission to *Iohn Cabot*, and his three sonnes, *Sebastian*, *Lewis*, and *Santius*. *Iohn* and *Sebastian* well provided, setting sayle, ranged a great part of this vnknowne world, in the yeare 1497. For though *Cullumbus* had found certaine Iles, it was 1498. ere he saw the Continent, which was a yeare after *Cabot*. Now *Americus* came a long time after, though the whole Continent to this day is called *America* after his name, yet *Sebastian Cabot* discovered much more then them all, for he sayled to about forty degrees Southward of the lyne, and to sixty-seauen towards the North: for which King *Henry* the eight Knighted him and made him grand Pilate of *England*. Being very aged King *Edward* the sixt gaue him a Pention of 166^l.13^s.4^d. yearely. By his directions Sir *Hugh Willowby* was sent to finde out the Country of *Russia*, but the next yeare he was found frozen to death in his Ship, and all his Company. 1497.

Mr *Martin Frobisher* was sent in the yeare 1576. by our most gracious Queene *Elizabeth*, to search for the Northwest passage, and *Meta incognita*: for which he was Knighted, honored, and well rewarded. 1576.

Sir *Humphrey Gilbert* a worthy Knight attempted a Plantation in some of those parts: and obtained Letters Pattents to his desire: but with this *Proviso*, He should 1583.

maintaine possession in some of those vast Countries within the tearme of sixe yeares. Yet when he was provided with a Navy able to incounter a Kings power, even here at home they fell in diuisions, and so into confusion, that they gaue over the Designe ere it was begun, notwithstanding all this losse, his vndanted spirit began againe, but his Fleet fell with *New-found land*, and he perished in his returne, as at large you may read in the third Volume of the English Voyages, written by Mr *Hackluit*.

Vpon all those Relations and inducements, Sir *Walter Raleigh*, a noble Gentleman, and then in great esteeme, vndertooke to send to discover to the Southward. And though his occasions and other imployments were such he could not goe himselfe, yet he procured her Maiesties Letters Pattents, and perswaded many worthy Knights and Gentlemen to adventure with him to finde a place fit for a Plantation. Their Proceedings followeth.

1584. The most famous, renowned, and euer worthy of all memory, for her courage, learning, iudgement, and vertue, Queene *Elizabeth*, granted her Letters Patents to Sir *Walter Raleigh* for the discovering and planting new Lands & Countries, not actually possessed by any Christians. This Patenty got to be his assistants Sir *Richard Grenvell* the valiant, Mr *William Sanderson* a great friend to all such noble and worthy actions, and divers other Gentlemen and Marchants, who with all speede prouided two small Barkes well furnished with all necessaries, vnder the command of Captaine *Philip Amidas* and Captaine *Barlow*. The 27. of Aprill they set sayle from the Thames, the tenth of May passed the *Canaries*, and the tenth of Iune the West Indies: which vnneedfull Southerly course, (but then no better was knowne) occasioned them in that season much sicknesse.

Their arrivall.

The second of Iuly they fell with the coast of *Florida* in shoule water, where they felt a most dilicate sweete smell, though they saw no land, which ere long they espied, thinking it the Continent: an hundred and twenty myles they sayled not finding any harbor. The first that appeared, with much difficulty they entred, and anchored, and after thankes to God they went to view the next Land adioyning to take possession of it for the Queenes most excellent Maiestie: which done, they found their first landing place very sandy and low, but so full of grapes that the very surge of the Sea sometimes over-flowed them: of which they found such plenty in all places, both on the sand, the greene soyle and hils, as in the plaines as well on euery little shrub, as also climbing towardes the tops of high Cedars, that they did thinke in the world were not the like abundance.

Abundance of Grapes.

The Ile of *Wokokon*.

We passed by the Sea-side towards the tops of the next hills being not high: from whence we might see the Sea on both sides, and found it an Ile of twentie myles in length, and six in breadth, the vallyes replenished with goodly tall Cedars. Discharging our Muskets, such a flocke of Cranes, the most white, arose by vs, with such a cry as if an Army of men had shouted altogether. This Ile hath many goodly Woods, and Deere, Conies, and Foule in incredible abundance, and vsing the Authors owne phrase, the Woods are not such as you finde in *Bohemia*, *Moscovia*, or *Hercinia*, barren and fruitlesse, but the highest and reddest Cedars of the world, bettering them of the Assores, Indies, or *Libanus*: Pynes, Cypres, Saxefras, the Lentisk that beareth Mastick, and many other of excellent smell and qualitie. Till the third day we saw not any of the people, then in a little Boat three of them appeared, one of them went on shore, to whom wee rowed, and he attended vs without any signe of feare; after he had spoke much though we vnderstood not a word, of his owne accord he came boldly aboord vs, we gaue him a shirt, a hat, wine and meate, which he liked well, and after he had well viewed the barkes and vs, he went away in his owne Boat, and within a quarter of a myle of vs in halfe an houre, had loaden his Boat with fish, with which he came againe to the poynt of land, and there devided it in two parts, poynting one part to the Ship, the other to the Pinnace, and so departed.

In *Lybanus* are not many.

Conference with a Salvage.

The

The next day came diuers Boats, and in one of them the Kings Brother, with forty or fifty men, proper people, and in their behauiour very ciuill; his name was *Granganameo*, the King is called *Wingina*, the Country *Wingandacoa*. Leauing his Boats a little from our Ships, he came with his trayne to the poynt: where spreading a Matte he sat downe. Though we came to him well armed, he made signes to vs to sit downe without any shew of feare, stroking his head and brest, and also ours, to expresse his loue. After he had made a long speech vnto vs, we presented him with diuers toyes, which he kindly accepted. He was greatly regarded by his people, for none of them did sit, nor speake a word, but foure, on whom we bestowed presents also, but he tooke all from them, making signes all things did belong to him.

The Arriuall of the Kings brother.

The King himselfe in a conflict with a King his next neighbour and mortall enemy, was shot in two places through the body, and the thigh, yet recouered: whereby he lay at his chiefe towne six dayes iourney from thence.

A day or two after shewing them what we had, *Granganameo* taking most liking to a Pewter dish, made a hole in it, hung it about his necke for a brest-plate: for which he gaue vs twenty Deere skins, worth twenty Crownes; and for a Copper Kettell, fiftie skins, worth fiftie Crownes. Much other trucke we had, and after two dayes he came aboord, and did eate and drinke with vs very merrily. Not long after he brought his wife and children, they were but of meane stature, but well fauoured and very bashfull; she had a long coat of Leather, and about her privities a peece of the same, about her forehead a band of white Corrall, and so had her husband, in her eares were bracelets of pearle, hanging downe to her middle, of the bignesse of great Pease; the rest of the women had Pendants of Copper, and the Noblemen fiue or sixe in an eare; his apparrell as his wiues, onely the women weare their haire long on both sides, and the men but on one; they are of colour yellow, but their hayre is blacke, yet we saw children that had very fayre Chesnut coloured hayre.

Trade with the Salvages.

After that these women had beene here with vs, there came downe from all parts great store of people, with Leather, Corrall, and diuers kinde of dyes, but when *Granganameo* was present, none durst trade but himselfe, and them that wore red Copper on their heads, as he did. When euer he came, he would signifie by so many fires he came with so many boats, that we might know his strength. Their Boats are but one great tree, which is but burnt in the forme of a trough with gins and fire, till it be as they would haue it. For an armour he would haue ingaged vs a bagge of pearle, but we refused, as not regarding it, that wee might the better learn where it grew. He was very iust of his promise, for oft we trusted him, and he would come within his day to keepe his word. He sent vs commonly euery day a brace of Bucks, Conies, Hares, and fish, sometimes Mellons, Walnuts, Cucumbers, Pease, and diuers rootes. This Author sayth, their corne groweth three times in fiue moneths; in May they sow, in Iuly reape; in Iune they sow, in August reape; in Iuly sow, in August reape. We put some of our Pease in the ground, which in ten dayes were 14. ynches high.

Note.

The soyle is most plentifull, sweete, wholesome, and fruitfull of all other, there are about 14. seuerall sorts of sweete smelling tymber trees: the most parts of the vnderwood, Bayes and such like: such Okes as we, but far greater and better. After this acquaintance, my selfe with seauen more went twenty myle into the Riuer *Occam*, that runneth toward the Cittie *Skicoack*, and the euening following we came to an Ile called *Roanoak*, from the harbour where we entred 7. leagues; at the North end was 9. houses, builded with Cedar, fortified round with sharpe trees, and the entrance like a Turnpik. When we came towards it, the wife of *Granganameo* came running out to meete vs, (her husband was absent) commanding her people to draw our Boat ashore for beating on the billowes, other she appoynted to carry vs on their backes aland, others to bring our Ores into the house for stealing.

The Ile *Roanoak*.

The great courtesie of a Woman.

stealing. When we came into the other roome, (for there was fiue in the house) she caused vs to sit downe by a great fire; after tooke off our clothes and washed them, of some our stockings, and some our feete in warme water, and she her selfe tooke much paines to see all things well ordered, and to provide vs victuall.

A banquet.

After we had thus dryed our selues, she brought vs into an Inner roome, where she set on the bord standing a long the house somewhat like frumentie, sodden venison, and rosted fish; in like manner mellons raw, boyled rootes and fruites of diuers kindes. There drinke is commonly water boyled with Ginger, sometimes with Saxefras, and wholsome herbes, but whilest the Grape lasteth they drinke wine. More loue she could not expresse to entertaine vs; they care but onely to defend themselues from the short winter, and feede on what they finde naturall in sommer. In this feasting house was their Idoll of whom they tould vs vncredible things. When we were at meate two or three of her men came amongst vs with their Bowes and Arrowes, which caused vs to take our armes in hand. She perceiuing our distrust, caused their Bowes and Arrowes to be broken, and they beaten out of the gate: but the euening approaching we returned to our boate, where at she much grieuing brought our supper halfe boyled, pots and all, but when she saw vs, but put our boat a little off from the shoar and lye at Anchor, perceiuing our Ielousie, she sent diuers men & 30. women to sit al night on the shoare side against vs, and sent vs fiue Mats to couer vs from the raine, doing all she could to perswade vs to her house. Though there was no cause of doubt, we would not aduenture: for on our safety depended the voyage: but a more kinde louing people cannot be. Beyond this Ile is the maine land and the great riuer *Occam*, on which standeth a Towne called *Pomeiock*, and six dayes higher, their City *Skicoak*: those people neuer saw it, but say there fathers affirme it to be aboue two houres iourney about. Into this riuer falleth an other called *Cipo*, where is found many Mustells wherein are Pearles: likewise another Riuer called *Nomapona*, on the one side whereof standeth a great towne called *Chawanock*, the Lord of the Country is not subiect to *Wingandacoa*. Beyond him an other king they cal *Menatonon*. These 3. are in league each with other. Towards the south. 4. dayes iourney is *Sequotan*, the southermost part of *Wingandacoa*.

Skicoac a great towne.

Adioyning to *Secotan* beginneth the country *Pomouik*, belonging to the King called *Piamacum*, in the Country *Nusiok* vpon the great riuer *News*. These haue mortall warres with *Wingina*, King of *Wingandacoa*. Betwixt *Piemacum* and the Lord of *Secotan*, a peace was concluded: notwithstanding there is a mortall malice in the *Secotans*, because this *Piemacum* invited diuers men, and 30. women to a feast, and when they were altogether merry before their Idoll, which is but a meere illusion of the Deuill, they sudainly slew all the men of *Secotan*, and kept the women for their vse. Beyond *Roanoak* are many Isles full of fruits and other Naturall increases, with many Townes a long the side of the Continent. Those Iles lye 200. myles in length, and betweene them and the mayne, a great long sea, in some places. 20. 40. or 50. myles broad, in other more, somewhere lesse. And in this sea are 100. Iles of diuers bignesses, but to get into it, you haue but 3. passages and they very dangerous. Though this you see for most part be but the relations of Saluages, because it is the first, I thought it not a misse to remember them as they are written by them that returned & arriued in *England* about the middest of *September* the same yeare. This discouery was so welcome into *England* that it pleased her Maiestie to call this Country of *Wingandacoa*, *Virginia*, by which name now you are to vnderstand how it was planted, disolued, reuned, and enlarged,

Pomovik.

How the Country was called *Virginia*.

The Performers of this voyage were these following.

Philip Amadas. } *Captaines*
Arthur Barlow. }

William Grenuill.
Iohn Wood.
Iames Browewich.
Henry Greene.
Beniamen Wood

Simon Ferdinando. } *Of the*
Nicholas Peryman. } *Companie.*
Iohn Hewes. }

Sir

Sir Richard Grenuills voyage to Virginia, for Sir Walter Raleigh. 1585.

THe 9. of *Aprill* he departed from *Plimouth* with 7. sayle: the chiefe men with him in command, were Master *Ralph Layne*, Master *Thomas Candish* Master *Iohn Arundel*, Master *Stukley*, Master *Bremige*, Master *Vincent*, Master *Heryot* and Master *Iohn Clarke*. The 14. day we fell with the *Canaries*, and the 7. of *May* with *Dominico* in the West *Indies*: we landed at *Portorico*, after with much a doe at *Izabella* on the north of *Hispaniola*, passing by many Iles. Vpon the 20. we fell with the mayne of *Florida*, and were put in great danger vpon Cape *Fear*. The 26. we Anchored at *Wocokon*, where the admiral had like to beene cast away, presently we sent to *Wingina* to *Roanoak*, and Master *Arundell* went to the mayne, with *Manteo* a saluage, and that day to *Crooton*. The 11. The Generall victualed for 8. dayes, with a selected company went to the maine, and discovered the Townes of *Pomeiok*, *Aquascogoc*, *Secotan*, and the great Lake called *Paquipe*. At *Aquascogoc* the Indians stole a siluer Cup, wherefore we burnt the Towne and spoyled their corne, so returned to our fleete at *Tocokon*. Whence we wayed for *Hatorask*, where we rested, and *Granganimeo*, King *Wingina's* brother with *Manteo* came abord our Admirall, the Admirall went for *Weapomeiok*, & Master *Iohn Arundell* for *England*. Our Generall in his way home tooke a rich loaden ship of 300. tunns, with which he arriued at *Plimouth* the 18. of *September*. 1585.

Sir Richard Grenvils voyage. 1585.

These were left vnder the command of Master *Ralph Layne* to inhabite the Country, but they returned within a yeare.

Philip Amidas Admirall.	*Master Kendall.*	*Master Antony Russe.*
Master Thomas Heryot.	*Master Gardiner.*	*Master Allen.*
Master Acton.	*Master Predeox.*	*Master Michaell Pollison.*
Master Stafford.	*Master Rogers.*	*Master Thomas Bockner.*
Master Thomas Luddington.	*Master Haruy.*	*Master Iames mason.*
Master Maruyn.	*Master Snelling.*	*Master Dauid Salter.*
Cap. Vaghan.		*Master Iames Skinner,*

With diuers others to the number of 108.

Touching the most remarkeable things of the Country and our proceeding from the 17. of *August* 1585. till the 18. of *Iune* 1586. we made *Roanoack* our habitation. The vtmost of our discouery Southward was *Secotan* as we esteemed 80. leagues from *Roanoacke*. The passage from thence was thought a broad sound within the maine, being without kenning of land, yet full of flats and shoulds that our Pinnasse could not passe, & we had but one boat with 4. ores, that would carry but 15. men with their prouisions for 7. dayes: so that because the winter approached we left those discoueries till a stronger supply. To the Northward; our farthest was to a Towne of the *Chesapeacks*, from *Roanoack* 130. myles. The passage is very shallow and dangerous by reason of the breadth of the sound and the little succour for a storme, but this teritory being 15. myle from the shoare, for pleasantnest of seate, for temporature of climate, fertility of soyle and comoditie of the Sea, besides beares, good woods, *Saxefras*, *Walnuts &c.* is not to be, excelled by any other whatsoeuer.

Their first Plantation.

There be sundry other Kings they call *Weroances* as the *Mangoacks*, *Trypaniks* and *opposians*, which came to visit vs.

To the northwest our farthest was *Chawonock* from *Roanoack* 130. myles our passage

Chawonock.

passage lyeth through a broad sound, but all fresh water, and the channell Nauigable for a Ship, but out of it full of shoules.

The townes by the way by the water, are *Passaquenock* the womens towne, *Chepanoc*, *Weapomeiok*; from *Muscamunge* wee enter the riuer and iurisdiction of *Chawonock*, there it beginneth to straiten, and at *Chawonock* it is as *Thames* at *Lambeth*: betwixt them as we passed is goodly high land on the left hand, and there is a towne called *Ohanock*, where is a great corne field, it is subiect to *Chawonock*, which is the greatest Prouince vpon the riuer, and the Towne it selfe can put seuen hundred men into the field, besides the forces of the rest. The King is lame, but hath more vnderstanding then all the rest.

Chawonock 700. men.

The riuer of *Moratoc* is more famous then all the rest, and openeth into the sound of *Weapomeiok*, and where there is but a very small currant in *Chawonock*, it hath so strong a currant from the Southwest, as we doubted how to row against it. Strange things they report of the head of this riuer, and of *Moratoc* it selfe, a principall towne on it, & is thirtie or fortie dayes Iourney to the head. This lame King is called *Menatonon*. When I had him prisoner two dayes, he told mee that 3. dayes Iourney in a Canow vp the riuer *Chawonock*, then landing & going foure dayes Iourney Northeast, there is a King whose Country lyeth on the Sea, but his best place of strength is an Iland in a Bay inuironed with deepe water, where he taketh that abundance of Pearle, that not onely his skins, and his nobles, but also his beds and houses are garnished therewith. This king was at *Chawonock* two yeares agoe to trade with blacke pearle, his worst sort whereof I had a rope, but they were naught; but that King he sayth hath store of white, and had trafficke with white men, for whom he reserued them; he promised me guides to him, but aduised me to goe strong, for he was vnwilling strangers should come in his Country, for his Country is populous and valiant men. If a supply had come in Aprill, I resolued to haue sent a small Barke to the Northward to haue found it, whilest I with small Boates and 200. men would haue gone to the head of the riuer *Chawonock*, with sufficient guides by land, inskonsing my selfe euery two dayes, where I would leaue Garrisons for my retreat till I came to this Bay.

Menatonon his Relations of the Ile of Pearle, and a rich Mine, & the Sea by it.

Very neare vnto it is the riuer of *Moratoc*, directly from the West, the head of it springeth out of a mayne Rocke, which standeth so neare the Sea, that in stormes the Sea beats ouer it into this fresh spring, that of it selfe at the surse is a violent streame. I intended with two Wherries and fortie persons to haue *Menatonons* sonne for guide, to try this presently, till I could meete with some of the *Moratocks*, or *Mangoaks*, but hoping of getting more victuall from the Saluages, we as narrowly escaped staruing in that Discouery as euer men did.

Pemissapan his trechery.

For *Pemissapan* who had changed his name of *Wingina* vpon the death of his brother *Granganameo*, had giuen both the *Chawonests*, and *Mangoaks* word of my purpose: also he told me the *Chawonocks* had assembled two or three thousand to assault me at *Roanok*, vrging me daily to goe against them, and them against vs; a great assembly I found at my comming thether, which suddaine approach did so dismay them, that we had the better of them: & this confederacy against vs was procured by *Pemissapan* himselfe our chiefe friend we trusted; he sent word also to the *Moratoks* and the *Mangoaks*, I came to inuade them, that they all fled vp into the high Country, so that where I assured my selfe both of succour and prouision, I found all abandoned. But being thus farre on my iourney 160. myles from home, and but victuals for two dayes, besides the casualties of crosse winds, stormes, and the Saluages trechery, though we intended no hurt to any: I gaue my Company to vnderstand we were onely drawne forth vpon these vaine hopes by the Saluages to bring vs to confusion: a Councell we held, to goe forward or returne, but they all were absolutely resolued but three, that whilst there was but one pynt of Corne for a man, they would not leaue the search of that riuer; for they had two Mastiue Dogs, which boyled with Saxefras leaues (if the worst fell out)

The discouery of the riuer *Moratoc*.

A noble resolution.

out) vpon them and the pottage they would liue two dayes, which would bring them to the sound, where they should finde fish for two dayes more to passe it to *Roanock*, which two dayes they had rather fast then goe backe a foote, till they had seene the *Mangoaks* either as friends or foes.

Though I did forsee the danger and misery, yet the desire I had to see the *Mangoaks* was, for that there is a prouince called *Chaunis Temoatan*, frequented by them and well knowne to all those Countries, where is a mine of Copper they call *Wassador*; they say they take it out of a riuer that falleth swiftly from high rocks in shallow water, in great Bowles, couered with leather, leauing a part open to receiue the mettall, which by the change of the colour of the water where the spout falleth, they suddainly chop downe, and haue the Bowle full, which they cast into the fire, it presently melteth, and doth yeeld in fiue parts at the first melting two parts mettall for three of Ore. The *Mangoaks* haue such plenty of it, they beautifie their houses with great plates thereof: this the Salvages report; and young *Skiko* the King of *Chawonocks* sonne my prisoner, that had beene prisoner among the *Mangoaks*, but neuer at *Chaunis Temoatan*, for he sayd that was twentie dayes iourney overland from the *Mangoaks*.

The strange Mine of *Chaunis Temoatan*.

Menatonon also confirmed all this, and promised me guids to this mettall Country; by Land to the *Mangoaks* is but one dayes iourney, but seauen by water, which made me so willing to haue met them for some assay of this mettall: but when we came there we found no creature, onely we might see where had beene their fires. After our two dayes iourney, and our victuals spent, in the euening we heard some call as we thought *Manteo*, who was with me in the boat; this made vs glad, he made them a friendly answer, which they answered with a song we thought for welcome, but he told vs they came to fight. Presently they did let flie their Arrowes about the boat, but did no hurt, the other boat scouring the shore we landed: but they all were fled, and how to finde them wee knew not. So the next morning we returned to the mouth of the riuer, that cost vs foure dayes rowing vp, and here our dogs pottage stood vs in good stead, for we had nothing els: the next day we fasted being windbound, and could not passe the sound, but the day following we came to *Chippanum*, where the people were fled, but their wires afforded vs fish: thus being neare spent, the next day God brought vs to *Roanocke*. I conclude a good Mine, or the South sea will make this Country quickly inhabited, and so for pleasure and profit comparable with any in the world: otherwise there will be nothing worth the fetching. Provided there be found a better harbour then yet there is, which must be Northward if there be any. Master *Vaughan*, no lesse hoped of the goodnesse of the Mine, then Master *Heriot* that the riuer *Moratocks* head, either riseth by the Bay of *Mexico*, or very neare the South Sea, or some part that openeth neare the same, which cannot with that facilitie be done as from the Bay of Pearles, by insconsing foure dayes iourney to the *Chawonoks*, *Mangoaks*, and *Moratocks*, &c.

The great currant of the river *Moratoc*.

The conspiracy of Pemissapan; *the Discouery of it; and our returne for* England *with Sir* Francis Drake.

ENsenore a Saluage, father to *Pemissapan*, the best friend we had after the death of *Granganimeo*, when I was in those Discoueries, could not prevaile any thing with the King from destroying vs, that all this time God had preserued, by his good counsell to the King to be friendly vnto vs. *Pemissapan* thinking as the brute was in this last iourney we were slaine and starued, began to blaspheme our God that would suffer it, and not defend vs, so that old *Ensenore* had no more credit for vs: for he began by all the deuises he could to inuade vs. But in the beginning of this brute, when they saw vs all returne, the report false,

The Conspiracy of *Pemissapan*.

and had *Manteo*, and three Saluages more with vs, how little we esteemed all the people we met, and feared neither hunger, killing, or any thing, and had brought their greatest Kings sonne prisoner with vs to *Roanock*: it a little asswaged all his deuises, and brought *Ensenore* in respect againe, that our God was good, and wee their friends, and our foes should perish, for we could doe them more hurt being dead, then liuing, and that being an hundred myles from them, shot, and strucke them sicke to death, and that when we die it is but for a time, then we returne againe. But that which wrought the most feare among them was the handy-worke of Almightie God. For certaine dayes after my returne, *Menatonon* sent messengers to me with Pearle, and *Okisco* King of *Weopomeoke*, to yeeld himselfe seruant to the Queene of *England*. *Okisco* with twenty-foure of his principall men came to *Pemissapan* to acknowledge this dutie and subiection, and would performe it. All which so changed the heart of *Pemissapan*, that vpon the aduise of *Ensenore*, when we were ready to famish they came and made vs wires, and planted their fields they intended to abandon (we not hauing one corne till the next haruest to sustaine vs). This being done our old friend *Ensenore* dyed the twenty of Aprill, then all our enemies wrought with *Pemissapan* to put in practise his deuises, which he easily imbraced, though they had planted corne by vs, and at *Dasamonpeack* two leagues from vs. Yet they got *Okisco* our tributary to get seuen or eight hundred (and the *Mandoages* with the *Chisapeans* should doe the like) to meete (as their custome is) to solemnize the Funerall of *Ensenore*. Halfe of whom should lye hid, to cut off the straglers, seeking crabs and prouision: the rest come out of the mayne vpon the Signall by fire. Twenty of the principall of *Pemissapans* men had charge in the night to beset my house, put fire in the Reeds that couered it, which might cause me run out so naked and amazed, they might without danger knocke out my braines. The same order for Mr *Heriots*, and the rest: for all should haue beene fired at an instant. In the meane time they should sell vs nothing, and in the night spoyle our wires, to make nenessitie disperse vs. For if we were but ten together, a hundred of them would not meddle with vs. So our famine increased, I was forced to send Captaine *Stafford* to *Croatan*, with twentie to feed himselfe, and see if he could espie any sayle passe the coast; Mr *Predeox* with ten to *Hatarask* vpon the same occasion: and other small parties to the Mayne to liue vpon rootes and Oysters.

The death of a most rare Salvage.

Pemissapan sequestring himselfe, I should not importune him for victuall, and to draw his troupes, found not the *Chawonests* so forward as he expected, being a people more faithfull and powerfull, and desired our friendships, and was offended with him for raising such tales, and all his proiects were revealed to me by *Skico* my prisoner; who finding himselfe as well vsed by me, as *Pemissapan* tould me all. These troubles caused me send to *Pemissapan*, to put suspition in his head, I was to goe presently to *Croatan* to meete a Fleete came to me, though I knew no such matter: and that he would lend me men to fish and hunt. He sent me word he would come himselfe to *Roanock*; but delaying time eight dayes that all his men were there to be assembled, not liking so much company, I resolued the next day to goe visit him, but first to giue them in the Ile a Canvisado, and at an instant to seaze on all their Canows about the Ile. But the towne tooke the Alarum before I ment it. For when I sent to take the Canows, he met one going from the shore, ouerthrew her and cut off two Salvages heads; wherevpon the cry arose, being by their spyes perceiued: for they kept as good watch over vs, as we of them. Vpon this they to their Bowes, and we to our Armes: three or foure of them at the first were slaine, the rest fled into the woods. The next morning I went to *Dassamonpeack*, and sent *Pemissapan* word I was going to *Croatan*, and tooke him in my way to complaine *Osocon* would haue stole my prisoner *Skico*. Herevpon he did abide my comming, & being among eight of the principallest, I gaue the watchword to my men, and immediately they had that they purposed

A slaughter of two Salvages.

for

for vs. Himselfe being shot through with a Pistoll fell downe as dead, but presently start vp and ran away from them all, till an Irish Boy shot him over the buttocks, where they tooke him and cut off his head. *Pemissapan slaine and 8. others.*

Seauen dayes after Captaine *Stufferton* sent to me he descryed twentie-three Sayle. The next day came to me himselfe (of whom I must say this, from the first to the last, he neither spared labour, or perill by land or sea, fayre weather, or foule, to performe any serious seruice committed to him.) He brought me a letter from Sir *Francis Drake*, whose generous mind offered to supply all my defects, of shipping, boats, munition, victuall, clothes, and men to further this action: and vpon good consultation and deliberation, he appointed me a ship of 70. tuns, with an hundred men, and foure moneths victuals, two Pinnaces, foure small Boats, with two sufficient Masters, with sufficient Gangs. All this being made ready for me, suddenly arose such a storme for foure dayes, that had like to haue driuen the whole Fleete on shore: many of them were forced to the Sea, whereof my ship so lately giuen me was one, with all my prouision and Company appoynted. *A most generous courtesie of Sir Francis Drake.*

Notwithstanding, the storme ceasing, the Generall appointed me a ship of 170. tuns, with all prouisions as before, to carry me into *England* the next August, or when I had performed such Discoueries as I thought fit. Yet they durst not vndertake to bring her into the harbour, but she must ride in the road, leauing the care of the rest to my selfe, advising me to consider with my Company what was fittest, and with my best speed returne him answer.

Herevpon calling my Company together, who were all as priuy of the Generals offer as my selfe; their whole request was, (in regard of all those former miseries, and no hope of the returne of Sir *Richard Grenvill*,) and with a generall consent, they desired me to vrge him, we might all goe with him for *England* in his Fleete; for whose reliefe in that storme he had sustained more perill of wrack, then in all his honorable actions against his enemies. So with prayses to God we set sayle in June 1586. and arriued in *Portsmouth* the 27. of July the same yeare: Leaving this remembrance to posteritie, *Virginia abandoned.*

To reason lend me thine attentive eares, Exempt thy selfe from mind-distracting cares:
Least that's here thus proiected for thy good; By thee reiected be, ere vnderstood.

Written by Mr *Ralph Layne*, Governour.

The Observations of Mr. Thomas Heriot *in this Voyage.*

For Marchandize and Victualls.

WHat before is writ, is also confirmed by that learned *Mathematician* Mr *Thomas Heriot*, with them in the Country, whose particular Relation of all the Beasts, Birds, Fishes, Foules, Fruites, and Rootes, and how they may be vsefull; because I haue writ it before for the most part in the Discourse of Captaine *Amidas*, and Captaine *Layne*, except Silk grasse, Wormesilke, Flax like Hempe, Allum, Wapeith, or *Terra sigillata*, Tar, Rosen, & Turpentine, Civet-cats, Iron ore, Copper that held Silver, Coprose and Pearle: Let those briefes suffice, because I would not trouble you with one thing twice. *Comodities.*

Dyes.

For Dyes, *Showmack*, the herbe *Wasebur*, little rootes called *Chapacor*, and the barke of a tree called by the Inhabitants *Tangomockonominge*, which are for divers sorts of Reds. *Dyes.*

What more then is related is an herbe in Dutch called *Melden*, described like an Orange, growing foure foote high; the seede will make good broth, and the *A strange Salt.*

ſtalke burnt to aſhes makes a kinde of Salt: other Salt they know not, and we vſed of it for Pot-herbs. Of their *Tobacco* we found plenty, which they eſteeme their chiefe Phyſicke.

Rootes. Ground nuts, *Tiſwaw* we call *China* roots; they grow in cluſters, and bring forth a bryer ſtalke, but the leafe is far vnlike, which will climbe vp to the top of the higheſt tree: the vſe knowne is to cut it in ſmall peeces, then ſtampe & ſtraine it with water, and boyled makes a gelly good to eate. *Caſſavia* growes in Mariſhes, which the *Indians* oft vſe for bread and broth. *Habaſcon* is like a Parſnip, naught of it ſelfe, except compounded: and their Leekes like thoſe in *England*.

Fruits thats ſtrange. *Sequenummener*, a kinde of Berry like Capers, and three kinde of Berries like Acornes, called *Sagatamenor*, *Oſamenor*, and *Pummuckoner*.

Beaſts extraordinary. *Saquenuckot* and *Maquowoc*, two kinde of beaſts, greater then Conies, and very good meate; in ſome places ſuch plenty of gray Conies, like hayres, that all the people make them mantels of their skins. I haue the names of 28. ſeverall ſorts that are diſperſed in the Country: of which 12. kindes we haue diſcouered and good to eate; but the Salvages ſometimes kill a Lyon and eate him.

Fiſh. There is plentie of Sturgeon in February, March, Aprill, and May; all Herings in abundance; ſome ſuch as ours, but the moſt part of 18.20. or 24. ynches long, and more. Trouts, Porpiſſes, Rayes, Mullets, Old-wiues, Plaice, Tortoiſes both by Sea and Land: Crabs, Oyſters, Muſſels, Scalops, Periwinckles, Creviſes, Secanank: we haue the Pictures of 12. ſorts more, but their names we know not.

Foules. Turkyes, Stockdoues, Partridges, Cranes, Hernes, Swans, Geeſe, Parrots, Faulcons, Merlins. I haue the names in their language of 86. ſeverall ſorts. Their woods are ſuch as ours in *England* for the moſt part, except *Rakeock*, a great ſweet tree, whereof they make their Canowes: and *Aſcopo*, a kinde of tree like Lowrell, and Saxefras.

Their Natures and Manners.

Their Clothing, Townes, Houſes, Warres, Arts, Tooles, handy crafts, and educations, are much like them in that part of *Virginia* we now inhabite: which at large you may reade in the Deſcription thereof. But the relation of their Religion is ſtrange, as this Author reporteth.

Their Religion. Some Religion they haue, which although it be farre from the truth, yet being as it is there is hope it may be the eaſier reformed. They beleeue there are many gods which they call *Mantoac*, but of different ſorts and degrees. Alſo that there is one chiefe God that hath beene from all eternitie, who as they ſay when he purpoſed firſt to make the world, made firſt other gods of a principall order, to be as inſtruments to be vſed in the Creation and government to follow: And after the Sunne, Moone, and Starres, as pettie gods; and the inſtruments of the other order more principall. Firſt (they ſay) were made waters, out of which by the gods were made all diverſitie of creatures that are viſible or inviſible.

How the world was made.

How man was made. For mankinde they ſay a Woman was made firſt, which by the working of one of the gods conceiued and brought forth children; and ſo they had their beginning, but how many yeares or ages ſince they know not; having no Records but onely Tradition from Father to ſonne.

How they vſe their gods. They thinke that all the gods are of humane ſhape, and therefore repreſent them by Images in the formes of men; which they call *Kewaſowok*: one alone is called *Kewaſa*; them they place in their Temples, where they worſhip, pray, ſing, and make many offerings. The common ſort thinke them alſo gods.

Whether they goe after death. They beleeue the immortalitie of the Soule, when life departing from the body, according to the good or bad workes it hath done, it is carried vp to the Tabernacles of the gods, to perpetuall happpineſſe, or to *Popoguſſo*, a great pit: which they thinke to be at the furtheſt parts of the world, where the Sunne ſets, and there burne continually.

To confirme this they told me of two men that had beene lately dead, and revived

vived againe; the one hapned but few yeares before our comming into the country; of a bad man, which being dead and buried, the next day the earth over him being seene to moue, was taken vp, who told them his soule was very neare entering into *Popogusso*, had not one of the gods saued him and gaue him leaue to returne againe, to teach his friends what they should doe to avoyd such torment. The other hapned the same yeare we were there, but sixtie myles from vs, which they told me for news, that one being dead, buried, & taken vp as the first, shewed, that although his body had layne dead in the graue, yet his soule liued, and had travailed far in a long broad way, on both sides whereof grew more sweet, fayre, and delicate trees and fruits, then ever he had seene before; at length he came to most braue and fayre houses, neare which he met his Father, that was dead long agoe, who gaue him charge to goe backe, to shew his friends what good there was to doe, to inioy the pleasures of that place; which when hee had done hee should come againe.

Two men risen from death.

What subtiltie so ever be in the *Weroances*, and *Priests*; this opinion worketh so much in the common sort, that they haue great respect to their Governours: and as great care to avoyde torment after death, and to enioy blisse. Yet they haue divers sorts of punishments according to the offence, according to the greatnesse of the fact. And this is the sum of their Religion, which I learned by having speciall familiaritie with their Priests, wherein they were not so sure grounded, nor gaue such credit, but through conversing with vs, they were brought into great doubts of their owne, and no small admiration of ours: of which many desired to learne more then we had meanes for want of vtterance in their Language to expresse.

The subtiltie of their Priests.

Most things they saw with vs as Mathematicall Instruments, Sea-Compasses; the vertue of the Loadstone, Perspectiue Glasses, burning Glasses: Clocks to goe of themselues; Bookes, writing, Guns, and such like; so far exceeded their capacities, that they thought they were rather the workes of gods then men; or at least the gods had taught vs how to make them, which loued vs so much better then them; & caused many of them giue credit to what we spake concerning our God. In all places where I came, I did my best to make his immortall glory knowne. And I told them, although the Bible I shewed them, contained all; yet of it selfe, it was not of any such vertue as I thought they did conceiue. Notwithstanding many would be glad to touch it, to kisse, and imbrace it, to hold it to their breasts, and heads, and stroke all their body over with it.

Their simplicitie.

The King *Wingina* where we dwelt, would oft be with vs at Prayer. Twice he was exceeding sicke and like to dye. And doubting of any helpe from his Priests, thinking he was in such danger for offending vs and our God, sent for some of vs to pray, and be a meanes to our God, he might liue with him after death. And so did many other in the like case. One other strange Accident (leauing others) will I mention before I end, which mooued the whole Country that either knew or heard of vs, to haue vs in wonderfull admiration.

Their desire of salvation.

There was no Towne where they had practised any villany against vs (we leaving it vnpunished, because we sought by all possible meanes to winne them by gentlenes) but within a few dayes after our departure, they began to dye; in some Townes twenty, in some forty, in some sixty, and in one an hundred and twenty, which was very many in respect of their numbers. And this hapned in no place (we could learn) where we had bin, but where they had vsed some practise to betray vs. And this disease was so strange, they neither knew what it was, nor how to cure it; nor had they knowne the like time out of minde; a thing specially observed by vs, as also by themselues, in so much that some of them who were our friends, especially *Wingina*, had observed such effects in foure or fiue Townes, that they were perswaded it was the worke of God through our meanes: and that we by him might kill and slay whom we would, without weapons, and not come

A wonderfull Accident.

neare them. And therevpon, when they had any vnderstanding, that any of their enemies abused vs in our Iourneyes, they would intreat vs, we would be a meanes to our God, that they, as the others that had dealt ill with vs, might dye in like sort: although we shewed them their requests were vngodly; and that our GOD would not subiect himselfe to any such requests of men, but all things as he pleased came to passe: and that we to shew our selues his true servants, ought rather to pray for the contrary: yet because the effect fell out so suddenly after, according to their desires, they thought it came to passe by our meanes, and would come giue vs thankes in their manner, that though we satisfied them not in words, yet in deeds we had fulfilled their desires.

Their strange opinions.

This marueilous Accident in all the Country wrought so strange opinions of vs, that they could not tell whether to thinke vs gods or men. And the rather that all the space of their sicknesse, there was no man of ours knowne to die, or much sicke. They noted also we had no women, nor cared for any of theirs: some therefore thought we were not borne of women, and therefore not mortall, but that we were men of an old generation many yeares past, & risen againe from immortalitie. Some would Prophesie there were more of our generation yet to come, to kill theirs and take their places. Those that were to come after vs they imagined to be in the ayre, yet invisible and without bodies: and that they by our intreaties, for loue of vs, did make the people die as they did, by shooting invisible bullets into them.

To confirme this, their Physicians to excuse their Ignorance in curing the disease, would make the simple people beleeue, that the strings of bloud they sucked out of the sicke bodies, were the strings wherein the invisible bullets were tyed, and cast. Some thought we shot them our selues from the place where we dwelt, and killed the people that had offended vs, as we listed, how farre distant soever. And others said it was the speciall worke of God for our sakes, as we had cause in some sort to thinke no lesse, whatsoever some doe, or may imagine to the contrary; especially some *Astrologers* by the eclipse of the Sunne we saw that yeare before our Voyage, and by a *Comet* which began to appeare but a few dayes before the sicknesse began: but to exclude them from being the speciall causes of so speciall an Accident, there are farther reasons then I thinke fit to present or alledge.

These their opinions I haue set downe, that you may see there is hope to imbrace the truth, and honor, obey, feare and loue vs, by good dealing and government: though some of our company towards the latter end, before we came away with Sir *Francis Drake* shewed themselues too furious, in slaying some of the people in some Townes, vpon causes that on our part might haue bin borne with more mildnesse; notwithstanding they iustly had deserued it. The best neverthelesse in this, as in all actions besides, is to be indevoured and hoped; and of the worst that may happen, notice to be taken with consideration; and as much as may be eschewed; the better to allure them hereafter to Civilitie and Christianitie.

Thus you may see, *How*

Palling

Nature her selfe delights her selfe in sundry Instruments,
That sundry things be done to decke the earth with Ornaments;
Nor suffers she her servants all should runne one race,
But wills the walke of every one frame in a divers pace;
That divers wayes and divers workes, the world might better grace.

Written by *Thomas Heriot*, one of the Voyage.

How Sir Richard Grenvill *went to relieue them.*

1586. IN the yeare of our Lord 1586. Sir *Walter Raleigh* and his Associates prepared a ship of a hundred tun, fraughted plentifully of all things necessary: but before they

they set sayle from *England* it was *Easter*. And arriving at *Hatorask*, they after some time spent in seeking the *Collony* vp in the Country, and not finding them, returned with all the prouision againe to *England*.

About 14. or 15. dayes after, Sir *Richard Grenvill* accompanied with three ships well appoynted, arrived there. Who not finding the aforesaid ship according to his expectation, nor hearing any newes of the *Collony* there seated, and left by him as is said 1585. travailing vp and downe to seeke them, but when he could heare no newes of them, and found their habitation abandoned, vnwilling to lose the possession of the Country, after good deliberation he landed fiftie men in the Ile of *Roanoak*, plentifully furnished with all manner of provision for two yeares: and so returned for *England*.

Sir *Richard Grenvill* left fiftie men.

Where many began strangely to discant of those crosse beginnings, and him; which caused me remember an old saying of *Euripides*.

Who broacheth ought thats new, to fooles vntaught,
Himselfe shall iudged be vnwise, and good for naught.

Three Ships more sent to relieue them by Mr. White.

Master *White* his Voyages. 1587.

WE went the old course by the west *Indies*, and *Simon Ferdinando* our continuall Pilot mistaking *Virginia* for Cape *Fear*, we sayled not much to haue beene cast away, vpon the conceit of our all-knowing *Ferdinando*, had it not beene prevented by the vigilancy of Captaine *Stafford*. We came to *Hatorask* the 22. of Iuly, and with fortie of our best men, intending at *Roanoack* to find the 50 men left by Sir *Richard Grenvill*. But we found nothing but the bones of a man, and where the Plantation had beene, the houses vnhurt, but overgrowne with weeds, and the Fort defaced, which much perplexed vs.

By the History it seemes *Simon Ferdinando* did what he could to bring this voyage to confusion; but yet they all arrived at *Hatorask*. They repayred the old houses at *Roanock*, and Master *George How*, one of the Councell, stragling abroad, was slaine by the Salvages. Not long after Master *Stafford* with 20. men went to *Croatan* with *Manteo*, whose friends dwelled there: of whom we thought to haue some newes of our 50 men. They at first made shew to fight, but when they heard *Manteo*, they threw away their Armes, and were friends, and desired there might be a token giuen to be knowne by, least we might hurt them by misprision, as the yeare before one had bin by Master *Layne*, that was ever their friend, and there present yet lame.

One of the Councell slaine.

The next day we had conference with them concerning the people of *Secotan*, *Aquascogoc*, and *Pomeiok*, willing them of *Croatan* to see if they would accept our friendship, and renew our old acquaintance: which they willingly imbraced, and promised to bring their King and Governours to *Roanoak*, to confirme it. We also vnderstood that Master *Howe* was slaine by the men of *Wingina*, of *Dassamonpeack*: and by them of *Roanoack*, that the fiftie men left by Sir *Richard Grenvill*, were suddainly set vpon by three hundred of *Secotan*, *Aquascogoc*, and *Dassamonpeack*. First they intruded themselues among 11 of them by friendship, one they slew, the rest retyring to their houses, they set them on fire, that our men with what came next to hand were forced to make their passage among them; where one of them was shot in the mouth, and presently dyed, and a Salvage slaine by him. On both sides more were hurt; but our men retyring to the water side, got their boat, & ere they had rowed a quarter of a myle towards *Hatorask*, they tooke vp foure of their fellowes, gathering Crabs and Oysters: at last they landed on a little Ile by *Hatorask*, where they remained a while, but after departed they

How the fiftie men were slaine.

knew not whether. So taking our leaues of the *Croatans*, we came to our Fleet at *Hatorask*.

The Governour having long expected the King and Governours of *Pomeiok*, *Secotan*, *Aquascogoc*, and *Dassamonpeack*, and the 7. dayes expired, and no newes of them, being also informed by those of *Croatan*, that they of *Dassamonpeack* slew Master *How*, and were at the driving our men from *Raonoack* he thought no longer to deferre the revenge. Wherefore about midnight, with Captaine *Stafford*, and twentie-foure men, whereof *Manteo* was one, for our guide, (that behaved himselfe towards vs as a most faithfull English man) he set forward.

An ill misprision.

The next day by breake of day we landed, and got beyond their houses, where seeing them sit by the fire we assaulted them. The miserable soules amazed fled into the Reeds, where one was shot through, and we thought to haue beene fully revenged, but we were deceiued, for they were our friends come from *Croatan* to gather their corne, because they vnderstood our enemies were fled after the death of Master *How*, and left all behinde them for the birds. But they had like to haue payd too deare for it, had we not chanced vpon a *Weroances* wife, with a childe at her backe, and a Salvage that knew Captaine *Stafford*, that ran to him calling him by his name. Being thus disappointed of our purpose, we gathered the fruit we found ripe, left the rest vnspoyled, and tooke *Menatonon* his wife with her childe, and the rest with vs to *Roanoak*. Though this mistake grieued *Manteo*, yet he imputed it to their own folly, because they had not kept promise to come to the governor at the day appointed. The 13. of August our Salvage *Manteo* was Christened, and called Lord of *Dassamonpeack*, in reward of his faithfulnesse. And the 18th, *Ellinor* the Governours daughter, and wife to *Ananias Dare*, was delivered of a daughter in *Roanoak*; which being the first Christian there borne, was called *Virginia*.

A child borne in *Virginia*.

Our ships being ready to depart, such a storme arose, as the Admirall was forced to cut her Cables: and it was six dayes ere she could recover the shore, that made vs doubt she had beene lost, because the most of her best men were on shore. At this time Controversies did grow betwixt our Governour and the Assistants, about choosing one of them 12. to goe as Factor for them all to *England*; for all refused saue one, whom all men thought most insufficient: the Conclusion was by a generall consent, they would haue the Governour goe himselfe, for that they thought none would so truly procure there supplyes as he. Which though he did what he could to excuse it, yet their importunitie would not cease till he vndertooke it, and had it vnder all their hands how vnwilling he was, but that necessity and reason did doubly constraine him. At their setting sayle for *England*, waighing Anchor, twelue of the men in the flyboat were throwne from the Capstern, by the breaking of a barre, and most of them so hurt, that some never recovered it. The second time they had the like fortune, being but 15. they cut the Cable and kept company with their Admirall to *Flowres* and *Coruos*; the Admirall stayed there looking for purchase: but the flyboats men grew so weake they were driuen to *Smerwick* in the West of *Ireland*. The Governour went for *England*; and *Simon Ferdinando* with much adoe at last arrived at *Portsmouth*. 1587.

A controversie who to send for Factor to *England*.

The Names of those were landed in this Plantation were,

Iohn White Governour.	*Christopher Couper.*	*Dionis Haruie.*
Roger Bayley.	*Thomas Stevens.*	*Roger Prat.*
Ananias Dare.	*Iohn Samson.*	*George How.*
Simon Ferdinando.	*Thomas Smith.*	*Antony Cage.*

With divers others to the number of about 115.

The

The fift Voyage to Virginia; *vndertaken by* M^r. Iohn White. 1589.

THe 20. of March three ſhips went from *Plimouth*, and paſſed betwixt *Barbary* and *Mogadoro* to *Dominico* in the Weſt *Indies*. After we had done ſome exployts in thoſe parts, the third of Auguſt wee fell with the low ſandy Iles weſtward of *Wokokon*. But by reaſon of ill weather it was the 11, ere we could Anchor there; and on the 12. we came to *Croatan*, where is a great breach in 35. degrees and a halfe, in the Northeaſt poynt of the Ile. The 15. we came to *Hatorask* in 36. degrees & a terſe, at 4. fadom, 3 leagues from ſhore: where we might perceiue a ſmoake at the place where I left the Colony, 1587. The next morning Captaine *Cooke*, Captaine *Spicer*, & their companies, with two boats left our ſhips, and diſcharged ſome Ordnance to giue them notice of our comming, but when we came there, we found no man, nor ſigne of any that had beene there lately: and ſo returned to our Boats. The next morning we prepared againe for *Roanoack*. Captaine *Spicer* had then ſent his Boat aſhore for water, ſo it was ten of the Clocke ere we put from the ſhips, which rode two myles from the ſhore. The Admirals boat, being a myle before the other, as ſhe paſſed the bar, a ſea broke into the boat and filled her halfe full of water: but by Gods good will, and the carefull ſtearage of Captaine *Cook*, though our proviſions were much wet we ſafe eſcaped, the wind blew hard at Northeaſt, which cauſed ſo great a current and a breach vpon the barre; Captaine *Spicer* paſſed halfe over, but by the indiſcreet ſteering of *Ralph Skinner*, their boat was overſet, the men that could catch hold hung about her, the next ſea caſt her on ground, where ſome let goe their hold to wade to ſhore, but the ſea beat them downe. The boat thus toſſed vp and downe Captaine *Spicer* and *Skinner* hung there till they were drowne; but 4. that could ſwim a little, kept themſelues in deeper water, were ſaued by the meanes of Captaine *Cook*, that preſently vpon the overſetting of their boat, ſhipped himſelfe to ſaue what he could. Thus of eleuen, ſeuen of the chiefeſt were drowned. This ſo diſcomfited all the Saylers, we had much to do to get them any more to ſeeke further for the Planters, but by their Captaines forwardnes at laſt they fitted themſelues againe for *Hatorask* in 2 boats, with 19. perſons. It was late ere we arrived, but ſeeing a fire through the woods, we ſounded a Trumpet, but no anſwer could we heare. The next morning we went to it, but could ſee nothing but the graſſe, and ſome rotten trees burning. We went vp and downe the Ile, and at laſt found three faire Romane Letters carved. *C.R.O.* which preſently we knew to ſignifie the place where I ſhould find them, according to a ſecret note betweene them & me: which was to write the name of the place they would be in, vpon ſome tree, dore, or poſt: and if they had beene in any diſtreſſe, to ſignifie it by making a croſſe over it. For at my departure they intended to goe fiftie myles into the mayne. But we found no ſigne of diſtreſſe; then we went to a place where they were left in ſundry houſes, but we found them all taken downe, and the place ſtrongly incloſed with a high Palizado, very Fortlike; and in one of the chiefe Poſts carued in fayre capitall Letters *CROATAN*, without any ſigne of diſtreſſe, and many barres of Iron, two pigs of Lead, foure Fowlers, Iron ſhot, and ſuch like heauie things throwne here and there, overgrowne with graſſe and weeds. We went by the ſhore to ſeeke for their boats but could find none, nor any of the Ordnance I left them. At laſt ſome of the Sailers found divers Chiſts had beene hidden and digged vp againe, and much of the goods ſpoyled, and ſcattered vp and downe, which when I ſaw, I knew three of them to be my owne; but bookes, pictures, and all things els were ſpoyled. Though it much grieued me, yet it did much comfort me that I did know they were at *Croatan*; ſo we returned to our Ships, but had like to haue bin caſt away by a great ſtorme that continued all that night.

1589. Maſter *White* his returne to *Virginia*.

Captaine *Spicer* and ſeauen others drowned.

They finde where they had buryed their proviſions.

The next morning we weighed Anchor for *Croatan*: having the Anchor a-pike, the Cable broke, by the meanes whereof we lost another: letting fall the third, the ship yet went so fast a drift, we fayled not much there to haue split. But God bringing vs into deeper water; considering we had but one Anchor, and our prouision neare spent, we resolued to goe forthwith to S. *Iohns* Ile, *Hispaniola*, or *Trinidado*, to refresh our selues and seeke for purchase that Winter, and the next Spring come againe to seeke our Country-men. But our *Vice Admirall* would not, but went directly for *England*, and we our course for *Trinidado*. But within two dayes after, the wind changing, we were constrained for the Westerne Iles to refresh our selues, where we met with many of the Queenes ships our owne consort, and diuers others, the 23. of Seeptember 1590. And thus we left seeking our Colony, that was neuer any of them found, nor seene to this day 1622. And this was the conclusion of this Plantation, after so much time, labour, and charge consumed. Whereby we see;

The end of this Plantation.

Not all at once, nor all alike, nor euer hath it beene,
That God doth offer and confer his blessings vpon men.

Written by Master *Iohn White*.

1602.

A briefe Relation of the Description of *Elizabeths* Ile, and some others towards the North part of *Virginia*; and what els they discovered in the yeare 1602. by Captaine *Bartholomew Gosnoll*, and Captaine *Bartholomew Gilbert*; and divers other Gentlemen their Associates.

12. yeares it lay dead.

ALL hopes of *Virginia* thus abandoned, it lay dead and obscured from 1590. till this yeare 1602. that Captaine *Gosnoll*, with 32. and himselfe in a small Barke, set sayle from **Dartmouth** vpon the 26. of March. Though the wind fauoured vs not at the first, but forced vs as far Southward as the *Asores*, which was not much out of our way; we ran directly west from thence, whereby we made our iourney shorter then heretofore by 500. leagues: the weaknesse of our ship, the badnes of our saylers, and our ignorance of the coast, caused vs carry but a low sayle, that made our passage longer then we expected.

On fryday the 11. of May we made land, it was somewhat low, where appeared certaine hummocks or hills in it: the shore white sand, but very rockie, yet overgrowne with fayre trees. Comming to an Anchor, 8 *Indians* in a Baske shallop, with mast and sayle came boldly aboord vs. It seemed by their signes & such things as they had, some Biskiners had fished there: being about the latitude of 43. But the harbour being naught, & doubting the weather, we went not ashore, but waighed, and stood to the Southward into the Sea. The next morning we found our selues imbayed with a mightie headland: within a league of the shore we anchored, and Captaine *Gosnoll*, my selfe, & three others went to it in our boat, being a white sand & a bold coast. Though the weather was hot, we marched to the highest hils we could see, where we perceiued this headland part of the mayn, neare inuironed with Ilands. As we were returning to our ship, a good proper, lusty young man came to vs, with whom we had but small conference, and so we left him. Here in 5. or 6. houres we tooke more Cod then we knew what to doe with, which made vs perswade our selues, there might be found a good fishing in March, Aprill, and May.

Their first landing.

At

At length we came among these fayre Iles, some a league, 2. 3. 5. or 6. from the Mayne, by one of them we anchored. We found it foure myles in compasse, without house or inhabitant. In it is a lake neare a myle in circuit; the rest overgrowne with trees, which so well as the bushes, were so overgrowne with Vines, we could scarce passe them. And by the blossomes we might perceiue there would be plenty of Strawberries, Respises, Gousberries, and divers other fruits: besides, Deere and other Beasts we saw, and Cranes, Hernes, with divers other sorts of fowle; which made vs call it *Martha's Vineyard.* Martha's Vineyard.

The rest of the Isles are replenished with such like; very rocky, and much tinctured stone like Minerall. Though we met many *Indians*, yet we could not see their habitations: they gaue vs fish, Tobacco, and such things as they had. But the next Isle we arrived at was but two leagues from the Maine, & 16. myle about, invironed so with creekes and coves, it seemed like many Isles linked together by small passages like bridges. In it is many places of plaine grasse, and such other fruits, and berries as before were mentioned. In mid-May we did sow Wheat, Barley, Oates, & Pease, which in 14. dayes sprung vp 9. inches. The soyle is fat and lusty: the crust therof gray, a foot or lesse in depth. It is full of high timbred Okes, their leaues thrise so broad as ours: Cedar straight and tall, Beech, Holly, Walnut, Hazell, Cherry trees like ours, but the stalke beareth the blossom or fruit thereof like a cluster of Grapes, forty or fiftie in a bunch. There is a tree of Orange colour, whose barke in the filing is as smooth as Velvet. There is a lake of fresh water three myles in compasse, in the midst an Isle containing an acre or thereabout, overgrowne with wood: here are many Tortoises, and abundance of all sorts of foules, whose young ones we tooke and eate at our pleasure. Grounds nuts as big as egges, as good as Potatoes, and 40. on a string, not two ynches vnder ground. All sorts of shell-fish, as Schalops, Mussels, Cockles, Crabs, Lobsters, Welks, Oysters, exceeding good and very great; but not to cloy you with particulars, what God and nature hath bestowed on those places, I refer you to the Authors owne writing at large. We called this Isle *Elizabeths* Isle, from whence we went right over to the mayne, where we stood a while as ravished at the beautie and dilicacy of the sweetnesse, besides divers cleare lakes, whereof we saw no end, & meadows very large and full of greene grasse, &c. *Elizabeths* Island.

Here we espyed 7. Salvages, at first they expressed some feare, but by our courteous vsage of them, they followed vs to the necke of Land, which we thought had beene severed from the Mayne, but we found it otherwise. Here we imagined was a river, but because the day was farre spent, we left to discover it till better leasure. But of good Harbours, there is no doubt, considering the Land is all rocky and broken lands. The next day we determined to fortifie our selues in the Isle in the lake. Three weekes we spent in building vs there a house. But the second day after our comming from the Mayne, 11. Canows with neare 50. Salvages came towards vs. Being vnwilling they should see our building, we went to, & exchanged with them Kniues, Hatchets, Beades, Bels, and such trifles, for some Bevers, Lyzards, Martins, Foxes, wilde Catte skinnes, and such like. We saw them haue much red Copper, whereof they make chaines, collars, and drinking cups, which they so little esteemed they would giue vs for small toyes, & signified vnto vs they had it out of the earth in the Mayne: three dayes they stayed with vs, but every night retyred two or three myle from vs: after with many signes of loue and friendship they departed, seaven of them staying behind, that did helpe vs to dig and carry Saxafras, and doe any thing they could, being of a comely proportion and the best condition of any Salvages we had yet incountred. They haue no Beards but counterfeits, as they did thinke ours also was: for which they would haue changed with some of our men that had great beards. Some of the baser sort would steale; but the better sort, we found very civill and iust. We saw but three of their women, and they were but of meane stature, attyred in skins like the men, A Copper Mine.

but fat and well favoured. The wholesomenesse and temperature of this climate, doth not onely argue the people to be answerable to this Description, but also of a perfect constitution of body, actiue, strong, healthfull, and very witty, as the sundry toyes by them so cunningly wrought may well testifie. For our selues, we found our selues rather increase in health and strength then otherwise, for all our toyle, bad dyet and lodging; yet not one of vs was touched with any sicknesse. Twelue intended here a while to haue stayed, but vpon better consideration, how

Their return. meanely we were provided, we left this Island (with as many true sorrowfull eyes as were before desirous to see it) the 18. of Iune, and arrived at ***Exmouth***, the 23 of Iuly.

But yet mans minde doth such it selfe explay,
As Gods great Will doth frame it every way.
And, *Such thoughts men haue, on earth that doe but liue,*
As men may craue, but God doth onely giue.

Written by *Iohn Brierton* one of the Voyage.

1603.

A Voyage of Captaine Martin Pring, *with two Barks from* Bristow, *for the Northpart of* Virginia. 1603.

BY the inducements and perswasions of Mr *Richard Hackluite*, Mr *Iohn Whitson* being Maior, with his brethren the Aldermen, & most of the Merchants of the Citie of *Bristow*, raised a stocke of 1000l. to furnish out two Barkes, the one of 50. tuns, with 30. men and boyes, the other 26. tuns, with 13. men and boyes, having *Martin Pring* an vnderstanding Gentleman, and a sufficient Mariner for Captaine, and *Robert Salterne* his Assistant, who had bin with Captaine *Gosnoll* there the yeare before for Pilot. Though they were much crossed by contrary windes vpon the coast of ***England***, and the death of that ever most memorable, miracle of the world, our most deare soveraigne Lady and Queene *Elizabeth*: yet at last they passed by the westerne Isles, and about the 7. of Iune, fell vpon the north part of *Virginia*, about the degrees of fortie three. Where they found plentie of most sorts of fish, and saw a high country full of great woods of sundry sorts. As they ranged the coast at a place they named ***Whitson Bay***, they were kindly vsed by the Natiues, that came to them, in troupes, of tens, twenties, & thirties, and sometimes more. But because in this Voyage for most part they followed the course of Captaine *Gosnoll*, and haue made no relation but to the same effect he writ before, we will thus conclude;

Lay hands vnto this worke with all thy wit,
But pray that God would speed and perfit it.

Robert Salterne.

1605.

A relation of a Discovery towards the Northward of Virginia, *by Captaine* George Waymouth 1605. *imployed thether by the right Honorable* Thomas Arundell, *Baron of* Warder, *in the Raigne of our most royall King* IAMES.

VPon tuesday the fift of March we set sayle from *Ratcliffe*, but by contrary winds we were forced into *Dartmouth* till the last of this moneth, then with 29. as good sea men, & all necessary provisiõs as could possibly be gotten, we put

to

to sea;and the 24 of Aprill fell with *Flowres* and *Coruos*. We intended as we were directed towards the Southward of 39. But the winds so crossed vs wee fell more Northwards about 41. and 20. minuits, we sounded at 100. fathom, & by that we had run 6 leagues we had but 5. yet saw no land; from the mayne top we descryed a whitish sandy clift, West North-west some 6. leagues from vs, but ere we had run two leagues further we found many shoules and breaches, sometimes in 4. fadom and the next throw 15. or 18. Being thus imbayed among those shoules, we were constrained to put back againe, which we did with no small danger, though both the winde and weather were as fayre as we could desire. Thus we parted from the Land, which we had not before so much desired, and at the first sight reioyced, as now we all ioyfully praysed God that he had delivered vs from so eminent danger. Here we found excellent Cod, and saw many Whales as we had done 2. or 3. daies before. Being thus constrained to put to sea, the want of wood & water caused vs take the best advantage of the winde, to fall with the shore wheresoever: but we found our Sea-cards most directly false. The 17. of May we made the Land againe, but it blew so hard, we durst not approach it. The next day it appeared to vs a mayne high land, but we found it an Island of 6. myles in compasse: within a league of it we came to an anchor, and went on shore for wood & water, of which we found sufficient. The water gushing forth downe the rocky clifts in many places, which are all overgrown with Firre, Birch, Beech, & Oke, as the Verge is with Gousberries, Strawberries, wild Pease, and Rose bushes, and much foule of divers sorts that breed among the rockes: here as in all places els where we came, we found Cod enough.

Dangerous sheules.

Cod and Whales.

Their first landing.

From hence we might discerne the mayne land and very high mountaines, the next day because we rode too open to the Sea, we waighed, and came to the Isles adioyning to the mayn: among which we found an excellent rode, defended from all windes, for ships of any burthen, in 6. 7. 8. 9. or 10. fadom vpon a clay oze. This was vpon a Whitsonday, wherefore we called it *Pentecost Harbour*. Here I cannot omit for foolish feare of imputation of flattery, the painfull industry of our Captaine, who as at Sea he was alwayes most carefull & vigilant, so at land he refused no paines: but his labour was ever as much or rather more then any mans; which not onely incouraged others with better content, but also effected much with great expedition. We digged a Garden the 22. of May, where among our garden-seeds we sowed Pease and Barley, which in 16. dayes grew vp 8. ynches, although this was but the crust of the ground, and much inferiour to the mould we after found in the mayne.

Pentecost harbour.

The Captains diligence.

After we had taken order for all our necessary businesses, we marched through two of these Isles. The biggest was 4. or 5. myles in compasse; we found here all sorts of ordinary trees, besides, Vines, Currants, Spruce, Yew, Angelica, and divers gummes: in so much many of our company wished themselues setled here. Vpon the 30. our Captaine with 13. went to discover the mayne: we in the ship espyed 3. Canowes that came towards the ship. Which after they had well viewed, one of them came aboord with 3. men, and by our good vsage of them not long after the rest, two dayes we had their companies, in all respects they are but like them at *Elizabeths* Isles, therefore this may suffice for their description. In this time our Captain had discovered a fayre river, trending into the mayne 40 myles, and returned backe to bring in the ship. The Salvages also kept their words and brought vs 40. Bever, Otter, and sable skins, for the value of 5. shillings in kniues, glasses, combes, and such toyes, and thus we vsed them so kindly as we could, because we intended to inhabit in their Country, they lying aboord with vs and we ashore with them; but it was but as changing man for man as hostages, and in this manner many times we had their companies.

Trade with the Salvages.

At last they desired our Captaine to goe with them to the mayne to trade with their *Bashabes*, which is their chiefe Lord, which we did, our boat well manned with

14.yet would they row faster with 3.Ores in their Canowes then we with 8. but when we saw our old acquaintance, would not stay aboord vs as before for hostage,but did what they could to draw vs into a narrow cirke,we exchanged one *Owen Griffin* with them for a yong fellow of theirs, that he might see if he could discover any trechery,as he did,for he found there assembled 283.Salvages with bowes & arrows,but not any thing at all to trade as they pretended.These things considered,we conceited them to be but as all Salvages ever had beene, kinde till they found opportunitie to do mischiefe.Wherefore we determined to take some of them, before they should suspect we had discovered their plot, lest they should absent themselues from vs,so the first that ever after came into the ship were three which we kept, and two we tooke on shore with much adoe,with two Canowes, their bowes and arrowes.

Their trechery.

Fiue Salvages surprised.

Some time we spent in sounding all the Isles, channels,and inlets thereabouts, and we found 4.severall waies a ship might be brought into this Bay.In the interim there came 2. Canowes more boldly aboord vs, signifying we should bring our ship to the place where he dwelt to trade. We excused our selues why we could not, but vsed them kindly, yet got them away with all the speed we could, that they should not be perceiued by them in the house, then we went vp the river 26.myles, of which I had rather not write, then by my relation detract from it, it is in breadth a myle,neare 40.myles;and a channell of 6.7.8.9.or 10.fadom, & on both sides every halfe myle gallant Coues,to containe in many of them 100 sayle, where they may lye on Oze without Cable or Anchor,onely mored with a Hanser, and it floweth 18. foot, that you may make,docke, or carine ships with much facilitie:besides the land is most rich,trending all along on both sides in an equall plaine, neither rocky nor mountainous, but verged with a greene border of grasse, doth make tender to the beholder her pleasant fertilitie,if by cleansing away the woods she were converted into meadow.

A description of the river.

The woods are great,and tall,such as are spoken of in the Islelands,and well watered with many fresh springs.Our men that had seene *Oranoque* so famous in the worlds eares,*Reogrande*,*Loyer*,& *Slion*,report, though they be great & goodly rivers, yet are not comparable to it. Leaving our ship we went higher, till we were 7.myles higher then the salt water flowed;we marched towards the mountains we had seene,but the weather was so hot, & our labour so great,as our Captaine was contented to returne:after we had erected a crosse we left this faire land and river, in which the higher we went the better we liked it,and returned to our ship. By the way we met a Canow that much desired one of our men to go vp to their *Basshabes*,but we knew their intents,and so turned them off;and though we had both time and provision to haue discovered much more,and might haue found peradventure good trade, yet because our company was but small, we would not hazzard so hopefull a businesse as this was, either for our private, or particular ends, being more regardfull of a publicke good,and promulgating Gods holy Church by planting Christianity,which was the intent of our adventurers so well as ours; returning by the Isles in the entry of the Sound we called them S[t] *Georges* Isles, & because on sunday we set out of *England*, on sunday also the 16.of Iune we departed hence. When we had run 30.leagues we had 40.fadom,then 70.then 100. After 2.or 3. watches more we were in 24.fadoms,where we tooke so much Cod as we did know what to doe with, and the 18.of Iuly came to *Dartmouth*,and all our men as well God be thanked as when they went forth.

Thus may you see;

God hath not all his gifts bestowed on all or any one,
Words sweetest,and wits sharpest,courage,strength of bone;
All rarities of minde and parts doe all concurre in none.

Written by *Iames Rosier* one of the Voyage.

The

Their triumph about him
C: Smith bound to a tree to be shott to death. 1607
A Coniurer.
Their Idoll
A Preist
Their Coniuration about C: Smith 1607
C. Smith taketh the King of Pamavnkee prisoner 1608
How they tooke him prisoner in the Oaze 1607
C: Smith bindeth a salvage to his arme, fighteth with the King of Pamaunkee and all his company, and slew 3 of them.
C: Smith takes the King of Paspahegh prisoner. Ao. 1609.
A description of part of the adventures of Cap: Smith in Virginia.
OULD VIRGINIA
Mountaynes forest
Waldens Oake
Masons bushe
LD: Lenox rocks
Richmonds
steps
Howards Mountaynes
Stuards reach
Bedfords valley
Anadales chase
Purchace Iles
Ramushonoq
L. Salvage Rocke
Beauchamps playne
Chawanok flu:
Alice
Smith feild
Segars grove
Chisapea
A Scale of 10 Leauges.
1 2 3 4 5 6 7 8 9 10
Vincere est Vivere
The Country wee now call Virginia beginneth at Cape Henry distant from Roanoack 60 miles, where was Sr. Walter Raleigh's plantation: and because the people differ very little from them of Powhatan in any thing, I have inserted those figures in this place because of the conveniency.
King Powhatan comands C: Smith to be slayne, his daughter Pokahontas beggs his life his thankfullness and how he subiected 39 of their kings reade ye history.
Graven and extracted out of ye generall history of Virginia, New England, and Somer Iles, by Robert Vaughan.
printed by James Reeve

The second Booke.

THE SIXT VOYAGE. 1606.

To another part of *Virginia*, where now are Planted our *English Colonies*, Whom God increase and preserue: Discovered and Described by Captaine IOHN SMITH, sometimes *Governour of the Countrey.*

BY these former relations you may see what incōveniences still crossed those good intents, and how great a matter it was all this time to finde but a Harbour, although there be so many. But this *Virginia* is a Country in *America* betweene the degrees of 34. and 45. of the North latitude. The bounds thereof on the East side are the great *Ocean*: on the South lyeth *Florida*: on the North *nova Francia*: as for the West thereof, the limits are vnknowne. Of all this Country we purpose not to speake, but onely of that part which was planted by the *English men* in the yeare of our Lord, 1606. *And this is vnder the degrees* 37. 38. *and* 39. The temperature of this Country doth agree well with *English* constitutions, being once seasoned to the Country. Which appeared by this, that though by many occasions our people fell sicke; yet did they recover by very small meanes, and continued in health, though there were other great causes, not onely to haue made them sicke, but even to end their dayes, &c. 1606. The latitude.

The Sommer is hot as in *Spaine*; the Winter cold as in *France* or *England*. The heat of sommer is in Iune, Iuly, and August, but commonly the coole Breeses asswage the vehemency of the heat. The chiefe of winter is halfe December, Ianuary, February, and halfe March. The colde is extreame sharpe, but here the Proverbe is true, that *no extreame long continueth.* The temperature.

In the yeare 1607. was an extraordinary frost in most of *Europe*, and this frost was found as extreame in *Virginia*. But the next yeare for 8. or 10. dayes of ill weather, other 14. dayes would be as Sommer.

The windes here are variable, but the like thunder and lightning to purifie the ayre, I haue seldome either seene or heard in *Europe*. From the Southwest came the greatest gusts with thunder and heat. The Northwest winde is commonly coole and bringeth faire weather with it. From the North is the greatest cold, and from the East and Southeast as from the *Barmudas*, fogs and raines. The windes.

Some times there are great droughts, other times much raine, yet great necessitie of neither, by reason we see not but that all the raritie of needfull fruits in *Europe*, may be there in great plentie, by the industry of men, as appeareth by those we there Planted.

There is but one entrance by Sea into this Country, and that is at the mouth of a very goodly Bay, 18. or 20. myles broad. The cape on the South is called *Cape Henry*, in honour of our most noble Prince. The land white hilly sands like vnto the Downes, and all along the shores great plentie of Pines and Firres. The entrances. *Cape Henry.*

The north *Cape* is called *Cape Charles*, in honour of the worthy Duke of *Yorke*. The Isles before it, *Smith's* Isles, by the name of the discover. Within is a country that *Cape Charles.*

may haue the prerogatiue over the most pleasant places knowne, for large and pleasant navigable Rivers, heaven & earth never agreed better to frame a place for mans habitation; were it fully manured and inhabited by industrious people. Here are mountaines, hils, plaines, valleyes, rivers, and brookes, all running most pleasantly into a faire Bay, compassed but for the mouth, with fruitfull and delightsome land. In the Bay and rivers are many Isles both great & small, some woody, some plaine, most of them low and not inhabited. This Bay lyeth North and South, in which the water floweth neare 200. myles, and hath a channell for 140 myles, of depth betwixt 6 and 15 fadome, holding in breadth for the most part 10 or 14 myles. From the head of the Bay to the Northwest, the land is mountanous, and so in a manner from thence by a Southwest line; So that the more Southward, the farther off from the Bay are those mountaines. From which fall certaine brookes which after come to fiue principall navigable rivers. These run from the Northwest into the South east, and so into the West side of the Bay, where the fall of every River is within 20 or 15 myles one of another.

The Country.

The mountaines are of divers natures: for at the head of the Bay the rockes are of a composition like Mill stones. Some of Marble, &c. And many peeces like Christall we found, as throwne downe by water from those mountaines. For in Winter they are covered with much snow, and when it dissolveth the waters fall with such violence, that it causeth great inundations in some narrow valleyes, which is scarce perceived being once in the rivers. These waters wash from the rocks such glistering tinctures, that the ground in some places seemeth as guilded, where both the rocks and the earth are so splendent to behold, *that better iudgements then ours might haue beene perswaded, they contained more then probabilities*. The vesture of the earth in most places doth manifestly proue the nature of the soyle to be lusty and very rich. The colour of the earth we found in diverse places, resembleth *bole Armoniac, terra sigillata*, and *Lemnia*, Fullers earth, Marle, and divers other such appearances. But generally for the most part it is a blacke sandy mould, in some places a fat slimy clay, in other places a very barren gravell. But the best ground is knowne by the vesture it beareth, as by the greatnesse of trees, or abundance of weeds, &c.

The mountaines.

The soyle.

The Country is not mountanous, nor yet low, but such pleasant plaine hils, and fertile valleyes, one prettily crossing another, & watered so conveniently with fresh brookes and springs, no lesse commodious, then delightsome. By the rivers are many plaine marishes, containing some 20 some 100. some 200 Acres, some more, some lesse. Other plaines there are few, but onely where the Salvages inhabit: but all overgrowne with trees & weeds, being a plaine wildernesse as God first made it.

The valleyes.

Plaines.

On the west side of the Bay, we sayd were 5. faire and delightfull navigable rivers. The first of those, and the next to the mouth of the Bay hath his course from the West Northwest. It is called *Powhatan*, according to the name of a principall country that lyeth vpon it. The mouth of this river is neare three myles in breadth, *yet doe the shoules force the Channell so neare the land, that a Sacre will overshoot it at point blanke. It is navigable* 150 *myles, the shouldes and soundings are here needlesse to be expressed*. It falleth from Rockes farre west in a Country inhabited by a nation they call *Monacans*. But where it commeth into our discovery it is *Powhatan*. In the farthest place that was diligently observed, are falles, rockes, shoules, &c. which makes it past navigation *any higher*. Thence in the running downeward, the river is enriched with many goodly brookes, which are maintained by an infinit number of small rundles and pleasant springs, that disperse themselues for best service, as do the veines of a mans body. From the South there fals into it: First, the pleasant river of *Apamatuck*. Next more to the East are two small rivers of *Quiyoughcohanocke*. A little farther is a Bay wherein falleth 3 or 4 prettie brookes & creekes that halfe intrench the Inhabitants of *Warraskoyac*, then the river of *Nandsamund*, and lastly the brooke of *Chisapeack*. From the North side is the river of *Chickahamania*, the backe river of *Iames* Towne; another by the *Cedar Isle*, where we liued ten weekes vpon Oysters, then a convenient harbour for Fisher boats at *Kecoughtan*, that so turneth it selfe into

The river *Powhatan*.

The branches

Bayes

Bayes and Creekes, it makes that place very pleasant to inhabit; their cornefields being girded therein in a manner as *Peninsulaes*. The most of these rivers are inhabited by severall nations, or rather families, of the name of the rivers They haue also over those some Governour, as their King, which they call *Werowances*. In a *Peninsula* on the North side of this river are the *English* Planted in a place by them called *Iames* Towne, in honour of the Kings most excellent Maiestie. *Iames Towne.*

The first and next the rivers mouth are the *Kecoughtans*, who besides their women & children, haue not past 20. fighting men. The *Paspaheghes* (on whose land is seated *Iames* Towne, some 40. myles from the *Bay*) haue not past 40. The river called *Chickahamania* neare 250. The *Weanocks* 100. The *Arrowhatocks* 30. The place called *Powhatan*, some 40. On the South side this river the *Appamatucks* haue sixtie fighting men. The *Quiyougcohanocks* 25. The *Nandsamūds* 200. The *Chesapeacks* 100. Of this last place the *Bay* beareth the name. In all these places is a severall commander, which they call *Werowance*, except the *Chickahamanians*, who are governed by the Priests and their Assistants, or their Elders called *Caw-cawwassoughes*. In sommer no place affordeth more plentie of *Sturgeon*, nor in winter more aboundance of foule, especially in the time of frost. I tooke once 52 Sturgeons at a draught, at another 68. From the later end of May till the end of Iune are taken few, but yong Sturgeons of two foot, or a yard long. From thence till the midst of September, them of two or three yards long and few others. And in 4 or 5, houres with one Net were ordinarily taken 7 or 8: often more, seldome lesse. In the small rivers all the yeare there is good plentie of small fish, so that with hookes those that would take paines had sufficient. The severall Inhabitants.

Foureteene myles Northward from the river *Powhatan*, is the river *Pamavnkee*, *which is navigable 60 or 70 myles, but with Catches and small Barkes 30 or 40 myles farther*. At the ordinary flowing of the salt water, it divideth it selfe into two gallant branches. On the South side inhabit the people of *Toughtanund*, who haue about 60 men for warres. On the North branch *Mattapament*, who haue 30 men. Where this river is divided the Country is called *Pamavnkee*, and nourisheth neare 300 able men. About 25. myles lower on the North side of this river is *Werawocomoco*, where their great King inhabited when I was delivered him prisoner; yet there are not past 40 able men. Ten or twelue myles lower, on the South side of this river, is *Chiskiack*, which hath some 40 or 50 men. These, as also *Apamatuck*, *Irrohatock*, and *Powhatan*, are their great Kings chiefe alliance, and inhabitants. The rest his Conquests. *R. Pamavnkee.* The inhabitants.

Before we come to the third river that falleth from the mountaines, there is another river (*some 30 myles navigable*) that commeth from the Inland, called *Payankatanke*, the Inhabitants are about 50 or 60 serviceable men. *Payankatank. R.*

The third navigable river is called *Toppahanock*. (*This is navigable some 130 myles*) At the top of it inhabit the people called *Mannahoacks* amongst the mountaines, but they are aboue the place we described. Vpon this river on the North side are the people *Cuttatawomen*, with 30 fighting men. Higher are the *Moraughtacunds*, with 80. Beyond them *Rapahanock* with 100. Far aboue is another *Cuttatawomen* with 20. On the South is the pleasant seat of *Nantaughtacund* having 150 men. This river also as the two former, is replenished with fish and foule. *Toppahanock R.* The inhabitants.

The fourth river is called *Patawomeke*, 6 or 7 myles in breadth. *It is navigable 140 myles*, and fed as the rest with many sweet rivers and springs, which fall from the bordering hils. These hils many of them are planted, and yeeld no lesse plentie and varietie of fruit, then the river exceedeth with abundance of fish. It is inhabited on both sides. First on the South side at the very entrance is *Wighcocomoco* & hath some 130 men, beyond them *Sekacawone* with 30. The *Onawmanient* with 100. And the *Patawomekes* more then 200. Here doth the river divide it selfe into 3 or 4 convenient branches. The greatest of the least is called *Quiyough*, trending Northwest, but the river it selfe turneth Northeast, and is still a navigable streame. On the Westerne side of this bought is *Tauxenent* with 40 men. On the North of this river is *Secowocomoco* with 40. Somewhat further *Potapaco* with 20. In the East part is *Pamacaeack* *Patawomek, R.* The inhabitants.

with 60. After *Moyowance* with 100. And lastly, *Nacotchtanke* with 80. The river aboue this place maketh his passage downe a low pleasant valley overshaddowed in many places with high rocky mountaines; from whence distill innumerable sweet and pleasant springs.

Pawtuxunt, R.

The fift river is called *Pawtuxunt*, of a lesse proportion then the rest; but the channell is 16 fadome deepe in some places. Here are infinit skuls of divers kindes of fish more then elswhere. Vpon this river dwell the people called *Acquintanacksuak*, *Pawtuxunt*, and *Mattapanient*. Two hundred men was the greatest strength that could be there perceived. But they inhabit together, and not so dispersed as the rest. These of all other we found most civill to giue intertainement.

Bolus, R. The head of the Bay. *Sasquesahanock*.

Thirtie leagues Northward is a river not inhabited, yet navigable; for the red clay resembling *bole Armoniack* we called it *Bolus*. At the end of the Bay where it is 6 or 7 myles in breadth, it divides it selfe into 4. branches, the best commeth Northwest from among the mountaines, but though Canows may goe a dayes iourney or two vp it, we could not get two myles vp it with our boat for rockes. Vpon it is seated the *Sasquesahanocks*, neare it North and by West runneth a creeke a myle and a halfe: at the head whereof the Eble left vs on shore, where we found many trees cut with hatchets. The next tyde keeping the shore to seeke for some Salvages; (for within thirtie leagues sayling, we saw not any, being a barren Country,) we went vp another small river like a creeke 6 or 7 myle. From thence returning we met 7 Canowes of the *Massowomeks*, with whom we had conference by signes, for we vnderstood one another scarce a word: the next day we discovered the small river & people of *Tockwhogh* trending Eastward.

Having lost our Grapnell among the rocks of *Sasquesahanocks*, we were then neare 200 myles from home, and our Barge about two tuns, and had in it but 12 men to performe this Discovery, wherein we lay aboue 12 weekes vpon those great waters in those vnknowne Countries, having nothing but a little meale, oatemeale and water to feed vs, and scarce halfe sufficient of that for halfe that time, but what provision we got among the Salvages, and such rootes and fish as we caught by accident, and Gods direction; nor had we a Mariner nor any had skill to trim the sayles but two saylers and my selfe, the rest being Gentlemen, or them were as ignorant in such toyle and labour. Yet necessitie in a short time by good words and examples made them doe that that caused them ever after to feare no colours. What I did with this small meanes I leaue to the Reader to iudge, and the Mappe I made of the Country, which is but a small matter in regard of the magnitude thereof. But to proceed, 60 of those *Sasquesahanocks* came to vs with skins, Bowes, Arrows, Targets, Beads, Swords, and Tobacco pipes for presents. Such great and well proportioned men are seldome seene, for they seemed like Giants to the English, yea and to the neighbours, yet seemed of an honest and simple disposition, with much adoe restrained from adoring vs as Gods. Those are the strangest people of all those Countries, both in language & attire; for their language it may well beseeme their proportions, sounding from them, as a voyce in a vault. Their attire is the skinnes of Beares, and Woolues, some haue Cassacks made of Beares heads & skinnes, that a mans head goes through the skinnes neck, and the eares of the Beare fastned to his shoulders, the nose and teeth hanging downe his breast, another Beares face split behind him, and at the end of the nose hung a Pawe, the halfe sleeues comming to the elbowes were the neckes of Beares, and the armes through the mouth with pawes hanging at their noses. One had the head of a Woolfe hanging in a chaine for a Iewell, his Tobacco pipe three quarters of a yard long, prettily carued with a Bird, a Deere, or some such devise at the great end, sufficient to beat out ones braines: with Bowes, Arrowes, and clubs, sutable to their greatnesse. These are scarse knowne to *Powhatan*. They can make neare 600 able men, and are pallisadoed in their Townes to defend them from the *Massawomekes* their mortall enemies. Fiue of their chiefe *Werowances* came aboord vs, and crossed the *Bay* in their Barge. The picture of the greatest of them is signified in the Mappe. The calfe of whose leg was three quarters of a yard about,

The description of a *Sasquesahanough*.

and

and all the rest of his limbes so answerable to that proportion, that he seemed the goodliest man we ever beheld. His hayre, the one side was long, the other shore close with a ridge over his crowne like a cocks combe. His arrowes were fiue quarters long, headed with the splinters of a white christall-like stone, in forme of a heart, an inch broad, and an inch and a halfe or more long. These he wore in a Woolues skinne at his backe for his Quiver, his bow in the one hand and his clubbe in the other, as is described.

On the East side the *Bay*, is the river *Tockwhogh*, and vpon it a people that can make 100 men, seated some seaven myles within the river: where they haue a Fort very well pallisadoed and mantelled with barkes of trees. Next them is *Ozinies* with sixty men. More to the South of that East side of the *Bay*, the river *Rapahanock*, neere vnto which is the river *Kuskarawaock*. Vpon which is seated a people with 200 men. After that, is the river *Tants Wighcocomoco*, & on it a people with 100 men. The people of those rivers are of little stature, of another language from the rest, & very rude. But they on the river *Acohanock* with 40 men, & they of *Accomack* 80 men doth equalize any of the Territories of *Powhatan*, and speake his language, who over all those doth rule as King.

Tockwhogh, R. *Rapahanock*, R. *Kuskarawaock*, R. *Wighcocomoco*, R. *Accomack*, R.

Southward we went to some parts of *Chawonock* and the *Mangoags* to search for them left by Mr *White*. Amongst those people are thus many severall Nations of sundry Languages, that environ *Powhatans* Territories. The *Chawonockes*, the *Mangoags*, the *Monacans*, the *Mannahokes*, the *Masawomekes*, the *Powhatans*, the *Sasquesahanocks*, the *Atquanachukes*, the *Tockwoghes*, and the *Kuscarawaokes*. All those not any one vnderstandeth another but by Interpreters. Their severall habitations are more plainly described by this annexed Mappe, which will present to the eye, the way of the mountaines, and current of the rivers, with their severall turnings, bayes, shoules, Isles, Inlets, and creekes, the breadth of the waters, the distances of places, and such like. In which Mappe obserue this, that as far as you see the little Crosses on rivers, mountaines, or other places haue beene discovered; the rest was had by information of the Savages, and are set downe according to their instructions.

Chawonock. The severall languages.

Thus haue I walkt a wayless way, with vncouth pace,
Which yet no Christian man did ever trace:
But yet I know this not affects the minde,
Which eares doth heare, as that which eyes doe finde.

Of such things which are naturally in Virginia, *and how they vse them.*

VIRGINIA doth afford many excellent vegetables, and liuing Creatures, yet grasse there is little or none, but what groweth in low Marishes: for all the Countrey is overgrowne with trees, whose droppings continually turneth their grasse to weeds, by reason of the rancknes of the ground, which would soone be amended by good husbandry. The wood that is most common is Oke and Walnut, many of their Okes are so tall & straight, that they will beare two foote and a halfe square of good timber for 20 yards long; Of this wood there is two or three severall kinds. The Acornes of one kinde, whose barke is more white then the other, & somewhat sweetish, which being boyled, at last affords a sweet oyle, that they keepe in gourds to annoint their heads and ioynts. The fruit they eate made in bread or otherwise. There is also some Elme, some blacke Walnut tree, and some Ash: of Ash and Elme they make sope Ashes. If the trees be very great, the Ashes will be good, and melt to hard lumps, but if they be small, it will be but powder, and not so good as the other. Of walnuts there is 2 or 3 kindes; there is a kinde of wood we called Cypres, because both the wood, the fruit, and leafe did most resemble it, and of those trees there are some neare three fadome about at the foot, very straight,

Why there is little grasse. Woods with their fruits. Elme. Walnuts. Supposed Cypres.

straight, and 50, 60, or 80 foot without a branch. By the dwelling of the Salvages are some great Mulbery trees, and in some parts of the Countrey, they are found growing naturally in prettie groues. There was an assay made to make silke, and surely the wormes prospered excellent well, till the master workeman fell sicke. During which time they were eaten with Rats.

Mulberries.

Chesnuts.

In some parts were found some Chesnuts, whose wild fruit equalize the best in *France, Spaine, Germany*, or *Italy*. Plums there are of three sorts. The red and white are like our hedge plums, but the other which they call *Putchamins*, grow as high as a *Palmeta*: the fruit is like a Medler; it is first greene, then yellow, and red when it is ripe; if it be not ripe, it will draw a mans mouth awry, with much torment, but when it is ripe, it is as delicious as an Apricot.

Cherries.

Vines.

They haue Cherries, and those are much like a Damson, but for their t. ; and colour we called them Cherries. We saw some few Crabs, but very small and bitter. Of vines great abundance in many parts that climbe the toppes of the highest trees in some places, but these beare but few grapes. Except by the rivers & savage habitations, where they are not overshadowed from the sunne, they are covered with fruit, though never pruined nor manured. Of those hedge grapes we made neere twentie gallons of wine, which was like our French Brittish wine, but certainely they would proue good were they well manured. There is another sort of grape neere as great as a Cherry, this they call *Messamins*, they be fatte, and the iuyce thicke. Neither doth the taste so well please when they are made in wine. They haue a small fruit growing on little trees, husked like a Chesnut, but the fruit most like a very small Acorne. This they call *Chechinquamins*, which they esteeme a great daintie. They haue a berry much like our Gooseberry, in greatnesse, colour, and tast; those they call *Rawcomens*, and doe eat them raw or boyled. Of these naturall fruits they liue a great part of the yeare, which they vse in this manner; The Walnuts, Chesnuts, Acornes, and *Chechinquamins* are dryed to keepe. When they need walnuts they breake them betweene two stones, yet some part of the shels will cleaue to the fruit. Then doe they dry them againe vpon a Mat over a hurdle. After they put it into a morter of wood, and beat it very small: that done they mix it with water, that the shels may sinke to the bottome. This water will be coloured as milke, which they call *Pawcohiccora*, and keepe it for their vse. The fruit like Medlers they call *Putchamins*, they cast vpon hurdles on a Mat, and preserue them as Pruines. Of their Chesnuts and *Chechinquamins* boyled, they make both broath and bread for their chiefe men, or at their greatest feasts. Besides those fruit trees, there is a white Popular, and another tree like vnto it, that yeeldeth a very cleare and an odoriferous *Gumme* like *Turpentine*, which some called *Balsom*. There are also *Cedars* and *Saxafras* trees. They also yeeld gummes in a small proportion of themselues. Wee tryed conclusions to extract it out of the wood, but nature afforded more then our arts.

Chechinquamins.

Rawcomens.

How they vse their fruits.

Walnut milke.

Gummes.
Cedars.
Saxafras trees.

Berries.

Matcum.

In the watry valleyes groweth a Berry which they call *Ocoughtanamnis* very much like vnto Caper:. These they dry in sommer. When they eat them they boile them neare halfe a day; for otherwise they differ not much from poyson. *Mattoum* groweth as our Bents. The seed is not much vnlike to Rie, though much smaller. This they vse for a daintie bread buttered with deare suet.

Strawberries.

During Sommer there are either Strawberries, which ripen in Aprill, or Mulberries which ripen in May and Iune. Raspises, hurts; or a fruit that the inhabitants call *Maracocks*, which is a pleasant wholsome fruit much like a Lemond. Many herbes in the spring are cōmonly dispersed throughout the woods, good for brothes and sallets, as Violets, Purslain, Sorrell, &c. Besides many we vsed whose names we know not.

Hearbes.

Rootes.

The chiefe root they haue for food is called *Tockawhoughe*. It groweth like a flagge in Marishes. In one day a Salvage will gather sufficient for a weeke. These roots are much of the greatnesse and taste of *Potatoes*. They vse to cover a great many of them with Oke leaues and Ferne, and then cover all with earth in the manner of a Colepit; over it, on each side, they continue a great fire 24 houres before they dare eat it.

Raw

Raw it is no better then poyson, and being rosted, except it be tender and the heat abated, or sliced and dryed in the Sunne, mixed with sorrell and meale or such like, it will prickle and torment the throat extreamely, and yet in sommer they vse this ordinarily for bread.

They haue another roote which they call *Wighsacan*: as th'other feedeth the body, so this cureth their hurts and diseases. It is a small root which they bruise and apply to the wound. *Pocones* is a small root that groweth in the mountaines, which being dryed and beate in powder turneth red. And this they vse for swellings, aches, annointing their ioynts, painting their heads and garments. They account it very precious, and of much worth. *Musquaspen* is a roote of the bignesse of a finger, and as red as bloud. In drying, it will wither almost to nothing. This they vse to paint their Mattes, Targets, and such like.

Wighsacan a roote. *Pocones* a small roote. *Musquaspen* a roote.

There is also *Pellitory of Spaine*, *Sasafrage*, and divers other simples, which the Apothecaries gathered, and commended to be good, and medicinable.

Pellitory. Sasafrage.

In the low Marishes grow plots of Onyons, containing an Acre of ground or more in many places; but they are small, not past the bignesse of the toppe of ones Thumbe.

Onyons.

Of beasts the chiefe are Deere, nothing differing from ours. In the deserts towards the heads of the rivers, there are many, but amongst the rivers few. There is a beast they call *Aroughcun*, much like a badger, but vseth to liue on trees as Squirrels doe. Their Squirrels some are neare as great as our smallest sort of wilde Rabbets, some blackish or blacke and white, but the most are gray.

Their chiefe beasts are Deere. *Aroughcun*. Squirrels.

A small beast they haue they call *Assapanick*, but we call them flying Squirrels, because spreading their legs, and so stretching the largenesse of their skins, that they haue beene seene to fly 30 or 40 yards. An *Opassom* hath a head like a Swine, and a taile like a Rat, and is of the bignesse of a Cat. Vnder her belly shee hath a bagge, wherein she lodgeth, carrieth, and suckleth her young. A *Mussascus* is a beast of the forme and nature of our water Rats, but many of them smell exceeding strongly of Muske. Their Hares no bigger then our Conies, and few of them to be found.

Assapanick, a Squirrel flying. *Opassom*. *Mussascus*.

Their Beares are very little in comparison of those of *Muscovia* and *Tartaria*. The Beaver is as big as an ordinary water dog, but his legs exceeding short. His forefeete like a dogs, his hinder feet like a Swans. His taile somewhat like the forme of a Racket, bare without haire, which to eat the Salvages esteeme a great delicate. They haue many *Otters*, which as the *Beavers* they take with snares, and esteeme the skins great ornaments, and of all those beasts they vse to feed when they catch them. An *Vtchunquoyes* is like a wilde Cat. Their Foxes are like our silver haired Conies, of a small proportion, and not smelling like those in *England*. Their Dogges of that Country are like their Woolues, and cannot barke but howle, and the Woolues not much bigger then our English Foxes. Martins, Powlecats, Weesels, and Minkes we know they haue, because we haue seene many of their skinnes, though very seldome any of them aliue. But one thing is strange, that we could never perceiue their Vermine destroy our Hennes, Egges, nor Chickens, nor doe any hurt, nor their flyes nor serpents any way pernicious, where in the South parts of *America* they are alwayes dangerous, and often deadly

Beares. The Beaver. Otters. *Vtchunquoyes* Foxes. Dogges. Martins. Polcats. Weesels, and Minkes.

Of Birds the Eagle is the greatest devourer. Hawkes there be of divers sorts, as our Falconers called them: *Sparrow-hawkes*, *Lanarets*, *Goshawkes*, *Falcons* and *Osperayes*, but they all prey most vpon fish. Their Partridges are little bigger then our Quailes. Wilde Turkies are as bigge as our tame. There are Woosels or Blackbirds with red shoulders, Thrushes and divers sorts of small Birds, some red, some blew, scarce so bigge as a Wrenne, but few in Sommer. In Winter there are great plentie of Swans, Cranes, gray and white with blacke wings, Herons, Geese, Brants, Ducke, Wigeon, Dotterell. Oxeies, Parrats, and Pigeons. Of all those sorts great abundance, and some other strange kinds, to vs vnknowne by name. But in Sommer not any, or a very few to be seene.

Birds.

Of fish we were best acquainted with Sturgeon, Grampus, Porpus, Seales, *Stingraies*,

Fish.

graies, whose tailes are very dangerous. Bretts, Mullets, white Salmonds, Trowts, Soles, Plaice, Herrings, Conyfish, Rockfish, Eeles, Lampreys, Catfish, Shades, Pearch of three sorts, Crabs, Shrimps, Creuises, Oysters, Cocles, and Muscles. But the most strange fish is a small one, so like the picture of St *George* his Dragon, as possible can be, except his legs and wings, and the Toadefish, which will swell till it be like to burst, when it commeth into the ayre.

The rockes.

Concerning the entrailes of the earth, little can be said for certaintie. There wanted good Refiners; for those that tooke vpon them to haue skill this way, tooke vp the washings from the mountaines, and some moskered shining stones and spangles which the waters brought downe, flattering themselues in their owne vaine conceits to haue beene supposed what they were not, by the meanes of that ore, if it proued as their arts and iudgements expected. Onely this is certaine, that many regions lying in the same latitude, afford Mines very rich of divers natures. The crust also of these rockes would easily perswade a man to beleeue there are other Mines then yron and steele, if there were but meanes and men of experience that knew the Mine from *Spar*.

Of their Planted fruits in Virginia, *and how they vse them.*

How they divide the yeare.

THey divide the yeare into fiue seasons. Their winter some call *Popanow*, the spring *Cattapeuk*, the sommer *Cohattayough*, the earing of their Corne *Nepinough*, the harvest and fall of leafe *Taquitock*. From September vntill the midst of November are the chiefe feasts & sacrifice. Then haue they plentie of fruits as well planted as naturall, as corne, greene and ripe, fish, fowle, and wilde beasts exceeding fat.

How they prepare the ground.

The greatest labour they take, is in planting their corne, for the Country naturally is overgrowne with wood. To prepare the ground they bruise the barke of the trees neare the root, then doe they scortch the roots with fire that they grow no more. The next yeare with a crooked peece of wood they beat vp the weeds by the rootes, and in that mould they plant their Corne. Their manner is this. They make a hole in the earth with a sticke, and into it they put foure graines of wheate and two of beanes These holes they make foure foote one from another; Their women and children do continually keepe it with weeding, and when it is growne middle high, they hill it about like a hop-yard.

How they plant.

In Aprill they begin to plant, but their chiefe plantation is in May, and so they continue till the midst of Iune. What they plant in Aprill they reape in August, for May in September, for Iune in October; Every stalke of their corne commonly beareth two eares, some three, seldome any foure, many but one, and some none. Every eare ordinarily hath betwixt 200 and 500 graines. The stalke being greene hath a sweet iuice in it, somewhat like a sugar Cane, which is the cause that when they gather their corne greene, they sucke the stalkes: for as we gather greene pease, so doe they their corne being greene, which excelleth their old. They plant also pease they call *Assentamens*, which are the same they call in *Italy*, *Fagioli*. Their Beanes are the same the Turkes call *Garnanses*, but these they much esteeme for dainties.

How they vse their Corne.

Their corne they rost in the eare greene, and bruising it in a morter of wood with a Polt, lap it in rowles in the leaues of their corne, and so boyle it for a daintie. They also reserue that corne late planted that will not ripe, by roasting it in hot ashes, the heat thereof drying it. In winter they esteeme it being boyled with beanes for a rare dish, they call *Pausarowmena*. Their old wheat they first steepe a night in hot water, in the morning pounding it in a morter. They vse a small basket for their Temmes, then pound againe the great, and so separating by dashing their hand in the basket, receiue the flower in a platter made of wood, scraped to that forme with burning and shels. Tempering this flower with water, they make it either in cakes, covering them with ashes till they be baked, and then washing them in faire water, they drie presently with their owne heat: or else boyle them in water, eating the broth with the bread which they call *Ponap*. The groutes and peeces of the cornes remaining, by fanning in a Platter or in the wind, away, the branne they boyle 3 or 4 houres with water, which is an ordinary food they call *Vstatahamen*. But some more thriftie then cleanly, doe burne the core of the eare to powder, which they call *Pungnough*, mingling that in their meale, but it never tasted well in bread, nor broth. Their fish & flesh they boyle either very tenderly, or boyle it so long on hurdles over the fire, or else after the *Spanish* fashion, putting it on a spit, they turne first the one side, then the other, till it be as drie as their ierkin Beefe in the west *Indies*, that they may keepe it a moneth or more without putrifying. The broth of fish or flesh they eat as commonly as the meat. How they vse their fish and flesh.

In May also amongst their corne they plant *Pumpeons*, and a fruit like vnto a muske mellon, but lesse and worse, which they call *Macocks*. These increase exceedingly, and ripen in the beginning of Iuly, and continue vntill September. They plant also *Maracocks* a wild fruit like a Lemmon, which also increase infinitely. They begin to ripe in September, and continue till the end of October. When all their fruits be gathered, little els they plant, and this is done by their women and children; neither doth this long suffice them, for neare three parts of the yeare, they onely obserue times and seasons, and liue of what the Country naturally affordeth from hand to mouth, &c. Planted fruits

The Commodities in Virginia, *or that may be had by Industrie.*

THe mildnesse of the ayre, the fertilitie of the soyle, and situation of the rivers are so propitious to the nature and vse of man, as no place is more convenient for pleasure, profit, and mans sustenance, vnder that latitude or climat. Here will liue any beasts, as horses, goats, sheepe, asses, hens, &c. as appeared by them that were carried thether. The waters, Isles, and shoales, are full of safe harbours for ships of warre or marchandize, for boats of all sorts, for transportation or fishing, &c. The Bay and rivers haue much marchantable fish, and places fit for Salt coats, building of ships, making of Iron, &c. A proofe cattell will liue well.

Muscovia and *Polonia* doe yearely receiue many thousands, for pitch, tarre, sopeashes, Rosen, Flax, Cordage, Sturgeon, Masts, Yards, Wainscot, Firres, Glasse, and such like; also *Swethland* for Iron and Copper. *France* in like manner, for Wine, Canvas, and Salt. *Spaine* asmuch for Iron, Steele, Figges, Reasons, and Sackes. *Italy* with Silkes and Velvets consumes our chiefe Commodities. *Holland* maintaines it selfe by fishing and trading at our owne doores. All these temporize with other for necessities, but all as vncertaine as peace or warres. Besides the charge, travell, and danger in transporting them, by seas, lands, stormes, and Pyrats. Then how much hath *Virginia* the prerogatiue of all those flourishing Kingdomes, for the benefit of our Land, when as within one hundred myles all those are to be had, either ready provided by nature, or else to be prepared, were there but industrious men to labour. Onely of Copper we may doubt is wanting, but there is good probabilitie that both Copper and better Minerals are there to be had for their labour. Other Countries haue it. So then here is a place, a nurse for souldiers, a practise for mariners, a trade for marchants, a reward for the good, and that which is most of all, a businesse (most acceptable to God) to bring such poore Infidels to the knowledge of God and his holy Gospell. The Commodities.

Of the naturall Inhabitants of VIRGINIA.

THe land is not populous, for the men be few; their far greater number is of women and children. Within 60 myles of *Iames* Towne, there are about some 5000 people, but of able men fit for their warres scarce 1500. To nourish so many The numbers

Seaven hundred men were the most were seene together when they thought to haue surprised Captaine Smith.

together they haue yet no meanes, because they make so small a benefit of their land, be it never so fertile. Six or seauen hundred haue beene the most hath beene seene together, when they gathered themselues to *haue surprised* mee *at Pamavnkee*, having but fifteene to withstand the worst of their fury. As small as the proportion of ground that hath yet beene discovered, is in comparison of that yet vnknowne: the people differ very much in stature, especially in language, as before is expressed. Some being very great as the *Sasquesahanocks*; others very little, as the *Wighcocomocoes*: but generally tall and straight, of a comely proportion, and of a colour browne when they are of any age, but they are borne white. Their hayre is generally blacke, but few haue any beards. The men weare halfe their beards shaven, the other halfe long; for Barbers they vse their women, who with two shels will grate away the hayre, of any fashion they please. The women are cut in many fashions, agreeable to their yeares, but ever some part remaineth long. They are very strong, of an able body and full of agilitie, able to endure to lie in the woods vnder a tree by the fire, in the worst of winter, or in the weedes and grasse, in Ambuscado in the Sommer. They are inconstant in every thing, but what feare constraineth them to keepe. Craftie, timerous, quicke of apprehension, and very ingenuous. Some are of disposition fearefull, some bold, most cautelous, all Savage. Generally covetous of Copper, Beads, and such like trash. They are soone moued to anger, and so malicious, that they seldome forget an iniury: they seldome steale one from another, least their coniurers should reveale it, and so they be pursued and punished. That they are thus feared is certaine, but that any can reueale their offences by coniuration I am doubtfull. Their women are carefull not to be suspected of dishonestie without the leaue of their husbands. Each houshold knoweth their owne lands, and gardens, and most liue of their owne labours. For their apparell, they are sometime covered with the skinnes of wilde beasts, which in Winter are dressed with the hayre, but in Sommer without. The better sort vse large mantels of Deare skins, not much differing in fashion from the Irish mantels. Some imbrodered with white beads, some with Copper, other painted after their manner. But the common sort haue scarce to cover their nakednesse, but with grasse, the leaues of trees, or such like. We haue seene some vse mantels made of Turky feathers, so prettily wrought & woven with threads that nothing could be discerned but the feathers. That was exceeding warme and very handsome. But the women are alwayes covered about their middles with a skin, and very shamefast to be seene bare. They adorne themselues most with copper beads and paintings. Their women, some haue their legs, hands, breasts and face cunningly imbrodered with divers workes, as beasts, serpents, artificially wrought into their flesh with blacke spots. In each eare commonly they haue 3 great holes, whereat they hang chaines, bracelets, or copper. Some of their men weare in those holes, a small greene and yellow coloured snake, neare halfe a yard in length, which crawling and lapping her selfe about his necke oftentimes familiarly would kisse his lips. Others weare a dead Rat tyed by the taile. Some on their heads weare the wing of a bird, or some large feather with a Rattell. Those Rattels are somewhat like the chape of a Rapier, but lesse, which they take from the taile of a snake. Many haue the whole skinne of a Hawke or some strange foule, stuffed with the wings abroad. Others a broad peece of Copper, and some the hand of their enemy dryed. Their heads and shoulders are painted red with the roote *Pocone* brayed to powder, mixed with oyle, this they hold in sommer to preserue them from the heate, and in winter from the cold. Many other formes of paintings they vse, but he is the most gallant that is the most monstrous to behold.

A description of the people. The Barbers. The constitution. The disposition. The possessions. Their attire. Their ornaments.

Their buildings.

Their buildings and habitations are for the most part by the rivers, or not farre distant from some fresh spring. Their houses are built like our Arbors, of small young springs bowed and tyed, and so close covered with Mats, or the barkes of trees very handsomely, that notwithstanding either winde, raine, or weather, they are as warme as stooues, but very smoaky, yet at the toppe of the house there is a hole made for the smoake to goe into right over the fire.

Against

Against the fire they lie on little hurdles of Reeds covered with a Mat, borne from the ground a foote and more by a hurdle of wood. On these round about the house they lie heads and points one by th'other against the fire, some covered with Mats, some with skins, and some starke naked lie on the ground, from 6 to 20 in a house. Their houses are in the midst of their fields or gardens, which are small plots of ground. Some 20 acres, some 40. some 100. some 200. some more, some lesse. In some places from 2 to 50 of those houses together, or but a little separated by groues of trees. Neare their habitations is little small wood or old trees on the ground by reason of their burning of them for fire. So that a man may gallop a horse amongst these woods any way, but where the creekes or Rivers shall hinder.

Their lodgings.

Their gardens

Men, women, and children haue their severall names according to the severall humor of their Parents. Their women (they say) are easily delivered of childe, yet doe they loue children very dearely. To make them hardie, in the coldest mornings they them wash in the rivers, and by painting and oyntments so tanne their skinnes, that after a yeare or two, no weather will hurt them.

How they vse their children.

The men bestow their times in fishing, hunting, warres, and such man-like exercises, scorning to be seene in any woman-like exercise, which is the cause that the women be very painefull, and the men often idle. The women and children doe the rest of the worke. They make mats, baskets, pots, morters, pound their corne, make their bread, prepare their victuals, plant their corne, gather their corne, beare all kind of burdens, and such like.

The industrie of their women.

Their fire they kindle presently by chafing a dry pointed sticke in a hole of a little square peece of wood, that firing it selfe, will so fire mosse, leaues, or any such like dry thing, that will quickly burne. In March and Aprill they liue much vpon their fishing wires; and feed on fish, Turkies, and Squirrels. In May and Iune they plant their fields, and liue most of Acornes, Walnuts, and fish. But to amend their dyet, some disperse themselues in small companies, and liue vpon fish, beasts, crabs, oysters, land Tortoises, strawberries, mulberries, and such like. In Iune, Iuly, and August, they feed vpon the rootes of *Tocknough* berries, fish, and greene wheat. It is strange to see how their bodies alter with their dyet, even as the deere & wilde beasts they seeme fat and leane, strong and weake. *Powhatan* their great King, and some others that are provident, rost their fish and flesh vpon hurdles as before is expressed, and keepe it till scarce times.

How they strike fire.

The order of dyet.

For fishing, hunting, and warres they vse much their bow and arrowes. They bring their bowes to the forme of ours by the scraping of a shell. Their arrowes are made some of straight young sprigs, which they head with bone, some 2 or 3 ynches long. These they vse to shoot at Squirrels on trees. Another sort of arrowes they vse made of Reeds. These are peeced with wood, headed with splinters of christall, or some sharpe stone, the spurres of a Turkey, or the bill of some bird. For his knife he hath the splinter of a Reed to cut his feathers in forme. With this knife also, he will ioynt a Deere, or any beast, shape his shooes, buskins, mantels, &c. To make the noch of his arrow he hath the tooth of a Beaver, set in a sticke, wherewith he grateth it by degrees. His arrow head he quickly maketh with a little bone, which he ever weareth at his bracert, of any splint of a stone, or glasse in the forme of a heart, and these they glew to the end of their arrowes. With the sinewes of Deere, and the tops of Deeres hornes boyled to a ielly, they make a glew that will not dissolue in cold water.

How they make their bowes and arrowes.

Their kniues.

For their warres also they vse Targets that are round and made of the barkes of trees, and a sword of wood at their backes, but oftentimes they vse for swords the horne of a Deere put through a peece of wood in forme of a Pickaxe. Some a long stone sharpned at both ends, vsed in the same manner. This they were wont to vse also for hatchets, but now by trucking they haue plentie of the same forme of yron. And those are their chiefe instruments and armes.

Their Targets and Swords.

Their fishing is much in Boats. These they make of one tree by burning and scratching away the coales with stones and shels, till they haue made it in forme of a

Their Boats.

Trough. Some of them are an elne deepe, and fortie or fiftie foote in length, and some will beare 40 men, but the most ordinary are smaller, and will beare 10, 20, or 30. according to their bignesse. In stead of Oares, they vse Paddles and stickes, with which they will row faster then our Barges. Betwixt their hands and thighes, their women vse to spin, the barkes of trees, Deere sinewes, or a kind of grasse they call **Pemmenaw**, of these they make a thread very even and readily. This thread serveth for many vses. As about their housing, apparell, as also they make nets for fishing, for the quantitie as formally braded as ours. They make also with it lines for angles. Their hookes are either a bone grated as they noch their arrowes in the forme of a crooked pinne or fish-hooke, or of the splinter of a bone tyed to the clift of a little sticke, and with the end of the line, they tie on the bait. They vse also long arrowes tyed in a line, wherewith they shoote at fish in the rivers. But they of *Accawmack* vse staues like vnto Iauelins headed with bone. With these they dart fish swimming in the water. They haue also many artificiall wires, in which they get abundance of fish.

How they spin.

Their fish-hookes.

In their hunting and fishing they take extreame paines; yet it being their ordinary exercise from their infancy, they esteeme it a pleasure and are very proud to be expert therein. And by their continuall ranging, and travell, they know all the advantages and places most frequented with Deere, Beasts, Fish, Foule, Roots, and Berries. At their huntings they leaue their habitations, and reduce themselues into companies, as the *Tartars* doe, and goe to the most desert places with their families, where they spend their time in hunting and fowling vp towards the mountaines, by the heads of their rivers, where there is plentie of game. For betwixt the rivers the grounds are so narrowe, that little commeth here which they devoure not. It is a marvell they can so directly passe these deserts, some 3 or 4 dayes iourney without habitation. Their hunting houses are like vnto Arbours covered with Mats. These their women beare after them, with Corne, Acornes, Morters, and all bag and baggage they vse. When they come to the place of exercise, every man doth his best to shew his dexteritie, for by their excelling in those qualities, they get their wiues. Fortie yards will they shoot levell, or very neare the marke, and 120 is their best at Random. At their huntings in the deserts they are commonly two or three hundred together. Having found the Deere, they environ them with many fires, & betwixt the fires they place themselues. And some take their stands in the midsts. The Deere being thus feared by the fires, and their voyces, they chase them so long within that circle, that many times they kill 6, 8, 10, or 15 at a hunting. They vse also to driue them into some narrow poynt of land, when they find that advantage; and so force them into the river, where with their boats they haue *Ambuscadoes* to kill them. When they haue shot a Deere by land, they follow him like bloud-hounds by the bloud, and straine, and oftentimes so take them. Hares, Partridges, Turkies, or Egges, fat or leane, young or old, they devoure all they can catch in their power. In one of these huntings they found me in the discovery of the head of the river of *Chickahamania*, where they slew my men, and tooke me prisoner in a Bogmire, where I saw those exercises, and gathered these Observations.

How they hunt.

One Salvage hunting alone, vseth the skinne of a Deere slit on the one side, and so put on his arme, through the neck, so that his hand comes to the head which is stuffed, and the hornes, head, eyes, eares, and every part as artificially counterfeited as they can devise. Thus shrowding his body in the skinne by stalking, he approacheth the Deere, creeping on the ground from one tree to another. If the Deere chance to find fault, or stand at gaze, he turneth the head with his hand to his best advantage to seeme like a Deere, also gazing and licking himselfe. So watching his best advantage to approach, having shot him, he chaseth him by his bloud and straine till he get him.

One Salvage hunting alone.

When they intend any warres, the **Werowances** vsually haue the advice of their their Priests and Coniurers, and their allies, and ancient friends, but chiefely the Priests determine their resolution. Every **Werowance**, or some lustie fellow, they appoin

Their Consultations.

point Captaine over every nation. They seldome make warre for lands or goods, but for women and children, and principally for revenge. They haue many enemies, namely, all their westernly Countries beyond the mountaines, and the heads of the rivers. Vpon the head of the *Powhatans* are the *Monacans*, whose chiefe habitation is at *Rasauweak*, vnto whom the *Mowhemenchughes*, the *Massinnacacks*, the *Monahassanughs*, the *Monasickapanoughs*, and other nations pay tributes. Vpon the head of the river of *Toppahanock* is a people called *Mannahoacks*. To these are contributers the *Tauxanias*, the *Shackaconias*, the *Ontponeas*, the *Tegninateos*, the *Whonkenteaes*, the *Stegarakes*, the *Hassinnungaes*, and divers others, all confederates with the *Monacans*, though many different in language, and be very barbarous, liuing for the most part of wild beasts and fruits. Beyond the mountaines from whence is the head of the river *Patawomeke*, the Salvages report inhabit their most mortall enemies, the *Massawomekes*, vpon a great salt water, which by all likelihood is either some part of *Cannada*, some great lake, or some inlet of some sea that falleth into the South sea. These *Massawomekes* are a great nation and very populous. For the heads of all those rivers, especially the *Pattawomekes*, the *Pautuxuntes*, the *Sasquesahanocks*, the *Tockwoughes* are continually tormented by them: of whose crueltie, they generally complained, and very importunate they were with me, and my company to free them from these tormentors. To this purpose they offered food, conduct, assistance, and continuall subiection. Which I concluded to effect. But the councell then present emulating my successe, would not thinke it fit to spare me fortie men to be hazzarded in those vnknowne regions, having passed (as before was spoken of) but with 12, and so was lost that opportunitie. Seaven boats full of these *Massawomekes* wee encountred at the head of the *Bay*; whose Targets, Baskets, Swords, Tobaccopipes, Platters, Bowes, and Arrowes, and every thing shewed, they much exceeded them of our parts, and their dexteritie in their small boats, made of the barkes of trees, sowed with barke and well luted with gumme, argueth that they are seated vpon some great water.

Their enemies.

Massawomekes.

Their offer of subiection.

Against all these enemies the *Powhatans* are constrained sometimes to fight. Their chiefe attempts are by Stratagems, trecheries, or surprisals. Yet the *Werowances* women and children they put not to death, but keepe them Captiues. They haue a method in warre, and for our pleasures they shewed it vs, and it was in this manner performed at *Mattapanient*.

Having painted and disguised themselues in the fiercest manner they could devise. They divided themselues into two Companies, neare a hundred in a company. The one company called *Monacans*, the other *Powhatans*. Either army had their Captaine. These as enemies tooke their stands a musket shot one from another; ranked themselues 15 a breast, and each ranke from another 4 or 5 yards, not in fyle, but in the opening betwixt their fyles. So the Reare could shoot as conveniently as the Front. Having thus pitched the fields: from either part went a messenger with these conditions, that whosoever were vanquished, such as escape vpon their submission in two dayes after should liue, but their wiues and children should be prize for the Conquerours. The messengers were no sooner returned, but they approached in their orders; On each flanke a Serieant, and in the Reare an Officer for Lieutenant, all duly keeping their orders, yet leaping and singing after their accustomed tune, which they onely vse in Warres. Vpon the first flight of arrowes they gaue such horrible shouts and screeches, as so many infernall hell-hounds could not haue made them more terrible. When they had spent their arrowes, they ioyned together prettily, charging and retyring, every ranke seconding other. As they got advantage they catched their enemies by the hayre of the head, and downe he came that was taken. His enemy with his wooden sword seemed to beat out his braines, and still they crept to the Reare, to maintaine the skirmish. The *Monacans* decreasing, the *Powhatans* charged them in the forme of a halfe Moone; they vnwilling to be inclosed, fled all in a troope to their *Ambuscadoes*, on whom they led them very cunningly. The *Monacans* disperse themselues among the fresh men, whereupon the

Their manner of Battell.

Powhatans retired, with all ſpeed to their ſeconds; which the *Monacans* ſeeing, tooke that advantage to retire againe to their owne battell, and ſo each returned to their owne quarter. All their actions, voyces, and geſtures, both in charging and retiring were ſo ſtrained to the height of their qualitie and nature, that the ſtrangeneſſe thereof made it ſeeme very delightfull.

Their Muſicke. For their Muſicke they vſe a thicke Cane, on which they pipe as on a Recorder. For their warres they haue a great deepe platter of wood. They cover the mouth thereof with a skin, at each corner they tie a walnut, which meeting on the backſide neere the bottome, with a ſmall rope they twitch them together till it be ſo tought and ſtiffe, that they may beat vpon it as vpon a drumme. But their chiefe inſtruments are Rattles made of ſmall gourds, or Pumpeons ſhels. Of theſe they haue Baſe, Tenor, Countertenor, Meane, and Treble. Theſe mingled with their voyces ſometimes twenty or thirtie together, make ſuch a terrible noiſe as would rather affright, then delight any man. If any great commander arriue at the habitation of a *Werowance*, they ſpread a Mat as the Turkes doe a Carpet for him to ſit vpon. Vpon another right oppoſite they ſit themſelues. Then doe all with a tunable voice of ſhouting bid him welcome. After this doe two or more of their chiefeſt men make an Oration, teſtifying their loue. Which they doe with ſuch vehemency, and ſo great paſſions, that they ſweat till they drop, and are ſo out of breath they can ſcarce ſpeake. So that a man would take them to be exceeding angry, or ſtark mad. Such victuall as they haue, they ſpend freely, and at night where his lodging is appointed, they ſet a woman freſh painted red with *Pocones* and oyle, to be his bed-fellow.

Their entertainement.

Their trade. Their manner of trading is for copper, beads, and ſuch like, for which they giue ſuch commodities as they haue, as skins, foule, fiſh, fleſh, and their Country Corne. But their victualls are their chiefeſt riches.

Their Phiſicke. Every ſpring they make themſelues ſicke with drinking the iuyce of a roote they call *Wighſacan*, and water; whereof they powre ſo great a quantitie, that it purgeth them in a very violent manner; ſo that in three or foure dayes after, they ſcarce recover their former health. Sometimes they are troubled with dropſies, ſwellings, aches, and ſuch like diſeaſes; for cure whereof they build a Stoue in the forme of a Doue-houſe with mats, ſo cloſe that a few coales therein covered with a pot, will make the patient ſweat extreamely. For ſwellings alſo they vſe ſmall peeces of touchwood, in the forme of cloues, which pricking on the griefe they burne cloſe to the fleſh, and from thence draw the corruption with their mouth. With this roote *Wighſacan* they ordinarily heale greene wounds. But to ſcarrifie a ſwelling, or make inciſion, their beſt inſtruments are ſome ſplinted ſtone. Old vlcers, or putrified hurts are ſeldome ſeene cured amongſt them. They haue many profeſſed Phiſicians, who with their charmes and Rattles, with an infernall rout of words and actions, will ſeeme to ſucke their inward griefe from their navels, or their grieued places; but of our Chirurgians they were ſo conceited, that they beleeued any Plaiſter would heale any hurt.

Their Chirurgery.

Their charms to cure.

But 'tis not alwayes in Phiſicians skill,
To heale the Patient that is ſicke and ill:
For ſometimes ſickneſſe on the Patients part,
Proues ſtronger farre then all Phiſicians art.

Of their Religion.

THere is yet in *Virginia* no place diſcovered to be ſo Savage, in which they haue not a Religion, Deere, and Bow, and Arrowes. All things that are able to doe them hurt beyond their prevention, they adore with their kinde of divine worſhip; as the fire, water, lightning, thunder, our Ordnance, peeces, horſes, &c. But their chiefe God they worſhip is the Devill. Him they call *Okee*, and

Their God.

and feare him more of feare then loue. They say they haue conference with him, and fashion themselues as neare to his shape as they can imagine. In their Temples they haue his image euill favouredly carved, and then painted and adorned with chaines of copper, and beads, and covered with a skin, in such manner as the deformitie may well suit with such a God. By him is commonly the sepulcher of their Kings. Their bodies are first bowelled, then dried vpon hurdles till they be very dry, and so about the most of their ioynts and necke they hang bracelets, or chaines of copper, pearle, and such like, as they vse to weare, their inwards they stuffe with copper beads, hatchets, and such trash. Then lappe they them very carefully in white skins, and so rowle them in mats for their winding sheets. And in the Tombe which is an arch made of mats, they lay them orderly. What remaineth of this kinde of wealth their Kings haue, they set at their feet in baskets. These Temples and bodies are kept by their Priests.

How they bury their Kings

For their ordinary burials, they dig a deepe hole in the earth with sharpe stakes, and the corpse being lapped in skins and mats with their iewels, they lay them vpon stickes in the ground, and so cover them with earth. The buriall ended, the women being painted all their faces with blacke cole and oyle, doe sit twenty-foure houres in the houses mourning and lamenting by turnes, with such yelling and howling, as may expresse their great passions.

Their ordinary burials.

In every Territory of a *Werowance* is a Temple and a Priest, two or three or more. Their principall Temple or place of superstition is at *Vttamussack* at *Pamavnkee*, neare vnto which is a house, Temple, or place of *Powhatans*.

Their Temples.

Vpon the top of certaine red sandy hils in the woods, there are three great houses filled with images of their Kings, and Devils, and Tombes of their Predecessors. Those houses are neare sixtie foot in length built arbour-wise, after their building. This place they count so holy as that but the Priests & Kings dare come into them; nor the Salvages dare not goe vp the river in boats by it, but they solemnly cast some peece of copper, white beads, or *Pocones* into the river, for feare their *Okee* should be offended and revenged of them.

Thus, *Feare was the first their Gods begot:*
Till feare began, their Gods were not.

In this place commonly are resident seauen Priests. The chiefe differed from the rest in his ornaments, but inferior Priests could hardly be knowne from the common people, but that they had not so many holes in their eares to hang their iewels at. The ornaments of the chiefe Priest were certaine attires for his head made thus. They tooke a dosen, or 16, or more snakes skins and stuffed them with mosse, and of Weesels and other Vermines skins a good many. All these they tie by their tailes, so as all their tailes meete in the toppe of their head like a great Tassell. Round about this Tassell is as it were a crowne of feathers, the skins hang round about his head, necke, and shoulders, and in a manner cover his face. The faces of all their Priests are painted as vgly as they can devise, in their hands they had every one his Rattle, some base, some smaller. Their devotion was most in songs, which the chiefe Priest beginneth and the rest followed him, sometimes he maketh invocations with broken sentences by starts and strange passions, and at every pause, the rest giue a short groane.

Their ornaments for their Priests

Thus seeke they in deepe foolishnesse,
To climbe the height of happinesse.

It could not be perceiued that they keepe any day as more holy then other; But onely in some great distresse of want, feare of enemies, times of triumph and gathering together their fruits, the whole Country of men, women, and children come together to solemnities. The manner of their devotion is, sometimes to make a great fire, in the house or fields, and all to sing and dance about it with Rattles and shouts

The times of solemnities.

together, foure or fiue houres. Sometimes they set a man in the midst, and about him they dance and sing, he all the while clapping his hands, as if he would keepe time, and after their songs and dauncings ended they goe to their Feasts.

Through God begetting feare,
Mans blinded minde did reare
A hell-god to the ghosts;
A heaven-god to the hoasts;
Yea God vnto the Seas:
Feare did create all these.

Their coniurations.

They haue also divers coniurations, one they made when I was their prisoner; of which hereafter you shall reade at large.

Their Altars.

They haue also certaine Altar stones they call *Pawcorances*, but these stand from their Temples, some by their houses, others in the woods and wildernesses, where they haue had any extraordinary accident, or incounter. And as you travell, at those stones they will tell you the cause why they were there erected, which from age to age they instruct their children, as their best records of antiquities. Vpon these they offer bloud, Deere suet, and Tobacco. This they doe when they returne from the Warres, from hunting, and vpon many other occasions. They haue also another superstition that they vse in stormes, when the waters are rough in the Rivers and Sea coasts. Their Coniurers runne to the water sides, or passing in their boats, after many hellish outcryes and invocations, they cast Tobacco, Copper, *Pocones*, or such trash into the water, to pacifie that God whom they thinke to be very angry in those stormes. Before their dinners and suppers the better sort will take the first bit, and cast it in the fire, which is all the grace they are knowne to vse.

Sacrifices to the water.

In some part of the Country they haue yearely a sacrifice of children. Such a one was at *Quiyoughcohanock* some ten myles from *Iames* Towne, and thus performed. Fifteene of the properest young boyes, betweene ten and fifteene yeares of age they painted white. Having brought them forth, the people spent the forenoone in dancing and singing about them with Rattles. In the afternoone they put those children to the roote of a tree. By them all the men stood in a guard, every one having a Bastinado in his hand, made of reeds bound together. This made a lane betweene them all along, through which there were appointed fiue young men to fetch these children: so every one of the fiue went through the guard to fetch a childe each after other by turnes, the guard fiercely beating them with their Bastinadoes, and they patiently enduring and receiuing all, defending the children with their naked bodies from the vnmercifull blowes, that pay them soundly, though the children escape. All this while the women weepe and cry out very passionately, prouiding mats, skins, mosse, and dry wood, as things fitting their childrens funerals. After the children were thus passed the guard, the guard tore down the trees, branches & boughs, with such violence that they rent the body, and made wreaths for their heads, or bedecked their hayre with the leaues. What els was done with the children, was not seene, but they were all cast on a heape, in a valley as dead, where they made a great feast for all the company. The *Werowance* being demanded the meaning of this sacrifice, answered that the children were not all dead, but that the *Okee* or *Divell* did sucke the bloud from their left breast, who chanced to be his by lot, till they were dead, but the rest were kept in the wildernesse by the young men till nine moneths were expired, during which time they must not converse with any, and of these were made their Priests and Coniurers. This sacrifice they held to be so necessary, that if they should omit it, their *Okee* or *Devill*, and all their other *Quiyoughcosughes*, which are their other Gods, would let them haue no Deere, Turkies, Corne, nor fish, and yet besides, he would make a great slaughter amongst them.

Their solemn Sacrifices of children, which they call Black-boyes.

Those Black-boyes are made so mad with a kind of drinke, that they will doe any mischiefe, at the command of their Keepers.

Their resurrection.

They thinke that their *Werowances* and Priests which they also esteeme *Quiyoughcosughes*, when they are dead, doe goe beyond the mountaines towards the setting of the sunne, and ever remaine there in forme of their *Okee*, with their heads painted

ted with oyle and *Pocones*, finely trimmed with feathers, and shall haue beads, hatchets, copper, and Tobacco, doing nothing but dance and sing, with all their Predecessors. But the common people they suppose shall not liue after death, but rot in their graues like dead dogs.

To divert them from this blind Idolatry, we did our best endevours, chiefly with the *Werowance* of *Quiyoughcohanock*, whose devotion, apprehension, and good disposition, much exceeded any in those Countries, with whom although we could not as yet prevaile, to forsake his false Gods, yet this he did beleeue that our God as much exceeded theirs, as our Gunnes did their Bowes & Arrowes, and many times did send to me to *Iames* Towne, intreating me to pray to my God for raine, for their Gods would not send them any. And in this lamentable ignorance doe these poore soules sacrifice themselues to the Devill, not knowing their Creator; and we had not language sufficient, so plainly to expresse it as make them vnderstand it; which God grant they may.

For, *Religion 'tis that doth distinguish vs,*
From their bruit humor, well we may it know;
That can with vnderstanding argue thus,
Our God is truth, but they cannot doe so.

Of the manner of the Virginians *Government.*

ALthough the Country people be very barbarous, yet haue they amongst them such government, as that their Magistrates for good commanding, and their people for due subiection, and obeying, excell many places that would be counted very civill. The forme of their Common-wealth is a Monarchicall government, one as Emperour ruleth ouer many Kings or Governours. Their chiefe ruler is called *Powhatan*, and taketh his name of his principall place of dwelling called *Powhatan*. But his proper name is *Wahunsonacock*. Some Countries he hath which haue beene his ancestors, and came vnto him by inheritance, as the Country called *Powhatan*, *Arrohateck*, *Appamatuck*, *Pamavnkee*, *Youghtanund*, and *Mattapanient*. All the rest of his Territories expressed in the Mappe, they report haue beene his severall Conquests. In all his ancient inheritances, he hath houses built after their manner like arbours, some 30. some 40. yards long, and at every house provision for his entertainement according to the time. At *Werowcomoco* on the Northside of the river *Pamavnkee*, was his residence, when I was delivered him prisoner, some 14 myles from *Iames* Towne, where for the most part, he was resident, but at last he tooke so little pleasure in our neare neighbourhood, that he retired himselfe to *Orapakes*, in the desert betwixt *Chickahamania* and *Youghtanund*. He is of personage a tall well proportioned man, with a sower looke, his head somwhat gray, his beard so thinne, that it seemeth none at all, his age neare sixtie; of a very able and hardy body to endure any labour. About his person ordinarily attendeth a guard of 40 or 50 of the tallest men his Country doth afford. Every night vpon the foure quarters of his house are foure Sentinels, each from other a flight shoot, and at every halfe houre one from the *Corps du guard* doth hollow, shaking his lips with his finger betweene them; vnto whom every Sentinell doth answer round from his stand: if any faile, they presently send forth an officer that beateth him extreamely.

A description of *Powhatan*.

His attendãce and watch.

A myle from *Orapakes* in a thicket of wood, he hath a house in which he keepeth his kinde of Treasure, as skinnes, copper, pearle, and beads, which he storeth vp against the time of his death and buriall. Here also is his store of red paint for oyntment, bowes and arrowes, Targets and clubs. This house is fiftie or sixtie yards in length, frequented onely by Priests. At the foure corners of this house stand foure

His treasury.

Images as Sentinels, one of a Dragon, another a Beare, the third like a Leopard, and the fourth like a giantlike man, all made evill favouredly, according to their best workemanship.

His wiues.

He hath as many women as he will, whereof when he lieth on his bed, one sitteth at his head, and another at his feet, but when he sitteth, one sitteth on his right hand and another on his left. As he is weary of his women, he bestoweth them on those that best deserue them at his hands. When he dineth or suppeth, one of his women before and after meat, bringeth him water in a wooden platter to wash his hands. Another waiteth with a bunch of feathers to wipe them in stead of a Towell, and the feathers when he hath wiped are dryed againe. His kingdomes descend not to his sonnes nor children, but first to his brethren, whereof he hath 3. namely, *Opitchapan*, *Opechancanough*, and *Catataugh*, and after their decease to his sisters. First to the eldest sister, then to the rest, and after them to the heires male or female of the eldest sister, but never to the heires of the males.

His successors

Their authoritie.

He nor any of his people vnderstand any letters, whereby to write or reade, onely the lawes whereby he ruleth is custome. Yet when he listeth his will is a law and must be obeyed: not onely as a King, but as halfe a God they esteeme him. His inferiour Kings whom they call *Werowances*, are tyed to rule by customes, and haue power of life and death at their command in that nature. But this word *Werowance*, which we call and construe for a King, is a common word, whereby they call all commanders: for they haue but few words in their language, and but few occasions to vse any officers more then one commander, which commonly they call *Werowance*, or *Caucorouse*, which is Captaine. They all know their severall lands, and habitations, and limits, to fish, foule, or hunt in, but they hold all of their great *Werowance Powhatan*, vnto whom they pay tribute of skinnes, beads, copper, pearle, deere, turkies, wild beasts, and corne. What he commandeth they dare not disobey in the least thing. It is strange to see with what great feare and adoration, all these people doe obey this *Powhatan*. For at his feet they present whatsoever he commandeth, and at the least frowne of his brow, their greatest spirits will tremble with feare: and no marvell, for he is very terrible & tyrannous in punishing such as offend him. For example, he caused certaine malefactors to be bound hand and foot, then having of many fires gathered great store of burning coales, they rake these coales round in the forme of a cockpit, and in the midst they cast the offenders to broyle to death. Sometimes he causeth the heads of them that offend him, to be laid vpon the altar or sacrificing stone, and one with clubbes beats out their braines. When he would punish any notorious enemy or malefactor, he causeth him to be tyed to a tree, and with Mussell shels or reeds, the executioner cutteth off his ioynts one after another, ever casting what they cut of into the fire; then doth he proceed with shels and reeds to case the skinne from his head and face; then doe they rip his belly and so burne him with the tree and all. Thus themselues reported they executed *George Cassen*. Their ordinary correction is to beate them with cudgels. We haue seene a man kneeling on his knees, and at *Powhatans* command, two men haue beate him on the bare skin, till he hath fallen senselesse in a sound, and yet never cry nor complained. And he made a woman for playing the whore, sit vpon a great stone, on her bare breech twenty-foure houres, onely with corne and water, every three dayes, till nine dayes were past, yet he loued her exceedingly: notwithstanding there are common whores by profession.

The tenor of their lands.

His manner of punishments.

In the yeare 1608, he surprised the people of *Payankatank* his neare neighbours and subiects. The occasion was to vs vnknowne, but the manner was thus. First he sent divers of his men as to lodge amongst them that night, then the *Ambuscadoes* environed all their houses, and at the houre appointed, they all fell to the spoyle, twenty-foure men they slew, the long haire of the one side of their heads, with the skinne cased off with shels or reeds, they brought away. They surprised also the women, and the children, and the *Werowance*. All these they presented to *Powhatan*. The *Werowance*, women and children became his prisoners, and doe him service.

The

The lockes of haire with their skinnes he hanged on a line betwixt two trees. And thus he made ostentation of his triumph at *Werowocomoco*, where he intended to haue done as much to mee and my company.

And this is as much as my memory can call to minde worthy of note; which I haue purposely collected, to satisfie my friends of the true worth and qualitie of *Virginia.* Yet some bad natures will not sticke to slander the Countrey, that will sloven1y spit at all things, especially in company where they can finde none to contradict them. Who though they were scarce euer ten myles from *Iames* Towne, or at the most but at the falles; yet holding it a great disgrace that amongst so much action, their actions were nothing, exclaime of all things, though they never adventured to know any thing; nor euer did any thing but devoure the fruits of other mens labours. Being for most part of such tender educations, and small experience in Martiall accidents, because they found not English Cities, nor such faire houses, nor at their owne wishes any of their accustomed dainties, with feather beds and downe pillowes, Tavernes and Alehouses in every breathing place, neither such plentie of gold and silver and dissolute libertie, as they expected, had little or no care of any thing, but to pamper their bellies, to fly away with our Pinnaces, or procure their meanes to returne for *England.* For the Country was to them a misery, a ruine, a death, a hell, and their reports here, and their actions there according.

Some other there were that had yearely stipends to passe to and againe for transportation: who to keepe the mysterie of the businesse in themselues, though they had neither time nor meanes to know much of themselues; yet all mens actions or relations they so formally tuned to the temporizing times simplicitie, as they could make their ignorances seeme much more, then all the true actors could by their experience. And those with their great words deluded the world with such strange promises, as abused the businesse much worse then the rest. For the businesse being builded vpon the foundation of their fained experience, the planters, the money and meanes haue still miscarried: yet they ever returning, and the planters so farre absent, who could contradict their excuses? which, still to maintaine their vaine glory and estimation, from time to time haue vsed such diligence as made them passe for truths, though nothing more false. And that the adventurers might be thus abused, let no man wonder; for the wisest liuing is soonest abused by him that hath a faire tongue and a dissembling heart.

There were many in *Virginia* meerely proiecting, verball, and idle contemplators, and those so devoted to pure idlenesse, that though they had liued two or three yeares in *Virginia*, lordly, necessitie it selfe could not compell them to passe the *Peninsula*, or *Pallisadoes* of *Iames* Towne, and those witty spirits, what would they not affirme in the behalfe of our transporters, to get victuall from their ships, or obtaine their good words in *England*, to get their passes. Thus from the clamors, and the ignorance of false informers, are sprung those disasters that sprung in *Virginia*: and our ingenious verbalists were no lesse plague to vs in *Virginia*, then the Locusts to the Egyptians. For the labour of twentie or thirtie of the best onely preserved in Christianitie by their industry, the idle livers of neare two hundred of the rest: who liuing neere ten moneths of such naturall meanes, as the Country naturally of it selfe afforded, notwithstanding all this, and the worst fury of the Salvages, the extremitie of sicknesse, mutinies, faction, ignorances, and want of victuall; in all that time I lost but seaven or eight men, yet subiected the salvages to our desired obedience, and receiued contribution from thirtie fiue of their Kings, to protect and assist them against any that should assault them, in which order they continued true and faithfull, and as subiects to his Maiestie, so long after as I did governe there, vntill I left the Countrey: since, how they haue revolted, the Countrie lost, and againe replanted, and the businesses hath succeded from time to time, I referre you to the relations of them returned from *Virginia*, that haue beene more diligent in such Observations.

Iohn Smith *writ this with his owne hand.*

Because many doe desire to know the manner of their Language, I haue inserted these few words.

KA ka torawines yowo. What call you this.
Nemarough, a man.
Crenepo, a woman.
Marowanchesso, a boy.
Yehawkans, Houses.
Matchcores, Skins, or garments.
Mockasins, Shooes.
Tussan, Beds. *Pokatawer*, Fire.
Attawp, A bow. *Attonce*, Arrowes.
Monacookes, Swords.
Aumouhhowgh, A Target.
Pawcussacks, Gunnes.
Tomahacks, Axes.
Tockahacks, Pickaxes.
Pamesacks, Kniues.
Accowprets, Sheares.
Pawpecones, Pipes. *Mattaßin*, Copper
Vssawassin, Iron, Brasse, Silver, or any white mettall. *Musses*, Woods.
Attasskuss, Leaues, weeds, or grasse.
Chepsin, Land. *Shacquohocan*. A stone.
Wepenter, A cookold.
Suckahanna, Water. *Noughmass*, Fish.
Copotone, Sturgeon.
Weghshaughes, Flesh.
Sawwehone, Bloud.
Netoppew, Friends.
Marrapough, Enemies.
Maskapow, the worst of the enemies.
Mawchick chammay, The best of friends
Casacunnakack, peya quagh acquintan vttasantasough, In how many daies will there come hither any more English Ships.

Their Numbers.

Necut, 1. *Ningh*, 2. *Nuss*, 3. *Yowgh*, 4.
Paranske, 5. *Comotinch*, 6. *Toppawoss*, 7
Nusswash, 8. *Kekatawgh*, 9. *Kaskeke* 10
They count no more but by tennes as followeth.
Case, how many.
Ninghsapooeksku, 20.
Nussapooeksku, 30.
Yowghapooeksku, 40.
Parankestassapooeksku, 50.
Comatinchtassapooeksku, 60.
Nussswashtassapooeksku, 70.
Kekataughtassapooeksku, 90.
Necuttoughtysinough, 100.
Necuttwevnquaough, 1000.
Rawcosowghs, Dayes.
Keskowghes, Sunnes:
Toppquough. Nights.
Nepawweshowghs, Moones.
Pawpaxsoughes, Yeares.
Pummahumps, Starres.
Osies, Heavens.
Okees, Gods.
Quiyoughcosoughs, Pettie Gods, and their affinities.
Righcomoughes, Deaths.
Kekughes, Liues.
Mowchick woyawgh tawgh noeragh kaquere mecher, I am very hungry? what shall I eate?
Tawnor nehiegh Powhatan, Where dwels Powhatan.
Mache, nehiegh yourowgh, Orapaks. Now he dwels a great way hence at Orapaks.
Vittapitchewayne anpechitchs nehawper Werowacomoco, You lie, he staid ever at Werowacomoco.
Kator nehiegh mattagh neer vttapitchewayne, Truely he is there I doe not lie.
Spaughtynere keragh werowance mawmarinough kekatē wawgh peyaquaugh. Run you then to the King Mawmarynough and bid him come hither.
Vtteke, e peya weyack wighwhip, Get you gone, & come againe quickly.
Kekaten Pokahontas patiaquagh ningh tanks manotyens neer mowchick rawrenock audowgh, Bid Pokahontas bring hither two little Baskets, and I will giue her white Beads to make her a Chaine. *FINIS.*

VIRGINIA
Massaw-omecks
Signification of these markes,
To the crosses hath bin discouerd what beyond is by relation
Kings howses
Ordinary howses
MONACANS
MANNAHOACKS
POWHATAN
Held this state & fashion when Capt. Smith was deliuered to him prisoner 1607
POWHATAN
The Sasquesahanougs are a Gyant like people & thus a-tyred
SASQUESAHANOUGH
CHESEPEACK BAY
TOCKWOGHS
KUSKARAWAOKS
ATQUANACHUKES
Cape Henry
Cape Charles
Poynt comfort
Scale of Leagues
and halfe
Leagues
Chickahokin
THE VIRGINIAN SEA
Discouered and Discribed by Captayn John Smith 1606
Grauen by William Hole

The third Booke.

THE PROCEEDINGS AND ACCIDENTS OF The English *Colony* in *Virginia*,

Extracted from the Authors following, by WILLIAM SIMONS, *Doctour of Divinitie.*

CHAPTER I.

IT might well be thought, a Countrie so faire (as *Virginia* is) and a people so tractable, would long ere this haue beene quietly possessed, to the satisfaction of the adventurers, & the eternizing of the memory of those that effected it. But because all the world doe see a defailement; this following Treatise shall giue satisfaction to all indifferent Readers, how the businesse hath bin carried: where no doubt they will easily vnderstand and answer to their question, how it came to passe there was no better speed and successe in those proceedings. 1606. Sir *Thomas Smith* Treasurer.

Captaine *Bartholomew Gosnoll*, one of the first movers of this plantation, having many yeares solicited many of his friends, but found small assistants; at last prevailed with some Gentlemen, as Captaine *Iohn Smith*, Mr *Edward-maria Wingfield*, Mr *Robert Hunt*, and divers others, who depended a yeare vpon his proiects, but nothing could be effected, till by their great charge and industrie, it came to be apprehended by certaine of the Nobilitie, Gentry, and Marchants, so that his Maiestie by his letters patents, gaue commission for establishing Councels, to direct here; and to governe, and to execute there. To effect this, was spent another yeare, and by that, three ships were provided, one of 100 Tuns, another of 40. and a Pinnace of 20. The transportation of the company was committed to Captaine *Christopher Newport*, a Marriner well practised for the Westerne parts of *America*. But their orders for government were put in a box, not to be opened, nor the governours knowne vntill they arrived in *Virginia*. The first mover of the action. Orders for government.

On the 19 of December, 1606. we set sayle from Blackwall, but by vnprosperous winds, were kept six weekes in the sight of *England*; all which time, Mr *Hunt* our Preacher, was so weake and sicke, that few expected his recovery. Yet although he were but twentie myles from his habitation (the time we were in the Downes) and notwithstanding the stormy weather, nor the scandalous imputations (of some few, little better then Atheists, of the greatest ranke amongst vs) suggested against him, all this could never force from him so much as a seeming desire to leaue the busines, but preferred the service of God, in so good a voyage, before any affection to contest with his godlesse foes, whose disasterous designes (could they haue prevailed)

had

had even then overthrowne the businesse, so many discontents did then arise, had he not with the water of patience, and his godly exhortations (but chiefly by his true devoted examples) quenched those flames of envie, and dissention.

We watered at the Canaries, we traded with the Salvages at *Dominica*; three weekes we spent in refreshing our selues amongst these west-India Isles; in *Gwardalupa* we found a bath so hot, as in it we boyled Porck as well as over the fire. And at a little Isle called *Monica*, we tooke from the bushes with our hands, neare two hogsheads full of Birds in three or foure houres. In *Mevis*, *Mona*, and the Virgin Isles, we spent some time, where, with a lothsome beast like a Crocodil, called a Gwayn, Tortoises, Pellicans, Parrots, and fishes, we daily feasted. Gone from thence in search of *Virginia*, the company was not a little discomforted, seeing the Marriners had 3 dayes passed their reckoning and found no land, so that Captaine *Ratliffe* (Captaine of the Pinnace) rather desired to beare vp the helme to returne for *England*, then make further search. But God the guider of all good actions, forcing them by an extreame storme to hull all night, did driue them by his providence to their desired Port, beyond all their expectations, for never any of them had seene that coast. The first land they made they called *Cape Henry*; where thirtie of them recreating themselues on shore, were assaulted by fiue Salvages, who hurt two of the English very dangerously. That night was the box opened, and the orders read, in which *Bartholomew Gosnoll, Iohn Smith, Edward Wingfield, Christopher Newport, Iohn Ratliffe, Iohn Martin*, and *George Kendall*, were named to be the Councell, and to choose a President amongst them for a yeare, who with the Councell should governe. Matters of moment were to be examined by a Iury, but determined by the maior part of the Councell, in which the President had two voyces. Vntill the 13 of May they sought a place to plant in, then the Councell was sworne, Mr *Wingfield* was chosen President, and an Oration made, why Captaine *Smith* was not admitted of the Councell as the rest.

Monica an vnfrequented Isle full of Birds.

Their first landing.

Matters of government.

Now falleth every man to worke, the Councell contriue the Fort, the rest cut downe trees to make place to pitch their Tents; some provide clapbord to relade the ships, some make gardens, some nets, &c. The Salvages often visited vs kindly. The Presidents overweening iealousie would admit no exercise at armes, or fortification, but the boughs of trees cast together in the forme of a halfe moone by the extraordinary paines and diligence of Captaine *Kendall. Newport, Smith*, and twentie others, were sent to discover the head of the river: by divers small habitations they passed, in six dayes they arrived at a Towne called *Powhatan*, consisting of some twelue houses, pleasantly seated on a hill; before it three fertile Isles, about it many of their cornefields, the place is very pleasant, and strong by nature, of this place the Prince is called *Powhatan*, and his people *Powhatans*, to this place the river is navigable: but higher within a myle, by reason of the Rockes and Isles, there is not passage for a small Boat, this they call the Falles, the people in all parts kindly intreated them, till being returned within twentie myles of *Iames* towne, they gaue iust cause of iealousie, but had God not blessed the discoverers otherwise then those at the Fort, there had then beene an end of that plantation; for at the Fort, where they arrived the next day, they found 17 men hurt, and a boy slaine by the Salvages, and had it not chanced a crosse barre shot from the Ships strooke downe a bough from a tree amongst them, that caused them to retire, our men had all beene slaine, being securely all at worke, and their armes in dry fats.

The discovery of the *Falles & Powhatan.*

The Fort assaulted by the Salvages.

Herevpon the President was contented the Fort should be pallisadoed, the Ordnance mounted, his men armed and exercised, for many were the assaults, and ambuscadoes of the Salvages, & our men by their disorderly stragling were often hurt, when the Salvages by the nimblenesse of their heeles well escaped. What toyle we had, with so small a power to guard our workemen adayes, watch all night, resist our enemies, and effect our businesse, to relade the ships, cut downe trees, and prepare the ground to plant our Corne, &c, I referre to the Readers consideration. Six weekes being spent in this manner, Captaine *Newport* (who was hired onely for our transportation) was to returne with the ships. Now Captaine *Smith*, who all this time from their departure from the Canaries was restrained as a prisoner vpon the scandalous suggestions of some of the chiefe (envying his repute) who fained he intended to vsurpe the government, murther the Councell, and make himselfe King, that his confederats were dispersed in all the three ships, and that divers of his confederats that revealed it, would affirme it, for this he was committed as a prisoner: thirteene weekes he remained thus suspected, and by that time the ships should returne they pretended out of their commiserations, to referre him to the Councell in *England* to receiue a check, rather then by particulating his designes make him so odious to the world, as to touch his life, or vtterly overthrow his reputation. But he so much scorned their charitie, and publikely defied the vttermost of their crueltie, he wisely prevented their policies, though he could not suppresse their envies, yet so well he demeaned himselfe in this businesse, as all the company did see his innocency, and his adversaries malice, and those suborned to accuse him, accused his accusers of subornation; many vntruthes were alledged against him; but being so apparently disproved, begat a generall hatred in the hearts of the company against such vniust Commanders, that the President was adiudged to giue him 200^{l}. so that all he had was seized vpon, in part of satisfaction, which *Smith* presently returned to the Store for the generall vse of the *Colony*. Many were the mischiefes that daily sprung from their ignorant (yet ambitious) spirits; but the good Doctrine and exhortation of our Preacher Mr *Hunt* reconciled them, and caused Captaine *Smith* to be admitted of the Councell; the next day all receiued the Communion, the day following the Salvages voluntarily desired peace, and Captaine *Newport* returned for *England* with newes; leaving in *Virginia* 100. the 15 of Iune 1607. Captain *Newports* returne for *England*.

By this obserue;

Good men did ne'r their Countries ruine bring.
But when evill men shall iniuries beginne;
Not caring to corrupt and violate
The iudgements-seats for their owne Lucr's sake:
Then looke that Country cannot long haue peace,
Though for the present it haue rest and ease.

The names of them that were the first Planters, were these following.

1607. Sir *Thomas Smith* Treasurer.

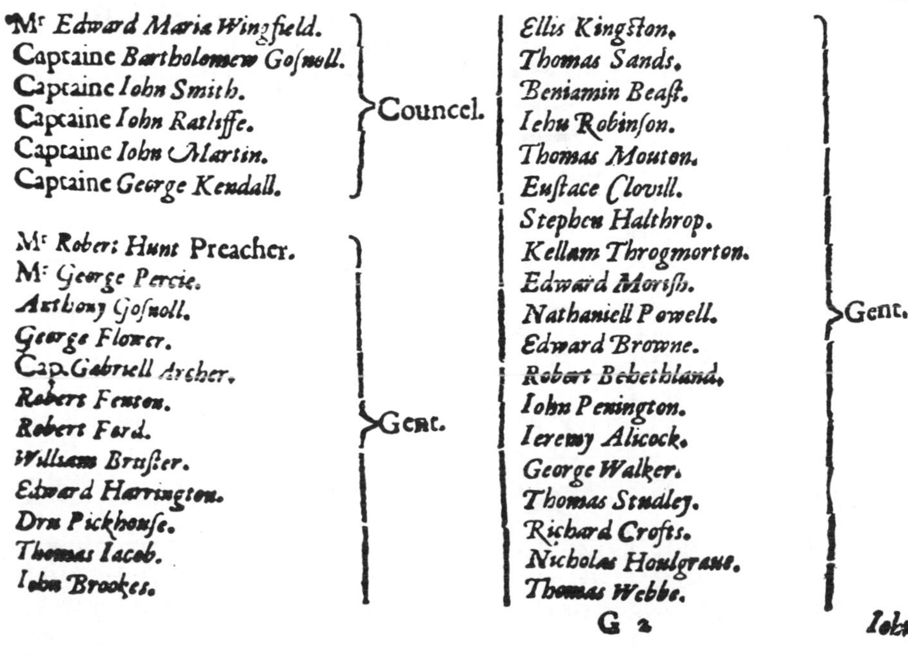

Councel:
- Mr *Edward Maria Wingfield.*
- Captaine *Bartholomew Gosnoll.*
- Captaine *Iohn Smith.*
- Captaine *Iohn Ratliffe.*
- Captaine *Iohn Martin.*
- Captaine *George Kendall.*

Gent.:
- Mr *Robert Hunt* Preacher.
- Mr *George Percie.*
- *Anthony Gosnoll.*
- *George Flower.*
- Cap. *Gabriell Archer.*
- *Robert Fenton.*
- *Robert Ford.*
- *William Bruster.*
- *Edward Harrington.*
- *Dru Pickhouse.*
- *Thomas Iacob.*
- *Iohn Brookes.*

Gent.:
- *Ellis Kingston.*
- *Thomas Sands.*
- *Beniamin Beast.*
- *Iehu Robinson.*
- *Thomas Mouton.*
- *Eustace Clovill.*
- *Stephen Halthrop.*
- *Kellam Throgmorton.*
- *Edward Morish.*
- *Nathaniell Powell.*
- *Edward Browne.*
- *Robert Bebethland.*
- *Iohn Penington.*
- *Ieremy Alicock.*
- *George Walker.*
- *Thomas Studley.*
- *Richard Crofts.*
- *Nicholas Houlgraue.*
- *Thomas Webbe.*

John Waller.
John Short.
William Tankard.
William Smethes.
Francis Snarsbrough.
Richard Simons.
Edward Brookes.
Richard Dixon.
John Martin.
Roger Cooke.
Anthony Gosnold.
Tho: Wotton, Chirurg.
John Stevenson.
Thomas Gore.
Henry Adling.
Francis Midwinter.
Richard Frith.
} Gent.

William Laxon.
Edward Pising.
Thomas Emry.
Robert Small.
} Carpenters.

John Laydon.
William Cassen.
George Cassen.
Thomas Cassen.
William Rodes.
William White.
Old Edward.
Henry Tavin.
George Goulding.
John Dods.
William Johnson.
William Vnger.
} Labourers.

Iam: Read, Blacksmith.
Ionas Profit, Sailer.
Tho: Cowper, Barber.
Will: Garret, Bricklayer.
Edward Brinto, Mason.
William Loue, Taylor.
Nic: Scot, Drum.
Wil: Wilkinson, Chirurg.

Samuell Collier, boy.
Nat. Pecock, boy.
James Brumfield, boy.
Richard Mutton, boy.

With divers others to the number of 100.

Chap. II.

What happened till the first supply.

The occasion of sicknesse.

BEing thus left to our fortunes, it fortuned that within ten dayes scarce ten amongst vs could either goe, or well stand, such extreame weaknes and sicknes oppressed vs. And thereat none need marvaile, if they consider the cause and reason, which was this; whilest the ships stayed, our allowance was somewhat bettered, by a daily proportion of Bisket, which the sailers would pilfer to sell, giue, or exchange with vs, for money, Saxefras, furres, or loue. But when they departed, there remained neither taverne, beere-house, nor place of reliefe, but the common Kettell. Had we beene as free from all sinnes as gluttony, and drunkennesse, we might haue beene canonized for Saints; But our President would never haue beene admitted, for ingrossing to his private, Oatmeale, Sacke, Oyle, *Aquavitæ*, Beefe, Egges, or what not, but the Kettell; that indeed he allowed equally to be distributed, and that was halfe a pint of wheat, and as much barley boyled with water for a man a day, and this having fryed some 26. weekes in the ships hold, contained as many wormes as graines; so that we might truely call it rather so much bran then corne, our drinke was water, our lodgings Castles in the ayre: with this lodging and dyet, our extreame toile in bearing and planting Pallisadoes, so strained and bruised vs, and our continuall labour in the extremitie of the heat had so weakned vs, as were cause sufficient to haue made vs as miserable in our natiue Countrey, or any other place in the world. From May, to September, those that escaped, liued vpon Sturgeon, and Sea-crabs, fiftie in this time we buried, the rest seeing the Presidents proiects to escape these miseries in our Pinnace by flight (who all this time had neither felt want nor sicknes) so moved our dead spirits, as we deposed him; and established *Ratcliffe* in his place, (*Gosnoll* being dead) *Kendall* deposed, *Smith* newly recovered, *Martin* and *Ratcliffe* was by his care preserved and relieued, and the most of the souldiers recovered, with the skilfull diligence of Mr *Thomas Wotton* our Chirurgian generall. But now was all our provision spent, the Sturgeon gone, all helps abandoned, each houre expecting the fury of the Salvages; when God the patron of all good indevours, in that desperate extremitie so changed the hearts of the Salvages, that they brought such plenty of their fruits, and provision, as no man wanted.

The Sailers abuses.

A bad President.

Plentie vnexpected.

And now where some affirmed it was ill done of the Councell to send forth men so badly provided, this incontradictable reason will shew them plainely they are too ill advised to nourish such ill conceits; first, the fault of our going was our owne, what

what could be thought fitting or necessary we had, but what we should find, or want, or where we should be, we were all ignorant, and supposing to make our passage in two moneths, with victuall to liue, and the advantage of the spring to worke; we were at Sea fiue moneths, where we both spent our victuall and lost the opportunitie of the time, and season to plant, by the vnskilfull presumption of our ignorant transporters, that vnderstood not at all, what they vndertooke.

Such actions haue ever since the worlds beginning beene subiect to such accidents, and every thing of worth is found full of difficulties, but nothing so difficult as to establish a Common-wealth so farre remote from men and meanes, and where mens mindes are so vntoward as neither doe well themselues, nor suffer others. But to proceed.

The new President and *Martin*, being little beloved, of weake iudgement in dangers, and lesse industrie in peace, committed the managing of all things abroad to Captaine *Smith*: who by his owne example, good words, and faire promises, set some to mow, others to binde thatch, some to build houses, others to thatch them, himselfe alwayes bearing the greatest taske for his owne share, so that in short time, he provided most of them lodgings, neglecting any for himselfe. This done, seeing the Salvages superfluitie beginne to decrease (with some of his workemen) shipped himselfe in the Shallop to search the Country for trade. The want of the language, knowledge to mannage his boat without sailes, the want of a sufficient power, (knowing the multitude of the Salvages) apparell for his men, and other necessaries, were infinite impediments, yet no discouragement. Being but six or seauen in company he went downe the river to *Kecoughtan*, where at first they scorned him, as a famished man, and would in derision offer him a handfull of Corne, a peece of bread, for their swords and muskets, and such like proportions also for their apparell. But seeing by trade and courtesie there was nothing to be had, he made bold to try such conclusions as necessitie inforced, though contrary to his Commission: Let fly his muskets, ran his boat on shore, whereat they all fled into the woods. So marching towards their houses, they might see great heapes of corne: much adoe he had to restraine his hungry souldiers from present taking of it, expecting as it hapned that the Salvages would assault them, as not long after they did with a most hydeous noyse. Sixtie or seaventie of them, some blacke, some red, some white, some party-coloured, came in a square order, singing and dauncing out of the woods, with their *Okee* (which was an Idoll made of skinnes, stuffed with mosse, all painted and hung with chaines and copper) borne before them: and in this manner being well armed, with Clubs, Targets, Bowes and Arrowes, they charged the English, that so kindly receiued them with their muskets loaden with Pistoll shot, that downe fell their God, and divers lay sprauling on the ground; the rest fled againe to the woods, and ere long sent one of their *Quiyoughkasoucks* to offer peace, and redeeme their *Okee*. *Smith* told them, if onely six of them would come vnarmed and loade his boat, he would not only be their friend, but restore them their *Okee*, and giue them Beads, Copper, and Hatchets besides: which on both sides was to their contents performed: and then they brought him Venison, Turkies, wild-foule, bread, and what they had, singing and dauncing in signe of friendship till they departed. In his returne he discovered the Towne and Country of *Warraskoyack*.

The building of *Iames Towne*.

The beginning of Trade abroad.

Thus God vnboundlesse by his power,
Made them thus kind, would vs devour.

Smith perceiving (notwithstanding their late miserie) not any regarded but from hand to mouth (the company being well recovered) caused the Pinnace to be provided with things fitting to get provision for the yeare following; but in the interim he made 3. or 4. iournies and discovered the people of *Chickahamania*: yet what he carefully provided the rest carelesly spent. *Wingfield* and *Kendall* liuing in disgrace, seeing all things at randome in the absence of *Smith*, the companies dislike of their Presidents

Amoris, a Salvage his best friend slaine for loving vs.

The Discovery of *Chickahamina*.

Presidents weaknes, and their small loue to *Martins* never-mending sicknes, strengthened themselues with the sailers, and other confederates to regaine their former credit and authority, or at least such meanes abord the Pinnace, (being fitted to saile as *Smith* had appointed for trade) to alter her course and to goe for *England*. *Smith* vnexpectedly returning had the plot discovered to him, much trouble he had to prevent it, till with store of sakre and musket shot he forced them stay or sinke in the riuer, which action cost the life of captaine *Kendall*. These brawles are so disgustfull, as some will say they were better forgotten, yet all men of good iudgement will conclude, it were better their basenes should be manifest to the world, then the busines beare the scorne and shame of their excused disorders. The President and captaine *Archer* not long after intended also to haue abandoned the country, which proiect also was curbed, and suppressed by *Smith*. The *Spaniard* never more greedily desired gold then he victuall, nor his souldiers more to abandon the Country, then he to keepe it. But finding plentie of Corne in the riuer of *Chickahamania* where hundreds of Salvages in diuers places stood with baskets expecting his comming. And now the winter approaching, the rivers became so covered with swans, geese, duckes, and cranes, that we daily feasted with good bread, Virginia pease, pumpions, and putchamins, fish, fowle, and diverse sorts of wild beasts as fat as we could eate them: so that none of our Tuftaffaty humorists desired to goe for *England*. But our *Comædies* never endured long without a *Tragedie*; some idle exceptions being muttered against Captaine *Smith*, for not discovering the head of *Chickahamania* river, and taxed by the Councell, to be too slow in so worthy an attempt. The next voyage hee proceeded so farre that with much labour by cutting of trees in sunder he made his passage, but when his Barge could passe no farther, he left her in a broad bay out of danger of shot, commanding none should goe a shore till his returne: himselfe with two English and two Salvages went vp higher in a Canowe, but hee was not long absent, but his men went a shore, whose want of government, gaue both occasion and opportunity to the Salvages to surprise one *George Cassen*, whom they slew, and much failed not to haue cut of the boat and all the rest. *Smith* little dreaming of that accident, being got to the marshes at the rivers head, twentie myles in the desert, had his * two men slaine (as is supposed) sleeping by the Canowe, whilst himselfe by fowling sought them victuall, who finding he was beset with 200. Salvages, two of them hee slew, still defending himselfe with the ayd of a Salvage his guid, whom he bound to his arme with his garters, and vsed him as a buckler, yet he was shot in his thigh a little, and had many arrowes that stucke in his cloathes but no great hurt, till at last they tooke him prisoner. When this newes came to *Iames* towne, much was their sorrow for his losse, fewe expecting what ensued. Sixe or seuen weekes those Barbarians kept him prisoner, many strange triumphes and coniurations they made of him, yet hee so demeaned himselfe amongst them, as he not onely diverted them from surprising the Fort, but procured his owne libertie, and got himselfe and his company such estimation amongst them, that those Salvages admired him more then their owne *Quiyouckosucks*. The manner how they vsed and deliuered him, is as followeth.

Another proiect to abandon the country.

* *Iehu Robinson* and *Thomas Emry* slaine.

Captaine *Smith* taken prisoner.

The Salvages hauing drawne from *George Cassen* whether Captaine *Smith* was gone, prosecuting that oportunity they followed him with. 300. bowmen, conducted by the King of *Pamavnkee*, who in diuisions searching the turnings of the riuer, found *Robinson* and *Emry* by the fire side, those they shot full of arrowes and slew. Then finding the Captaine, as is said, that vsed the Salvage that was his guide as his shield (three of them being slaine and diuers other so gauld) all the rest would not come neere him. Thinking thus to haue returned to his boat, regarding them, as he marched, more then his way, slipped vp to the middle in an oasie creeke & his Salvage with him, yet durst they not come to him till being neere dead with cold, he threw away his armes. Then according to their composition they drew him forth and led him to the fire, where his men were slaine. Diligently they chafed his benummed

nummed limbs. He demanding for their Captaine, they shewed him *Opechankanough*, King of *Pamavnkee*, to whom he gaue a round Ivory double compass Dyall. Much they marvailed at the playing of the Fly and Needle, which they could see so plainely, and yet not touch it, because of the glasse that covered them. But when he demonstrated by that Globe-like Iewell, the roundnesse of the earth, and skies, the spheare of the Sunne, Moone, and Starres, and how the Sunne did chase the night round about the world continually; the greatnesse of the Land and Sea, the diversitie of Nations, varietie of complexions, and how we were to them *Antipodes*, and many other such like matters, they all stood as amazed with admiration. Notwithstanding, within an houre after they tyed him to a tree, and as many as could stand about him prepared to shoot him, but the King holding vp the Compass in his hand, they all laid downe their Bowes and Arrowes, and in a triumphant manner led him to *Orapaks*, where he was after their manner kindly feasted, and well vsed.

The order they observed in their trivmph.

Their order in conducting him was thus; Drawing themselues all in fyle, the King in the middest had all their Peeces and Swords borne before him. Captaine *Smith* was led after him by three great Salvages, holding him fast by each arme: and on each side six went in fyle with their Arrowes nocked. But arriving at the Towne (which was but onely thirtie or fortie hunting houses made of Mats, which they remoue as they please, as we our tents) all the women and children staring to behold him, the souldiers first all in fyle performed the forme of a *Bissom* so well as could be; and on each flanke, officers as Serieants to see them keepe their orders. A good time they continued this exercise, and then cast themselues in a ring, dauncing in such severall Postures, and singing and yelling out such hellish notes and screeches; being strangely painted, every one his quiver of Arrowes, and at his backe a club; on his arme a Fox or an Otters skinne, or some such matter for his vambrace; their heads and shoulders painted red, with Oyle and *Pocones* mingled together, which Scarlet-like colour made an exceeding handsome shew; his Bow in his hand, and the skinne of a Bird with her wings abroad dryed, tyed on his head, a peece of copper, a white shell, a long feather, with a small rattle growing at the tayles of their snaks tyed to it, or some such like toy. All this while *Smith* and the King stood in the middest guarded, as before is said, and after three dances they all departed. *Smith* they conducted to a long house, where thirtie or fortie tall fellowes did guard him, and ere long more bread and venison was brought him then would haue served twentie men, I thinke his stomacke at that time was not very good; what he left they put in baskets and tyed over his head. About midnight they set the meate againe before him, all this time not one of them would eate a bit with him, till the next morning they brought him as much more, and then did they eate all the old, & reserved the new as they had done the other, which made him thinke they would fat him to eat him. Yet in this desperate estate to defend him from the cold, one *Maocassater* brought him his gowne, in requitall of some beads and toyes *Smith* had given him at his first arrivall in *Virginia*.

How he should haue beene slaine at *Orapacks*.

Two dayes after a man would haue slaine him (but that the guard prevented it) for the death of his sonne, to whom they conducted him to recover the poore man then breathing his last. *Smith* told them that at *Iames* towne he had a water would doe it, if they would let him fetch it, but they would not permit that; but made all the preparations they could to assault *Iames* towne, crauing his advice, and for recompence he should haue life, libertie, land, and women. In part of a Table booke he writ his minde to them at the Fort, what was intended, how they should follow that direction to affright the messengers, and without fayle send him such things as he writ for. And an Inventory with them. The difficultie and danger, he told the Salvages, of the Mines, great gunnes, and other Engins exceedingly affrighted them, yet according to his request they went to *Iames* towne, in as bitter weather as could be of frost and snow, and within three dayes returned with an answer.

How he saued *Iames* towne from being surprised.

But when they came to *Iame* towne, seeing men sally out as he had told them they would, they fled; yet in the night they came againe to the same place where he had told

told them they should receiue an answer, and such things as he had promised them, which they found accordingly, and with which they returned with no small expedition, to the wonder of them all that heard it, that he could either divine, or the paper could speake: then they led him to the *Youthtanunds*, the *Mattapanients*, the *Payankatanks*, the *Nantaughtacunds*, and *Onawmanients* vpon the rivers of *Rapahanock*, and *Patawomek*, over all those rivers, and backe againe by divers other severall Nations, to the Kings habitation at *Pamavnkee*, where they entertained him with most strange and fearefull Coniurations; *As if neare led to hell,*
Amongst the Devils to dwell.

How they did Coniure him at *Pamavnkee*.

Not long after, early in a morning a great fire was made in a long house, and a mat spread on the one side, as on the other, on the one they caused him to sit, and all the guard went out of the house, and presently came skipping in a great grim fellow, all painted over with coale, mingled with oyle; and many Snakes and Wesels skins stuffed with mosse, and all their tayles tyed together, so as they met on the crowne of his head in a tassell; and round about the tassell was as a Coronet of feathers, the skins hanging round about his head, backe, and shoulders, and in a manner covered his face; with a hellish voyce and a rattle in his hand. With most strange gestures and passions he began his invocation, and environed the fire with a circle of meale; which done, three more such like devils came rushing in with the like antique tricks, painted halfe blacke, halfe red: but all their eyes were painted white, and some red stroakes like Mutchato's, along their cheekes: round about him those fiends daunced a pretty while, and then came in three more as vgly as the rest; with red eyes, and white stroakes over their blacke faces, at last they all sat downe right against him; three of them on the one hand of the chiefe Priest, and three on the other. Then all with their rattles began a song, which ended, the chiefe Priest layd downe fiue wheat cornes: then strayning his armes and hands with such violence that he sweat, and his veynes swelled, he began a short Oration: at the conclusion they all gaue a short groane; and then layd down three graines more. After that, began their song againe, and then another Oration, ever laying downe so many cornes as before, till they had twice incirculed the fire; that done, they tooke a bunch of little stickes prepared for that purpose, continuing still their devotion, and at the end of every song and Oration, they layd downe a sticke betwixt the divisions of Corne. Till night, neither he nor they did either eate or drinke, and then they feasted merrily, with the best provisions they could make. Three dayes they vsed this Ceremony; the meaning whereof they told him, was to know if he intended them well or no. The circle of meale signified their Country, the circles of corne the bounds of the Sea, and the stickes his Country. They imagined the world to be flat and round, like a trencher, and they in the middest. After this they brought him a bagge of gunpowder, which they carefully preserved till the next spring, to plant as they did their corne; because they would be acquainted with the nature of that seede. *Opitchapam* the Kings brother invited him to his house, where, with as many platters of bread, foule, and wild beasts, as did environ him, he bid him wellcome; but not any of them would eate a bit with him, but put vp all the remainder in Baskets. At his returne to *Opechancanoughs*, all the Kings women, and their children, flocked about him for their parts, as a due by Custome, to be merry with such fragments.

But his waking mind in hydeous dreames did oft see wondrous shapes,
Of bodies strange, and huge in growth, and of stupendious makes.

How *Powhatan* entertained him.

At last they brought him to *Meronocomoco*, where was *Powhatan* their Emperor. Here more then two hundred of those grim Courtiers stood wondering at him, as he had beene a monster; till *Powhatan* and his trayne had put themselues in their greatest braveries. Before a fire vpon a seat like a bedsted, he sat covered with a great robe, made of *Rarowcun* skinnes, and all the tayles hanging by. On either hand did sit a young wench of 16 or 18 yeares, and along on each side the house, two rowes of of men, and behind them as many women, with all their heads and shoulders painted red; many of their heads bedecked with the white downe of Birds; but every one with something: and a great chayne of white beads about their necks. At his entrance before the King, all the people gaue a great shout. The Queene of *Appamatuck* was appointed to bring him water to wash his hands, and another brought him a bunch of feathers, in stead of a Towell to dry them: having feasted him after their best barbarous manner they could, a long consultation was held, but the conclusion was, two great stones were brought before *Powhatan*: then as many as could layd hands on him, dragged him to them, and thereon laid his head, and being ready with their clubs, to beate out his braines, *Pocahontas* the Kings dearest daughter, when no intreaty could prevaile, got his head in her armes, and laid her owne vpon his to saue him from death: whereat the Emperour was contented he should liue to make him hatchets, and her bells, beads, and copper; for they thought him aswell of all occupations as themselues. For the King himselfe will make his owne robes, shooes, bowes, arrowes, pots; plant, hunt, or doe any thing so well as the rest.

How *Pocahontas* saved his life.

They say he bore a pleasant shew,
But sure his heart was sad.
For who can pleasant be, and rest,
That liues in feare and dread:
And having life suspected, doth
It still suspected lead.

Two dayes after, *Powhatan* having disguised himselfe in the most fearefullest manner he could, caused Capt: *Smith* to be brought forth to a great house in the woods, and there vpon a mat by the fire to be left alone. Not long after from behinde a mat that divided the house, was made the most dolefullest noyse he ever heard; then *Powhatan* more like a devill then a man with some two hundred more as blacke as himselfe, came vnto him and told him now they were friends, and presently he should goe to *Iames* towne, to send him two great gunnes, and a gryndstone, for which he would giue him the Country of *Capahowosick*, and for ever esteeme him as his sonne *Nantaquond*. So to *Iames* towne with 12 guides *Powhatan* sent him. That night they quarterd in the woods, he still expecting (as he had done all this long time of his imprisonment) every houre to be put to one death or other: for all their feasting. But almightie God (by his divine providence) had mollified the hearts of those sterne *Barbarians* with compassion. The next morning betimes they came to the Fort, where *Smith* having vsed the Salvages with what kindnesse he could, he shewed *Rawhunt*, *Powhatans* trusty servant two demi-Culverings & a millstone to carry *Powhatan*: they found them somewhat too heavie; but when they did see him discharge them, being loaded with stones, among the boughs of a great tree loaded with Isickles, the yce and branches came so tumbling downe, that the poore Salvages ran away halfe dead with feare. But at last we regained some conference with them, and gaue them such toyes; and sent to *Powhatan*, his women, and children such presents, as gaue them in generall full content. Now in *Iames* Towne they were all in combustion, the strongest preparing once more to run away with the Pinnace; which with the hazzard of his life, with Sakre falcon and musket shot, *Smith* forced now the third time to stay or sinke. Some no better then they should be, had plotted with the President, the next day to haue put him to death by the Leviticall law, for the liues of *Robinson* and *Emry*, pretending the fault was his that had led them to their ends: but he quickly tooke such order with such Lawyers, that he layd them by the heeles till he sent some of them prisoners for *England*. Now ever once in foure or fiue dayes, *Pocahontas* with her attendants, brought him so much provision, that saved many of their liues, that els for all this had starved with hunger.

How *Powhatan* sent him to *Iames* Towne.

The third proiect to abandon the Countrey.

Thus from numbe death our good God sent reliefe,
The sweete asswager of all other griefe.

H

His

A true proofe of Gods loue to the action.

His relation of the plenty he had seene, especially at *Werawocomoco*, and of the state and bountie of *Powhatan*, (which till that time was vnknowne) so revived their dead spirits (especially the loue of *Pocahontas*) as all mens feare was abandoned. Thus you may see what difficulties still crossed any good indevour: and the good successe of the businesse being thus oft brought to the very period of destruction; yet you see by what strange means God hath still delivered it. As for the insufficiency of them admitted in Commission, that error could not be prevented by the Electors; there being no other choise, and all strangers to each others education, qualities, or disposition. And if any deeme it a shame to our Nation to haue any mention made of those inormities, let them peruse the Histories of the Spanyards Discoveries and Plantations, where they may see how many mutinies, disorders, and dissentions haue accompanied them, and crossed their attempts: which being knowne to be particular mens offences; doth take away the generall scorne and contempt, which malice, presumption, covetousnesse, or ignorance might produce; to the scandall and reproach of those, whose actions and valiant resolutions deserue a more worthy respect.

Of two evils the lesse was chosen.

Now whether it had beene better for Captaine *Smith*, to haue concluded with any of those severall proiects, to haue abandoned the Countrey, with some ten or twelue of them, who were called the better sort, and haue left M[r] *Hunt* our Preacher, Master *Anthony Gosnoll*, a most honest, worthy, and industrious Gentleman, Master *Thomas Wotton*, and some 27 others of his Countrymen to the fury of the Salvages, famine, and all manner of mischiefes, and inconveniences, (for they were but fortie in all to keepe possession of this large Country;) or starue himselfe with them for company, for want of lodging: or but adventuring abroad to make them provision, or by his opposition to preserue the action, and saue all their liues; I leaue to the censure of all honest men to consider. But

We men imagine in our Iolitie,
That 'tis all one, or good or bad to be.
But then anone wee alter this againe,
If happily wee feele the sence of paine;
For then we're turn'd into a mourning vaine.

Written by *Thomas Studley*, the first Cape Merchant in *Virginia*,
Robert Fenton, *Edward Harrington*, and *I. S.*

Chap. III.

The Arrivall of the first supply, with their Proceedings, and the Ships returne.

ALL this time our care was not so much to abandon the Countrey; but the Treasurer and Councell in *England*, were as diligent & carefull to supply vs. Two good ships they sent vs, with neare a hundred men, well furnished with all things could be imagined necessary, both for them and vs; The one commanded by Captaine *Newport*: the other by Captaine *Francis Nelson*, an honest man, and an expert Marriner. But such was the lewardnesse of his Ship (that though he was within the sight of *Cape Henry*) by stormy contrary winds was he forced so farre to Sea, that the West *Indies* was the next land, for the repaire of his Masts, and reliefe of wood and water. But *Newport* got in and arrived at *Iames* Towne, not long after the redemption of Captaine *Smith*. To whom the Salvages, as is sayd, every other day repaired, with such provisions that sufficiently did serue them from hand to mouth: part alwayes they brought him as Presents from their Kings, or *Pocahontas*; the rest he as their Market Clarke set the price himselfe, how they should sell: so he had

The *Phœnix* from Cape *Henry* forced to the West *Indies*.

had inchanted these poore soules being their prisoner; and now *Newport*, whom he called his Father arriving, neare as directly as he foretold, they esteemed him as an Oracle, and had them at that submission he might command them what he listed. That God that created all things they knew he adored for his God: they would also in their discourses tearme the God of Captaine *Smith*.

Thus the Almightie was the bringer on,
The guide, path, terme, all which was God alone.

Their opinion of our God.

But the President and Councell so much envied his estimation among the Salvages, (though we all in generall equally participated with him of the good thereof,) that they wrought it into the Salvages vnderstandings (by their great bounty in giving foure times more for their commodities then *Smith* appointed) that their greatnesse and authoritie as much exceeded his, as their bountie and liberalitie. Now the arrivall of this first supply so overioyed vs, that wee could not devise too much to please the Marriners. We gaue them libertie to trucke or trade at their pleasures. But in a short time it followed, that could not be had for a pound of Copper, which before was sould vs for an ounce: thus ambition and sufferance cut the throat of our trade, but confirmed their opinion of the greatnesse of Capt. *Newport*, (wherewith *Smith* had possessed *Powhatan*) especially by the great presents *Newport* often sent him, before he could prepare the Pinnace to goe and visit him: so that this great Savage desired also to see him. A great coyle there was to set him forward. When he went he was accompanied with Captaine *Smith*, & Mr *Scrivener*, a very wise vnderstanding Gentleman, newly arrived and admitted of the Councell, with thirtie or fortie chosen men for their guard. Arriving at *Werowocomoco*, *Newports* conceit of this great Savage bred many doubts and suspitions of trecheries, which *Smith* to make appeare was needlesse, with twentie men well appointed, vndertooke to encounter the worst that could happen: Knowing

Smiths revisiting Powhatan.

All is but one, and selfe-same hand, that thus
Both one while scourgeth, and that helpeth vs.

Nathaniell Powell.	Gent.	*Anthony Gosnoll.*	Gent.	*Thomas Coe.*	Gent.
Robert Behethland.		*Richard Wyffin.*		*Thomas Hope.*	
Michell Phittiplace.		*John Taverner.*		*Anas Todkill.*	
William Phittiplace.		*William Dyer.*			

These, with nine others (whose names I haue forgotten) comming a-shore, landed amongst a many of creekes, over which they were to passe such poore bridges, onely made of a few cratches, thrust in the ose, and three or foure poles laid on them, and at the end of them the like, tyed together onely with barkes of trees, that it made them much suspect those bridges were but traps. Which caused *Smith* to make diverse Salvages goe over first, keeping some of the chiefe as hostage till halfe his men were passed, to make a guard for himselfe and the rest. But finding all things well, by two or three hundred Salvages they were kindly conducted to their towne. Where *Powhatan* strained himselfe to the vtmost of his greatnesse to entertaine them, with great shouts of ioy, Orations of protestations; and with the most plenty of victualls he could provide to feast them. Sitting vpon his bed of mats, his pillow of leather imbrodered (after their rude manner with pearle and white Beads) his attyre a faire robe of skinnes as large as an Irish mantell: at his head and feete a handsome young woman: on each side his house sat twentie of his Concubines, their heads and shoulders painted red, with a great chaine of white beads about each of their neckes. Before those sat his chiefest men in like order in his arbour-like house, and more then fortie platters of fine bread stood as a guard in two fyles on each side the doore. Foure or fiue hundred people made a guard behinde them for our passage; and Proclamation was made, none vpon paine of death to presume to doe vs any wrong or discourtesie. With many pretty Discourses to re-

Powhatan his entertainement.

new their old acquaintance, this great King and our Captaine spent the time, till the ebbe left our Barge aground. Then renewing their feasts with feates, dauncing and singing, and such like mirth, we quartered that night with *Powhatan.* The next day *Newport* came a shore and receiued as much content as those people could giue him: a boy named *Thomas Salvage* was then giuen vnto *Powhatan*, whom *Newport* called his sonne; for whom *Powhatan* gaue him *Namontack* his trustie servant, and one of a shrewd, subtill capacitie. Three or foure dayes more we spent in feasting, dauncing, and trading, wherein *Powhatan* carried himselfe so proudly, yet discreetly (in his saluage manner) as made vs all admire his naturall gifts, considering his education. As scorning to trade as his subiects did; he bespake *Newport* in this manner.

The exchãge of a Christian for a Salvage.

Powhatans speech.

Captaine Newport *it is not agreeable to my greatnesse, in this pedling manner to trade for trifles; and I esteeme you also a great Werowance. Therefore lay me downe all your commodities together; what I like I will take, and in recompence giue you what I thinke fitting their value.* Captaine *Smith* being our interpreter, regarding *Newport* as his father, knowing best the disposition of *Powhatan*, tould vs his intent was but onely to cheate vs; yet Captaine *Newport* thinking to out braue this Salvage in ostentation of greatnesse, and so to bewitch him with his bountie, as to haue what he listed, it so hapned, that *Powhatan* hauing his desire, valued his corne at such a rate, that I thinke it better cheape in *Spaine*: for we had not foure bushells for that we expected to haue twentie hogsheads. This bred some vnkindnesse betweene our two Captaines; *Newport* seeking to please the vnsatiable desire of the Salvage, *Smith* to cause the Salvage to please him; but smothering his distast to avoyd the Saluages suspition, glanced in the eyes of *Powhatan* many trifles, who fixed his humor vpon a few blew beades. A long time he importunately desired them, but *Smith* seemed so much the more to affect them, as being composed of a most rare substance of the coulour of the skyes, and not to be worne but by the greatest kings in the world. This made him halfe madde to be the owner of such strange Iewells: so that ere we departed, for a pound or two of blew beades, he brought ouer my king for 2. or 300. Bushells of corne; yet parted good friends. The like entertainment we found of *Opechankanough* king of *Pamavnkee*, whom also he in like manner fitted (at the like rates) with blew beads, which grew by this meanes, of that estimation, that none durst weare any of them but their great kings, their wiues and children. And so we returned all well to *Iames* towne, where this new supply being lodged with the rest, accidentally fired their quarters and so the towne, which being but thatched with reeds, the fire was so fierce as it burnt their Pallisado's, (though eight or ten yards distant) with their Armes, bedding, apparell, and much priuate prouision. Good Master *Hunt* our Preacher lost all his Library and all he had but the cloathes on his backe: yet none neuer heard him repine at his losse. This happned in the winter in that extreame frost. 1607. Now though we had victuall sufficient I meane onely of Oatmeale, meale and corne, yet the Ship staying 14. weekes when shee might as wel haue beene gone in 14. dayes, spent a great part of that, and neare all the rest that was sent to be landed. When they departed what there discretion could spare vs, to make a little poore meale or two, we called feastes, to relish our mouthes: of each somwhat they left vs, yet I must confesse, those that had either money, spare clothes credit to giue billes of paiment, gold rings, furrs, or any such commodities, were euer welcome to this remouing tauerne, such was our patience to obay such vile Commanders, and buy our owne provisions at 15. times the value, suffering them feast (we bearing the charge) yet must not repine, but fast, least we should incurre the censure of factious and seditious persons: and then leakage, ship-rats, and other casualties occasioned them losse, but the vessels and remnants (for totals) we were glad to receaue with all our hearts to make vp the account, highly commending their prouidence for preseruing that, least they should discourage any more to come to vs. Now for all this plenty our ordynary was but meale and water, so that this great charge little releeued our wants, whereby with the extremitie of the

Differences of opinions.

Iames towne burnt.

A ship Idely loytering 14. weekes.

bitter cold frost and those defects, more then halfe of vs dyed; I cannot deny but both *Smith* and *Skriuener* did their best to amend what was amisse, but with the President went the maior part, that there hornes were to short. But the worst was our guilded refiners with their golden promises made all men their slaues in hope of recompences; there was no talke, no hope, no worke, but dig gold, wash gold, refine gold, loade gold, such a bruit of gold, that one mad fellow desired to be buried in the sands least they should by there art make gold of his bones: little neede there was and lesse reason, the ship should stay, there wages run on, our victualls consume 14. weekes, that the Mariners might say, they did helpe to build such a golden Church that we can say the raine washed neere to nothing in 14. dayes. Were it that captaine *Smith* would not applaude all those golden inventions, because they admitted him not to the sight of their trialls nor golden consultations, I know not; but I haue heard him oft question with Captaine *Martin* & tell him, except he could shew him a more substantiall triall, he was not inamoured with their durty skill, breathing out these and many other passions, neuer any thing did more torment him, then to see all necessary busines neglected, to fraught such a drunken ship with so much guilded durt. Till then we neuer accounted, Captaine *Newport* a refiner, who being ready to set saile for *England*, & we not hauing any vse of Parliaments, Plaies, Petitions, Admiralls, Recorders, Interpreters, Chronologers, Courts of Plea, nor Iustices of peace, sent Master *Wingfield* and Captaine *Archer* home with him, that had ingrossed all those titles, to seeke some better place of imployment.

The effect of meere Verbalists.

A needlesse charge.

A returne to England.

Oh cursed gold those, hunger-starved movers,
To what misfortunes lead'st thou all those lovers!
For all the China *wealth, nor* Indies *can*
Suffice the minde of an av'ritious man.

CHAP. IIII.

The Arrivall of the Phoenix; *her returne; and other Accidents.*

THe authoritie now consisting in Captaine *Martin*, and the still sickly President, the sale of the Stores commodities maintained his estate, as an inheritable revenew. The spring approaching, and the Ship departing, Mr *Scrivener* and Captaine *Smith* devided betwixt them the rebuilding *Iames* towne; the repairing our Pallizadoes; the cutting downe trees; preparing our fields; planting our corne, and to rebuild our Church, and recover our Store house. All men thus busie at their severall labours, Master *Nelson* arrived with his lost *Phœnix*; lost (I say) for that we all deemed him lost. Landing safely all his men, (so well he had mannaged his ill hap,) causing the *Indian Isles* to feede his company, that his victuall to that we had gotten, as is said before, was neare after our allowance sufficient for halfe a yeare. He had not any thing but he freely imparted it, which honest dealing (being a Marriner) caused vs admire him: we would not haue wished more then he did for vs. Now to relade this ship with some good tydings, the President (not holding it stood with the dignitie of his place to leaue the Fort) gaue order to Captaine *Smith* to discover and search the commodities of the *Monacans* Countrey beyond the Falls. Sixtie able men was allotted them, the which within six dayes, *Smith* had so well trained to their armes and orders, that they little feared with whom they should incounter: yet so vnseasonable was the time, and so opposit was Captaine *Martin* to any thing, but onely to fraught this ship also with his phantasticall gold, as Captaine *Smith* rather desired to relade her with Cedar, (which was a present dispatch) then either with durt, or the hopes and reports of an vncertaine discovery, which he would performe when they had lesse charge and more leisure.

The rebuilding *Iames* Towne.

Sixtie appointed to discover the *Monacans.*

But, *The God of Heav'n, He eas'ly can*
Immortalize a mortall man,
With glory and with fame.
The same God, ev'n as eas'ly may
Afflict a mortall man, I say,
With sorrow and with shame.

Whilst the conclusion was a resolving, this hapned.

An ill example to sell swords to Salvages.

Powhatan (to expresse his loue to *Newport*) when he departed, presented him with twentie Turkies, conditionally to returne him twentie swords, which immediately was sent him; now after his departure he presented Captaine *Smith* with the like luggage, but not finding his humor obeyed in not sending such weapons as he desired, he caused his people with twentie devices to obtaine them. At last by ambuscadoes at our very Ports they would take them perforce, surprise vs at worke, or any way; which was so long permitted, they became so insolent there was no rule; the command from *England* was so strait not to offend them, as our authoritie-bearers (keeping their houses) would rather be any thing then peace-breakers. This charitable humor prevailed, till well it chanced they medled with Captaine *Smith*, who without farther deliberation gaue them such an incounter, as some he so hunted vp and downe the Isle, some he so terrified with whipping, beating, and imprisonment, as for revenge they surprised two of our forraging disorderly souldiers, and having assembled their forces, boldly threatned at our Ports to force *Smith* to redeliver seven Salvages, which for their villanies he detained prisoners, or we were all but dead men. But to try their furies he sallied out amongst them, and in lesse then an houre, he so hampred their insolencies, they brought them his two men, desiring peace without any further composition for their prisoners. Those he examined, and caused them all beleeue, by severall vollies of shot one of their companions was shot to death, because they would not confesse their intents and plotters of those villanies. And thus they all agreed in one point, they were directed onely by *Powhatan* to obtaine him our weapons, to cut our owne throats, with the manner where, how, and when, which we plainly found most true and apparant: yet he sent his messengers, and his dearest daughter *Pocahontas* with presents to excuse him of the iniuries done by some rash vntoward Captaines his subiects, desiring their liberties for this time, with the assurance of his loue for ever. After *Smith* had given the prisoners what correction he thought fit, vsed them well a day or two after, & then delivered them *Pocahontas*, for whose sake onely he fayned to haue saued their liues, and gaue them libertie. The patient Councell that nothing would moue to warre with the Salvages, would gladly haue wrangled with Captaine *Smith* for his crueltie, yet none was slaine to any mans knowledge, but it brought them in such feare and obedience, as his very name would sufficiently affright them; where before, wee had sometime peace and warre twice in a day, and very seldome a weeke, but we had some trecherous villany or other.

The Presidents weaknesse.

Smiths attempt to suppresse the Salvages insolencies.

Powhatans excuse.

A ship fraught with Cedar.

The fraught of this Ship being concluded to be Cedar, by the diligence of the Master, and Captaine *Smith*, she was quickly reladed: Master *Scrivener* was neither idle nor slow to follow all things at the Fort; the Ship being ready to set sayle, Captaine *Martin* being alwayes very sickly, and vnserviceable, and desirous to inioy the credit of his supposed Art of finding the golden Mine, was most willingly admitted to returne for *England*. For

He hath not fill'd his lapp,
That still doth hold it oap.

From the writings of *Thomas Studley*,
and *Anas Todkill*.

Their

Their Names that were landed in this Supply.

1608. Sir *Thomas Smith* Treasurer.

Mathew Scrivener appointed to be one of the Councell.

Gent.:
Michaell Phittiplace.
William Phittiplace.
Ralph Morton.
Richard Wyffing.
John Taverner.
William Cantrell.
Robert Barnes.
Richard Fetherstone.
George Hill.
George Pretty.
Nathaniell Causy.
Peter Pory.
Robert Cutler.
Michaell Sicklemore.
William Bentley.
Thomas Coe.
Doctor *Russell.*
Ieffrey Abbot.
Edward Gurgana.
Richard Worley.
Timothy Leeds.
Richard Killingbeck.
William Spence.
Richard Prodger.
Richard Pots.
Richard Mullinax.
William Bayley.

Gent.:
Francis Perkins.
Iohn Harper.
George Forest.
Iohn Nichols.
William Griuell.

Labourers:
Raymōd Goodison.
William Simons.
Iohn Spearman.
Richard Bristow.
William Perce.
Iames Watkins.
Iohn Bouth.
Christopher Rods.
Richard Burket.
Iames Burre.
Nicholas Ven.
Francis Perkins.
Richard Gradon.
Rawland Nelstrop.
Richard Savage.
Thomas Savage.
Richard Milmer.
William May.
Vere.
Michaell.
Bishop Wiles.

Taylers:
Thomas Hope.
William Ward.
Iohn Powell.
William Yong.
William Beckwith.
Larence Towtales.

Apothecaries:
Thomas Field.
Iohn Harford.

Dani: Stallings, Ieweller.
Will: Dawson, a refiner.
Abram Ransack, a refiner.
Wil: Iohnson, a Goldsmith.
Peter Keffer, a gunsmith.
Rob: Alberton, a perfumer.
Richard Belfield, a Goldsmith.
Post Ginnat, a Chirurg.
Iohn Lewes, a Cooper.
Robert Cotton, a Tobacco-pipe-maker.
Richard Dole, a Blacksmith.

And divers others to the number of 120.

CHAPTER V.

The Accidents that hapned in the Discovery of the Bay of Chisapeack.

THe prodigalitie of the Presidents state went so deepe into our small store, that *Smith* and *Scrivener* tyed him and his Parasites to the rules of proportion. But now *Smith* being to depart, the Presidents authoritie so overswayed the discretion of Mr *Scrivener*, that our store, our time, our strength and labours were idely consumed to fulfill his phantasies. The second of Iune 1608. *Smith* left the Fort to performe his Discovery with this Company.

Walter Russell, Doctor of Physicke.

Gentlemen:
Ralfe Murton.
Thomas Momford.
William Cantrill.
Richard Fetherston.
Iames Burne.
Michell Sicklemore.

Souldiers:
Ionas Profit.
Anas Todkill.
Robert Small.
Iames Watkins.
Iohn Powell.
Iames Read.
Richard Keale.

These being in an open Barge neare three tuns burthen, leaving the *Phœnix* at Cape *Henry*, they crossed the Bay to the Easterne shore, and fell with the Isles called *Smiths Isles*, after our Captaines name. The first people we saw were two grim and stout Salvages vpon Cape *Charles*, with long poles like Iauelings, headed with bone, they boldly demanded what we were, and what we would; but after many circumstances they seemed very kinde, and directed vs to *Accomack*, the habitation of their *Werowance*, where we were kindly intreated. This King was the comliest, proper, civill Salvage we incountred. His Country is a pleasant fertile clay soyle, some small creekes; good Harbours for small Barks, but not for Ships. He told vs of a strange accident lately happened him, and it was, two children being dead; some extreame passions, or dreaming visions, phantasies, or affection moued their parents againe to revisit their dead carkases, whose benummed bodies reflected to the eyes of the beholders such delightfull countenances, as though they had regained their vitall spirits. This as a miracle drew many to behold them, all which being a great part of his people, not long after dyed, and but few escaped. They spake the language of *Powhatan*, wherein they made such descriptions of the Bay, Isles, and rivers, that often did vs exceeding pleasure. Passing along the coast, searching every inlet, and Bay, fit for harbours and habitations. Seeing many Isles in the midst of the Bay we bore vp for them, but ere we could obtaine them, such an extreame gust of wind, rayne, thunder, and lightening happened, that with great danger we escaped the vnmercifull raging of that Ocean-like water. The highest land on the mayne, yet it was but low, we called *Keales* hill, and these vninhabited Isles, *Russels* Isles. The next day searching them for fresh water, we could find none, the defect whereof forced vs to follow the next Easterne Channell, which brought vs to the river of *Wighcocomoco*. The people at first with great fury seemed to assault vs, yet at last with songs and daunces and much mirth became very tractable, but searching their habitations for water, we could fill but three barricoes, & that such puddle, that never till then we ever knew the want of good water. We digged and searched in many places, but before two daies were expired, we would haue refused two barricoes of gold for one of that puddle water of *Wighcocomoco*. Being past these Isles which are many in number, but all naught for habitation, falling with a high land vpon the mayne, we found a great Pond of fresh water, but so exceeding hot wee supposed it some bath; that place we called poynt *Ployer*, in honor of that most honourable House of *Mousay* in *Britaine*, that in an extreame extremitie once relieued our Captaine. From *Wighcocomoco* to this place, all the coast is low broken Isles of Morap, growne a myle or two in breadth, and ten or twelue in length, good to cut for hay in Summer, and to catch fish and foule in Winter: but the Land beyond them is all covered over with wood, as is the rest of the Country.

A strange mortalitie of Salvages.

Russels Isles.

Wighcocomoco.

An extreame want of fresh water.

Being thus refreshed in crossing ouer from the maine to other Isles, we discouered the winde and waters so much increased with thunder, lightning, and raine, that our mast and sayle blew ouerbord and such mighty waues ouerracked vs in that small barge that with great labour we kept her frō sinking by freeing out the water. Two dayes we were inforced to inhabite these vninhabited Isles which for the extremitie of gusts, thunder, raine, stormes, and ill wether we called *Limbo*. Repairing our saile with our shirts, we set sayle for the maine and fell with a pretty convenient riuer on the East called *Cuskarawaok*, the people ran as amazed in troups from place to place, and diuers got into the tops of trees, they were not sparing of their arrowes, nor the greatest passion they could expresse of their anger. Long they shot, we still ryding at an Anchor without there reatch making all the signes of friendship we could. The next day they came vnarmed, with euery one a basket, dancing in a ring, to draw vs on shore: but seeing there was nothing in them but villany, we discharged a volly of muskets charged with pistoll shot, whereat they all lay tumbling on the grownd, creeping some one way, some another into a great cluster of reedes hard by; where there companies lay in Ambuscado. Towards the euening we wayed, & approaching the shoare, discharging fiue or six shot among the reedes, we landed where there lay a many of baskets and much bloud, but saw not a Salvage. A smoake appearing on the other side the riuer, we rowed thither, where we found two or three little houses, in each a fire, there we left some peeces of copper, beads, bells, and looking glasses, and then went into the bay, but when it was darke we came backe againe. Early in the

Their Barge neare sunke in a gust.

Cuskarawaock.

the morning foure Salvages came to vs in their Canow, whom we vsed with such courtesie, not knowing what we were, nor had done, hauing beene in the bay a fishing, bade vs stay and ere long they would returne, which they did and some twentie more with them; with whom after a little conference, two or three thousand men women & childrẽ came clustring about vs, euery one presẽting vs with something, which a little bead would so well requite, that we became such friends they would contend who should fetch vs water, stay with vs for hostage, conduct our men any whither, and giue vs the best content. Here doth inhabite the people of *Sarapinagh*, *Nause*, *Arseek*, and *Nantaquak* the best Marchants of all other Salvages. They much extolled a great nation called *Massawomekes*, in search of whom we returned by *Limbo*: this riuer but onely at the entrance is very narrow, and the people of small stature as them of *Wightcocomoco*, the Land but low, yet it may proue very commodious, because it is but a ridge of land betwixt the Bay and the maine Ocean. Finding this Easterne shore, shallow broken Isles, and for most part without fresh water, we passed by the straites of *Limbo* for the Westerne shore: so broad is the bay here, we could scarce perceiue the great high clifts on the other side: by them we Anchored that night and called them *Riccards Cliftes*. 30. leagues we sayled more Northwards not finding any inhabitants, leauing all the Easterne shore, lowe Islandes, but ouergrowne with wood, as all the Coast beyond them so farre as wee could see: the Westerne shore by which we sayled we found all along well watered, but very mountanous and barren, the vallies very fertill, but extreame thicke of small wood so well as trees, and much frequented with Wolues, Beares, Deere and other wild beasts. We passed many shallow creekes, but the first we found Nauigable for a ship, we called *Bolus*, for that the clay in many places vnder the clifts by the high water marke, did grow vp in red and white knots as gum out of trees; and in some places so participated together as though they were all of one nature, excepting the coulour, the rest of the earth on both sides being hard sandy grauell, which made vs thinke it *Bole-Armoniack* and *Terra sigillata*. When we first set sayle some of our Gallants doubted nothing but that our Captaine would make too much hast home, but hauing lien in this small barge not aboue 12. or 14. dayes, oft tyred at the Oares, our bread spoyled with wet so much that it was rotten (yet so good were their stomacks that they could disgest it) they did with continuall complaints so importune him now to returne, as caused him bespeake them in this manner.

The first notice of the *Massawomeks*.

Bolus Riuer.

Gentlemen if you would remember the memorable history of Sir Ralph Layne, *how his company importuned him to proceed in the discovery of* Moratico, *alleadging they had yet a dog, that being boyled with Saxafras leaues, would richly feede them in their returnes; then what a shame would it be for you (that haue bin so suspitious of my tendernesse) to force me returne, with so much provision as we haue, and scarce able to say where we haue beene, nor yet heard of that we were sent to seeke? You cannot say but I haue shared with you in the worst which is past; and for what is to come, of lodging, dyet, or whatsoeuer, I am contented you allot the worst part to my selfe. As for your feares that I will lose my selfe in these vnknowne large waters, or be swallowed vp in some stormie gust; abandon these childish feares, for worse then is past is not likely to happen: and there is as much danger to returne as to proceede. Regaine therefore your old spirits for returne I will not (if God please) till I haue seene the* Massawomeks, *found* Patawomek, *or the head of this water you conceit to be endlesse.* Two or 3. dayes we expected winde & wether, whose aduerse extremities added such discouragement, that three or foure fell sicke, whose pittifull complaints caused vs to to returne, leauing the bay some nine miles broad, at nine and ten fadome water.

Smiths speech to his souldiers.

The discouery of *Patawomek*.

The 16. of *Iune* we fell with the riuer *Patowomek*: feare being gone, and our men recovered, we were all content to take some paines, to know the name of that seuen mile broad riuer: for thirtie myles sayle, we could see no inhabitants: then we were conducted by two Savages vp a little bayed creeke, towards *Onawmanient*, where all the woods were layd with ambuscado's to the number of three or foure thousand Salvages, so strangely paynted, grimed and disguised, shouting, yelling and crying

Ambuscadoes of Salvages.

as so many spiritsfrom hell could not haue shewed more terrible. Many brauado's they made, but to appease their fury, our Captaine prepared with as seeming a willingnesse (as they) to incounter them. But the grazing of our bullets vpon the water (many being shot on purpose they might see them) with the Ecco of the of the woods so amazed them, as downe went their bowes and arrowes; (and exchanging hostage) *Iames Watkins* was sent six myles vp the woods to their Kings habitation. We were kindly vsed of those Salvages, of whom we vnderstood, they were commanded to betray vs, by the direction of *Powhatan*, and he so directed from the discontents at *Iames* towne, because our Captaine did cause them stay in their country against their wills.

A trecherous proiect.

The like incounters we found at *Patowomek, Cecocawonee* and diuers other places: but at *Moyaones, Nacotchtant* and *Toags* the people did their best to content vs. Hauing gone so high as we could with the bote, we met diuers Saluages in Canowes, well loaden with the flesh of Beares, Deere and other beasts, whereof we had part, here we found mighty Rocks, growing in some places aboue the grownd as high as the shrubby trees, and diuers other solid quarries of diuers tinctures: and diuers places where the waters had falne from the high mountaines they had left a tinctured spāgled skurfe, that made many bare places seeme as guilded. Digging the growne aboue in the highest clifts of rocks, we saw it was a claie sand so mingled with yeallow spangles as if it had beene halfe pin-dust. In our returne inquiring still for this *Matchqueon*, the king of *Patawomeke* gaue vs guides to conduct vs vp a little riuer called *Quiyough*, vp which we rowed so high as we could. Leauing the bote, with six shot, and diuers Salvages, he marched seuen or eight myle before they came to the mine: leading his hostages in a small chaine they were to haue for their paines, being proud so richly to be adorned. The mine is a great Rocky mountaine like *Antimony*; wherein they digged a great hole with shells & hatchets: and hard by it, runneth a fayre brooke of *Christal*-like water, where they wash a way the drosse and keepe the remainder, which they put in little baggs and sell it all ouer the country to paint there bodyes, faces, or Idols; which makes them looke like Blackmores dusted over with siluer. With so much as we could carry we returned to our bote, kindly requiting this kinde king and all his kinde people. The cause of this discovery was to search this mine, of which *Newport* did assure vs that those small baggs (we had giuen him) in *England* he had tryed to hold halfe siluer; but all we got proued of no value: also to search what furrs, the best whereof is at *Cuscarawaoke*, where is made so much *Rawranoke* or white beads that occasion as much dissention among the the Salvages, as gold and siluer amongst Christians; and what other mineralls, riuers, rocks, nations, woods, fishings, fruites, victuall, and what other commodities the land afforded: and whether the bay were endlesse or how farre it extended: of mines we were all ignorant, but a few Beuers, Otters, Beares, Martins and minkes we found, and in diuers places that aboundance of fish, lying so thicke with their heads aboue the water, as for want of nets (our barge driuing amongst them) we attempted to catch them with a frying pan: but we found it a bad instrument to catch fish with: neither better fish, more plenty, nor more variety for smal fish, had any of vs euer seene in any place so swimming in the water, but they are not to be caught with frying pans: some small codd also we did see swim close by the shore by *Smiths* Iles, and some as high as *Riccards* Clifts. And some we haue found dead vpon the shore.

A myne like *Antimony*.

An aboundant plenty of fish.

How to deale with the Salvages.

To exprest all our quarrels, trecheries and incounters amongst those Salvages I should be too tedious: but in breefe, at all times we so incountred them, and curbed their insolencies, that they concluded with presents to purchase peace; yet we lost not a man: at our first meeting our Captaine euer obserued this order to demand their bowes and arrowes, swordes, mantells and furrs, with some childe or two for hostage, whereby we could quickly perceiue, when they intended any villany. Hauing finished this discouery (though our victuall was neere spent) he intended to see his imprisonment-acquaintances vpon the riuer of *Rapahanock*, by

many

many called *Toppahanock*, but our bote by reaſon of the ebbe, chanſing to grownd vpon a many ſhoules lying in the entrances, we ſpyed many fiſhes lurking in the reedes: our Captaine ſporting himſelfe by nayling them to the grownd with his ſword, ſet vs all a fiſhing in that manner: thus we tooke more in owne houre then we could eate in a day. But it chanſed our Captaine taking a fiſh from his ſword (not knowing her condition) being much of the faſhion of a Thornback, but a long tayle like a ryding rodde, whereon the middeſt is a moſt poyſoned ſting, of two or three inches long, bearded like a ſaw on each ſide, which ſhe ſtrucke into the wreſt of his arme neere an inch and a halfe: no bloud nor wound was ſeene, but a little blew ſpot, but the torment was inſtantly ſo extreame, that in foure houres had ſo ſwolen his hand, arme and ſhoulder, we all with much ſorrow concluded his funerall, and prepared his graue in an Iſland by, as himſelfe directed: yet it pleaſed God by a precious oyle Docter *Ruſſell* at the firſt applyed to it when he ſounded it with probe (ere night) his tormenting paine was ſo well aſſwaged that he eate of the fiſh to his ſupper, which gaue no leſſe ioy and content to vs then eaſe to himſelfe, for which we called the Iſland *Stingray* Iſle after the name of the fiſh.

Captaine *Smith* neare killed with a *Stingray*.

Hauing neither Chirurgian, nor Chirurgery, but that preſeruatiue oyle we preſently ſet ſayles for *Iames* towne, paſſing the mouthes of the riuers of *Payankatank*, & *Pamavnkee*, the next day we ſafely arriued at *Kecougtan*. The ſimple Salvages ſeeing our Captaine hurt, and an other bloudy by breaking his ſhinne, our numbers of bowes, arrowes, ſwords, mantles, and furrs, would needes imagine we had beene at warres (the truth of theſe accidents would not ſatisfie them) but impatiently importuned vs to know with whom. Finding their aptneſſe to beleeue we fayled not (as a great ſecret) to tell them any thing that might affright them, what ſpoyle we had got and made of the *Maſſawomeks*. This rumor went faſter vp the river then our Barge, that arrived at *Waraskoyack* the 20 of Iuly; where trimming her with painted ſtreamers, and ſuch deviſes as we could, we made them at *Iames* towne iealous of a Spaniſh Frigot, where we all God be thanked ſafely arrived the 21 of Iuly. There we found the laſt Supply were all ſicke, the reſt ſome lame, ſome bruiſed, all vnable to doe any thing but complaine of the pride and vnreaſonable needleſſe crueltie of the ſilly Preſident, that had riotouſly conſumed the ſtore: and to fulfill his follies about building him an vnneceſſary building for his pleaſure in the woods, had brought them all to that miſery; that had we not arrived, they had as ſtrangely tormented him with revenge: but the good newes of our Diſcovery, and the good hope we had by the Salvages relation, that our Bay had ſtretched into the South Sea, or ſomewhat neare it, appeaſed their fury; but conditionally that *Ratliffe* ſhould be depoſed, and that Captaine *Smith* would take vpon him the government, as by courſe it did belong. Their requeſt being effected, he ſubſtituted Mr *Scrivener* his deare friend in the Preſidency, equally diſtributing thoſe private proviſions the other had ingroſſed, appointing more honeſt officers to aſſiſt maſter *Scrivener* (who then lay exceeding ſicke of a Callenture) and in regard of the weakneſſe of the company, and heate of the yeare, they being vnable to worke, he left them to liue at eaſe, to recover their healths, but imbarked himſelfe to finiſh his Diſcovery.

The Salvages affrighted with their owne ſuſpition.

Needleſſe miſery at *Iames* towne.

Written by Walter Ruſſell, Anas Todkill, *and* Thomas Momford.

Chap. VI.

The Government ſurrendred to Maſter Scrivener.

What happened the ſecond Voyage in diſcovering the Bay.

THe 24 of Iuly, Captaine *Smith* ſet forward to finiſh the diſcovery with twelue men: their names were

Nathaniell Powell.	Gentlemen.	*Ionas Profit.*	Souldiers.
Thomas Momford.		*Anas Todkill.*	
Richard Fetherston.		*Edward Pising.*	
Michell Sicklemore.		*Richard Keale.*	
Iames Bourne.		*Iames Watkins.*	
Anthony Bagnall, Chir.		*William Ward.*	

The wind being contrary caused our stay two or three dayes at *Kecoughtan*: the King feasted vs with much mirth, his people were perswaded we went purposely to be revenged of the *Massawomeks*. In the evening we fired a few rackets, which flying in the ayre so terrified the poore Salvages, they supposed nothing vnpossible we attempted; and desired to assist vs. The first night we anchored at *Stingray* Isle. The next day crossed *Patawomeks* river, and hasted to the river *Bolus*. We went not much further before we might see the Bay to divide in two heads, and arriving there we found it divided in foure, all which we searched so farre as we could sayle them. Two of them we found inhabited, but in crossing the Bay, we incountred 7 or 8 Canowes full of *Massawomeks*, we seeing them prepare to assault vs, left our Oares and made way with our sayle to incounter them, yet were we but fiue with our Captaine that could stand, for within 2 dayes after we left *Kecoughtan*, the rest (being all of the last supply) were sicke almost to death, vntill they were seasoned to the Country. Having shut them vnder our Tarpawling, we put their hats vpon stickes by the Barges side, and betwixt two hats a man with two peeces, to make vs seeme many, and so we thinke the *Indians* supposed those hats to be men, for they fled with all possible speed to the shore, and there stayed, staring at the sayling of our barge till we anchored right against them. Long it was ere we could draw them to come vnto vs. At last they sent two of their company vnarmed in a Canow, the rest all followed to second them if neede required. These two being but each presented with a bell, brought aboord all their fellowes, presenting our Captaine with venison, beares flesh, fish, bowes, arrowes, clubs, targets, and beares-skinnes. We vnderstood them nothing at all, but by signes, whereby they signified vnto vs they had beene at warres with the *Tockwoghes*, the which they confirmed by shewing vs their greene wounds, but the night parting vs, we imagined they appointed the next morning to meete, but after that we never saw them.

The Salvages admire fire-workes.

An Incounter with the *Massawomeks* at the head of the Bay.

Entring the river of *Tockwogh*, the Salvages all armed, in a fleete of boats, after their barbarous manner, round invironed vs; so it chanced one of them could speake the language of *Powhatan*, who perswaded the rest to a friendly parley. But when they saw vs furnished with the *Massawomeks* weapons, and we faining the invention of *Kecoughtan*, to haue taken them perforce; they conducted vs to their pallizadoed towne, mantelled with the barkes of trees, with scaffolds like mounts, brested about with brests very formally. Their men, women, and children with daunces, songs, fruits, furres, and what they had, kindly welcommed vs, spreading mats for vs to sit on, stretching their best abilities to expresse their loues.

An Incounter with the *Tockwhoghs*.

Many hatchets, kniues, peeces of iron, and brasse, we saw amongst them, which they reported to haue from the *Sasquesahanocks*, a mightie people and mortall enemies with the *Massawomeks*. The *Sasquesahanocks* inhabit vpon the chiefe Spring of these foure branches of the Bayes head, two dayes iourney higher then our barge could passe for rocks, yet we prevailed with the Interpreter to take with him another Interpreter, to perswade the *Sasquesahanocks* to come visit vs, for their language are different. Three or foure dayes we expected their returne, then sixtie of those gyant-like people came downe, with presents of Venison, Tobacco-pipes three foot in length, Baskets, Targets, Bowes and Arrowes. Fiue of their chiefe *Werowances* came boldly aboord vs to crosse the Bay for *Tockwhogh*, leaving their men and Canowes; the wind being so high they durst not passe.

Hatchets from the *Sasquesahanocks*.

Our order was daily to haue Prayer, with a Psalme, at which solemnitie the poore Salvages much wondred, our Prayers being done, a while they were busied with a consultation till they had contrived their businesse. Then they began in a most pas-

sionate

nonate manner to hold vp their hands to the Sunne, with a most fearefull song, then imbracing our Captaine, they began to adore him in like manner: though he rebuked them, yet they proceeded till their song was finished: which done with a most strange furious action, and a hellish voyce, began an Oration of their loues; that ended, with a great painted Beares skin they covered him: then one ready with a great chayne of white Beads, weighing at least six or seaven pound, hung it about his necke, the others had 18 mantels, made of divers sorts of skinnes sowed together; all these with many other toyes they layd at his feete, stroking their ceremonious hands about his necke for his Creation to be their Governour and Protector, promising their aydes, victualls, or what they had to be his, if he would stay with them, to defend and revenge them of the *Massawomeks*. But we left them at *Tockwhogh*, sorrowing for our departure, yet we promised the next yeare againe to visit them. Many descriptions and discourses they made vs, of *Atquanachuck*, *Massawomek*, & other people, signifying they inhabit vpon a great water beyond the mountaines, which we vnderstood to be some great lake, or the river of *Canada*: and from the French to haue their hatchets and Commodities by trade. These know no more of the territories of *Powhatan*, then his name, and he as little of them, but the *Atquanachuks* are on the Ocean Sea.

The *Sasquesahanocks* offer to the *English*.

The highest mountaine we saw Northward wee called *Perigrines* mount, and a rocky river, where the *Massawomeks* went vp, *Willowbyes* river, in honor of the towne our Captaine was borne in, and that honorable house the Lord *Willowby*, his most honored good friend. The *Sasquesahanocks* river we called *Smiths* falles; the next poynt to *Tockwhogh*, *Pisings* poynt; the next it poynt *Bourne*. *Powells* Isles and *Smals* poynt is by the river *Bolus*; and the little Bay at the head *Profits* poole; *Watkins*, *Reads*, and *Momfords* poynts are on each side *Limbo*; *Ward*, *Cantrell*, and *Sicklemore*, betwixt *Patawomek* and *Pamavnkee*, after the names of the discoverers. In all those places and the furthest we came vp the rivers, we cut in trees so many crosses as we would, and in many places made holes in trees, wherein we writ notes, and in some places crosses of brasse, to signifie to any, Englishmen had beene there.

Thus having sought all the inlets and rivers worth noting, we returned to discover the river of *Pawtuxunt*; these people we found very tractable, and more civill then any, we promised them, as also the *Patawomeks* to revenge them of the *Massawomeks*, but our purposes were crossed.

Pawtuxunt, R.

In the discovery of this river some call *Rapahanock*, we were kindly entertained by the people of *Moraughtacund*; here we incountered our old friend *Mosco*, a lusty Salvage of *Wighcocomoco* vpō the river of *Patawomek*, we supposed him some *French* mans sonne, because he had a thicke blacke bush beard, and the Salvages seldome haue any at all, of which he was not a little proud, to see so many of his Countrymen. Wood and water he would fetch vs, guide vs any whether, nay, cause divers of his Countrymen helpe vs towe against winde or tyde from place to place till we came to *Patawomek*: there he rested till we returned from the head of the river, and occasioned our conduct to the mine we supposed *Antimony*. And in the place he fayled not to doe vs all the good he could, perswading vs in any case not to goe to the *Rapahanocks*, for they would kill vs for being friends with the *Moraughtacunds* that but lately had stolne three of the Kings women. This we did thinke was but that his friends might onely haue our trade: so we crossed the river to the *Rapahanocks*. There some 12 or 16 standing on the shore, directed vs a little Creeke where was good landing, and Commodities for vs in three or foure Canowes we saw lie there: but according to our custome, we demanded to exchange a man in signe of loue, which after they had a little consulted, foure or fiue came vp to the middles, to fetch our man, and leaue vs one of them, shewing we need not feare them, for they had neither clubs, bowes, nor arrowes. Notwithstanding, *Anas Todkill*, being sent on shore to see if he could discover any Ambuscadoes, or what they had, desired to goe over the playne to fetch some wood, but they were vnwilling, except we would come into the Creeke, where the boat might come close ashore. *Todkill* by degrees

Rapahanock, R.

The exceeding loue of the Salvage *Mosco*.

Our fight with the *Rapahanocks*.

having got some two stones throwes vp the playne, perceived two or three hundred men (as he thought) behind the trees, so that offering to returne to the Boat, the Salvages assayed to carry him away perforce, that he called to vs we were betrayed, and by that he had spoke the word, our hostage was over-boord, but *Watkins* his keeper slew him in the water. Immediatly we let fly amongst them, so that they fled, & *Todkill* escaped, yet they shot so fast that he fell flat on the ground ere he could recover the boat. Here the *Massawomek* Targets stood vs in good stead, for vpon *Mosco's* words, we had set them about the forepart of our Boat like a forecastle, from whence we securely beat the Salvages from off the plaine without any hurt: yet they shot more then a thousand Arrowes, and then fled into the woods. Arming our selues with these light Targets (which are made of little small sticks woven betwixt strings of their hempe and silke grasse, as is our Cloth, but so firmely that no arrow can possibly pierce them:) we rescued *Todkill*, who was all bloudy by some of them who were shot by vs that held him, but as God pleased he had no hurt; and following them vp to the woods, we found some slaine, and in divers places much bloud. It seems all their arrowes were spent, for we heard no more of them. Their Canows we tooke; the arrowes we found we broke, saue them we kept for *Mosco*, to whom we gaue the Canowes for his kindnesse, that entertained vs in the best trivmphing manner, and warlike order in armes of conquest he could procure of the *Moraughtacunds*.

The Salvages disguised like bushes fight.

The rest of the day we spent in accomodating our Boat, in stead of thoules wee made stickes like Bedstaues, to which we fastened so many of our *Massawomek* Targets, that invironed her as wast clothes. The next morning we went vp the river, and our friend *Mosco* followed vs along the shore, and at last desired to goe with vs in our Boat. But as we passed by *Pisacack*, *Matchopeak*, and *Mecuppom*, three Townes situated vpon high white clay clifts; the other side all a low playne marish, and the river there but narrow. Thirtie or fortie of the *Rapahanocks*, had so accommodated themselues with branches, as we tooke them for little bushes growing among the sedge, still seeing their arrowes strike the Targets, and dropped in the river: whereat *Mosco* fell flat in the Boat on his face, crying the *Rapahanocks*, which presently we espied to be the bushes, which at our first volley fell downe in the sedge: when wee were neare halfe a myle from them, they shewed themselues dauncing and singing very merrily.

The Kings of *Pissassack*, *Nandtaughtacund*, and *Cuttatawomen*, vsed vs kindly, and all their people neglected not any thing to *Mosco* to bring vs to them. Betwixt *Secobeck* and *Massawteck* is a small Isle or two, which causeth the river to be broader then ordinary; there it pleased God to take one of our Company called Mr *Fetherstone*, that all the time he had beene in this Country, had behaved himselfe, honestly, valiantly, and industriously, where in a little Bay we called *Fetherstones* Bay wee buryed him with a volley of shot: the rest notwithstanding their ill dyet, and bad lodging, crowded in so small a Barge, in so many dangers never resting, but alwayes tossed to and againe, had all well recovered their healths. The next day wee sayled so high as our Boat would float, there setting vp crosses, and graving our names in the trees. Our Sentinell saw an arrow fall by him, though we had ranged vp and downe more then an houre in digging in the earth, looking of stones, herbs, and springs, not seeing where a Salvage could well bide himselfe.

Our fight with the *Manahoacks*.

Vpon the alarum by that we had recovered our armes, there was about an hundred nimble *Indians* skipping from tree to tree, letting fly their arrows so fast as they could: the trees here served vs for Baricadoes as well as they. But *Mosco* did vs more service then we expected, for having shot away his quiver of Arrowes, he ran to the Boat for more. The Arrowes of *Mosco* at the first made them pause vpon the matter, thinking by his bruit and skipping, there were many Salvages. About halfe an houre this continued, then they all vanished as suddainly as they approached. *Mosco* followed them so farre as he could see vs, till they were out of sight. As we returned there lay a Salvage as dead, shot in the knee, but taking him vp we found he had

A Salvage shot and taken prisoner.

life,

lie, which *Mosco* seeing, never was Dog more furious against a Beare, then *Mosco* was to haue beat out his braines, so we had him to our Boat, where our Chirurgian who went with vs to cure our Captaines hurt of the *Stingray*, so dressed this Salvage that within an houre after he looked somewhat chearefully, and did eate and speake. In the meane time we contented *Mosco* in helping him to gather vp their arrowes, which were an armefull, whereof he gloried not a little. Then we desired *Mosco* to know what he was, and what Countries were beyond the mountaines; the poore Salvage mildly answered, he and all with him were of *Hasinninga*, where there are three Kings more, like vnto them, namely the King of *Stegora*, the King of *Tauxuntania*, and the King of *Shakahonea*, that were come to *Mohaskahod*, which is onely a hunting Towne, and the bounds betwixt the Kingdome of the *Mannahocks*, and the *Nandtaughtacunds*, but hard by where we were. We demanded why they came in that manner to betray vs, that came to them in peace, and to seeke their loues; he answered, they heard we were a people come from vnder the world, to take their world from them. We asked him how many worlds he did know, he replyed, he knew no more but that which was vnder the skie that covered him, which were the *Powhatans*, with the *Monacans*, and the *Massawomeks*, that were higher vp in the mountaines. Then we asked him what was beyond the mountaines, he answered the Sunne: but of any thing els he knew nothing; *because the woods were not burnt.

His relation of their countries.

*They cannot trauell but where the woods are burnt.

These and many such questions wee demanded, concerning the *Massawomeks*, the *Monacans*, their owne Country, and where were the Kings of *Stegora*, *Tauxsintania*, and the rest. The *Monacans* he sayd were their neighbours and friends, and did dwell as they in the hilly Countries by small rivers, liuing vpon rootes and fruits, but chiefly by hunting. The *Massawomeks* did dwell vpon a great water, and had many boats, & so many men that they made warre with all the world. For their Kings, they were gone every one a severall way with their men on hunting: But those with him came thither a fishing till they saw vs, notwithstanding they would be altogether at night at *Mahaskahod*. For his relation we gaue him many toyes, with perswasions to goe with vs, and he as earnestly desired vs to stay the comming of those Kings that for his good vsage should be friends with vs, for he was brother to *Hasinninga*. But *Mosco* advised vs presently to be gone, for they were all naught, yet we told him we would not till it was night. All things we made ready to entertain what came, & *Mosco* was as diligent in trimming his arrowes. The night being come we all imbarked, for the riuer was so narrow, had it beene light the land on the one side was so high, they might haue done vs exceeding much mischiefe. All this while the K. of *Hasinninga* was seeking the rest, and had consultation a good time what to doe. But by their espies seeing we were gone, it was not long before we heard their arrowes dropping on every side the Boat; we caused our Salvages to call vnto them, but such a yelling & hallowing they made that they heard nothing, but now and then a peece, ayming so neare as we could where we heard the most voyces. More then 12 myles they followed vs in this manner; then the day appearing, we found our selues in a broad Bay, out of danger of their shot, where wee came to an anchor, and fell to breakfast. Not so much as speaking to them till the Sunne was risen; being well refreshed, we vntyed our Targets that couered vs as a Deck, and all shewed our selues with those shields on our armes, and swords in our hands, and also our prisoner *Amoroleck*; a long discourse there was betwixt his Countrimen and him, how good wee were, how well wee vsed him, how wee had a *Patawomek* with vs, loued vs as his life, that would haue slaine him had we not preserued him, and that he should haue his libertie would they be but friends; and to doe vs any hurt it was impossible. Vpon this they all hung their Bowes and Quivers vpon the trees, and one came swimming aboord vs with a Bow tyed on his head, and another with a Quiver of Arrowes, which they deliuered our Captaine as a present, the Captaine hauing vsed them so kindly as he could, told them the other three Kings should doe the like, and then the great King of our world should be their friend, whose men we were. It was no sooner demanded but performed, so

How we concluded peace with the foure kings of *Monahoke*.

vpon a low Moorish poynt of Land we went to the shore, where those foure Kings came and receiued *Amoroleck*: nothing they had but Bowes, Arrowes, Tobacco-bags, and Pipes: what we desired, none refused to giue vs, wondering at every thing we had, and heard we had done: our Pistols they tooke for pipes, which they much desired, but we did content them with other Commodities, and so we left foure or fiue hundred of our merry *Mannahocks*, singing, dauncing, and making merry, and set sayle for *Moraughtacund*.

How we became friends with the *Rapahanocks*.

In our returnes we visited all our friends, that reioyced much at our Victory against the *Mannahocks*, who many times had Warres also with them, but now they were friends, and desired we would be friends with the *Rapahanocks*, as we were with the *Mannahocks*. Our Captaine told them, they had twise assaulted him that came onely in loue to doe them good, and therefore he would now burne all their houses, destroy their corne, and for euer hold them his enemies, till they made him satisfaction; they desired to know what that should be: he told them they should present him the Kings Bow and Arrowes, and not offer to come armed where he was; that they should be friends with the *Moraughtacunds* his friends, and giue him their Kings sonne in pledge to performe it, and then all King *Iames* his men should be their friends. Vpon this they presently sent to the *Rapahanocks* to meete him at the place where they first fought, where would be the Kings of *Nantautacund* and *Pissassac*: which according to their promise were there so soone as we; where *Rapahanock* presented his Bow and Arrowes, and confirmed all we desired, except his sonne, hauing no more but him he could not liue without him, but in stead of his sonne he would giue him the three women *Moraughtacund* had stolne. This was accepted: and so in three or foure Canowes, so many as could went with vs to *Moraughtacund*, where *Mosco* made them such relations, and gaue to his friends so many Bowes and Arrowes, that they no lesse loued him then admired vs. The 3 women were brought our Captaine, to each he gaue a chayne of Beads: and then causing *Moraughtacund*, *Mosco*, and *Rapahanock* stand before him, bid *Rapahanock* take her he loued best, and *Moraughtacund* chuse next, & to *Mosco* he gaue the third. Vpon this away went their Canowes over the water, to fetch their venison, and all the provision they could, and they that wanted Boats swam over the river: the darke commanded vs then to rest. The next day there was of men, women, and children, as we coniectured, six or seauen hundred, dauncing, & singing, and not a Bow nor Arrow seene amongst them. *Mosco* changed his name *Vttasantasough*, which we interpret *Stranger*, for so they call vs. All promising ever to be our friends, and to plant Corne purposely for vs; and we to provide hatchets, beads, and copper for them, we departed, giuing them a Volley of shot, and they vs as loud shouts and cryes as their strengths could vtter. That night we anchored in the river of *Payankatank*, and discovered it so high as it was navigable, but the people were most a hunting, saue a few old men, women, and children, that were tending their corne, of which they promised vs part when we would fetch it, as had done all the Nations where ever we had yet beene.

The discovery of *Payankatank*.

In a fayre calme, rowing towards poynt *Comfort*, we anchored in *Gosnolls* Bay, but such a suddaine gust surprised vs in the night with thunder and rayne, that we never thought more to haue seene *Iames* Towne. Yet running before the wind, we sometimes saw the Land by the flashes of fire from heaven, by which light onely we kept from the splitting shore, vntill it pleased God in that blacke darknesse to preserue vs by that light to finde poynt *Comfort*: there refreshing our selues, because we had onely but heard of the *Chisapeacks* & *Nandsamunds*, we thought it as fit to know all our neighbours neare home, as so many Nations abroad.

A notable trechery of the *Nandsamunds*.

So setting sayle for the Southerne shore, we sayled vp a narrow river vp the country of *Chisapeack*; it hath a good channell, but many shoules about the entrance. By that we had sayled six or seauen myles, we saw two or three little garden plots with their houses, the shores overgrowne with the greatest Pyne and Firre trees wee ever saw in the Country. But not seeing nor hearing any people, and the riuer very narrow, we returned to the great riuer, to see if we could finde any of them. Coasting the

the shore towards *Nandsamund*, which is most Oyster-bankes; at the mouth of that riuer, we espied six or seauen Salvages making their wires, who presently fled: ashore we went, and where they wrought we threw diuers toyes, and so departed. Farre we were not gone ere they came againe, and began to sing, and daunce, and recall vs: and thus we began our first acquaintance. At last one of them desired vs to goe to his house vp that riuer, into our Boat voluntarily he came, the rest ran after vs by the shore with all shew of loue that could be. Seauen or eight myles we sayled vp this narrow riuer: at last on the Westerne shore we saw large Cornefields, in the midst a little Isle, and in it was abundance of Corne; the people he told vs were all a hunting, but in the Isle was his house, to which he inuited vs with much kindnesse: to him, his wife, and children, we gaue such things as they seemed much contented them. The others being come, desired vs also to goe but a little higher to see their houses: here our host left vs, the rest rowed by vs in a Canow, till we were so far past the Isle the riuer became very narrow. Here we desired some of them to come abord vs, wherat pausing a little, they told vs they would but fetch their bows and arrowes and goe all with vs, but being a-shore and thus armed, they perswaded vs to goe forward, but we could neither perswade them into their Canow, nor into our Boat. This gaue vs cause to prouide for the worst. Farre we went not ere seauen or eight Canowes full of men armed appeared following vs, staying to see the conclusion. Presently from each side the riuer came arrowes so fast as two or three hundred could shoot them, whereat we returned to get the open. They in the Canowes let fly also as fast, but amongst them we bestowed so many shot, the most of them leaped overboord and swam ashore, but two or three escaped by rowing, being against their playnes: our Muskets they found shot further then their Bowes, for wee made not twentie shot ere they all retyred behind the next trees. Being thus got out of their trap, we seised on all their Canowes, and moored them in the midst of the open. More then an hundred arrowes stucke in our Targets, and about the boat, yet none hurt, onely *Anthony Bagnall* was shot in his Hat, and another in his sleeue. But seeing their multitudes, and suspecting as it was, that both the *Nandsamunds*, and the *Chisapeacks* were together, we thought it best to ryde by their Canowes a while, to bethinke if it were better to burne all in the Isle, or draw them to composition, till we were prouided to take all they had, which was sufficient to feed all our *Colony*: but to burne the Isle at night it was concluded. In the interim we began to cut in peeces their Canowes, and they presently to lay downe their bowes, making signes of peace: peace we told them we would accept, would they bring vs their Kings bowes and arrowes, with a chayne of pearle; and when we came againe giue vs foure hundred baskets full of Corne, otherwise we would breake all their boats, and burne their houses, and corne, and all they had. To performe all this they alledged onely the want of a Canow; so we put one a drift & bad them swim to fetch her: and till they performed their promise, wee would but onely breake their Canowes. They cryed to vs to doe no more, all should be as we would: which presently they performed, away went their bowes and arrowes, and tagge and ragge came with their baskets: so much as we could carry we tooke, and so departing good friends, we returned to *Iames* Towne, where we safely arriued the 7. of September, 1608. There we found Mr *Scrivener*, and divers others well recovered: many dead; some sicke: the late President prisoner for mutiny: by the honest diligence of Master *Scrivener*, the haruest gathered, but the provision in the store much spoyled with rayne. Thus was that summer (when little wanted) consumed and spent, and nothing done (such was the gouernment of Captaine *Ratliffe*) but onely this discovery; wherein to expresse all the dangers, accidents, and incounters this small number passed in that small Barge, by the scale of proportion, about three thousand myles, with such watery dyet in those great waters and barbarous Countries (till then to any Christian vtterly vnknowne) I rather referre their merit to the censure of the courteous and experienced Reader, then I would be tedious or partiall being a partie.

The fight with the *Chisapeacks* and *Nandsamunds*.

How they became friends.

The proceeding at *Iames* Towne.

But to this place to come who will adventure,
with iudgements guide and reason how to enter:
Finds in this worlds broad sea, with winde and tyde,
Ther's safer sayle then any where beside.
But 'cause to wanton novices it is
A Province full of fearefulnesse I wiss;
Into the great vast deepe to venter out:
Those shallow rivers let them coast about.
And by a small Boat learne there first, and marke,
How they may come to make a greater Barke.

Written by *Anthony Bagnall*, *Nathanaell Powell*, and *Anas Todkill*.

Chapter VII.

The Presidency surrendred to Captaine Smith: *the Arrivall and returne of the second Supply. And what happened.*

THe tenth of September, by the Election of the Councell, and request of the Company, Captaine *Smith* receiued the Letters Patents: which till then by no meanes he would accept, though he was often importuned thereunto. Now the building of *Ratliffes* Pallace stayed as a thing needlesse; the Church was repaired; the Store-house recouered; buildings prepared for the Supplyes, we expected; the Fort reduced to a fiue-square forme; the order of the Watch renewed; the squadrons (each setting of the Watch) trained; the whole Company euery Saturday exercised, in the plaine by the west Bulwarke, prepared for that purpose, we called *Smithfield*: where sometimes more then an hundred Salvages would stand in an amazement to behold, how a fyle would batter a tree, where he would make them a marke to shoot at; the boats trimmed for trade, which being sent out with Lieutenant *Percy*, in their Iourney incountred the second Supply, that brought them backe to discover the Country of *Monacan*. How or why Captaine *Newport* obtained such a private Commission, as not to returne without a lumpe of gold, a certaintie of the South sea, or one of the lost company sent out by Sir *Water Raleigh*, I know not; nor why he brought such a fiue peeced Barge, not to beare vs to that South sea, till we had borne her over the mountaines, which how farre they extend is yet vnknowne. As for the Coronation of *Powhatan*, and his presents of Bason and Ewer, Bed, Bedstead, Clothes, and such costly nouelties, they had beene much better well spared then so ill spent, for wee had his favour much better onely for a playne peece of Copper, till this stately kinde of soliciting, made him so much overvalue himselfe, that he respected vs as much as nothing at all. As for the hyring of the *Poles* and *Dutch*-men, to make Pitch, Tar, Glasse, Milles, and Sope ashes, when the Country is replenished with people, and necessaries, would haue done well, but to send them and seauentie more without victualls to worke, was not so well aduised nor considered of, as it should haue beene. Yet this could not haue hurt vs had they beene 200. though then we were 130 that wanted for our selues. For we had the Salvages in that *decorum* (their harvest being newly gathered,) that we feared not to get victuals for 500. Now was there no way to make vs miserable, but to neglect that time to make prouision whilst it was to be had, the which was done by the direction from *England* to performe this strange discovery, but a more strange Coronation to loose that time, spend that victualls we had, tyre and starue our men, hauing no meanes to carry victuals, munition, the hurt or sicke, but on their owne backes. How or by whom they were inuented I know not: but Captaine *Newport* we onely accounted the Author, who to effect these proiects, had so guilded mens hopes with great promises, that both Company and Councell concluded his resolution

Powhatans scorne when his courtesie was most deserved.

No better way to overthrow the busines then by our instructors.

tion for the most part: God doth know they little knew what they did, nor vnderstood their owne estates to conclude his conclusions, against all the inconveniences the foreseeing President alledged. Of this Supply there was added to the Councell, one Captaine *Richard Waldo*, and Captaine *Wynne*, two auncient Souldiers, and valiant Gentlemen, but yet ignorant of the busines, (being but newly arriued.) *Ratliffe* was also permitted to haue his voyce, & Mr *Scrivener*, desirous to see strange Countries: so that although *Smith* was President, yet the Maior part of the Councell had the authoritie and ruled it as they listed. As for clearing *Smiths* obiections, how Pitch and Tarre, Wainscot, Clapbord, Glasse, and Sope ashes, could be provided, to relade the ship, or provision got to liue withall, when none was in the Country, and that we had, spent, before the ship departed to effect these projects. The answer was, Captaine *Newport* vndertooke to fraught the Pinnace of twentie tunnes with Corne in going and returning in his Discovery, and to refraught her againe from *Werowocomoco* of *Powhatan*. Also promising a great proportion of victualls from the Ship; inferring that *Smiths* propositions were onely devices to hinder his iourney, to effect it himselfe; and that the crueltie he had vsed to the Salvages, might well be the occasion to hinder these Designes, and seeke revenge on him. For which taxation all workes were left, and 120 chosen men were appointed for *Newports* guard in this Discovery. But Captaine *Smith* to make cleare all those seeming suspitions, that the Salvages were not so desperate as was pretended by Captaine *Newport*, and how willing (since by their authoritie they would haue it so) he was to assist them what he could, because the Coronation would consume much time, he vndertooke himselfe their message to *Powhatan*, to intreat him to come to *Iames* Towne to receiue his presents. And where *Newport* durst not goe with lesse then 120. he onely tooke with him Captaine *Waldo*, Mr *Andrew Buckler*, *Edward Brinton*, and *Samuel Collier*: with these foure he went over land to *Werowocomoco*, some 12 myles; there he passed the river of *Pamavnkee* in a Salvage Canow. *Powhatan* being 30 myles of, was presently sent for: in the meane time, *Pocahontas* and her women entertained Captaine *Smith* in this manner.

A consultation, where all the Councell was against the President.

Capt. *Smith* goeth with 4. to *Powhatan*, when *Newport* feared with 120.

In a fayre plaine field they made a fire, before which, he sitting vpon a mat, suddainly amongst the woods was heard such a hydeous noise and shreeking, that the English betooke themselues to their armes, and seized on two or three old men by them, supposing *Powhatan* with all his power was come to surprise them. But presently *Pocahontas* came, willing him to kill her if any hurt were intended, and the beholders, which were men, women, and children, satisfied the Captaine there was no such matter. Then presently they were presented with this anticke; thirtie young women came naked out of the woods, onely covered behind and before with a few greene leaues, their bodies all painted, some of one colour, some of another, but all differing, their leader had a fayre payre of Bucks hornes on her head, and an Otters skinne at her girdle, and another at her arme, a quiver of arrowes at her backe, a bow and arrowes in her hand; the next had in her hand a sword, another a club, another a pot-sticke; all horned alike: the rest every one with their severall devises. These fiends with most hellish shouts and cryes, rushing from among the trees, cast themselues in a ring about the fire, singing and dauncing with most excellent ill varietie, oft falling into their infernall passions, and solemnly againe to sing and daunce; having spent neare an houre in this Mascarado, as they entred in like manner they departed.

A *Virginia* Maske.

Having reaccōmodated themselues, they solemnly invited him to their lodgings, where he was no sooner within the house, but all these Nymphes more tormented him then ever, with crowding, pressing, and hanging about him, most tediously crying, Loue you not me? loue you not me? This salutation ended, the feast was set, consisting of all the Salvage dainties they could devise: some attending, others singing and dauncing about them; which mirth being ended, with fire-brands in stead of Torches they conducted him to his lodging.

The Womens entertainement.

Thus did they shew their feats of armes, and others art in dauncing:
Some other vs'd there oaten pipe, and others voyces chanting.

The

Captaine *Smiths* message.

The next day came *Powhatan. Smith* delivered his message of the presents sent him, and redelivered him *Namontack* he had sent for *England*, desiring him to come to his Father *Newport*, to accept those presents, and conclude their revenge against the *Monacans*. Whereunto this subtile Savage thus replyed.

Powhatans answer.

If your King haue sent me Presents, I also am a King, and this is my land: eight dayes I will stay to receiue them. Your Father is to come to me, not I to him, nor yet to your Fort, neither will I bite at such a bait: as for the Monacans *I can revenge my owne iniuries, and as for* Atquanachuk, *where you say your brother was slaine, it is a contrary way from those parts you suppose it; but for any salt water beyond the mountaines, the Relations you haue had from my people are false.* Whereupon he began to draw plots vpon the ground (according to his discourse) of all those Regions. Many other discourses they had (yet both content to giue each other content in complementall Courtesies) and so Captaine *Smith* returned with this Answer.

Powhatans Coronation.

Vpon this the Presents were sent by water which is neare an hundred myles, and the Captains went by land with fiftie good shot. All being met at *Werowocomoco*, the next day was appointed for his Coronation, then the presents were brought him, his Bason and Ewer, Bed and furniture set vp, his scarlet Cloke and apparell with much adoe put on him, being perswaded by *Namontack* they would not hurt him: but a foule trouble there was to make him kneele to receiue his Crowne, he neither knowing the maiesty nor meaning of a Crowne, nor bending of the knee, endured so many perswasions, examples, and instructions, as tyred them all; at last by leaning hard on his shoulders, he a little stooped, and three having the crowne in their hands put it on his head, when by the warning of a Pistoll the Boats were prepared with such a volley of shot, that the King start vp in a horrible feare, till he saw all was well. Then remembring himselfe, to congratulate their kindnesse, he gaue his old shooes and his mantell to Captaine *Newport*: but perceiving his purpose was to discover the *Monacans*, he laboured to divert his resolution, refusing to lend him either men or guides more then *Namontack*; and so after some small complementall kindnesse on both sides, in requitall of his presents he presented *Newport* with a heape of wheat eares that might containe some 7 or 8 Bushels, and as much more we bought in the Towne, wherewith we returned to the Fort.

The discovery of *Monacan*.

The Ship having disburdened her selfe of 70 persons, with the first Gentlewoman and woman-seruant that arrived in our *Colony*. Captaine *Newport* with 120 chosen men, led by Captaine *Waldo*, Lieutenant *Percie*, Captaine *Winne*, Mr *West*, and Mr *Scrivener*, set forward for the discovery of *Monacan*, leaving the President at the Fort with about 80. or 90. (such as they were) to relade the Ship. Arriving at the Falles we marched by land some fortie myles in two dayes and a halfe, and so returned downe the same path we went. Two townes we discovered of the *Monacans*, called *Massinacak* and *Mowhemenchouch*, the people neither vsed vs well nor ill, yet for our securitie we tooke one of their petty Kings, and led him bound to conduct vs the way. And in our returnes searched many places we supposed Mines, about which we spent some time in refyning, having one *William Callicut*, a refyner fitted for that purpose. From that crust of earth we digged, he perswaded vs to beleeue he extracted some small quantitie of silver; and (not vnlikely) better stuffe might be had for the digging. With this poore tryall, being contented to leaue this fayre, fertile, well watered Country; and comming to the Falles, the Salvages fayned there were divers ships come into the Bay, to kill them at *Iames* Towne. Trade they would not, and finde their Corne we could not; for they had hid it in the woods: and being thus deluded, we arrived at *Iames* Towne, halfe sicke, all complaining, and tyred with toyle, famine, and discontent, to haue onely but discovered our guilded hopes, and such fruitlesse certainties, as Captaine *Smith* fortold vs.

How the Salvages deluded Cap. *Newport*.

But those that hunger seeke to slake,
Which thus abounding wealth would rake:
Not all the gemmes of Ister *shore,*
Nor all the gold of Lydia's *store,*

Can

Can fill their greedie appetite;
It is a thing so infinite.

No sooner were we landed, but the President dispersed so many as were able, some for Glasse, others for Tarre, Pitch, and Sope-ashes, leauing them with the Fort to the Councels oversight, but 30 of vs he conducted downe the river some 5 myles from *Iames* towne, to learne to make Clapbord, cut downe trees, and lye in woods. Amongst the rest he had chosen *Gabriel Beadle*, and *Iohn Russell*, the onely two gallants of this last Supply, and both proper Gentlemen. Strange were these pleasures to their conditions; yet lodging, eating, and drinking, working or playing, they but doing as the President did himselfe. All these things were carried so pleasantly as within a weeke they became Masters: making it their delight to heare the trees thunder as they fell; but the Axes so oft blistered their tender fingers, that many times every third blow had a loud othe to drowne the eccho; for remedie of which sinne, the President devised how to haue every mans othes numbred, and at night for every othe to haue a Cann of water powred downe his sleeue, with which every offender was so washed (himselfe and all) that a man should scarce heare an othe in a weeke.

A punishment for swearing.

For he who scornes and makes but iests of cursings, and his othe,
He doth contemne, not man but God, nor God, nor man, but both.

By this, let no man thinke that the President and these Gentlemen spent their times as common Wood-haggers at felling of trees, or such other like labours, or that they were pressed to it as hirelings, or common slaues; for what they did, after they were but once a little invred, it seemed and some conceited it, onely as a pleasure and recreation, yet 30 or 40 of such voluntary Gentlemen would doe more in a day then 100 of the rest that must be prest to it by compulsion, but twentie good workemen had beene better then them all.

3. Men better then 100.

Master *Scrivener*, Captaine *Waldo*, and Captaine *Winne* at the Fort, every one in like manner carefully regarded their charge. The President returning from amongst the woods, seeing the time consumed and no provision gotten, (and the Ship lay idle at a great charge and did nothing) presently imbarked himselfe in the discovery barge, giving order to the Councell to send Lieutenant *Percie* after him with the next barge that arrived at the Fort; two Barges he had himselfe and 18 men, but arriving at *Chickahamania*, that dogged Nation was too well acquainted with our wants, refusing to trade, with as much scorne and insolency as they could expresse. The President perceiuing it was *Powhatans* policy to starue vs, told them he came not so much for their Corne, as to revenge his imprisonment, and the death of his men murthered by them, and so landing his men and readie to charge them, they immediately fled: and presently after sent their Ambassadors with corne, fish, foule, and what they had to make their peace, (their Corne being that yeare but bad) they complained extreamely of their owne wants, yet fraughted our Boats with an hundred Bushels of Corne, and in like manner Lieutenant *Percies*, that not long after arrived, and having done the best they could to content vs, we parted good friends, and returned to *Iames* towne.

The *Chickahamania's* forced to contribution.

Though this much contented the Company, (that feared nothing more then starving) yet some so envied his good successe, that they rather desired to hazzard a starving, then his paines should proue so much more effectuall then theirs. Some proiects there were invented by *Newport* and *Ratliffe*, not onely to haue deposed him, but to haue kept him out of the Fort; for that being President, he would leaue his place and the Fort without their consents, but their hornes were so much too short to effect it, as they themselues more narrowly escaped a greater mischiefe.

A bad reward for well-doing.

All this time our old Taverne made as much of all them that had either money or ware as could be desired: by this time they were become so perfect on all sides (I meane the souldiers, saylers, and Salvages) as there was tenne times more care to maintaine their damnable and private trade, then to provide for the *Colony* things

A good Taverne in *Virginia*.

A bad trade of the masters and saylers.

that were necessary. Neither was it a small policy in *Newport* and the Marriners to report in *England* we had such plentie, and bring vs so many men without victuals, when they had so many priuate Factors in the Fort, that within six or seauen weeks, of two or three hundred Axes, Chissels, Hows, and Pick-axes, scarce twentie could be found: and for Pike-heads, shot, Powder, or any thing they could steale from their fellowes, was vendible; they knew as well (and as secretly) how to convey them to trade with the Salvages for Furres, Baskets, *Mussanceks*, young Beasts, or such like Commodities, as exchange them with the Saylers for Butter, Cheese, Beefe, Porke, *Aqua vitæ*, Beere, Bisket, Oatmeale, and Oyle: and then fayne all was sent them from their friends. And though *Virginia* affoorded no Furres for the Store, yet one Master in one voyage hath got so many by this indirect meanes, as he confessed to haue sold in *England* for 30[l].

Those are the Saint-seeming Worthies of *Virginia*, that haue notwithstanding all this meate, drinke, and wages; but now they begin to grow weary, their trade being both perceived and prevented; none hath beene in *Virginia* that hath observed any thing, which knowes not this to be true, and yet the losse, the scorne, the misery, and shame, was the poore Officers, Gentlemen, and carelesse Governours, who were all thus bought & sold; the adventurers cousened, and the action overthrowne by their false excuses, informations, and directions. By this let all men iudge, how this businesse could prosper, being thus abused by such pilfring occasions. And had not Captaine *Newport* cryed *Peccavi*, the President would haue discharged the ship, and caused him to haue stayed one yeare in *Virginia*, to learne to speake of his owne experience.

Master *Scriveners* voyage to *Werowocomoco.*

Master *Scrivener* was sent with the Barges and Pinnace to *Werowocomoco*, where he found the Salvages more readie to fight then trade; but his vigilancy was such as prevented their proiects, and by the meanes of *Namontack* got three or foure hogsheads of Corne, and as much *Pocones*, which is a red roote, which then was esteemed an excellent Dye.

Captaine *Newport* being dispatched, with the tryals of Pitch, Tarre, Glasse, Frankincense, Sope ashes; with that Clapboord and Waynscot that could be provided: met with M[r] *Scrivener* at poynt *Comfort*, and so returned for *England*. We remaining were about two hundred.

¶ The Copy of a Letter sent to the Treasurer and Councell of *Virginia* from Captaine *Smith*, then President in VIRGINIA.

Right Honorable, &c.

I Received your Letter, wherein you write, that our minds are so set vpon faction, and idle conceits in diuiding the Country without your consents, and that we feed You *but with ifs & ands, hopes, & some few proofes; as if we would keepe the mystery of the businesse to our selues: and that we must expresly follow your instructions sent by Captain* Newport: *the charge of whose voyage amounts to neare two thousand pounds, the which if we cannot defray by the Ships returne, we are like to remain as banished men. To these particulars I humbly intreat your Pardons if I offend you with my rude Answer.*

For our factions, vnlesse you would haue me run away and leaue the Country, *I cannot prevent them: because I do make many stay that would els fly any whether. For the idle Letter sent to my Lord of* Salisbury, *by the President and his confederats, for diuiding the Country &c. What it was I know not, for you saw no hand of of mine to it; nor euer dream't I of any such matter. That we feed you with hopes, &c. Though I be no scholer, I am past a schoole-boy; and I desire but to know, what either you, and these here doe know, but that I haue learned to tell you by the continuall hazard of my life. I haue not concealed from you any thing I know; but I feare some cause you to beleeue much more then is true.*

Expresly to follow your directions by Captaine Newport, *though they be performed, I was directly against it; but according to our Commission, I was content to be overruled by the maior part of the Councell, I feare to the hazard of vs all; which now is generally confessed when it is too late. Onely Captaine* Winne *and Captaine* Waldo *I haue sworne of the Councell, and Crowned* Powhatan *according to your instructions.*

For the charge of this Voyage of two or three thousand pounds, we haue not receiued the value of an hundred pounds. And for the quartred Boat to be borne by the Souldiers over the Falles, Newport *had* 120 *of the best men he could chuse. If he had burnt her to ashes, one might haue carried her in a bag; but as she is, fiue hundred cannot, to a navigable place aboue the Falles. And for him at that time to find in the South Sea, a Mine of gold; or any of them sent by Sir* Walter Raleigh: *at our Consultation I told them was as likely as the rest. But during this great discovery of thirtie myles, (which might as well haue beene done by one man, and much more, for the value of a pound of Copper at a seasonable tyme) they had the Pinnace and all the Boats with them, but one that remained with me to serue the Fort. In their absence I followed the new begun workes of Pitch and Tarre, Glasse, Sope-ashes, and Clapboord, whereof some small quantities we haue sent you. But if you rightly consider, what an infinite toyle it is in* Russia *and* Swethland, *where the woods are proper for naught els, and though there be the helpe both of man and beast in those ancient Common-wealths, which many an hundred yeares haue vsed it, yet thousands of those poore people can scarce get necessaries to liue, but from hand to mouth. And though your Factors there can buy as much in a week as will fraught you a ship, or as much as you please; you must not expect from vs any such matter, which are but a many of ignorant miserable soules, that are scarce able to get wherewith to liue, and defend our selues against the inconstant* Salvages: *finding but here and there a tree fit for the purpose, and want all things els the* Russians *haue. For the Coronation of* Powhatan, *by whose advice you sent him such presents, I know not; but this giue me leaue to tell you, I feare they will be the confusion of vs all ere we heare from you againe. At your Ships arrivall, the* Salvages *harvest was newly gathered, and we going to buy it, our owne not being halfe sufficient for so great a number. As for the two ships loading of Corne* Newport *promised to provide vs from* Powhatan, *he brought vs but foureteene Bushels; and from the* Monacans *nothing, but the most of the men sicke and neare famished. From your Ship we had not provision in victuals worth twenty pound, and we are more then two hundred to liue vpon this: the one halfe sicke, the other little better. For the Saylers (I confesse) they daily make good cheare, but our dyet is a little meale and water, and not sufficient of that. Though there be fish in the Sea, foules in the ayre, and Beasts in the woods, their bounds are so large, they so wilde, and we so weake and ignorant, we cannot much trouble them. Captaine* Newport *we much suspect to be the Authour of those inventions. Now that you should know, I haue made you as great a discovery as he, for lesse charge then he spendeth you every meale; I haue sent you this Mappe of the Bay and Rivers, with an annexed*

Relation of the Countries and Nations that inhabit them, as you may see at large. Also two barrels of stones, and such as I take to be good Iron ore at the least; so devided, as by their notes you may see in what places I found them. The Souldiers say many of your officers maintaine their families out of that you send vs: and that Newport *hath an hundred pounds a yeare for carrying newes. For every master you haue yet sent can find the way as well as he, so that an hundred pounds might be spared, which is more then we haue all, that helpe to pay him wages. Cap.* Ratliffe *is now called* Sicklemore, *a poore counterfeited Imposture. I haue sent you him home, least the company should cut his throat. What he is, now every one can tell you: if he and* Archer *returne againe, they are sufficient to keepe vs alwayes in factions. When you send againe I intreat you rather send but thirty Carpenters, husbandmen, gardiners, fisher men, blacksmiths, masons, and diggers vp of trees, roots, well provided; then a thousand of such as we haue: for except wee be able both to lodge them, and feed them, the most will consume with want of necessaries before they can be made good for any thing. Thus if you please to consider this account, and of the vnnecessary wages to Captaine* Newport, *or his ships so long lingering and staying here (for notwithstanding his boasting to leaue vs victuals for 12 moneths, though we had 89 by this discovery lame and sicke, and but a pinte of Corne a day for a man, we were constrained to giue him three hogsheads of that to victuall him homeward) or yet to send into* Germany *or* Poleland *for glasse-men & the rest, till we be able to sustaine our selues, and relieue them when they come. It were better to giue fiue hundred pound a tun for those grosse Commodities in* Denmarke, *then send for them hither, till more necessary things be provided. For in over-toyling our weake and vnskilfull bodies, to satisfie this desire of present profit, we can scarce ever recover our selues from one Supply to another. And I humbly intreat you hereafter, let vs know what we should receiue, and not stand to the Saylers courtesie to leaue vs what they please, els you may charge vs with what you will, but we not you with any thing. These are the causes that haue kept vs in* Virginia, *from laying such a foundation, that ere this might haue given much better content and satisfaction; but as yet you must not looke for any profitable returnes: so I humbly rest.*

The Names of those in this Supply, were these: with their Proceedings and Accidents.

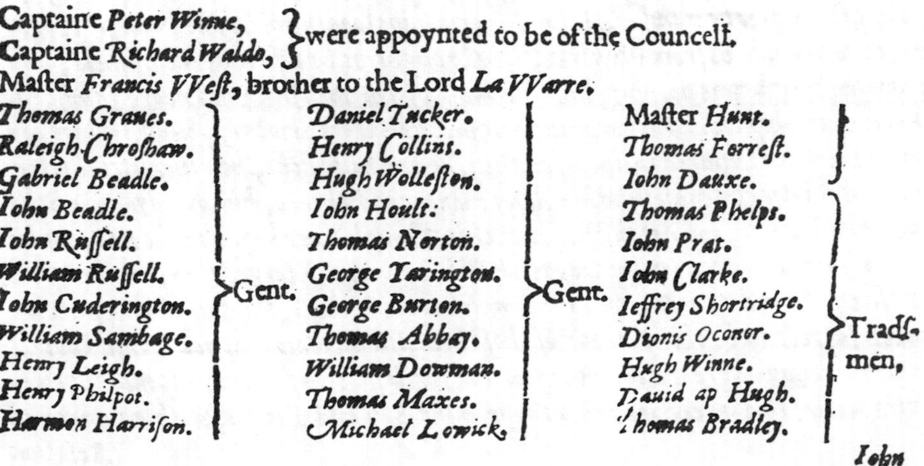

Captaine *Peter Winne*, Captaine *Richard Waldo*, } were appoynted to be of the Councell.

Master *Francis West*, brother to the Lord *La Warre*.

Gent.	Gent.	
Thomas Graues.	*Daniel Tucker.*	Master *Hunt.*
Raleigh Chroshaw.	*Henry Collins.*	*Thomas Forrest.*
Gabriel Beadle.	*Hugh Wolleston.*	*Iohn Dauxe.*
Iohn Beadle.	*Iohn Hoult.*	*Thomas Phelps.*
Iohn Russell.	*Thomas Norton.*	*Iohn Prat.*
William Russell.	*George Yarington.*	*Iohn Clarke.*
Iohn Cuderington.	*George Burton.*	*Ieffrey Shortridge.*
William Sambage.	*Thomas Abbay.*	*Dionis Oconor.*
Henry Leigh.	*William Dowman.*	*Hugh Winne.*
Henry Philpot.	*Thomas Maxes.*	*David ap Hugh.*
Harmon Harrison.	*Michael Lowick.*	*Thomas Bradley.*

(Thomas Phelps … Thomas Bradley: Tradsmen,)

Iohn

Iohn Burras.	*Thomas Mallard.*		*Morley.*	
Thomas Lavander.	*William Tayler.*		*Rose.*	
Henry Bell.	*Thomas Fox.*	La-	*Scot.*	
Master *Powell.*	*Nicholas Hancock.*	bou-	*Hardwyn.*	
David Ellis.	*Walker.*	rers.	*Milman.*	Boyes.
Thomas Gibson.	*Williams.*		*Hilliard.*	
Thomas Dawse.	*Floud.*			

Mistresse *Forrest*, and *Anne Burras* her maide; eight *Dutch* men and *Poles*, with some others, to the number of seaventie persons, &c.

These poore conclusions so affrighted vs all with famine, that the President provided for *Nandsamund*, and tooke with him Captaine *Winne*, and Mr *Scrivener*, then returning from Captaine *Newport*. These people also long denied him not onely the 400 Baskets of Corne they promised, but any trade at all; (excusing themselues they had spent most they had, and were commanded by *Powhatan* to keepe that they had, and not to let vs come into their river) till we were constrained to begin with them perforce. Vpon the discharging of our Muskets they all fled and shot not an Arrow; the first house we came to we set on fire, which when they perceiued, they desired we would make no more spoyle, and they would giue vs halfe they had: how they collected it I know not, but before night they loaded our three Boats; and so we returned to our quarter some foure myles downe the River, which was onely the open woods vnder the lay of a hill, where all the ground was covered with snow, and hard frozen; the snow we digged away and made a great fire in the place; when the ground was well dryed, we turned away the fire; and covering the place with a mat, there we lay very warme. To keepe vs from the winde we made a shade of another Mat; as the winde turned we turned our shade, and when the ground grew cold we remoued the fire. And thus many a cold winter night haue wee laine in this miserable manner, yet those that most commonly went vpon all those occasions, were alwayes in health, lusty, and fat. For sparing them this yeare, the next yeare they promised to plant purposely for vs; and so we returned to *Iames* towne. About this time there was a marriage betwixt *Iohn Laydon* and *Anne Burras*; which was the first marriage we had in *Virginia*.

Nandsamund forced to contribution.

The first marriage in *Virginia*.

Long he stayed not, but fitting himselfe and Captaine *Waldo* with two Barges. From *Chawopoweanock*, and all parts thereabouts, all the people were fled, as being iealous of our intents; till we discovered the river and people of *Apamatuck*; where we found not much, that they had we equally divided, but gaue them copper, and such things as contented them in consideration. Master *Scrivener* and Lieutenant *Percie* went also abroad, but could find nothing.

***Apamatuck* discovered.**

The President seeing the procrastinating of time, was no course to liue, resolved with Captaine *Waldo* (whom he knew to be sure in time of need) to surprise *Powhatan*, and all his provision, but the vnwillingnesse of Captaine *Winne*, and Master *Scrivener*, for some private respect, plotted in *England* to ruine Captaine *Smith*, did their best to hinder their proiect; but the President whom no perswasions could perswade to starue, being invited by *Powhatan* to come vnto him: and if he would send him but men to build him a house, giue him a gryndstone, fiftie swords, some peeces, a cock and a hen, with much copper and beads, he would load his Ship with Corne. The President not ignorant of his devises and subtiltie, yet vnwilling to neglect any opportunitie, presently sent three *Dutch*-men and two *English*, having so small allowance, few were able to doe any thing to purpose: knowing there needed no better a Castle to effect this proiect, tooke order with Captaine *Waldo* to second him, if need required; *Scrivener* he left his substitute, and set forth with the Pinnace, two Barges, and fortie-six men, which onely were such as voluntarily offered themselues for his Iourney, the which by reason of Mr *Scriveners* ill successe, was censured very desperate, they all knowing *Smith* would not returne emptie, if it were to be had; howsoever, it caused many of those that he had appointed, to find excuses to stay behinde.

Chap. VIII.

Captaine Smiths *Iourney to* Pamavnkee.

THe twentie-nine of December he set forward for *Werowocomoco*: his Company were these;

In the Discovery Barge himselfe.

Robert Behethland.
Nathanael Graues.
Iohn Russell.
Raleigh Chrashow.
Michael Sicklemore.
Richard Worley. } Gent.

Anas Todkill.
William Loue.
William Bentley.
Ieffrey Shortridge.
Edward Pising.
William Ward. } Souldiers.

In the Pinnace.

Lieutenant *Percie*, brother to the Earle of Northumberland.
Master *Francis West*, brother to the Lord *La Warre.*
William Phittiplace, Captaine of the Pinnace.

Michael Phittiplace.
Ieffrey Abbot, Serieant.
William Tankard.
George Yarington. } Gent.

Ionas Profit, Master.
Robert Ford, Clarke of the Councell.

Iames Browne.
Edward Brinton.
George Burton.
Thomas Coe. } Souldiers.

Iohn Dods, Souldier.
Henry Powell, Souldier.

Thomas Gipson, David Ellis, Nathanael Peacock, Saylers. *Iohn Prat, George Acrig, Iames Read, Nicholas Hancock, Iames Watkins, Thomas Lambert*, foure *Dutch*-men, and *Richard Salvage* were sent by land before to build the house for *Powhatan* against our Arrivall.

This company being victualled but for three or foure dayes, lodged the first night at *Warraskoyack*, where the President tooke sufficient provision. This kind King did his best to divert him from seeing *Powhatan*, but perceiuing he could not prevaile, he advised in this manner. Captaine *Smith*, you shall find *Powhatan* to vse you kindly, but trust him not, and be sure he haue no oportunitie to seize on your Armes; for he hath sent for you onely to cut your throats. The Captaine thanking him for his good counsell: yet the better to try his loue, desired guides to *Chawwonock*; for he would send a present to that King, to bind him his friend. To performe this iourney was sent Mr *Sicklemore*, a very valiant, honest, and a painefull Souldier: with him two guides, and directions how to seeke for the lost company of Sir *Walter Raleighs*, and silke Grasse. Then we departed thence, the President assuring the King perpetuall loue; and left with him *Samuel Collier* his Page to learne the Language.

The good counsell of *Warraskoyack.*

So this Kings deeds by sacred Oath adiur'd.
More wary proues, and circumspect by ods:
Fearing at least his double forfeiture;
To offend his friends, and sin against his Gods.

The next night being lodged at *Kecoughtan*; six or seaven dayes the extreame winde, rayne, frost and snow caused vs to keepe Christmas among the Salvages, where we were never more merry, nor fed on more plentie of good Oysters, Fish, Flesh, Wild-foule, and good bread; nor never had better fires in *England*, then in the dry smoaky houses of *Kecoughtan*: but departing thence, when we found no houses we were not curious in any weather to lye three or foure nights together vnder the trees by a fire, as formerly is sayd. An hundred fortie eight foules the President, *Anthony Bagnall*, and Serieant *Pising* did kill at three shoots. At *Kiskiack* the frost & contrary winds forced vs three or foure dayes also (to suppresse the insolency of those proud Salvages) to quarter in their houses, yet guard our Barge, and cause them giue vs what we wanted; though we were but twelue and himselfe, yet we never wanted shelter where we found any houses. The 12 of Ianuary we arrived at *Werowocomoco*, where the river was frozen neare halfe a myle from the shore; but to neglect

Plentie of victualls.

148 Foules killed at three shootes.

left no time, the President with his Barge so far had approached by breaking the ice, as the ebbe left him amongst those oasie shoules, yet rather then to lye there froze to death, by his owne example he taught them to march neere middle deepe, a flight shot through this muddy frozen oase. When the Barge floated, he appoynted two or three to returne her aboord the Pinnace. Where for want of water in melting the ice, they made fresh water, for the river there was salt. But in this march Mr *Russell*, (whom none could perswade to stay behinde) being somewhat ill, and exceeding heauie, so overtoyled himselfe as the rest had much adoe (ere he got ashore) to regaine life into his dead benummed spirits. Quartering in the next houses we found, we sent to *Powhatan* for provision, who sent vs plentie of bread, Turkies, and Venison; the next day having feasted vs after his ordinary manner, he began to aske vs when we would be gone: fayning he sent not for vs, neither had he any corne; and his people much lesse: yet for fortie swords he would procure vs fortie Baskets. The President shewing him the men there present that brought him the message and conditions, asked *Powhatan* how it chanced he became so forgetfull; thereat the King concluded the matter with a merry laughter, asking for our Commodities, but none he liked without gunnes and swords, valuing a Basket of Corne more precious then a Basket of Copper; saying he could rate his Corne, but not the Copper.

Captaine *Smith* seeing the intent of this subtill Salvage began to deale with him after this manner. *Powhatan, though I had many courses to haue made my provision, yet beleeving your promises to supply my wants, I neglected all to satisfie your desire: and to testifie my loue, I sent you my men for your building, neglecting mine owne. What your people had you haue ingressed, forbidding them our trade: and now you thinke by consuming the time, we shall consume for want, not having to fulfill your strange demands. As for swords and gunnes, I told you long agoe I had none to spare; and you must know those I haue can keepe me from want: yet steale or wrong you I will not, nor dissolue that friendship we haue mutually promised, except you constraine me by our bad vsage.*

Cap. *Smiths* discourse to *Powhatan*.

The King having attentiuely listned to this Discourse, promised that both he and his Country would spare him what he could, the which within two dayes they should receiue. Yet Captaine Smith, *sayth the King, some doubt I haue of your comming hither, that makes me not so kindly seeke to relieue you as I would: for many doe informe me, your comming hither is not for trade, but to invade my people, and possesse my Country, who dare not come to bring you Corne, seeing you thus armed with your men. To free vs of this feare, leaue aboord your weapons, for here they are needlesse, we being all friends, and for ever* Powhatans.

Powhatans reply and flattery.

With many such discourses they spent the day, quartering that night in the Kings houses. The next day he renewed his building, which hee little intended should proceede. For the *Dutch*-men finding his plentie, and knowing our want, and perceiving his preparations to surprise vs, little thinking we could escape both him and famine; (to obtaine his favour) revealed to him so much as they knew of our estates and proiects, and how to prevent them. One of them being of so great a spirit, judgement, and resolution, and a hireling that was certaine of his wages for his labour, and ever well vsed both he and his Countrymen; that the President knew not whom better to trust; and not knowing any fitter for that imployment, had sent him as a spy to discover *Powhatans* intent, then little doubting his honestie, nor could ever be certaine of his villany till neare halfe a yeare after.

Whilst we expected the comming in of the Country, we wrangled out of the King ten quarters of Corne for a copper Kettell, the which the President perceiving him much to affect, valued it at a much greater rate; but in regard of his scarcity he would accept it, provided we should haue as much more the next yeare, or els the Country of *Monacan*. Wherewith each seemed well contented, and *Powhatan* began to expostulate the difference of Peace and Warre after this manner.

Captaine Smith, *you may vnderstand that I having seene the death of all my people thrice, and not any one living of those three generations but my selfe; I know the difference of Peace and Warre better then any in my Country. But now I am old and ere long must die, my brethren*

Powhatans discourse of peace and warre.

thren, namely Opitchapam, Opechancanough, *and* Kekataugh, *my two sisters, and their two daughters, are distinctly each others successors. I wish their experience no lesse then mine, and your loue to them no lesse then mine to you. But this bruit from* Nandsamund, *that you are come to destroy my Country, so much affrighteth all my people as they dare not visit you. What will it availe you to take that by force you may quickly haue by loue, or to destroy them that provide you food. What can you get by warre, when we can hide our provisions and fly to the woods? whereby you must famish by wronging vs your friends And why are you thus iealous of our loues seeing vs vnarmed, and both doe, and are willing still to feede you, with that you cannot get but by our labours? Thinke you I am so simple, not to know it is better to eate good meate, lye well, and sleepe quietly with my women and children, laugh and be merry with you, haue copper, hatchets, or what I want being your friend: then be forced to flie from all, to lie cold in the woods, feede vpon Acornes, rootes, and such trash, and be so hunted by you, that I can neither rest, eate, nor sleepe; but my tyred men must watch, and if a twig but breake, every one cryeth there commeth Captaine* Smith: *then must I fly I know not whether: and thus with miserable feare, end my miserable life, leauing my pleasures to such youths as you, which through your rash vnaduisednesse may quickly as miserably end, for want of that, you never know where to finde. Let this therefore assure you of our loues, and every yeare our friendly trade shall furnish you with Corne; and now also, if you would come in friendly manner to see vs, and not thus with your guns and swords as to invade your foes.* To this subtill discourse, the President thus replyed.

Capt. *Smiths* Reply.

Seeing you will not rightly conceiue of our words, we striue to make you know our thoughts by our deeds; the vow I made you of my loue, both my selfe and my men haue kept. As for your promise I find it euery day violated by some of your subiects: yet we finding your loue and kindnesse, our custome is so far from being vngratefull, that for your sake onely, we haue curbed our thirsting desire of revenge; els had they knowne as well the crueltie we vse to our enemies, as our true loue and courtesie to our friends. And I thinke your iudgement sufficient to conceiue, as well by the adventures we haue vndertaken, as by the advantage we haue (by our Armes) of yours: that had we intended you any hurt, long ere this we could haue effected it. Your people comming to Iames *Towne are entertained with their Bowes and Arrowes without any exceptions; we esteeming it with you as it is with vs, to weare our armes as our apparell. As for the danger of our enemies, in such warres consist our chiefest pleasure: for your riches we haue no vse: as for the hiding your provision, or by your flying to the woods, we shall not so vnadvisedly starue as you conclude, your friendly care in that behalfe is needlesse, for we haue a rule to finde beyond your knowledge.*

Many other discourses they had, till at last they began to trade. But the King seeing his will would not be admitted as a law, our guard dispersed, nor our men disarmed, he (sighing) breathed his minde once more in this manner.

Powhatans importunity to haue vs vnarmed to betray vs.

Captaine Smith, *I neuer vse any Werowance so kindely as your selfe, yet from you I receiue the least kindnesse of any.* Captaine Newport *gaue me swords, copper, cloathes, a bed, towels, or what I desired; euer taking what I offered him, and would send away his gunnes when I intreated him: none doth deny to lye at my feet, or refuse to doe what I desire, but onely you; of whom I can haue nothing but what you regard not, and yet you will haue whatsoeuer you demand.* Captaine Newport *you call father, and so you call me; but I see for all vs both you will doe what you list, and we must both seeke to content you. But if you intend so friendly as you say, send hence your armes, that I may beleeue you; for you see the loue I beare you, doth cause me thus nakedly to forget my selfe.*

Smith seeing this Salvage but trifle the time to cut his throat, procured the salvages to breake the ice, that his Boate might come to fetch his corne and him: and gaue order for more men to come on shore, to surprise the King, with whom also he but trifled the time till his men were landed: and to keepe him from suspicion, entertained the time with this reply.

Cap. *Smiths* discourse to delay time, till he found oportunity to surprise the King.

Powhatan *you must know, as I haue but one God, I honour but one King; and I liue not here as your subiect, but as your friend to pleasure you with what I can. By the gifts you bestow on me, you gaine more then by trade: yet would you visit mee as I doe you, you should know it is not our custome, to sell our curtesies as a vendible commodity. Bring all your countrey*

countrey with you for your guard, I will not dislike it as being ouer iealous. But to content you, to morrow I will leaue my Armes, and trust to your promise. I call you father indeed, and as a father you shall see I will loue you: but the small care you haue of such a childe caused my men perswade me to looke to my selfe.

By this time *Powhatan* hauing knowledge his men were ready whilest the ice was a breaking, with his luggage women and children, fled. Yet to auoyd suspicion, left two or three of the women talking with the Captaine, whilest hee secretly ran away, and his men that secretly beset the house. Which being presently discouered to *Captaine Smith*, with his pistoll, sword, and target hee made such a passage among these naked Diuels; that at his first shoot, they next him tumbled one ouer another, and the rest quickly fled some one way some another: so that without any hurt, onely accompanied with *Iohn Russell*, hee obtained the *corps du guard.* When they perceiued him so well escaped, and with his eighteene men (for he had no more with him a shore) to the vttermost of their skill they sought excuses to dissemble the matter: and *Powhatan* to excuse his flight and the sudden comming of this multitude, sent our Captaine a great bracelet and a chaine of pearle, by an ancient Oratour that bespoke vs to this purpose, perceiuing euen then from our Pinnace, a Barge and men departing and comming vnto vs.

Powhatan plot to haue murdered *Smith.*

A chaine of pearle sent the Captaine for a present.

CaptaineSmith, *our Werowance is fled, fearing your gunnes, and knowing when the ice was broken there would come more men, sent these numbers but to guard his corne from stealing, that might happen without your knowledge: now though some bee hurt by your misprision, yet* Powhatan *is your friend and so will for euer continue. Now since the ice is open, he would haue you send away your corne, and if you would haue his company, send away also your gunnes, which so affrighteth his people, that they dare not come to you as hee promised they should.*

Then hauing prouided baskets for our men to carry our corne to the boats, they kindly offered their seruice to guard our Armes, that none should steale them. A great many they were of goodly well proportioned fellowes, as grim as Diuels; yet the very sight of cocking our matches, and being to let fly, a few wordes caused them to leaue their bowes and arrowes to our guard, and beare downe our corne on their backes; wee needed not importune them to make dispatch. But our Barges being left on the oase by the ebbe, caused vs stay till the next high-water, so that wee returned againe to our old quarter. *Powhatan* and his Dutch-men brusting with desire to haue the head of Captaine *Smith*, for if they could but kill him, they thought all was theirs, neglected not any oportunity to effect his purpose. The Indians with all the merry sports they could deuise, spent the time till night: then they all returned to *Powhatan*, who all this time was making ready his forces to surprise the house and him at supper. Notwithstanding the eternall all-seeing God did preuent him, and by a strange meanes. For *Pocahontas* his dearest iewell and daughter, in that darke night came through the irksome woods, and told our Captaine great cheare should be sent vs by and by: but *Powhatan* and all the power he could make, would after come kill vs all, if they that brought it could not kill vs with our owne weapons when we were at supper. Therefore if we would liue shee wished vs presently to bee gone. Such things as shee delighted in, he would haue giuen her: but with the teares running downe her cheekes, shee said shee durst not be seene to haue any: for if *Powhatan* should know it, she were but dead, and so shee ranne away by her selfe as she came. Within lesse then an houre came eight or ten lusty fellowes, with great platters of venison and other victuall, very importunate to haue vs put out our matches (whose smoake made them sicke) and sit down to our victuall. But the Captaine made them taste euery dish, which done hee sent some of them backe to *Powhatan*, to bid him make haste for hee was prepared for his comming. As for them hee knew they came to betray him at his supper: but hee would preuent them and all their other intended villanies: so that they might be gone. Not long after came more messengers, to see what newes; not long after them others. Thus wee spent the night as vigilantly as they, till it was high-water, yet seemed to the saluages

Pretending to kill our men loaded with baskets, we caused them do it themselues.

Pocahontas bewrayes her fathers deceit to kill vs.

as friendly as they to vs: and that wee were so desirous to giue *Powhatan* content, as hee requested, wee did leaue him *Edward Brynton* to kill him foule, and the Dutch-men to finish his house; thinking at our returne from *Pamavnkee* the frost would be gone, and then we might finde a better oportunity if necessity did occasion it, little dreaming yet of the Dutch-mens treachery, whose humor well suted this verse:

Is any free, that may not liue as freely as he list?
Let vs liue so, then w'are as free, and bruitish as the best.

CHAP. IX.

How wee escaped surprising at Pamavnkee.

The Dutch men deceiue Cap. *Winne*.

WE had no sooner set sayle but *Powhatan* returned, and sent *Adam* and *Francis* (two stout Dutch-men) to *Iames* towne: who faining to Captaine *Winne* that all things were well, and that Captaine *Smith* had vse of their armes, wherefore they requested new (the which were giuen them) they told him their comming was for some extraordinary tooles, and shift of apparell; by which colourable excuse they obtained sixe or seauen more to their confederacie, such expert theeues, that presently furnished them with a great many swords, pike-heads, peeces, shot, powder and such like: Saluages they had at hand to carry it away, and the next day they returned vnsuspected, leauing their confederates to follow, and in the interim to convay them such things as they could: for which seruice they should liue with *Powhatan* as his chiefe affected, free from those miseries that would happen the Colony. *Samuel* their other consort *Powhatan* kept for their pledge, whose diligence had prouided them three hundred of their kinde of hatchets; the rest fifty swords, eight peeces, and eight pikes. *Brynton* and *Richard Salvage* seeing the Dutch-men so diligent to accommodate the Saluages with weapons, attempted to haue gotten to *Iames* towne, but they were apprehended, and expected euer when to be put to death.

The Dutch men furnish the Saluages with Armes.

Within two or three dayes we arriued at *Pamavnkee*, the King as many dayes entertained vs with feasting and much mirth. And the day appointed to beginne our trade, the President, Lieutenant *Percie*, Mr. *West*, Mr. *Russell*, Mr. *Behethland*, Mr. *Crashaw*, Mr. *Powell*, Mr. *Ford*, and some others to the number of fifteene, went vp to *Opechancanoughs* house a quarter of a mile from the riuer) where wee found nothing but a lame fellow and a boy: and all the houses round about of all things abandoned. Not long wee stayed ere the King arriued, and after him came diuerse of his people loaden with bowes and arrowes: but such pinching commodities, and those esteemed at such a value, as our Captaine began with the King after this manner.

***Smiths* Speech to *Opechancanough*.**

Opechancanough, the great loue you professe with your tongue, seemes meere deceit by your actions. Last yeere you kindly fraughted out ship: but now you haue inuited mee to starue with hunger: you know my want, and I your plenty; of which by some meanes I must haue part: remember it is fit for Kings to keepe their promise. Here are my commodities, whereof take your choice, the rest I will proportion fit bargains for your people.

The King seemed kindly to accept his offer, and the better to colour his proiect, sold vs what they had to our owne content, promising the next day more company, better prouided. The Barges and Pinnace being committed to the charge of Mr. *Phetiplace*; the President with his old fifteene marched vp to the Kings house, where wee found foure or fiue men newly arriued, each with a great basket. Not long after came the King, who with a strained cheerfulnesse held vs with discourse what paines he had taken to keep his promise; till Mr. *Russell* brought vs in newes that we were all betrayed: for at least seuen hundred Saluages well armed, had inuironed the

700. Saluages beset the English being but 16.

the house, and beset the fields. The King coniecturing what *Russell* related, wee could well perceiue how the extremity of his feare bewrayed his intent: whereat some of our company seeming dismaied with the thought of such a multitude; the Captaine encouraged vs to this effect.

Worthy Countrey-men, were the mischiefes of my seeming friends no more then the danger of these enemies, I little cared were they as many more: if you dare doe, but as I. But this is my torment, that if I escape them, our malicious Councell with their open mouthed Minions, will make me such a peace breaker (in their opinions in England) as will breake my necke. I could wish those here, that make these seeme Saints, and me an oppressor. But this is the worst of all, wherein I pray you aid mee with your opinions. Should wee beginne with them and surprise the King, we cannot keepe him and defend well our selues. If wee should each kill our man, and so proceed with all in the house; the rest will all fly: then shall wee get no more then the bodies that are slaine, and so starue for victuall. As for their fury it is the least danger, for well you know, being alone assaulted with two or three hundred of them, I made them by the helpe of God compound to saue my life. And wee are sixteene, and they but seauen hundred at the most; and assure your selues, God will so assist vs, that if you dare stand but to discharge your pieces, the very smoake will bee sufficient to affright them. Yet howsoeuer, let vs fight like men, and not die like sheepe: for by that meanes you know God hath oft deliuered mee, and so I trust will now. But first, I will deale with them, to bring it to passe wee may fight for something, and draw them to it by conditions. If you like this motion, promise me you will be valiant.

Smiths speech to his Company.

The time not permitting any argument, all vowed to execute whatsoeuer hee attempted, or die: whereupon the Captaine in plaine tearmes told the King this.

I see Opechancanough *your plot to murder me, but I feare it not. As yet your men and mine haue done no harme, but by our direction. Take therefore your Armes, you see mine, my body shall bee as naked as yours: the Isle in your riuer is a fit place, if you be contented: and the conquerour (of vs two) shall be Lord and Master ouer all our men. If you haue not enough, take time to fetch more, and bring what number you will; so euery one bring a basket of corne, against all which I will stake the value in copper, you see I haue but fifteene, and our game shall be, the Conquerour take all.*

Smiths offer to Opechancanough.

The King being guarded with forty or fifty of his chiefe men, seemed kindly to appease *Smiths* suspicion of vnkindnesse, by a great present at the doore, they intreated him to receiue. This was to draw him out of the doore, where the bait was guarded with at least two hundred men, and thirty lying vnder a great tree (that lay thwart as a barricado) each his arrow nocked ready to shoot. The President commanded one to go see what what kind of deceit this was, and to receiue the present; but hee refused to doe it: yet the Gentlemen and all the rest were importunate to goe, but he would not permit them, being vexed at that Coward: and commanded Lieutenant *Percie*, Master *West*, and the rest to make good the house; Master *Powell* and Master *Behethland* he commanded to guard the doore, and in such a rage snatched the King by his long locke in the middest of his men, with his Pistoll readie bent against his brest. Thus he led the trembling King, neare dead with feare amongst all his people: who delivering the Captaine his Vambrace, Bow, and Arrowes, all his men were easily intreated to cast downe their Armes, little dreaming any durst in that manner haue vsed their King: who then to escape himselfe bestowed his presents in good sadnesse, and causing a great many of them come before him vnarmed, holding the King by the hayre (as is sayd) he spake to them to this effect.

Opechancanoughs deuice to betray Smith.

Smith taketh the King prisoner.

I see (you Pamavnkees*) the great desire you haue to kill me, and my long suffering your iniuries hath imboldened you to this presumption. The cause I haue forborne your insolencies, is the promise I made you (before the God I serue) to be your friend, till you giue me iust cause to be your enemy. If I keepe this vow, my God will keepe me, you cannot hurt me, if I breake it, he will destroy me. But if you shoot but one Arrow to shed one drop of bloud of any of my men, or steale the least of these Beads, or Copper, I spurne here before you with my foot; you shall see I will not cease revenge (if once I begin) so long as I can heare where to finde one of*

Smiths discourse to the Pamavnkees.

your Nation that will not deny the name of Pamavnk. *I am not now at* Rassaweak *halfe drowned with myre, where you tooke me prisoner; yet then for keeping your promise and your good vsage and saving my life, I so affect you, that your denyals of your trechery, doe halfe perswade me to mistake my selfe. But if I be the marke you ayme at, here I stand, shoot he that dare. You promised to fraught my Ship ere I departed, and so you shall, or I meane to load her with your dead carcasses, yet if as friends you will come and trade, I once more promise not to trouble you, except you giue me the first occasion, and your King shall be free and be my friend, for I am not come to hurt him or any of you.*

The Salvages dissemble their intent.

Vpon this away went their Bowes and Arrowes, and men, women, and children brought in their Commodities: two or three houres they so thronged about the President and so overwearied him, as he retyred himselfe to rest, leauing Mr *Behethland* and Mr *Powell* to receiue their presents, but some Salvages perceiuing him fast asleepe, & the guard somewhat carelesly dispersed, fortie or fiftie of their choise men each with a club, or an English sword in his hand began to enter the house with two or three hundred others, that pressed to second them. The noyse and hast they made in, did so shake the house they awoke him from his sleepe, and being halfe amazed with this suddaine sight, betooke him strait to his sword and Target; Mr *Chrashaw* and some others charged in like manner; whereat they quickly thronged faster backe then before forward. The house thus cleansed, the King and some of his auncients we kept yet with him, who with a long Oration, excused this intrusion. The rest of the day was spent with much kindnesse, the companie againe renewing their presents with their best provisions, and whatsoever he gaue them they seemed therewith well contented.

Their excuse and reconcilement.

Now in the meane while since our departure, this hapned at our Fort. Master *Scrivener* having receiued Letters from *England* to make himselfe either *Cæsar* or nothing, he began to decline in his affection to Captaine *Smith*, that ever regarded him as himselfe, and was willing to crosse the surprising of *Powhatan*. Some certaine daies after the Presidents departure, he would needs goe visit the Isle of Hogs, and tooke with him Captaine *Waldo* (though the President had appointed him to be ready to second his occasions) with Mr *Anthony Gosnoll* and eight others; but so violent was the wind (that extreame frozen time) that the Boat sunke, but where or how none doth know. The Skiff was much over-loaden, and would scarce haue liued in that extreame tempest had she beene empty: but by no perswasion he could be diverted, though both *Waldo* and an hundred others doubted as it hapned. The Salvages were the first that found their bodies, which so much the more encouraged them to effect their proiects. To advertise the President of this heavie newes, none could be found would vndertake it, but the Iorney was often refused of all in the Fort, vntill Master *Richard Wyffin* vndertooke alone the performance thereof.

The losse of Mr. *Scrivener* and others with a Skiff.

In this Iourney he was incountred with many dangers and difficulties in all parts as he passed. As for that night he lodged with *Powhatan*, perceiuing such preparation for warre, not finding the President there: he did assure himselfe some mischiefe was intended. *Pocahontas* hid him for a time, and sent them who pursued him the cleane contrary way to seeke him; but by her meanes and extraordinary bribes and much trouble in three dayes travell, at length he found vs in the middest of these turmoyles. This vnhappy newes the President swore him to conceale from the company, and so dissembling his sorrow with the best countenances he could, when the night approched went safely aboord with all his Souldiers; leauing *Opechancanough* at libertie, according to his promise, the better to haue *Powhatan* in his returne.

Master *Wyffins* desperate iourney.

Now so extreamely *Powhatan* had threatned the death of his men, if they did not by some meanes kill Captaine *Smith*: that the next day they appointed all the countrey should come to trade vnarmed: yet vnwilling to be trecherous, but that they were constrained, hating fighting with him almost as ill as hanging, such feare they had of bad successe. The next morning the Sunne had not long appeared, but the fields appeared covered with people and Baskets, to tempt vs on shore: but nothing was to be had without his presence, nor they would not indure the sight of a gun.

Powhatan constraineth his men to be trecherous.

When

When the President saw them begin to depart, being vnwilling to loose such a bootie, he so well contrived the Pinnace, and his Barges with Ambuscadoes, as onely with Lieutenant *Percie*, Mr *West*, and Mr *Russell*, with their Armes went on shore; others he appointed vnarmed to receiue what was brought. The Salvages flocked before him in heapes, and the banke serving as a trench for a retreat, he drew them fayre open to his Ambuscado's. For he not being to be perswaded to goe visit their King, the King knowing the most of them vnarmed, came to visit him with two or three hundred men, in the forme of two halfe Moones; and with some twentie men, and many women loaden with painted Baskets. But when they approached somewhat neare vs, their women and children fled. For when they had environed and beset the fields in this manner, they thought their purpose sure, yet so trembled with feare as they were scarse able to nock their Arrowes: *Smith* standing with his three men ready bent, beholding them till they were within danger of our Ambuscado's, who vpon the word discovered themselues, and he retyred to the Barge. Which the Salvages no sooner perceived, then away they fled, esteeming their heeles for their best advantage.

The third attempt to betray vs.

That night we sent Mr *Chrashaw*, and Mr *Ford* to *Iames* towne to Cap. *Winne*. In the way betweene *Werowocomoco* and the Fort they met foure or fiue of the *Dutchmens* Confederates going to *Powhatan*: the which to excuse those Gentlemens suspition of their running to the Salvages, returned to the Fort and there continued.

The Salvages hearing our Barge goe downe the river in the night, were so terribly affrayde, that we sent for more men (we having so much threatned their ruine, and the rasing of their houses, boats, and wires) that the next day the King sent our Captaine a chayne of Pearle, to alter his purpose and stay his men: promising though they wanted themselues, to fraught our ship and bring it aboord to avoyd suspition. So that fiue or six dayes after, from all parts of the Country within ten or twelue myles in the extreame frost and snow, they brought vs provision on their naked backes.

A chayne of pearle sent to obtaine peace.

Yet notwithstanding this kindnesse and trade, had their art and poyson beene sufficient, the President, with Mr *West*, and some others had beene poysoned; it made them sicke, but expelled it selfe. *Wecuttanow*, a stout young fellow, knowing he was suspected for bringing this present of poyson, with fortie or fiftie of his chiefe companions (seeing the President but with a few men at *Potavncak*) so proudly braued it, as though he expected to incounter a revenge. Which the President perceiving in the midst of his company, did not onely beate, but spurned him like a dogge, as scorning to doe him any worse mischiefe. Wherevpon all of them fled into the woods, thinking they had done a great matter to haue so well escaped: and the townsmen remaining presently fraughted our Barge to be rid of our companies, framing many excuses to excuse *Wecuttanow*, (being sonne to their chiefe King, but *Powhatan*) and told vs if we would shew them him that brought the poyson, they would deliver him to vs to punish as we pleased. Men may thinke it strange there should be such a stirre for a little corne, but had it beene gold with more ease wee might haue got it; and had it wanted, the whole *Colony* had starued. Wee may be thought very patient to endure all those iniuries, yet onely with fearing them wee got what they had. Whereas if we had taken revenge, then by their losse, we should haue lost our selues. We searched also the Countries of *Youghtanund* and *Mattapanient*, where the people imparted that little they had with such complaints and teares from the eyes of women and children, as he had beene too cruell to haue beene a Christian, that would not haue beene satisfied and moued with compassion. But had this hapned in October, November, and December, when that vnhappie discovery of *Monacan* was made, and when we might haue fraughted a ship of fortie tuns, and twice as much might haue beene had from the Rivers of *Rapahanock*, *Patawomek*, and *Pawtuxunt*.

The President poysoned: the offender punished.

The Salvages want and povertie.

The maine occasion of our thus temporizing with them was, to part friends as we did, to giue the lesse cause of suspition to *Powhatan* to fly, by whom we now returned with a purpose to haue surprised him and his provision. For effecting whereof (when we came against the Towne) the President sent Mr *Wyffin* and Mr *Coe* ashore to discover and make way for his intended proiect. But they found that those damned *Dutch*-men had caused *Powhatan* to abandon his new house and *Werowocomoco*, and to carry away all his corne and provision: and the people they found so ill affected, that they were in great doubt how to escape with their liues. So the President finding his intent frustrated, and that there was nothing now to be had, and therefore an vnfit time to revenge their abuses, sent Master *Michael Phittiplace* by Land to *Iames* towne, whether we sayled with all the speed we could; wee having in this Iourney (for 25l. of Copper, and 50l. of Iron & Beads) enough to keepe 46 men six weekes, and every man for his reward a moneths provision extraordinary (no Trade being allowed but for the store) we got neare 200l waight of deere suet, and delivered to the Cape Merchant 479 Bushels of Corne.

The Dutchmen did much hurt.

Those temporizing proceedings to some may seeme too charitable, to such a daily daring trecherous people: to others not pleasing, that we washed not the ground with their blouds, nor shewed such strange inventions in mangling, murdering, ransacking, and destroying (as did the *Spanyards*) the simple bodies of such ignorant soules; nor delightfull, because not stuffed with Relations of heapes and mynes of gold and silver, nor such rare commodities, as the *Portugals* and *Spanyards* found in the East and West *Indies*. The want whereof hath begot vs (that were the first vndertakers) no lesse scorne and contempt, then the noble conquests and valiant adventures beautified with it, prayse and honour. Too much I confesse the world cannot attribute to their ever memorable merit: and to cleare vs from the blind worlds ignorant censure, these few words may suffice any reasonable vnderstanding.

An Apology for the first Planters.

It was the *Spanyards* good hap to happen in those parts where were infinite numbers of people, who had manured the ground with that providence, it affoorded victualls at all times. And time had brought them to that perfection, they had the vse of gold and silver, and the most of such commodities as those Countries affoorded: so that, what the *Spanyard* got was chiefely the spoyle and pillage of those Countrey people, and not the labours of their owne hands. But had those fruitfull Countries beene as salvage, as barbarous, as ill peopled, as little planted, laboured, and manured, as *Virginia*: their proper labours it is likely would haue produced as small profit as ours. But had *Virginia* beene peopled, planted, manured, and adorned with such store of precious Iewels, and rich commodities as was the *Indies*: then had we not gotten and done as much as by their examples might be expected from vs, the world might then haue traduced vs and our merits, and haue made shame and infamy our recompence and reward.

But we chanced in a Land even as God made it, where we found onely an idle, improvident, scattered people, ignorant of the knowledge of gold or silver, or any commodities, and carelesse of any thing but from hand to mouth, except bables of no worth; nothing to incourage vs, but what accidentally we found Nature afforded. Which ere we could bring to recompence our paines, defray our charges, and satisfie our Adventurers; we were to discover the Countrey, subdue the people, bring them to be tractable, civill, and industrious, and teach them trades, that the fruits of their labours might make vs some recompence, or plant such *Colonies* of our owne, that must first make prouision how to liue of themselues, ere they can bring to perfection the commodities of the Country: which doubtlesse will be as commodious for *England* as the west *Indies* for *Spaine*, if it be rightly mannaged: notwithstanding all our home-bred opinions, that will argue the contrary, as formerly some haue done against the *Spanyards* and *Portugalls*. But to conclude, against all rumor of opinion, I onely say this, for those that the three first yeares began this Plantation; notwithstanding all their factions, mutinies, and miseries, so gently corrected, and well prevented: peruse the *Spanish Decades*; the Relations of Master *Hackluit*, and tell me how many ever with such small meanes as a Barge of 22 tuns, sometimes with seauen, eight, or nine, or but at most, twelue or sixteene men, did ever discover so

many

many fayre and navigable Rivers, subiect so many severall Kings, people, and Nations, to obedience, and contribution, with so little bloudshed.

And if in the search of those Countries we had hapned where wealth had beene, we had as surely had it as obedience and contribution, but if we haue overskipped it, we will not enuie them that shall find it: yet can we not but lament, it was our fortunes to end when we had but onely learned how to begin, and found the right course how to proceed.

By *Richard Wyffin*, *William Phittiplace*, *Ieffrey Abbot*, and *Anas Todkill*.

Chap. X.

How the Salvages *became subiect to the* English.

WHen the Ships departed, all the provision of the Store (but that the President had gotten) was so rotten with the last Summers rayne, and eaten with Rats and Wormes, as the Hogges would scarcely eate it. Yet it was the Souldiers dyet till our returnes, so that we found nothing done, but our victuals spent, and the most part of our tooles, and a good part of our Armes conveyed to the Salvages. But now casting vp the Store, and finding sufficient till the next harvest, the feare of starving was abandoned, and the company divided into tens, fifteens, or as the businesse required; six houres each day was spent in worke, the rest in Pastime and merry exercises, but the vntowardnesse of the greatest number caused the President advise as followeth.

Countrymen, the long experience of our late miseries, I hope is sufficient to perswade every one to a present correction of himselfe, and thinke not that either my pains, nor the Adventurers purses, will ever maintaine you in idlenesse and sloath. I speake not this to you all, for divers of you I know deserue both honour and reward, better then is yet here to be had: but the greater part must be more industrious, or starue, how euer you haue beene heretofore tolerated by the authoritie of the Councell, from that I haue often commanded you. You see now that power resteth wholly in my selfe: you must obey this now for a Law, that he that will not worke shall not eate (except by sicknesse he be disabled:) for the labours of thirtie or fortie honest and industrious men shall not be consumed to maintaine an hundred and fiftie idle loyterers. And though you presume the authoritie here is but a shadow, and that I dare not touch the liues of any but my owne must answer it: the Letters patents shall each weeke be read to you, whose Contents will tell you the contrary. I would wish you therefore without contempt seeke to obserue these orders set downe, for there are now no more Counsellers to protect you, nor curbe my endevours. Therefore he that offendeth, let him assuredly expect his due punishment.

The Presidents advice to the Company.

He made also a Table, as a publicke memoriall of every mans deserts, to incourage the good, and with shame to spurre on the rest to amendment. By this many became very industrious, yet more by punishment performed their businesse, for all were so tasked, that there was no excuse could prevaile to deceiue him: yet the *Dutch*-mens consorts so closely convayed them powder, shot, swords, and tooles, that though we could find the defect, we could not finde by whom, till it was too late.

All this time the *Dutch* men remaining with *Powhatan*, (who kindly entertained them to instruct the Salvages the vse of our Armes) and their consorts not following them as they expected; to know the cause, they sent *Francis* their companion, a stout young fellow, disguised like a Salvage, to the Glasse-house, a place in the woods neare a myle from *Iames* Towne; where was their *Rendezvous* for all their vnsuspected villany. Fortie men they procured to lie in Ambuscado for Captaine *Smith*, who no sooner heard of this *Dutch*-man, but he sent to apprehend him (but he was gone) yet to crosse his returne to *Powhatan*, the Captaine presently dispatched 20.

The *Dutch*-mens plot to murther Cap. *Smith*.

shot after him, himselfe returning from the Glasse-house alone. By the way he incountred the King of *Paspahegh*, a most strong stout Salvage, whose perswasions not being able to perswade him to his Ambush, seeing him onely armed but with a faucheon, attempted to haue shot him, but the President prevented his shoot by grapling with him, and the Salvage as well prevented him for drawing his faucheon, and perforce bore him into the River to haue drowned him. Long they strugled in the water, till the President got such hold on his throat, he had neare strangled the King; but having drawne his faucheon to cut off his head, seeing how pittifully he begged his life, he led him prisoner to *Iames* Towne, and put him in chaynes.

Smith taketh the King of *Paspahegh* prisoner.

The *Dutch*-man ere long was also brought in, whose villany though all this time it was suspected, yet he fayned such a formall excuse, that for want of language Captaine *Winne* vnderstood him not rightly, and for their dealings with *Powhatan*, that to saue their liues they were constrained to accommodate his armes, of whom he extreamely complained to haue detained them perforce, and that he made this escape with the hazard of his life, and meant not to haue returned, but was onely walking in the woods to gather Walnuts. Yet for all this faire tale, there was so small appearance of truth, and the plaine confession of *Paspahegh* of his trechery, he went by the heeles: *Smith* purposing to regaine the *Dutch*-men, by the saving his life. The poore Salvage did his best by his daily messengers to *Powhatan*, but all returned that the *Dutch*-men would not returne, neither did *Powhatan* stay them; and to bring them fiftie myles on his mens backes they were not able. Daily this Kings wiues, children, and people came to visit him with presents, which he liberally bestowed to make his peace. Much trust they had in the Presidents promise: but the King finding his guard negligent, though fettered yet escaped. Captaine *Winne* thinking to pursue him found such troupes of Salvages to hinder his passage, as they exchanged many vollies of shot for flights of Arrowes. Captaine *Smith* hearing of this in returning to the Fort, tooke two Salvages prisoners, called *Kemps* and *Tussore*, the two most exact villaines in all the Country. With these he sent Captaine *Winne* and fiftie choise men, and Lieutenant *Percie*, to haue regained the King, and revenged this iniury, and so had done, if they had followed his directions, or beene advised with those two villaines, that would haue betrayed both King & kindred for a peece of Copper, but he trifling away the night, the Salvages the next morning by the rising of the Sunne, braved him to come ashore to fight: a good time both sides let fly at other, but we heard of no hurt, onely they tooke two Canowes, burnt the Kings house, and so returned to *Iames* towne.

Cap. *Smith* taketh two Salvages prisoners.

The President fearing those Bravado's would but incourage the Salvages, began againe himselfe to try his conclusions; whereby six or seauen were slaine, as many made prisoners. He burnt their houses, tooke their Boats, with all their fishing wires, and planted some of them at *Iames* towne for his owne vse, and now resolved not to cease till he had revenged himselfe of all them had iniured him. But in his iourney passing by *Paspahegh* towards *Chickahamania*, the Salvages did their best to draw him to their Ambuscadoes; but seeing him regardlesly passe their Country, all shewed themselues in their bravest manner. To try their valours he could not but let fly, and ere he could land, they no sooner knew him, but they threw downe their armes and desired peace. Their Orator was a lustie young fellow called *Okaning*, whose worthy discourse deserveth to be remembred. And thus it was:

The Salvages desire Peace.

Okaning his Oration.

Captaine Smith, *my Master is here present in the company, thinking it Capt.* Winne, *and not you, (of him he intended to haue beene revenged) having never offended him. If he hath offended you in escaping your imprisonment, the fishes swim, the foules fly, and the very beasts striue to escape the snare and liue. Then blame not him being a man. He would intreat you remember, you being a prisoner, what paines he tooke to saue your life. If since he hath iniured you he was compelled to it: but howsoever, you haue revenged it with our too great losse. We perceiue and well know you intend to destroy vs, that are here to intreat and desire your friendship, and to enioy our houses and plant our fields, of whose fruit you shall participate: otherwise you will haue the worse by our absence; for we can plant any where,*

though

though with more labour, and we know you cannot liue if you want our harvest, and that reliefe we bring you. If you promise vs peace, we will beleeue you; if you proceed in revenge we will abandon the Country.

Vpon these tearmes the President promised them peace, till they did vs iniury, vpon condition they should bring in provision. Thus all departed goods friends, and so continued till *Smith* left the Countrey.

Arriving at *Iames* Towne, complaint was made to the President, that the *Chickahamanians*, who all this while continued trade and seemed our friends, by colour thereof were the onely theeues. And amongst other things a Pistoll being stolne and the theefe fled, there was apprehended two proper young fellowes, that were brothers, knowne to be his confederates. Now to regaine this Pistoll, the one was imprisoned, the other was sent to returne the Pistoll againe within twelue houres, or his brother to be hanged. Yet the President pittying the poore naked Salvage in the dungeon, sent him victuall and some Char-coale for a fire: ere midnight his brother returned with the Pistoll, but the poore Salvage in the dungeon was so smoothered with the smoake he had made, and so pittiously burnt, that wee found him dead. The other most lamentably bewayed his death, and broke forth into such bitter agonies, that the President to quiet him, told him that if hereafter they would not steale, he would make him aliue againe: but he little thought he could be recovered. Yet we doing our best with *Aqua vitæ* and *Vineger*, it pleased God to restore him againe to life, but so drunke & affrighted, that he seemed Lunaticke, the which as much tormented and grieued the other, as before to see him dead. Of which maladie vpon promise of their good behaviour, the President promised to recover him: and so caused him to be layd by a fire to sleepe, who in the morning having well slept, had recovered his perfect senses, and then being dressed of his burning, and each a peece of Copper giuen them, they went away so well contented, that this was spread among all the Salvages for a miracle, that Captaine *Smith* could make a man aliue that was dead.

A Salvage smoothered at *Iames* towne, and recovered.

Another ingenuous Salvage of *Powhatans*, having gotten a great bag of Powder, and the backe of an Armour, at *Werowocomoco* amongst a many of his companions, to shew his extraordinary skill, he did dry it on the backe as he had seene the Souldiers at *Iames* Towne. But he dryed it so long, they peeping over it to see his skill, it tooke fire, and blew him to death, and one or two more, and the rest so scorched, they had little pleasure to meddle any more with powder.

Two or three Salvages slaine in drying Powder.

These and many other such pretty Accidents, so amazed and affrighted both *Powhatan*, and all his people, that from all parts with presents they desired peace; returning many stolne things which we never demanded nor thought of; and after that, those that were taken stealing, both *Powhatan* and his people haue sent them backe to *Iames* towne, to receiue their punishment; and all the Country became absolute as free for vs, as for themselues.

Chap. XI.

What was done in three moneths having Victualls. The Store devoured by Rats, how we liued three moneths of such naturall fruits as the Country affoorded.

Now we so quietly followed our businesse, that in three moneths wee made three or foure Last of Tarre, Pitch, and Sope ashes; produced a tryall of Glasse; made a Well in the Fort of excellent sweet water, which till then was wanting; built some twentie houses; recovered our Church; provided Nets and Wires for fishing; and to stop the disorders of our disorderly theeues, and the Salvages, built a Blockhouse in the neck of our Isle, kept by a Garrison to entertaine the

the Saluages trade, and none to passe nor repasse Saluage nor Christian without the presidents order. Thirtie or forty Acres of ground we digged and planted. Of three sowes in eighteene moneths, increased 60, and od Piggs. And neere 500. chickings brought vp themselues without hauing any meat giuen them: but the Hogs were transported to Hog. Isle: where also we built a block-house with a garison to giue vs notice of any shipping, and for their exercise they made Clapbord and waynscot, and cut downe trees. We built also a fort for a retreat neere a conuenient Riuer vpon a high commanding hill, very hard to be assalted and easie to be defended, but ere it was finished this defect caused a stay.

Great extremitie by Rats.

In searching our casked corne, we found it halfe rotten, and the rest so consumed with so many thousands of Rats that increased so fast, but there originall was from the ships, as we knew not how to keepe that little we had. This did driue vs all to our wits end, for there was nothing in the country but what nature afforded. Vntill this time *Kemps* and *Tassore* were fettered prisoners, and did double taske and taught vs how to order and plant our fields: whom now for want of victuall we set at liberty, but so well they liked our companies they did not desire to goe from vs. And to expresse their loues for 16. dayes continuance, the Countrie people brought vs (when least) 100. a day, of Squirrils, Turkyes, Deere and other wilde beasts: But this want of corne occasioned the end of all our works, it being worke sufficient to provide victuall. 60. or 80. with *Ensigne Laxon* was sent downe the riuer to liue vpon Oysters, and 20. with liutenant *Percy* to try for fishing at *Poynt Comfort*: but in six weekes they would not agree once to cast out the net, he being sicke and burnt sore with Gunpouder. Master *West* with as many went vp to the falls, but nothing could be found but a few Acornes; of that in store euery man had their equall proportion. Till this present, by the hazard and indeuours of some thirtie or fortie, this whole Colony had ever beene fed. We had more Sturgeon, then could be deuoured by Dog and Man, of which the industrious by drying and pounding, mingled with Caviare, Sorell and other wholesome hearbes would make bread and good meate: others would gather as much *Tockwhogh* roots, in a day as would make them bread a weeke, so that of those wilde fruites, and what we caught, we liued very well in regard of such a diet, But such was the strange condition of some 150, that had they not beene forced *nolens, volens*, perforce to gather and prepare their victuall they would all haue starued or haue eaten one another. Of those wild fruits the Salvages often brought vs, and for that, the President would not fullfill the vnreasonable desire, of those distracted Gluttonous Loyterers, to sell not only out kettles, hows, tooles, and Iron, nay swords, pieces, and the very Ordnance and howses, might they haue prevayled to haue beene but Idle: for those Saluage fruites, they would haue had imparted all to the Saluages, especially for one basket of Corne they heard of to be at *Powhatās*, fifty myles from our Fort. Though he bought neere halfe of it to satisfie their humors, yet to haue had the other halfe, they would haue sould their soules, though not sufficient to haue kept them a weeke. Thousands were there exclamations, suggestions and deuises, to force him to those base inventions to haue made it an occasion to abandon the Country. Want perforce constrained him to indure their exclaiming follies, till he found out the author, one *Dyer* a most crafty fellow and his ancient Maligner, whom he worthily punished, and with the rest he argued the case in this maner.

Bread made of dried Sturgeon.

Their desire to destroy themselues.

The Presidents order for the drones

Fellow souldiers, I did little thinke any so false to report, or so many to be so simple to be perswaded, that I either intend to starue you, or that Powhatan *at this present hath corne for himselfe, much lesse for you; or that I would not haue it, if I knew where it were to be had. Neither did I thinke any so malitious as now I see a great many; yet it shal not so passionate me, but I will doe my best for my most maligner. But dreame no longer of this vaine hope from* Powhatan, *not that I will longer forbeare to force you, from your Idlenesse, and punish you if you rayle. But if I finde any more runners for Newfoundland with the Pinnace, let him assuredly looke to arive at the Gallows. You cannot deny but that by the hazard of my life many a time I haue saued yours, when (might your owne wills haue prevailed) you would*

would haue starued; and will doe still whether I will or noe; But I protest by that God that made me, since necessitie hath not power to force you to gather for your selues those fruites the earth doth yeeld, you shall not onely gather for your selues, but those that are sicke. As yet I neuer had more from the store then the worst of you: and all my English extraordinary prouision that I haue, you shall see me diuide it amongst the sick. And this Saluage trash you so scornfully repine at; being put in your mouthes your stomackes can disgest, if you would haue better you should haue brought it; and therefore I will take a course you shall prouide what is to be had. The sick shall not starue, but equally share of all our labours; and he that gathereth not every day as much as I doe, the next day shall be set beyond the riuer, and be banished from the Fort as a drone, till he amend his conditions or starue. But some would say with *Seneca.*

I know those things thou sayst are true good Nurse,
But fury forceth me to follow worse.
My minde is hurried headlong vp and downe:
Desiring better counsell, yet finds none.

This order many murmured was very cruell, but it caused the most part so well bestirre themselues, that of 200. (except they were drowned) there died not past seuenas: for Captaine *Winne* and Master *Leigh* they were dead ere this want hapned, and the rest dyed not for want of such as preserued the rest. Many were billetted amongst the Saluages, whereby we knew all their passages, fields and habitations, how to gather and vse there fruits as well as themselues; for they did know wee had such a commanding power at *Iames* towne they durst not wrong vs of a pin.

But seuen of 200 dyed in nine moneths.

So well those poore Salvages vsed vs that were thus billetted, that diuers of the Souldiers ran away to search *Kemps* & *Tassore* our old prisoners. Glad were these Salvages to haue such an oportunity to testifie their loue vnto vs, for in stead of entertaining them, and such things as they had stollen, with all their great Offers, and promises they made them how to reuenge their iniuryes vpon Captaine *Smith*; *Kemps* first made himselfe sport, in shewing his countrie men (by them) how he was vsed, feeding thē with this law, who would not work must not eat, till they were neere starued indeede, continually threatning to beate them to death: neither could they get from him, till hee and his consorts brought them perforce to our Captaine, that so well contented him and punished them, as many others that intended also to follow them, were rather contented to labour at home, then aduenture to liue idlely amongst the Salvages; (of whom there was more hope to make better Christians & good subiects, then the one halfe of those that counterfeited themselues both.) For so affraide was al those kings and the better sort of the people to displease vs, that some of the baser sort that we haue extreamly hurt and punished for there villanies would hire vs, we should not tell it to their kings, or countrymen, who would also repunish them, and yet returne them to *Iames* towne to content the President for a testimony of their loues.

The Salvages returne our fugitiues.

Master *Sicklemore* well returned from *Chawwonoke*; but found little hope and lesse certaintie of them were left by Sir *Walter Raleigh*. The riuer, he saw was not great, the people few, the countrey most over growne with pynes, where there did grow here and there straglingly *Pemminaw*, we call silke grasse. But by the riuer the ground was good, and exceeding furtill;

Master *Sicklemores* Iourney to *Chawwonoke*

Master *Nathanael powell* and *Anas Todkill* were also by the *Quiyoughqnohanocks* conducted to the *Mangoags* to search them there: but nothing could they learne but they were all dead. This honest proper good promise-keeping king, of all the rest did euer best affect vs, and though to his false Gods he was very zealous, yet he would confesse our God as much exceeded his as our Gunns did his Bow and Arrowes, often sending our President may presents, to pray to his God for raine or his corne would perish, for his Gods were angry. Three dayes iorney they conducted them

Master *Powels* iorney to the *Mangoags*.

them through the woods, into a high country towards the Southwest: where they saw here and there a little corne field, by some little spring or smal brooke, but no riuer they could see: the people in all respects like the rest, except there language: they liue most vpon rootes, fruites and wilde beasts; and trade with them towards the sea and the fatter countrys for dryed fish and corne, for skins.

The *Dutch* mens proiects.

All this time to recouer the *Dutch*-men and one *Bentley* another fugitiue, we imployed one *William Volday*, a *Zwitzar* by birth, with Pardons & promises to regaine them. Little we then suspected this double villane, of any villany; who plainly taught vs, in the most trust was the greatest treason; for this wicked hypocrite, by the seeming hate he bore to the lewd conditions of his cursed country men, (hauing this oportunity by his imployment to regaine them) conuayed them euery thing they desired to effect their proiects, to distroy the Colony. With much deuotion they expected the *Spaniard*, to whom they intended good seruice, or any other, that would but carry them from vs. But to begin with the first oportunity; they seeing necessitie thus inforced vs to disperse our selues, importuned *Powhatan* to lend them but his forces, and they would not onely distroy our Hoggs, fire our towne, and betray our Pinnace; but bring to his seruice and subiection the most of our company. With this plot they had acquainted many Discontents, and many were agreed to there Deuilish practise. But one *Thomas Douse*, and *Thomas Mallard* (whose christian hearts relented at such an vnchristian act) voluntarily reuealed it to Captaine *Smith*, who caused them to conceale it, perswading *Douse* and *Mallard* to proceed in their confedracie: onely to bring the irreclamable *Dutch* men and the inconstant Salvages in such a maner amongst such Ambuscado's as he had prepared, that not many of thē should returne from our *Peninsula*. But this brute cōming to the eares of the impatiēt multitude they so importuned the President to cut of those *Dutch* men, as amongst māy that offered to cut their throats before the face of *Powhatā*, the first was Lieutenāt *Percy*, and M^r. *Iohn Cuderington*, two Gentlemen of as bold resolute spirits as could possibly be foūd. But the Presidēt had occasiō of other imploiment for them, & gaue gaue way to Master *Wyffin* and Sarieant *Ieffrey Abbot*, to goe and stab them or shoot them. But the *Dutch* men made such excuses, accusing *Volday* whom they supposed had reuealed their proiect, as *Abbot* would not, yet *Wyffing* would, perceiuing it but deceit. The King vnderstanding of this their imployment, sent presently his messengers to Captaine *Smith* to signifie it was not his fault to detaine them, nor hinder his men from executing his command: nor did he nor would he mantaine them, or any to occasion his displeasure.

Two Gentlemen sent to the *Germans*.

The first arriuall of Captaine *Argall*.

But whilst this businesse was in hand, Arriued one Captaine *Argall*, and Master *Thomas Sedan*, sent by Master *Cornelius* to truck with the *Collony*, and fish for Sturgeon, with a ship well furnished, with wine and much other good provision. Though it was not sent vs, our necessities was such as inforced vs to take it. He brought vs newes of a great supply and preparation for the Lord *La Warre*, with letters that much taxed our President for his heard dealing with the Salvages, and not returning the shippes fraughted. Notwithstanding we kept this ship tell the fleete arriued. True it is *Argall* lost his voyage, but we reuictualled him, and sent him for England, with a true relation of the causes of our defailments, and how imposible it was to returne that wealth they expected, or obserue there instructions to indure the Salvages insolencies, or doe any thing to any purpose, except they would send vs men and meanes that could produce that they so much desired: otherwises all they did was lost, and could not but come to confusion. The villany of *Volday* we still dissembled. *Adam* vpon his pardon came home but *Samuell* still stayed with *Powhahan* to heare further of there estates by this supply. Now all their plots *Simth* so well vnderstood, they were his best advantages to secure vs from any trechery, could be done by them or the Salvages: which with facillity he could revenge when he would, because all those countryes more feared him then *Powhatan*, and hee had such parties with all his bordering neighbours: and many of the rest for loue or feare would haue done any thing he would haue them, vpon any commotion,

though

though these fugitiues had done all they could to perswade *Powhatan*, King *Iames* would kill *Smith*, for vsing him and his people so vnkindly.

By this you may see for all those crosses, trecheries, and dissentions, how hee wrestled and overcame (without bloudshed) all that happened: also what good was done; how few dyed; what food the Countrey naturally affoordeth; what small cause there is men should starue, or be murthered by the Salvages, that haue discretion to mannage them with courage and industrie. The two first yeares, though by his adventures, he had oft brought the Salvages to a tractable trade, yet you see how the envious authoritie ever crossed him, and frustrated his best endevours. But it wrought in him that experience and estimation amongst the Salvages, as otherwise it had bin impossible, he had ever effected that he did. Notwithstanding the many miserable, yet generous and worthy adventures, he had oft and long endured in the wide world, yet in this case he was againe to learne his Lecture by experience. Which with thus much adoe having obtained, it was his ill chance to end, when he had but onely learned how to begin. And though he left those vnknowne difficulties (made easie and familiar) to his vnlawfull successors, (who onely by liuing in *Iames* Towne, presumed to know more then all the world could direct them:) Now though they had all his Souldiers, with a tripple power, and twice tripple better meanes; by what they haue done in his absence, the world may see what they would haue done in his presence, had he not prevented their indiscretions: it doth iustly proue, what cause he had to send them for *England*; and that he was neither factious, mutinous, nor dishonest. But they haue made it more plaine since his returne for *England*; having his absolute authoritie freely in their power, with all the advantages and opportunitie that his labours had effected. As I am sorry their actions haue made it so manifest, so I am vnwilling to say what reason doth compell me, but onely to make apparant the truth, least I should seeme partiall, reasonlesse, and malicious.

Note these inconveniences.

CHAPTER XII.
The Arrivall of the third Supply.

TO redresse those jarres and ill proceedings, the Treasurer, Councell, and Company of *Virginia*, not finding that returne, and profit they expected; and them ingaged there, not having meanes to subsist of themselues, made meanes to his Maiestie, to call in their Commission, and take a new in their owne names, as in their owne publication, 1610. you may reade at large. Having thus annihilated the old by vertue of a Commission made to the right Honourable, Sir *Thomas West*, Lord *de la Warre*, to be Generall of *Virginia*; Sir *Thomas Gates*, his Lieutenant; Sir *George Somers*, Admirall; Sir *Thomas Dale*, high Marshall; Sir *Fardinando Waitman*, Generall of the Horse; and so all other offices to many other worthy Gentlemen, for their liues: (though not any of them had ever beene in *Virginia*, except Captaine *Newport*, who was also by Patent made vice Admirall:) those noble Gentlemen drew in such great summes of money, that they sent Sir *Thomas Gates*, Sir *George Somers*, and Captaine *Newport* with nine shippes, and fiue hundred people, who had each of them a Commission, who first arrived to call in the old, without the knowledge or consent of them, that had endured all those former dangers to beat the path, not any regard had at all of them. All things being ready, because those three Captaines could not agree for place, it was concluded they should goe all in one ship, so all their three Commissions were in that Ship with them called the *Sea-Venture*. They set sayle from *England* in May 1609. A small Catch perished at Sea in a Hericano: the Admirall with an hundred and fiftie men, with the two Knights, and their new Commission, their Bils of Loading, with all manner of directions, and the most part of their provision arrived not. With the o-

The alteration of the government.

1609. Sir *Thomas Smith* Treasurer.

ther

The losse of *Virginia.*

ther seaven Ships as Captaines arrived *Ratliffe,* whose right name (as is sayd) was *Sicklemore, Martin,* and *Archer,* with Captaine *Wood,* Captaine *Webbe,* Captaine *Moone,* Captaine *King,* Captaine *Davis,* and divers Gentlemen of good meanes, and great parentage. But the first as they had beene troublesome at Sea, began againe to marre all ashore: for though (as is said) they were formerly sent for *England,* yet now returning againe, graced by the titles of Captaines of the passengers, seeing the Admirall wanting, and great probabilitie of her losse, strengthened themselues with those new companies, so exclaiming against Captaine *Smith,* that they mortally hated him ere ever they saw him. Who vnderstanding by his Scouts the arrivall of such a Fleet, little dreaming of any such supply, supposed them *Spanyards.* But he quickly so determined and ordered our affaires, as we little feared their Arrivall, nor the successe of our incounter; nor were the Salvages any way negligent for the most part, to ayd and assist vs with their best power. Had it so beene we had beene happy; for we would not haue trusted them but as our foes, where receiuing them as our Countreymen and friends, they did what they could to murther our President, to surprise the Store, the Fort, and our lodgings, to vsurpe the government, and make vs all their servants and slaues, till they could consume vs and our remembrance; and rather indeed to supplant vs then supply vs, as master *William Box* an honest Gentleman in this voyage thus relateth.

The Salvages offer to fight vnder our colours.

In the tayle of a *Hericano* wee were separated from the Admirall, which although it was but the remainder of that Storme, there is seldome any such in *England,* or those Northerne parts of *Europe.* Some lost their Masts, some their Sayles blowne from their Yards; the Seas so over-raking our Ships, much of our prouision was spoyled, our Fleet separated, and our men sicke, and many dyed, and in this miserable estate we arrived in *Virginia.*

But in this Storme,

When ratling Thunder ran along the Clouds;
Did not the Saylers poore, and Masters proud
A terror feele as strucke with feare of God?
Did not their trembling ioynts then dread his rod?
Least for foule deeds and black mouth'd blasphemies,
The rufull time be come that vengeance cryes.

Mutinies.

To a thousand mischiefes those lewd Captaines led this lewd company, wherein were many vnruly Gallants, packed thither by their friends to escape ill destinies, and those would dispose and determine of the government, sometimes to one, the next day to another; to day the old Commission must rule, to morrow the new, the next day neither, in fine they would rule all, or ruine all: yet in charitie we must endure them thus to destroy vs, or by correcting their follies, haue brought the worlds censure vpon vs to be guiltie of their blouds. Happie had we beene had they never arrived, and we for ever abandoned, and as we were left to our fortunes: for on earth for the number was never more confusion, or misery, then their factions occasioned.

The President seeing the desire those Braues had to rule; seeing how his authoritie was so vnexpectedly changed, would willingly haue left all, and haue returned for *England.* But seeing there was small hope this new Commission would arriue, longer he would not suffer those factious spirits to proceede. It would be too tedious, too strange, and almost incredible; should I particularly relate the infinite dangers, plots, and practices, he daily escaped amongst this factious crew; the chiefe whereof he quickly layd by the heeles, till his leasure better served to doe them iustice: and to take away all occasions of further mischiefe, Master *Percie* had his request granted to returne for *England,* being very sicke; and Mr *West* with an hundred and twentie of the best he could chuse, he sent to the Falles; *Martin* with neare as many to *Nandsamund,* with their due proportions of all provisions according to thir numbers.

The planting Nandsamund.

Now

Now the Presidents yeare being neare expired, he made Captaine *Martin* President to follow the order for the election of a President every yeare: but he knowing his owne insufficiency, and the companies vntowardnesse and little regard of him, within three houres after resigned it againe to Captaine *Smith*, and at *Nandsamund* thus proceeded. The people being contributers vsed him kindly; yet such was his iealous feare, in the midst of their mirth, he did surprise this poore naked King, with his Monuments, houses, and the Isle he inhabited, and there fortified himselfe; but so apparantly distracted with feare, as imboldened the Salvages to assault him, kill his men, release their King, gather and carry away a thousand bushels of Corne, he not once offering to intercept them; but sent to the President then at the Falles for thirtie good shot; which from *Iames* Towne immediately was sent him. But he so well imployed them they did iust nothing, but returned complaining of his tendernesse: yet he came away with them to *Iames* Towne, leauing his company to their fortunes.

The breach of peace with the Salvages.

Here I cannot omit the courage of *George Forrest*, that had seauenteene Arrowes sticking in him, and one shot through him, yet liued sixe or seauen dayes, as if he had small hurt, then for want of Chirurgery dyed.

Master *West* having seated his men by the Falles, presently returned to reuisit *Iames* Towne: the President followed him to see that company seated; met him by the way, wondering at his so quicke returne; and found his company planted so inconsiderately, in a place not onely subiect to the rivers invndation, but round inuironed with many intollerable inconueniences.

For remedie whereof he presently sent to *Powhatan* to sell him the place called *Powhatan*, promising to defend him against the *Monacans*. And these should be his Conditions (with his people) to resigne him the Fort and houses, and all that Countrey for a proportion of Copper; that all stealing offenders should be sent him, there to receiue their punishment; that every house as a Custome should pay him a Bushell of Corne for an inch square of Copper, and a proportion of *Pocones*, as a yearely tribute to King *Iames* for their protection, as a dutie; what else they could spare to barter at their best discretions.

Powhatan bought for Copper.

But both this excellent place and those good Conditions did those furies refuse, contemning both him, his kinde care and authoritie. So much they depended on the Lord Generals new Commission, as they regarded none: the worst they could doe to shew their spights they did; supposing all the *Monacans* Country, gold; and none should come there but whom they pleased. I doe more then wonder to thinke how onely with fiue men, he either durst or would adventure as he did, (knowing how greedie they were of his bloud) to land amongst them, and commit to imprisonment all the Chieftaines of those mutinies, till by their multitudes being an hundred and twentie they forced him to retyre: yet in that interim he surprised one of their Boates, wherewith he returned to their ship; where in deed was their prouision, which also he tooke, and well it chanced he found the Marriners so tractable and constant, or there had beene small possibilitie he had ever escaped. There were divers other of better reason and experience, that from their first landing, hearing the generall good report of his old Souldiers, and seeing with their eyes his actions so well mannaged with discretion, as Captaine *Wood*, Captaine *Webbe*, Cap. *Moone*, Captaine *Fitz Iames*, Master *William Powell*, Master *Partridge*, Master *White*, and divers others, when they perceiued the malice of *Ratliffe* and *Archer*, and their faction, left their companies, and ever rested his faithfull friends. But the worst was, that the poore Salvages, that daily brought in their contribution to the President, that disorderly company so tormented those poore soules, by stealing their corne, robbing their gardens, beating them, breaking their houses and keeping some prisoners; that they daily complained to Captaine *Smith*, he had brought them for Protectors, worse enemies then the *Monacans* themselues: which though till then, for his loue they had endured, they desired pardon if hereafter they defended themselues; since he would not correct them, as they had long expected he would. So

Mutinies.

Fiue suppresse an hundred and twentie.

Breach of peace with the Salvages at the Falles.

much they importuned him to punish their misdemeanors, as they offered (if he would leade them) to fight for him against them. But having spent nine dayes in seeking to reclaime them; shewing them how much they did abuse themselues with these great guilded hopes of the South Sea Mines, commodities, or victories, they so madly conceived; then seeing nothing would prevaile, he set sayle for *Iames* Towne.

Thus oft we see from small greene wounds, and from a little griefe,
A greater sore and sicknesse growes, then will admit reliefe:
For thus themselues they did beguile, and with the rest play'd theefe.

An assalt by the Salvages

Now no sooner was the Ship vnder sayle, but the Salvages assaulted those hundred and twentie in their Fort, finding some stragling abroad in the woods: they slew many, and so affrighted the rest, as their prisoners escaped, and they safely retyred, with the swords and cloakes of those they had slaine. But ere wee had sayled halfe a league, our ship grounding, gaue vs once more libertie to summon them to a parley; where we found them all so strangely amazed with this poore silly assault of twelue Saluages, that they submitted themselues vpon any tearmes to the Presidents mercy; who presently put by the heeles sixe or seauen of the chiefe offenders: the rest he seated gallantly at *Powhatan*, in that Salvage Fort, readie built, and prettily fortified with poles and barkes of trees, sufficient to haue defended them from all the Salvages in *Virginia*, dry houses for lodgings and neere two hundred acres of ground ready to be planted, and no place we knew so strong, so pleasant and delightfull in *Virginia* for which we called it *Non-such*. The Salvages also hee presently appeased, redeliuering to either party their former losses. Thus all were friends.

The planting of *Non-such*.

The Salvages appeased.

New officers appointed to command, and the President againe ready to depart, at that instant arriued Captaine *West*, whose gentle nature (by the perswasions and compassion of those mutinous prisoners, alledging they had onely done this for his honor) was so much abused, that to regaine their old hopes, new turboyles did arise. For they a-shore being possessed of all there victuall, munition, and euery thing, grew to that height in their former factions, as the President left them to their fortunes: they returned againe to the open ayre at *Wests* Fort, abandoning *Non-such*, and he to *Iames* towne with his best expedition, but this happned him in that Iourney.

Captaine *Smith* blowne vp with powder.

Sleeping in his Boate, (for the ship was returned two daies before) accidentallie, one fired his powder-bag, which tore the flesh from his body and thighes, nine or ten inches square in a most pittifull manner; but to quench the tormenting fire, frying him in his cloaths he leaped over-boord into the deepe river, where ere they could recouer him he was neere drowned. In this estate without either Chirurgian, or Chirurgery he was to goe neere an hundred myles. Arriving at *Iames* towne, causing all things to be prepared for peace or warres to obtaine provision, whilest those things were providing, *Ratliffe*, *Archer*, & the rest of their Confederates, being to come to their trials; their guiltie consciences, fearing a iust reward for their deserts, seeing the President, vnable to stand, and neere bereft of his senses by reason of his torment, they had plotted to haue murdered him in his bed. But his heart did faile him that should haue giuen fire to that mercilesse Pistoll. So not finding that course to be the best, they ioyned together to vsurpe the government, thereby to escape their punishment. The President, had notice of their proiects, the which to withstand, though his old souldiers importuned him but permit them to take their heads that would resist his command, yet he would not suffer them, but sent for the Masters of the ships, and tooke order with them for his returne for England. Seeing there was neither Chirurgian, nor Chirurgery in the Fort to cure his hurt, and the ships to depart the next day, his Commission to be suppressed he knew not why, himselfe and souldiers to be rewarded he knew not how, and a new

A bloudy intent.

new commission granted they knew not to whom (the which disabled that authority he had, as made them presume so oft to those mutinies as they did:) besides so grievous were his wounds, and so cruell his torments (few expecting he could liue) nor was hee able to follow his busines to regaine what they had lost, suppresse those factions, and range the countries for provision as he intended; and well he knew in those affaires his owne actions and presence was as requisit as his directions, which now could not be, he went presently abroad, resoluing there to appoint them governours, and to take order for the mutiners, but he could finde none hee thought fit for it would accept it. In the meane time, seeing him gone, they perswaded Master *Perry* to stay, who was then to goe for England, and be their President. Within lesse then an houre was this mutation begun and concluded. For when the Company vnderstood *Smith* would leaue them, & saw the rest in Armes called Presidents & Councellors, divers began to fawne on those new commanders, that now bent all their wits to get him resigne them his Commission: who after much adoe and many bitter repulses; that their confusion (which he tould them was at their elbowes) should not be attributed to him, for leauing the Colony without a Commission, he was not vnwilling they should steale it, but never would he giue it to such as they.

The causes why *Smith* left the Countrey and his Commission.

And thus, *Strange violent forces drew vs on vnwilling:*
Reason perswading 'gainst our loues rebelling.
We saw and knew the better, ah curse accurst!
That notwithstanding we imbrace the worst.

But had that vnhappie blast not hapned, he would quickly haue qualified the heate of those humors, and factions, had the ships but once left them and vs to our fortunes; and haue made that provision from among the Salvages, as we neither feared *Spanyard*, Salvage, nor famine; nor would haue left *Virginia*, nor our lawfull authoritie, but at as deare a price as we had bought it, and payd for it. What shall I say but thus, we left him, that in all his proceedings, made Iustice his first guide, and experience his second, even hating basenesse, sloath, pride, and indignitie, more then any dangers; that neuer allowed more for himselfe, then his souldiers with him; that vpon no danger would send them where he would not lead them himselfe; that would never see vs want, what he either had, or could by any meanes get vs; that would rather want then borrow, or starue then not pay; that loued action more then words, and hated falshood and covetousnesse worse then death; whose adventures were our liues, and whose losse our deaths.

Leaving vs thus with three ships, seaven boats, commodities readie to trade, the harvest newly gathered, ten weeks provision in the store, foure hundred nintie and od persons, twentie-foure Peeces of Ordnance, three hundred Muskets, Snaphances, and Firelockes, Shot, Powder, and Match sufficient, Curats, Pikes, Swords, and Morrios, more then men; the Salvages, their language, and habitations well knowne to an hundred well trayned and expert Souldiers; Nets for fishing; Tooles of all sorts to worke; apparell to supply our wants; six Mares and a Horse; fiue or sixe hundred Swine; as many Hennes and Chickens; some Goats; some sheepe; what was brought or bred there remained. But they regarding nothing but from hand to mouth, did consume that wee had, tooke care for nothing, but to perfect some colourable complaints against Captaine *Smith*. For effecting whereof three weekes longer they stayed the Ships, till they could produce them. That time and charge might much better haue beene spent, but it suted well with the rest of their discretions.

Besides *Iames* towne that was strongly Pallizadoed, containing some fiftie or sixtie houses, he left fiue or sixe other severall Forts and Plantations: though they were not so sumptuous as our successors expected, they were better then they provided any for vs. All this time we had but one Carpenter in the Countrey, and three others

thers that could doe little, but desired to be learners: two Blacksmiths; two saylers, & those we write labourers were for most part footmen, and such as they that were Adventurers brought to attend them, or such as they could perswade to goe with them, that neuer did know what a dayes worke was, except the *Dutch*-men and *Poles*, and some dozen other. For all the rest were poore Gentlemen, Tradsmen, Serving-men, libertines, and such like, ten times more fit to spoyle a Common-wealth, then either begin one, or but helpe to maintaine one. For when neither the feare of God, nor the law, nor shame, nor displeasure of their friends could rule them here, there is small hope ever to bring one in twentie of them ever to be good there. Notwithstanding, I confesse divers amongst them, had better mindes and grew much more industrious then was expected: yet ten good workemen would haue done more substantiall worke in a day, then ten of them in a weeke. Therefore men may rather wonder how we could doe so much, then vse vs so badly, because we did no more, but leaue those examples to make others beware, and the fruits of all, we know not for whom.

The ends of the *Dutch*-men.

But to see the iustice of God vpon these *Dutch*-men; *Valdo* before spoke of, made a shift to get for *England*, where perswading the Merchants what rich Mines he had found, and great service he would doe them, was very well rewarded, and returned with the Lord *La Warre*: but being found a meere Impostor, he dyed most miserably. *Adam* and *Francis* his two consorts were fled againe to *Powhatan*, to whom they promised at the arrivall of my Lord, what wonders they would doe, would he suffer them but to goe to him. But the King seeing they would be gone, replyed; You that would haue betrayed Captaine *Smith* to mee, will certainely betray me to this great Lord for your peace: so caused his men to beat out their braines.

To conclude, the greatest honour that ever belonged to the greatest Monarkes, was the inlarging their Dominions, and erecting Common-weales. Yet howsoever any of them haue attributed to themselues, the Conquerors of the world: there is more of the world never heard of them, then ever any of them all had in subiection: for the *Medes*, *Persians*, and *Assyrians*, never Conquered all *Asia*, nor the *Grecians* but part of *Europe* and *Asia*. The *Romans* indeed had a great part of both, as well as *Affrica*: but as for all the Northerne parts of *Europe* and *Asia*, the interior Southern and Westerne parts of *Affrica*, all *America* & *Terra incognita*, they were all ignorant: nor is our knowledge yet but superficiall. That their beginnings, ending, and limitations were proportioned by the Almightie is most evident: but to consider of what small meanes many of them haue begun is wonderfull. For some write that even *Rome* her selfe, during the Raigne of *Romulus*, exceeded not the number of a thousand houses. And *Carthage* grew so great a Potentate, that at first was but incirculed in the thongs of a Bulls skinne, as to fight with *Rome* for the Empire of the world. Yea *Venice* at this time the admiration of the earth, was at first but a Marish, inhabited by poore Fishermen. And likewise *Ninivie*, *Thebes*, *Babylon*, *Delus*, *Troy*, *Athens*, *Mycena* and *Sparta*, grew from small beginnings to be most famous States, though now they retaine little more then a naked name. Now this our yong Common-wealth in *Virginia*, as you haue read once consisted but of 38 persons, and in two yeares increased but to 200. yet by this small meanes so highly was approved the Plantation in *Virginia*, as how many Lords, with worthy Knights, and braue Gentlemen pretended to see it, and some did, and now after the expence of fifteene yeares more, and such massie summes of men and money, grow they disanimated? If we truely consider our Proceedings with the *Spanyards*, and the rest, we haue no reason to despayre, for with so small charge, they never had either greater Discoveries, with such certaine tryals of more severall Commodities, then in this short time hath beene returned from *Virginia*, and by much lesse meanes. *New England* was brought out of obscuritie, and affoorded fraught for neare 200 sayle of ships, where there is now erected a braue Plantation. For the happines of *Summer Isles*, they are no lesse then either, and yet those haue had a far lesse, and a more difficult beginning, then either *Rome*, *Carthage*, or *Venice*.

Written by *Richard Pots*, Clarke of the Councell, *William Tankard*, and *G.P.*

Now seeing there is this much Paper here to spare, that you should not be altogether cloved with Prose; such Verses as my worthy Friends bestowed upon New England, *I here present you, because with honestie I can neither reiect, nor omit their courtesies.*

In the deserued Honour of the Author, Captaine *Iohn Smith*, and his Worke.

DAmn'd Envie *is a sp'rite, that ever haunts*
Beasts, mis-nam'd Men; Cowards, or Ignorants.
But, onely such shee followes, whose deare WORTH
(Maugre her malice) sets their glory forth.
If this faire Overture, then, take not; It
Is Envie's *spight (deare friend) in men of wit;*
Or Feare, *lest morsels, which our mouths possesse,*
Might fall from thence; or else, tis Sottishnesse.
If either; (I hope neither) thee they raise;
Thy Letters are as Letters in thy praise;*
Who, by their vice, improue *(when they* reprooue*)*
Thy vertue; so, in hate, procure thee Loue.
Then, On firme Worth: this Monument I frame;
Scorning for any Smith to forge such fame. Iohn Davies, *Heref:*

*Hinderers.

To his worthy Captaine the Author

THat which wee call the subiect of all Storie,
Is Truth: which in this Worke of thine giues glorie
To all that thou hast done. Then, scorne the spight
Of Envie; *which doth no mans Merits right.*
My sword may helpe the rest: my Pen no more
Can doe, but this; I'aue said enough before.

Your sometime Souldier, *I. Codrinton,* now Templer.

To my Worthy Friend and Cosen, Captaine *Iohn Smith.*

IT over-ioyes my heart, when as thy Words
Of these designes, with deeds I doe compare.
Here is a Booke, such worthy truth affords,
None should the due desert thereof impare:
Sith thou, the man, deserving of these Ages,
Much paine hast ta'en for this our Kingdomes good,
In Climes vnknowne, 'Mongst Turks *and Salvages,*
T'inlarge our bounds; though with thy losse of blood.
Hence damn'd Detraction: *stand not in our way.*
Envie, it selfe, will not the Truth gainesay. N. Smith.

In the deserved Honour of my honest and worthy Captaine, *Iohn Smith*, and his Worke.

CAptaine and friend; when I peruse thy Booke
(With Iudgements *eyes) into my* heart *I looke:*
And there I finde (what sometimes Albion *knew)*
A Souldier, *to his* Countries-honour, *true.*
Some fight for wealth; *and some for* emptie praise;
But thou alone thy Countries Fame *to raise.*

With

With due discretion, *and* vndanted heart,
I (oft) so well haue seene thee act thy Part
In deepest plunge of hard extreamitie,
As forc't the troups of proudest foes to flie.
Though men of greater Ranke *and lesse* desert
Would Pish-*away thy* Praise, *it can not start*
From the true Owner: *for, all good mens tongues*
Shall keepe the same. To them that Part belongs.
If, then, Wit, Courage, *and* Successe *should get*
Thee Fame; *the Muse for* that *is in thy* debt:
A part whereof (least able though I be)
Thus here I doe disburse, to honor Thee. Raleigh Crashaw.

Michael Phettiplace, Wil: Phettiplace, and *Richard Wiffing,* Gentlemen, and Souldiers vnder Captaine *Smiths* command: In his deserved honour for his Worke, and Worth.

WHy may not wee in this Worke haue our Mite,
That had our share in each black day and night,
When thou Virginia *foild'st, yet kept'st vnstaind;*
And held'st the King of Paspeheh *enchaind.*
Thou all alone this Salvage *sterne didst take.*
Pamavnkees *King wee saw thee captiue make*
Among seauen hundred of his stoutest men,
To murther thee and vs resolved; when
Fast by the hayre thou ledst this Salvage grim,
Thy Pistoll at his breast to governe him:
Which did infuse such awe in all the rest
(Sith their drad Soveraigne thou had'st so distrest)
That thou and wee (poore sixteene) safe retir'd
Vnto our helplesse Ships. *Thou (thus admir'd)*
Didst make proud Powhatan, *his subiects send*
To Iames *his Towne, thy censure to attend:*
And all Virginia's *Lords, and pettie Kings,*
Aw'd by thy vertue, crouch, and Presents brings
To gaine thy grace; so dreaded thou hast beene:
And yet a heart more milde is seldome seene;
So, making Valour Vertue, really;
Who hast nought in thee counterfeit, or slie;
If in the sleight be not the truest Art,
That makes men famoused for faire desert.
Who saith of thee, this savors of vaine-glorie,
Mistakes both thee and vs, and this true Storie.
If it be ill in Thee, so well to doe;
Then, is ill in Vs, to praise thee too.
But, if the first be well done; it is well,
To say it doth (if so it doth) excell.
Praise is the guerdon of each deare desert
Making the praised act the praised part
With more alacritie: Honours *Spurre is* Praise;
Without which, it (regardlesse) soone decaies.
And for this paines of thine wee praise thee rather,
That future Times may know who was the father
*Of that rare Worke (*New England*) which may bring,*
Praise to thy God, *and profit to thy* King.

THE FOVRTH BOOKE.

TO MAKE PLAINE THE TRVE PROCEEDINGS of the Historie for 1609. we must follow the examinations of Doctor *Simons*, and two learned Orations published by the Companie; with the relation of the Right Honourable the Lord *De la Ware*.

What happened in the first gouernment after the alteration in the time of Captaine George Piercie *their Gouernour.*

THE day before Captaine *Smith* returned for *England* with the ships, Captaine *Dauis* arriued in a small Pinace, with some sixteene proper men more: To these were added a company from *Iames* towne, vnder the command of Captaine *Iohn Sickelmore* alias *Ratliffe*, to inhabit *Point Comfort*. Captaine *Martin* and Captaine *West*, hauing lost their boats and neere halfe their men among the Saluages, were returned to *Iames* towne; for the Saluages no sooner vnderstood *Smith* was gone, but they all reuolted, and did spoile and murther all they incountered. Now wee were all constrained to liue onely on that *Smith* had onely for his owne Companie, for the rest had consumed their proportions, and now they had twentie Presidents with all their appurtenances: Master *Piercie* our new President, was so sicke hee could neither goe nor stand. But ere all was consumed, Captaine *West* and Captaine *Sickelmore*, each with a small ship and thirtie or fortie men well appointed, sought abroad to trade. *Sickelmore* vpon the confidence of *Powhatan*, with about thirtie others as carelesse as himselfe, were all slaine, onely *Ieffrey Shortridge* escaped, and *Pokahontas* the Kings daughter saued a boy called *Henry Spilman*, that liued many yeeres after, by her meanes, amongst the *Patawomekes*. *Powhatan* still as he found meanes, cut off their Boats, denied them trade, so that Captaine *West* set saile for *England*. Now we all found the losse of Captaine *Smith*, yea his greatest maligners could now curse his losse: as for corne, prouision and contribution from the Saluages, we had nothing but mortall wounds, with clubs and arrowes; as for our Hogs, Hens, Goats, Sheepe, Horse, or what liued, our commanders, officers & Saluages daily consumed them, some small proportions sometimes we tasted, till all was deuoured; then swords, armes, pieces, or any thing, wee traded with the Saluages, whose cruell fingers were so oft imbrewed in our blouds, that what by their crueltie, our Gouernours indiscretion, and the losse of our ships, of fiue hundred within six moneths after Captaine *Smiths* departure, there remained not past sixtie men, women and children, most miserable and poore creatures; and those were preserued for the most part, by roots, herbes, acornes, walnuts, berries, now and then a little fish: they that had starch in these extremities, made no small vse of it; yea, euen the very skinnes of our horses. Nay, so great was our famine, that a Saluage we slew, and buried, the poorer sort tooke him vp againe and eat him, and so did diuers

The planting *Point Comfort.*

1609

one

one another boyled and ſtewed with roots and herbs: And one amongſt the reſt did kill his wife, powdered her, and had eaten part of her before it was knowne, for which hee was executed, as hee well deſerued; now whether ſhee was better roaſted, boyled or carbonado'd, I know not, but of ſuch a diſh as powdered wife I neuer heard of. This was that time, which ſtill to this day we called the staruing time; it were too vile to ſay, and ſcarce to be beleeued, what we endured: but the occaſion was our owne, for want of prouidence, induſtrie and gouernment, and not the barrenneſſe and defect of the Countrie, as is generally ſuppoſed; for till then in three yeeres, for the numbers were landed vs, we had neuer from *England* prouiſion ſufficient for ſix moneths, though it ſeemed by the bils of loading ſufficient was ſent vs, ſuch a glutton is the Sea, and ſuch good fellowes the Mariners; we as little taſted of the great proportion ſent vs, as they of our want and miſeries, yet notwithſtanding they euer ouer-ſwayed and ruled the buſineſſe, though we endured all that is ſaid, and chiefly liued on what this good Countrie naturally afforded; yet had wee beene euen in Paradice it ſelfe with theſe Gouernours, it would not haue beene much better with vs; yet there was amongſt vs, who had they had the gouernment as Captaine *Smith* appointed, but that they could not maintaine it, would ſurely haue kept vs from thoſe extremities of miſeries. This in ten daies more, would haue ſupplanted vs all with death.

The arriuall of Sir *Thomas Gates*. But God that would not this Countrie ſhould be vnplanted, ſent Sir *Thomas Gates*, and Sir *George Sommers* with one hundred and fiftie people moſt happily preſerued by the *Bermudas* to preſerue vs: ſtrange it is to ſay how miraculouſly they were preſerued in a leaking ſhip, as at large you may reade in the inſuing Hiſtorie of thoſe Ilands.

The gouernment reſigned to Sir Thomas Gates, 1610.

1610. WHen theſe two Noble Knights did ſee our miſeries, being but ſtrangers in that Countrie, and could vnderſtand no more of the cauſe, but by coniecture of our clamours and complaints, of accuſing and excuſing one another: They embarked vs with themſelues, with the beſt meanes they could, and abandoning *Iames* towne, ſet ſaile for *England*, whereby you may ſee the euent of the gouernment of the former Commanders left to themſelues; although they had liued there many yeeres as formerly hath beene ſpoken (who hindred now their proceedings, Captaine *Smith* being gone.)

Iames towne abandoned.

At noone they fell to the Ile of *Hogs*, and the next morning to *Mulbery point*, at what time they deſcried the Long-boat of the Lord *la Ware*, for God would not haue it ſo abandoned. For this honourable Lord, then Gouernour of the Countrie, met them with three ſhips exceedingly well furniſhed with all neceſſaries fitting, who againe returned them to the abandoned *Iames* towne. *Out of the obſeruations of* William Simmons *Doctor of Diuinitie*.

The gouernment deuolued to the Lord la Ware.

The arriuall of the Lord *la Ware*. HIs Lordſhip arriued the ninth of Iune 1610. accompanied with Sir *Ferdinando Waynman*, Captaine *Houlcroft*, Captaine *Lawſon*, and diuers other Gentlemen of ſort; the tenth he came vp with his fleet, went on ſhore, heard a Sermon, read his Commiſſion, and entred into conſultation for the good of the Colonie, in which ſecret counſell we will a little leaue them, that we may duly obſerue the reuealed counſell of God. Hee that ſhall but turne vp his eie, and behold the ſpangled canopie of heauen, or ſhall but caſt downe his eie, and conſider the embroydered carpet of the earth, and withall ſhall marke how the heauens heare the earth, and the earth the Corne and Oile, and they relieue the neceſſities of man, that man will acknowledge Gods infinite prouidence:

prouidence: But hee that shall further obserue, how God inclineth all casuall euents to worke the necessary helpe of his Saints, must needs adore the Lords infinite goodnesse; neuer had any people more iust cause, to cast themselues at the very foot-stoole of God, and to reuerence his mercie, than this distressed Colonie; for if God had not sent Sir *Thomas Gates* from the *Bermudas*, within foure daies they had almost beene famished; if God had not directed the heart of that noble Knight to saue the Fort from fiering at their shipping, for many were very importunate to haue burnt it, they had beene destitute of a present harbour and succour: if they had abandoned the Fort any longer time, and had not so soone returned, questionlesse the Indians would haue destroied the Fort, which had beene the meanes of our safeties amongst them and a terror. If they had set saile sooner, and had lanched into the vast Ocean, who would haue promised they should haue incountered the Fleet of the Lord *la Ware*, especially when they made for *New found land*, as they intended, a course contrarie to our Nauie approaching. If the Lord *la Ware* had not brought with him a yeeres prouision, what comfort would those poore soules haue receiued, to haue beene relanded to a second distruction? This was the arme of the Lord of Hosts, who would haue his people passe the red Sea and Wildernesse, and then to possesse the land of *Canaan*: It was diuinely spoken of Heathen *Socrates*, If God for man be carefull, why should man bee ouer-distrustfull? for he hath so tempered the contrary qualities of the Elements,

That neither cold things want heat, nor moist things dry,
Nor sad things spirits, to quicken them thereby,
Yet make they musicall content of contrarietie,
Which conquer'd, knits them in such links together;
They doe produce euen all this whatsoeuer.

The Lord Gouernour, after mature deliberation, deliuered some few words to the Companie, laying iust blame vpon them, for their haughtie vanities and sluggish idlenesse, earnestly intreating them to amend those desperate follies, lest hee should be compelled to draw the sword of Iustice, and to cut off such delinquents, which he had rather draw, to the shedding of his vitall bloud, to protect them from iniuries; heartning them with relation of that store hee had brought with him, constituting officers of all conditions, to rule ouer them, allotting euery man his particular place, to watch vigilantly, and worke painfully: This Oration and direction being receiued with a generall applause, you might shortly behold the idle and restie diseases of a diuided multitude, by the vnitie and authoritie of this gouernment to be substantially cured. Those that knew not the way to goodnesse before, but cherished singularitie and faction, can now chalke out the path of all respectiue dutie and seruice: euery man endeuoureth to outstrip other in diligence: the *French* preparing to plant the Vines, the *English* labouring in the Woods and grounds; euery man knoweth his charge, and dischargeth the same with alacritie. Neither let any man be discouraged, by the relation of their daily labour (as though the sap of their bodies should bee spent for other mens profit) the setled times of working, to effect all themselues, or as the Aduenturers need desire, required no more paines than from six of the clocke in the morning, vntill ten, and from two in the afternoone, till foure, at both which times they are prouided of spirituall and corporall reliefe. First, they enter into the Church, and make their praiers vnto God, next they returne to their houses and receiue their proportion of food. Nor should it bee conceiued that this businesse excludeth Gentlemen, whose breeding neuer knew what a daies labour meant, for though they cannot digge, vse the Spade, nor practice the Axe, yet may the staied spirits of any condition, finde how to imploy the force of knowledge, the exercise of counsell, the operation and power of their best breeding and qualities. The houses which are built, are as warme and defensiue against wind and

 weather,

weather, as if they were tiled and slated, being couered aboue with strong boards, and some matted round with Indian mats. Our forces are now such as are able to tame the furie and trecherie of the Saluages: Our Forts assure the Inhabitants, and frustrate all assaylants. And to leaue no discouragement in the heart of any, who personally shall enter into this great action, I will communicate a double comfort; first, Sir *George Sommers*, that worthy Admirall hath vndertaken a dangerous adueuture for the good of the Colonie.

Sir *George Sommers* returne to the *Bermudas.*

Vpon the 15. of Iune, accompanied with Captaine *Samuel Argall*, hee returned in two Pinaces vnto the *Bermudas*, promising (if by any meanes God will open a way to that Iland of Rocks) that he would soone returne with six moneths prouision of flesh; with much crosse weather at last hee there safely arriued, but Captaine *Argall* was forced backe againe to *Iames* towne, whom the Lord *De la Ware* not long after sent to the Riuer of *Patawomeke*, to trade for Corne; where finding an *English* boy, one *Henry Spilman*, a young Gentleman well descended, by those people preserued from the furie of *Powhatan*, by his acquaintance had such good vsage of those kinde Saluages, that they fraughted his ship with Corne, wherewith he returned to *Iames* towne.

The building Fort *Henry* and Fort *Charles.*

The other comfort is, that the Lord *la Ware* hath built two new Forts, the one called Fort *Henry*, the other Fort *Charles*, in honour of our most noble Prince, and his hopefull brother, vpon a pleasant plaine, and neare a little Riuilet they call *Southampton* Riuer; they stand in a wholsome aire, hauing plentie of Springs of sweet water, they command a great circuit of ground, containing Wood, Pasture and Marsh, with apt places for Vines, Corne and Gardens; in which Forts it is resolued, that all those that come out of *England*, shall be at their first landing quartered, that the wearisomnesse of the Sea, may bee refreshed in this pleasing part of the Countrie, and Sir *Thomas Gates* hee sent for *England*. But to correct some iniuries of the *Paspahegs*, he sent Captaine *Pearcie*, Master *Stacy*, and fiftie or threescore shot, where the Saluages flying, they burnt their houses, tooke the Queene and her children prisoners, whom not long after they slew.

The fertilitie of the soile, the temperature of the climate, the forme of gouernment, the condition of our people, their daily inuocating of the Name of God being thus expressed; why should the successe, by the rules of mortall iudgement, bee disparaged? why should not the rich haruest of our hopes be seasonably expected? I dare say, that the resolution of *Cæsar* in *France*, the designes of *Alexander*, the discoueries of *Hernando Cortes* in the West, and of *Emanuel* King of *Portugal* in the East, were not encouraged vpon so firme grounds of state and possibilitie.

But his Lordship being at the fales, the Saluages assaulted his troopes and slew three or foure of his men. Not long after, his Honour growing very sicke, he returned for *England* the 28. of March; in the ship were about fiue and fiftie men, but ere we arriued at *Fyall*, fortie of vs were neare sicke to death, of the Scuruie, Callenture, and other diseases: the Gouernour being an *English-man*, kindly vsed vs, but small reliefe we could get, but Oranges, of which we had plenty, whereby within eight daies wee recouered, and all were well and strong by that they came into *England*. *Written by* William Box.

The Counsell of *Virginia* finding the smalnesse of that returne which they hoped should haue defrayed the charge of a new supply, entred into a deep consultation, whether it were fit to enter into a new Contribution, or in time to send for them home, and giue ouer the action, and therefore they adiured Sir *Thomas Gates* to deale plainly with them, who with a solemne and a sacred oath replyed, That all things before reported were true, and that all men know that wee stand at the deuotion of politicke Princes and States, who for their proper vtilitie, deuise all courses to grind our Merchants, and by all pretences to confiscate their goods, and to draw from vs all manner of gaine by their inquisitiue inuentions, when in *Virginia*, a few yeeres labour by planting and husbandry, will furnish all

our

our defects with honour and securitie. *Out of a Declaration published by the Councell, 1610.*

The gouernment left againe to Captaine George Piercie, *and the returne of the Lord* la Ware, *with his Relation to the Councell.*

1611. Sir *Thomas Smith* Treasurer.

The Relation of the Lord *la Ware.*

MY Lords, now by accident returned from my charge at *Virginia,* contrary either to my owne desire, or other mens expectations, who spare not to censure me, in point of dutie, and to discourse and question the reason, though they apprehend not the true cause of my returne, I am forced out of a willingnesse to satisfie euery man, to deliuer vnto your Lordships and the rest of this assemblie, in what state I haue liued euer since my arriuall to the Colonie, what hath beene the iust cause of my sudden departure, and on what tearmes I haue left the same, the rather because I perceiue, that since my comming into *England,* such a coldnesse and irresolution is bred in many of the Aduenturers, that some of them seeke to withdraw their payments, by which the action must be supported, making this my returne colour of their needlesse backwardnesse and vniust protraction: which that you may the better vnderstand, I was welcomed to *James* towne by a violent ague; being cured of it, within three weekes after I began to be distempered with other grieuous sicknesses which successiuely and seuerally assailed me, for besides a relapse into the former disease, which with much more violence held me more than a moneth, and brought me to greater weaknesse; the flux surprised mee, and kept me many daies, then the crampe assaulted my weake body with strong paines, and after, the gout; all those drew me to that weaknesse, being vnable to stirre, brought vpon me the scuruie, which though in others it be a sicknesse of slothfulnesse, yet was it in me an effect of weaknesse, which neuer left me, till I was ready to leaue the world.

In these extremities I resolued to consult with my friends, who finding nature spent in me, and my body almost consumed, my paines likewise daily increasing, gaue me aduice to preferre a hopefull recouerie, before an assured ruine, which must necessarily haue ensued, had I liued but twentie daies longer in *Virginia,* wanting at that instant both food and Physicke, fit to remedie such extraordinary diseases; wherefore I shipped my selfe with Doctor *Bohun* and Captaine *Argall,* for *Meuis* in the West *Indies,* but being crossed with Southerly winds, I was forced to shape my course for the Westerne Iles, where I found helpe for my health, and my sicknesse asswaged, by the meanes of fresh dyet, especially Oranges and Limons, and vndoubted remedie for that disease: then I intended to haue returned backe againe to *Virginia,* but I was aduised not to hazard my selfe, before I had perfectly recouered my strength: so I came for *England;* in which accident, I doubt not but men of iudgement will imagine, there would more preiudice haue happened by my death there, than I hope can doe by my returne.

For the Colony I left it to the charge of Captaine *George Piercie,* a Gentleman of honour and resolution, vntill the comming of Sir *Thomas Dale,* whose Commission was likewise to bee determined vpon the arriuall of Sir *Thomas Gates,* according to the order your Lordships appointed: the number I left were about two hundred, the most in health, and prouided of at least ten moneths victuall, and the Countrie people tractable and friendly. What other defects they had, I found by Sir *Thomas Gates* at the Cowes; his Fleet was sufficiently furnished with supplies, but when it shall please God that Sir *Thomas Dale,* and Sir *Thomas Gates* shall arriue in *Virginia* with the extraordinarie supply of 100. Kine, and 200. Swine, besides store of other prouision, for the maintenance of the Colonie, there will appeare that successe in the action, as shall giue no man cause of distrust, that hath already aduentured, but incourage euery good minde to further so good a worke, as will redound both to the glory of God, to the credit of our nation,

100. Kine and 200. Swine sent to *Virginia.*

nation, and the comfort of all those that haue beene instruments in the furthering of it. *Out of the Lord* la Wares *discourse, published by Authoritie,* 1611.

The gouernment surrendred to Sir Thomas Dale, *who arriued in* Virginia *the tenth of May,* 1611. *out of Master* Hamors *Booke.*

1611. Sir *Thomas Smith* Treasurer. The arriuall of Sir *Thomas Dale.*

BEfore the Lord *la Ware* arriued in *England*, the Councell and Companie had dispatched away Sir *Thomas Dale* with three ships, men and cattell, and all other prouisions necessarie for a yeere; all which arriued well the tenth of May 1611. where he found them growing againe to their former estate of penurie, being so improuident as not to put Corne in the ground for their bread, but trusted to the store, then furnished but with three moneths prouision; his first care therefore was to imploy all hands about setting of Corne, at the two Forts at *Kecoughtan*, *Henry* and *Charles*, whereby, the season then not fully past, though about the end of May, wee had an indifferent crop of good Corne.

His preparation to build a new towne.

This businesse taken order for, and the care and trust of it committed to his vnder-Officers, to *Iames* towne he hastened, where most of the companie were at their daily and vsuall works, bowling in the streets; these hee imployed about necessarie workes, as felling of Timber, repayring their houses ready to fall on their heads, and prouiding pales, posts and railes, to impale his purposed new towne, which by reason of his ignorance, being but newly arriued, hee had not resolued where to seat; therefore to better his knowledge, with one hundred men he spent some time in viewing the Riuer of *Nausamund*, in despight of the *Indians* then our enemies; then our owne Riuer to the Fales, where vpon a high land, inuironed with the maine Riuer, some twelue miles from the Fales, by *Arsahattock*, he resolued to plant his new towne.

It was no small trouble to reduce his people so timely to good order, being of so ill a condition, as may well witnesse his seueritie and strict imprinted booke of Articles, then needfull with all extremitie to be executed; now much mitigated; so as if his Lawes had not beene so strictly executed, I see not how the vtter subuersion of the Colonie should haue beene preuented, witnesse *Webbes* and *Prices* designe the first yeere, since that of *Abbots*, and others, more dangerous than the former. Here I entreat your patience for an Apologie, though not a pardon. This *Ieffrey Abbots*, how euer this Author censures him, and the Gouernour executes him, I know he had long serued both in *Ireland* and *Netherlands*, here hee was a Sargeant of my Companie, and I neuer saw in *Virginia* a more sufficient Souldier, lesse turbulent, a better wit, more hardy or industrious, nor any more forward to cut off them that sought to abandon the Countrie, or wrong the Colonie; how ingratefully those deserts might bee rewarded, enuied or neglected, or his farre inferiors preferred to ouer-top him, I know not, but such occasions might moue a Saint, much more a man, to an vnaduised passionate impatience, but how euer, it seemes he hath beene punished for his offences, that was neuer rewarded for his deserts. And euen this Summer *Cole* and *Kitchins* plot with three more, bending their course to *Ocanahowan*, fiue daies iourney from vs, where they report are *Spaniards* inhabiting. These were cut off by the Saluages, hired by vs to hunt them home to receiue their deserts: So as Sir *Thomas Dale* hath not beene so tyrannous nor seuere by the halfe, as there was occasion, and iust cause for it, and though the manner was not vsuall, wee were rather to haue regard to those, whom we would haue terrified and made fearefull to commit the like offences, than to the offenders iustly condemned, for amongst them so hardned in euill, the feare of a cruell, painfull and vnusuall death more restraines them, than death it selfe. Thus much I haue proceeded of his endeuours, vntill the comming of Sir *Thomas Gates*, in preparing himselfe to proceed as he intended.

Diuers mutinie suppressed.

Now

Now in *England* againe to second this noble Knight, the Counsell and Companie with all possible expedition prepared for Sir *Thomas Gates* six tall ships, with three hundred men, and one hundred Kine and other Cattell, with munition and all other manner of prouision that could be thought needfull; and about the first or second of August, 1611. arriued safely at *Iames* towne.

The gouernment returned againe to Sir Thomas Gates, 1611.

THese worthy Knights being met, after their welcoming salutations, Sir *Thomas Dale* acquainted him what he had done, and what he intended, which designe Sir *Thomas Gates* well approuing, furnished him with three hundred and fiftie men, such as himselfe made choice of. In the beginning of September, 1611. hee set saile, and arriued where hee intended to build his new towne: within ten or twelue daies he had inuironed it with a pale, and in honour of our noble Prince *Henry*, called it *Henrico*. The next worke he did, was building at each corner of the Towne, a high commanding Watch-house, a Church, and Store-houses; which finished, hee began to thinke vpon conuenient houses for himselfe and men, which with all possible speed hee could he effected, to the great content of his companie, and all the Colonie.

The second arriuall of Sir *Thomas Gates*.

This towne is situated vpon a necke of a plaine rising land, three parts inuironed with the maine Riuer, the necke of land well impaled, makes it like an Ile; it hath three streets of well framed houses, a handsome Church, and the foundation of a better laid, to bee built of Bricke, besides Store-houses, Watch-houses, and such like: Vpon the verge of the Riuer there are fiue houses, wherein liue the honester sort of people, as Farmers in *England*, and they keepe continuall centinell for the townes securitie. About two miles from the towne, into the Maine, is another pale, neere two miles in length, from Riuer to Riuer, guarded with seuerall Commanders, with a good quantitie of Corne-ground impailed, sufficiently secured to maintaine more than I suppose will come this three yeeres.

The building of *Henrico*.

On the other side of the Riuer, for the securitie of the towne, is intended to be impaled for the securitie of our Hogs, about two miles and a halfe, by the name of *Hope in Faith*, and *Coxendale*, secured by fiue of our manner of Forts, which are but Palisadoes, called *Charitie* Fort, *Mount Malado*, a guest house for sicke people, a high seat and wholsome aire, *Elisabeth* Fort, and Fort *Patience*: And here hath Master *Whitaker* chosen his Parsonage, impaled a faire framed Parsonage, and one hundred acres called *Rocke hall*, but these are not halfe finished.

About Christmas following, in this same yeere 1611. in regard of the iniurie done vs by them of *Apamatuck*, Sir *Thomas Dale*, without the losse of any, except some few Saluages, tooke it and their Corne, being but fiue miles by land from *Henrico*, and considering how commodious it might be for vs, resolued to possesse and plant it, and at the instant called it the new *Bermudas*, whereunto hee hath laid out and annexed to the belonging freedome and corporation for euer, many miles of Champian and Woodland ground in seuerall hundreds, as the vpper and nether hundreds, *Rochdale* hundred, West *Sherly* hundred, and *Digs* his hundred. In the nether hundred he first began to plant, for there is the most Corne-ground, and with a pale of two miles, cut ouer from Riuer to Riuer, whereby we haue secured eight *English* miles in compasse; vpon which circuit, within halfe a mile of each other, are many faire houses already built, besides particular mens houses neere to the number of fiftie. *Rochdale*, by a crosse pale welnigh foure miles long, is also planted with houses along the pale, in which hundred our Hogs and Cattell haue twentie miles circuit to graze in securely. The building of the Citie is referred till our haruest be in, which he intends to make a retreat against any forraigne enemie.

The building the *Bermudas*.

About fiftie miles from these is *Iames* towne, vpon a fertill *peninsula*, which although

though somerly scandaled for an vnhealthfull aire, wee finde it as healthfull as any other part of the Countrie; it hath two rowes of houses of framed timber, and some of them two stories, and a garret higher, three large Store-houses ioined together in length, and hee hath newly strongly impaled the towne. This Ile, and much ground about it, is much inhabited: To *Kecoughtan* we accounted it fortie miles, where they liue well with halfe that allowance the rest haue from the store, because of the extraordinarie quantitie of Fish, Fowle and Deere; as you may reade at large in the Discoueries of Captaine *Smith*. And thus I haue truly related vnto you the present estate of that small part of *Virginia* wee frequent and possesse.

1612. Sir *Thomas Smith* Treasurer. Captaine *Argals* arriuall.

Since there was a ship fraughted with prouision, and fortie men; and another since then with the like number and prouision, to stay twelue moneths in the Countrie, with Captaine *Argall*, which was sent not long after. After hee had recreated and refreshed his Companie, hee was sent to the Riuer *Patawomeake*, to trade for Corne, the Saluages about vs hauing small quarter, but friends and foes as they found aduantage and opportunitie: But to conclude our peace, thus it happened. Captaine *Argall*, hauing entred into a great acquaintance with *Iapazaws*, an old friend of Captaine *Smiths*, and so to all our Nation, euer since hee discouered the Countrie: hard by him there was *Pocahontas*, whom Captaine *Smiths* Relations intituleth the Numparell of *Virginia*, and though she had beene many times a preseruer of him and the whole Colonie, yet till this accident shee was neuer seene at *Iames* towne since his departure, being at *Patawomeke*, as it seemes, thinking her selfe vnknowne, was easily by her friend *Iapazaws* perswaded to goe abroad with him and his wife to see the ship, for Captaine *Argall* had promised him a Copper Kettle to bring her but to him, promising no way to hurt her, but keepe her till they could conclude a peace with her father; the Saluage for this Copper Kettle would haue done any thing, it seemed by the Relation; for though she had seene and beene in many ships, yet hee caused his wife to faine how desirous she was to see one, and that hee offered to beat her for her importunitie, till she wept. But at last he told her, if *Pocahontas* would goe with her, hee was content: and thus they betraied the poore innocent *Pocahontas* aboord, where they were all kindly feasted in the Cabbin. *Iapazaws* treading oft on the Captaines foot, to remember he had done his part, the Captaine when he saw his time, perswaded *Pocahontas* to the Gun-roome, faining to haue some conference with *Iapazaws*, which was onely that she should not perceiue hee was any way guiltie of her captiuitie: so sending for her againe, hee told her before her friends, she must goe with him, and compound peace betwixt her Countrie and vs, before she euer should see *Powhatan*, whereat the old Iew and his wife began to howle and crie as fast as *Pocahontas*, that vpon the Captaines faire perswasions, by degrees pacifying her selfe, and *Iapazaws* and his wife, with the Kettle and other toies, went merrily on shore, and shee to *Iames* towne. A messenger forthwith was sent to her father, that his daughter *Pocahontas* he loued so dearely, he must ransome with our men, swords, peeces, tooles, &c. hee trecherously had stolne.

How *Pocahontas* was taken prisoner.

This vnwelcome newes much troubled *Powhatan*, because hee loued both his daughter and our commodities well, yet it was three moneths after ere hee returned vs any answer: then by the perswasion of the Councell, he returned seuen of our men, with each of them an vnseruiceable Musket, and sent vs word, that when wee would deliuer his daughter, hee would make vs satisfaction for all iniuries done vs, and giue vs fiue hundred bushels of Corne, and for euer be friends with vs. That he sent, we receiued in part of payment, and returned him this answer: That his daughter should be well vsed, but we could not beleeue the rest of our armes were either lost or stolne from him, and therefore till hee sent them, we would keepe his daughter.

Seuen *English* returned from *Powhatan* prisoners.

This answer, it seemed, much displeased him, for we heard no more from him a long

long time after, when with Captaine *Argals* ship, and some other vessels belonging to the Colonie, Sir *Thomas Dale*, with a hundred and fiftie men well appointed, went vp into his owne Riuer, to his chiefe habitation, with his daughter; with many scornfull brauado's they affronted vs, proudly demanding why wee came thither; our reply was, Wee had brought his daughter, and to receiue the ransome for her that was promised, or to haue it perforce. They nothing dismayed thereat, told vs, We were welcome if wee came to fight, for they were prouided for vs, but aduised vs, if wee loued our liues to retire; else they would vse vs as they had done Captaine *Ratcliffe*: We told them, wee would presently haue a better answer; but we were no sooner within shot of the shore than they let flie their Arrowes among vs in the ship.

Sir *Thomas Dale* his voyage to *Pamavuke*.

Being thus iustly prouoked, wee presently manned our Boats, went on shore, burned all their houses, and spoiled all they had we could finde; and so the next day proceeded higher vp the Riuer, where they demanded why wee burnt their houses, and wee, why they shot at vs: They replyed, it was some stragling Saluage, with many other excuses, they intended no hurt, but were our friends: We told them, wee came not to hurt them, but visit them as friends also. Vpon this we concluded a peace, and forthwith they dispatched messengers to *Powhatan*, whose answer, they told vs, wee must expect foure and twentie houres ere the messengers could returne: Then they told vs, our men were runne away for feare we would hang them, yet *Powhatans* men were runne after them; as for our Swords and Peeces, they should be brought vs the next day, which was only but to delay time; for the next day they came not. Then we went higher, to a house of *Powhatans*, called *Matchot*, where we saw about foure hundred men well appointed; here they dared vs to come on shore, which wee did; no shew of feare they made at all, nor offered to resist our landing, but walking boldly vp and downe amongst vs, demanded to conferre with our Captaine, of his comming in that manner, and to haue truce till they could but once more send to their King to know his pleasure, which if it were not agreeable to their expectation, then they would fight with vs, and defend their owne as they could, which was but onely to deferre the time, to carrie away their prouision; yet wee promised them truce till the next day at noone, and then if they would fight with vs, they should know when we would begin by our Drums and Trumpets.

A man shot in the forehead.

Vpon this promise, two of *Powhatans* sonnes came vnto vs to see their sister, at whose sight, seeing her well, though they heard to the contrarie, they much reioiced, promising they would perswade her father to redeeme her, and for euer be friends with vs. And vpon this, the two brethren went aboord with vs, and we sent Master *Iohn Rolfe* and Master *Sparkes* to *Powhatan*, to acquaint him with the businesse; kindly they were entertained, but not admitted the presence of *Powhatan*, but they spoke with *Opechaucanough*, his brother and successor; hee promised to doe the best he could to *Powhatan*, all might be well. So it being Aprill, and time to prepare our ground and set our Corne, we returned to *Iames* Towne, promising the forbearance of their performing their promise, till the next haruest.

Two of *Powhatans* sonnes come to see *Pocahontas*.

Long before this, Master *Iohn Rolfe*, an honest Gentleman, and of good behauiour, had beene in loue with *Pocahontas*, and she with him, which thing at that instant I made knowne to Sir *Thomas Dale* by a letter from him, wherein hee intreated his aduice, and she acquainted her brother with it, which resolution Sir *Thomas Dale* well approued: the brute of this mariage came soone to the knowledge of *Powhatan*, a thing acceptable to him, as appeared by his sudden consent, for within ten daies he sent *Opachisco*, an old Vncle of hers, and two of his sons, to see the manner of the mariage, and to doe in that behalfe what they were requested, for the confirmation thereof, as his deputie; which was accordingly done about the first of Aprill: And euer since wee haue had friendly trade and commerce, as well with *Powhatan* himselfe, as all his subiects.

The mariage of *Pocahontas* to Master *Iohn Rolfe*.
1613.
Sir *Thomas Smith* Treasurer.

The *Chicahamaniae* desire friendship.

Besides this, by the meanes of *Powhatan*, we became in league with our next neighbours, the *Chicahamanias*, a lustie and a daring people, free of themselues. These people, so soone as they heard of our peace with *Powhatan*, sent two messengers with presents to Sir *Thomas Dale*, and offered them his seruice, excusing all former iniuries, hereafter they would euer be King *Iames* his subiects, and relinquish the name of *Chickahamania*, to be called *Tassautessus*, as they call vs, and Sir *Thomas Dale* there Gouernour, as the Kings Deputie; onely they desired to be gouerned by their owne Lawes, which is eight of their Elders as his substitutes. This offer he kindly accepted, and appointed the day hee would come to visit them.

When the appointed day came, Sir *Thomas Dale* and Captaine *Argall* with fiftie men well appointed, went to *Chickahamania*, where wee found the people expecting our comming, they vsed vs kindly, and the next morning sate in counsell, to conclude their peace vpon these conditions:

Articles of Peace

First, they should for euer bee called Englishmen, *and bee true subiects to King* Iames *and his Deputies.*

Secondly, neither to kill nor detaine any of our men, nor cattell, but bring them home.

Thirdly, to bee alwaies ready to furnish vs with three hundred men, against the Spaniards or any.

Fourthly, they shall not enter our townes, but send word they are new Englishmen.

Fiftly, that euery fighting man, at the beginning of haruest, shall bring to our store two bushels of Corne, for tribute, for which they shall receiue so many Hatchets.

Lastly, the eight chiefe men should see all this performed, or receiue the punishment themselues: for their diligence they should haue a red coat, a copper chaine, and King Iames *his picture, and be accounted his Noblemen.*

All this they concluded with a generall assent, and a great shout to confirme it: then one of the old men began an Oration, bending his speech first to the old men, then to the young, and then to the women and children, to make them vnderstand how strictly they were to obserue these conditions, and we would defend them from the furie of *Powhatan*, or any enemie whatsoeuer, and furnish them with Copper, Beads, and Hatchets; but all this was rather for feare *Powhatan* and we, being so linked together, would bring them againe to his subiection; the which to preuent, they did rather chuse to be protected by vs, than tormented by him, whom they held a Tyrant. And thus wee returned againe to *Iames* towne.

The benefit of libertie in the planters.

When our people were fed out of the common store, and laboured iointly together, glad was he could slip from his labour, or slumber ouer his taske he cared not how, nay, the most honest among them would hardly take so much true paines in a weeke, as now for themselues they will doe in a day, neither cared they for the increase, presuming that howsoeuer the haruest prospered, the generall store must maintaine them, so that wee reaped not so much Corne from the labours of thirtie, as now three or foure doe prouide for themselues. To preuent which, Sir *Thomas Dale* hath allotted euery man three Acres of cleare ground, in the nature of Farmes, except the *Bermudas*, who are exempted, but for one moneths seruice in the yeere, which must neither bee in seed-time, nor haruest; for which doing, no other dutie they pay yeerely to the store, but two barrels and a halfe of Corne (from all those Farmers, whereof the first was *William Spence*, an honest, valiant, and an industrious man, and hath continued from 1607. to this present) from those is expected such a contribution to the store, as wee shall neither want for our selues, nor to entertaine our supplies; for the rest, they are to worke eleuen moneths for the store, and hath one moneth onely allowed them to get prouision to keepe them for twelue, except two bushels of Corne they haue out of the store; if those can liue so, why should any feare staruing, and it were much better to denie them passage, that would not ere they come, bee content to ingage themselues to those conditions: for onely from the slothfull and idle drones,

Ensigne *Spence* the first Farmer in *Virginia*.

drones, and none else, hath sprung the manifold imputations, *Virginia* innocently hath vndergone; and therefore I would deter such from comming here, that cannot well brooke labour, except they will vndergoe much punishment and penurie, if they escape the skuruie: but for the industrious, there is reward sufficient, and if any thinke there is nothing but bread, I referre you to his relations that discouered the Countrie first.

The gouernment left to Sir Thomas Dale *vpon Sir* Thomas Gates *returne for* England.

Captaine *Argals* voyage to Port *Royall.*

SIr *Thomas Dale* vnderstanding there was a plantation of *Frenchmen* in the north part of *Virginia*, about the degrees of 45. sent Captaine *Argall* to Port *Royall* and *Sancta Crux*, where finding the *Frenchmen* abroad dispersed in the Woods, surprized their Ship and Pinnace, which was but newly come from *France*, wherein was much good apparel, and other prouision, which he brought to *Iames* towne, but the men escaped, and liued among the Saluages of those Countries.

1614. Sir *Thomas Smith* Treasurer.

It pleased Sir *Thomas Dale*, before my returne to *England*, because I would be able to speake somewhat of my owne knowledge, to giue mee leaue to visit *Powhatan* and his Court: being prouided, I had *Thomas Salnage* with mee, for my Interpreter, with him and two Saluages for guides, I went from the *Bermuda* in the morning, and came to *Matchot* the next night, where the King lay vpon the Riuer of *Pamavuke*; his entertainment was strange to me, the boy he knew well, and told him; My child, I gaue you leaue, being my boy, to goe see your friends, and these foure yeeres I haue not seene you, nor heard of my owne man *Namoutack* I sent to *England*, though many ships since haue beene returned thence: Hauing done with him, hee began with mee, and demanded for the chaine of pearle he sent his brother Sir *Thomas Dale* at his first arriuall, which was a token betwixt them, when euer hee should send a messenger from himselfe to him, he should weare that chaine about his necke, since the peace was concluded, otherwaies he was to binde him and send him home.

Master *Hamars* iourney to *Powhatan.*

It is true Sir *Thomas Dale* had sent him such word, and gaue his Page order to giue it me, but he forgot it, and till this present I neuer heard of it, yet I replyed I did know there was such an order, but that was when vpon a sudden he should haue occasion to send an *Englishman* without an *Indian* Guide; but if his owne people should conduct his messenger, as two of his did me who knew my message, it was sufficient; with which answer he was contented, and so conducted vs to his house, where was a guard of two hundred Bow-men, that alwaies attend his person. The first thing he did, he offered me a pipe of Tobacco, then asked mee how his brother Sir *Thomas Dale* did, and his daughter, and vnknowne sonne, and how they liued, loued and liked; I told him his brother was well, and his daughter so contented, she would not liue againe with him; whereat he laughed, and demanded the cause of my comming: I told him my message was priuate, and I was to deliuer it onely to himselfe and *Papaschicher*, one of my guides that was acquainted with it; instantly he commanded all out of the house, but onely his two Queenes, that alwaies sit by him, and bade me speake on.

His message to *Powhatan.*

I told him, by my Interpreter, Sir *Thomas Dale* hath sent you two pieces of Copper, fiue strings of white and blue Beads, fiue woodden Combes, ten Fishhookes, a paire of Kniues, and that when you would send for it, hee would giue you a Grind-stone; all this pleased him: but then I told him his brother *Dale*, hearing of the fame of his youngest daughter, desiring in any case he would send her by me vnto him, in testimonie of his loue, as well for that he intended to marry her, as the desire her sister had to see her, because being now one people, and hee desirous for euer to dwell in his Countrie, he conceiued there could not be a truer assurance of peace and friendship, than in such a naturall band of an vnited vnion.

I needed not entreat his answer by his oft interrupting mee in my speech, and presently with much grauitie he thus replyed.

Powhatans answer.

I gladly accept your salute of loue and peace, which while I liue, I shall exactly keepe, his pledges thereof I receiue with no lesse thanks, although they are not so ample as formerly he had receiued; but for my daughter, I haue sold herwithin this few daies to a great Werowance, for two bushels of Rawrenoke, three daies iournie from me. I replyed, I knew his greatnesse in restoring the Rawrenoke, might call her againe to gratifie his brother, and the rather, because she was but twelue yeeres old, assuring him, besides the band of peace, hee should haue for her, three times the worth of the Rawrenoke, in Beads, Copper, Hatchets, &c. His answer was, he loued his daughter as his life, and though hee had many children, hee delighted in none so much as shee, whom if he should not often behold, he could not possibly liue, which she liuing with vs he could not do, hauing resolued vpon no termes to put himselfe into our hands, or come amongst vs; therefore desired me to vrge him no further, but returne his brother this answer: That I desire no former assurance of his friendship, than the promise hee hath made, from me he hath a pledge, one of my daughters, which so long as she liues shall be sufficient, when she dies, he shall haue another: I hold it not a brotherly part to desire to bereaue me of my two children at once. Farther, tell him though he had no pledge at all, hee need not distrust any iniurie from me or my people; there haue beene too many of his men and mine slaine, and by my occasion there shall neuer be more, (I which haue power to performe it, haue said it) although I should haue iust cause, for I am now old, & would gladly end my daies in peace; if you offer me iniurie, my countrie is large enough to goe from you: Thus much I hope will satisfie my brother. Now because you are wearie, and I sleepie, wee will thus end. So commanding vs victuall and lodging, we rested that night, and the next morning he came to visit vs, and kindly conducted vs to the best cheere hee had. *William Parker.*

William Parker recouered.

While I here remained, by chance came an *Englishman*, whom there had beene surprized three yeeres agoe at Fort *Henry*, growne so like, both in complexion and habit like a Saluage, I knew him not, but by his tongue: hee desired mee to procure his libertie, which I intended, and so farre vrged *Powhatan*, that he grew discontented, and told mee, You haue one of my daughters, and I am content, but you cannot see one of your men with mee, but you must haue him away, or breake friendship; if you must needs haue him, you shall goe home without guides, and if any euill befall you, thanke your selues: I told him I would, but if I returned not well, hee must expect a reuenge, and his brother might haue iust cause to suspect him. So in passion he left me till supper, and then gaue me such as hee had with a cheerefull countenance: About midnight hee awaked vs, and promised in the morning my returne with *Parker*; but I must remember his brother to send him ten great pieces of Copper, a Shauing-knife, a Frowe, a Grindstone, a Net, Fish-hookes, and such toies; which lest I should forget, he caused me write in a table-booke he had; how euer he got it, it was a faire one, I desired hee would giue it me; he told me, no, it did him much good in shewing to strangers, yet in the morning when we departed, hauing furnished vs well with prouision, he gaue each of vs a Bucks skin as well dressed as could be, and sent two more to his sonne and daughter: And so we returned to *Iames* towne. *Written by Master* Ralph Hamor *and* Iohn Rolph.

From a letter of Sir *Thomas Dale* and Master *Whitakers.*

I haue read the substance of this relation, in a Letter written by Sir *Thomas Dale*, another by Master *Whitaker*, and a third by Master *Iohn Rolfe*; how carefull they were to instruct her in Christianity, and how capable and desirous shee was thereof, after she had beene some time thus tutored, shee neuer had desire to goe to her father, nor could well endure the society of her owne nation: the true affection she constantly bare her husband was much, and the strange apparitions and violent passions he endured for her loue, as he deeply protested, was wonderfull, ful,and she openly renounced her countries idolatry,confessed the faith of Christ, and was baptized, but either the coldnesse of the aduenturers, or the bad vsage of that was collected, or both, caused this worthy Knight to write thus. Oh why should so many Princes and Noblemen ingage themselues, and thereby intermedling herein, haue caused a number of soules transport themselues, and be transported hither? Why should they, I say, relinquish this so glorious an action: for if their ends be to build God a Church, they ought to perseuere; if otherwise, yet their honour ingageth them to be constant; howsoeuer they stand affected, here is enough to content them. These are the things haue animated me to stay a little season from them, I am bound in conscience to returne vnto; leauing all contenting pleasures and mundall delights, to reside here with much turmoile, which I will rather doe than see Gods glory diminished, my King and Country dishonoured, and these poore soules I haue in charge reuiued, which would quickly happen if I should leaue them; so few I haue with me fit to command or manage the businesse: Master *Whitaker* their Preacher complaineth, and much museth, that so few of our English Ministers, that were so hot against the surplice and subscription come hether, where neither is spoken of. Doe they not wilfully hide their talents, or keepe themselues at home, for feare of losing a few pleasures; be there not any among them of *Moses* his minde, and of the Apostles,that forsooke all to follow Christ,but I refer them to the Iudge of all hearts, and to the King that shall reward euery one according to his talent. *From Virginia, Iune* 18. 1614.

The businesse being brought to this perfection, Captaine *Argall* returned for *England*, in the latter end of *Iune*, 1614. ariuing in *England*, and bringing this good tidings to the Councell and company by the assistances of Sir *Thomas Gates*, that also had returned from *Virginia* but the March before; it was presently concluded, that to supply this good successe with all expedition, the standing Lottery should be drawne with all diligent conueniency, and that posterity may remember vpon occasion to vse the like according to the declaration, I thinke it not amisse to remember thus much.

The Contents of the declaration of the Lottery published by the Counsell.

IT is apparent to the world, by how many former Proclamations, we manifested our intents, to haue drawn out the great standing Lottery long before this, which not falling out as we desired, and others expected, whose monies are aduentured therein, we thought good therefore for the auoiding all vniust and sinister constructions, to resolue the doubts of all indifferent minded, in three speciall points for their better satisfaction. 1615. Sir *Thomas Smith* Treasurer.

But ere I goe any farther, let vs remember there was a running Lottery, vsed a long time in Saint *Pauls* Church-yard, where this stood, that brought into the Treasury good summes of mony dayly, though the Lot was but small.

Now for the points, the first is, for as much as the Aduenturers came in so slackly for the yeere past, without preiudice to the generality, in losing the blankes and prises, we were forced to petition to the honourable Lords, who out of their noble care to further this Plantation, haue recommended their Letters to the Countries, Cities, and good townes in *England*, which we hope by sending in their voluntary Aduenturers, will sufficiently supply vs.

The second for satisfaction to all honest well affected minds, is, that though this expectation answer not our hopes, yet wee haue not failed in our Christian care, the good of that Colony, to whom we haue lately sent two sundry supplies, and were they but now supplied with more hands, wee should soone resolue the diuision of the Country by Lot, and so lessen the generall charge.

The third is our constant resolution, that seeing our credits are so farre ingaged to to the honourable Lords and the whole State, for the drawing this great Lottery, which we intend ſhall be without delay, the 26. of Iune next, deſiring all ſuch as haue vndertaken with bookes to ſolicit their friends, that they will not with-hold their monies till the laſt moneth be expired, leſt we be vnwillingly forced to proportion a leſſe value and number of our Blankes and Priſes which hereafter followeth.

Welcomes.

	Crownes.
TO him that firſt ſhall be drawne out with a blanke,	100
To the ſecond,	50
To the third,	25
To him that euery day during the drawing of this Lottery, ſhall bee firſt drawne out with a blanke,	10

Prizes.

	Crownes.
1 Great Prize of	4500
2 Great Prizes, each of	2000
4 Great Prizes, each of	1000
6 Great Prizes, each of	500
10 Prizes, each of	300
20 Prizes, each of	200
100 Prizes, each of	100
200 Prizes, each of	50
400 Prizes, each of	20
1000 Prizes, each of	10
1000 Prizes, each of	8
1000 Prizes, each of	6
4000 Prizes, each of	4
1000 Prizes, each of	3
1000 Prizes, each of	2

Rewards.

	Crownes
TO him that ſhall be laſt drawne out with a blanke,	25
To him that putteth in the greateſt Lot, vnder one name,	400
To him that putteth in the ſecond greateſt number,	300
To him that putteth in the third greateſt number,	200
To him that putteth in the fourth greateſt number,	100

If diuers be of equall number, their rewards are to be diuided proportionally.

Addition of new Rewards.

	Crownes.
THe blanke that ſhall bee drawne out next before the great Prize ſhall haue	25
The blanke that ſhall be drawne out next after the ſaid great Prize	25
The blancks that ſhall be drawne out immediatly before the two next great Prizes, ſhall haue each of them	20
The ſeuerall blankes next after them, each ſhall haue	20
The ſeuerall blankes next before the foure great Prizes, each ſhall haue	15
The ſeuerall blankes next after them, each ſhall haue	15
The ſeuerall blankes next before the ſix great Prizes, each ſhall haue	10
The ſeuerall blankes next after them, each ſhall haue	10

The prizes, welcomes, and rewards, shall be payed in ready Mony, Plate, or other goods reasonably rated; if any dislike of the plate or goods, he shall haue mony, abating only the tenth part, except in small prizes of ten Crownes or vnder.

The mony for the Aduenturers is to be paied to Sir *Thomas Smith*, Knight, and Treasurer for *Virginia*, or such Officers as he shall apoint in City or Country, vnder the common seale of the company for the receit thereof.

All prizes, welcomes and rewards drawne where euer they dwell, shall of the Treasurer haue present pay, and whosoeuer vnder one name or poesie payeth three pound in ready money, shall receiue six shillings and eight pence, or a siluer spoone of that value at his choice.

About this time it chanced a Spanish ship, beat too and againe before point *Comfort*, and at last sent a shore their boat, as desirous of a Pilot. Captaine *Iames Dauis* the gouernor, immediatly gaue them one, but he was no sooner in the boat, but a way they went with him, leauing three of their companions behind them; this sudden accident occasioned some distrust, and a strict examination of those three thus left, yet with as good vsage as our estate could afford them. They only confessed hauing lost their Admirall, accident had forced them into those parts, and two of them were Captaines, and in chiefe authority in the fleet, thus they liued till one of them was found to be an Englishman, and had been the Spaniards Pilot for *England* in 88. and hauing here induced some male-contents, to beleeue his proiects, to run away with a small barke, which was apprehended, some executed, and he expecting but the Hangmans curtesie, directly confessed that two or three Spanish ships was at Sea, purposely to discouer the estate of the Colony, but their Commission was not to be opened till they arriued in the Bay, so that of any thing more he was vtterly ignorant. One of the Spaniards at last dyed, the other was sent for *England*, but this reprieued, till Sir *Thomas Dale* hanged him at Sea in his voyage homeward; the English Pilot they carried for Spaine, whom after a long time imprisonment, with much sute was returned for *England*.

A Spanish Ship in *Virginia*.

Whilst those things were effecting, Sir *Thomas Dale*, hauing setled to his thinking all things in good order, made choice of one Master *George Yearly*, to be Deputy Gouernour in his absence, and so returned for *England*, accompanied with *Pocahontas* the Kings Daughter, and Master *Rolfe* her husband, and arriued at *Plimmoth* the 12. of *Iune*. 1616.

1616. Sir *Thomas Smith* Treasurer.

The gouernment left to Captaine Yearly.

NOw a little to commentary vpon all these proceedings, let me leaue but this as a caueat by the way; if the alteration of gouernment hath subuerted great Empires, how dangerous is it then in the infancy of a commonweale? The multiplicity of Gouernors is a great damage to any State, but vncertaine daily changes are burdensome, because their entertainments are chargeable, and many will make hay whilst the sunne doth shine, how euer it shall faire with the generality.

A degression.

This deare bought Land with so much bloud and cost, hath onely made some few rich, and all the rest losers. But it was intended at the first, the first vndertakers should be first preferred and rewarded, and the first aduenturers satisfied, and they of all the rest are the most neglected; and those that neuer aduentured a groat, neuer see the Country, nor euer did any seruice for it, imploied in their places, adorned with their deserts, and inriched with their ruines; and when they are fed fat, then in commeth others so leane as they were, who through their omnipotency doth as much. Thus what one Officer doth, another vndoth, only ayming at their owne ends, thinking all the world derides his dignity, cannot fill his Coffers being in authority with any thing. Euery man hath his minde free, but he can neuer be a true member to that estate, that to enrich himselfe beggers

gers all the Countrie. Which bad course, there are many yet in this noble plantation, whose true honour and worth as much scornes it, as the others loues it; for the Nobilitie and Gentrie, there is scarce any of them expects any thing but the prosperitie of the action: and there are some Merchants and others, I am confidently perswaded, doe take more care and paines, nay, and at their continuall great charge, than they could be hired to for the loue of money, so honestly regarding the generall good of this great worke, they would hold it worse than sacrilege, to wrong it but a shilling, or extort vpon the common souldier a penny. But to the purpose, and to follow the Historie.

The gouernment of Captaine *Yearley.*

Mr. *George Yearly* now inuested Deputie Gouernour by Sr. *Thomas Dale*, applied himselfe for the most part in planting Tobacco, as the most present commoditie they could deuise for a present gaine, so that euery man betooke himselfe to the best place he could for the purpose: now though Sir *Thomas Dale* had caused such an abundance of corne to be planted, that euery man had sufficient, yet the supplies were sent vs, came so vnfurnished, as quickly eased vs of our superfluitie. To relieue their necessities, he sent to the *Chickahamanias* for the tribute Corne Sir *Thomas Dale* and Captaine *Argall* had conditioned for with them: But such a bad answer they returned him, that hee drew together one hundred of his best shot, with whom he went to *Chickahamania*; the people in some places vsed him indifferently, but in most places with much scorne and contempt, telling him he was but Sir *Thomas Dales* man, and they had payed his Master according to condition, but to giue any to him they had no such order, neither would they obey him as they had done his Master; after he had told them his authoritie, and that he had the same power to enforce them that *Dale* had, they dared him to come on shore to fight, presuming more of his not daring, than their owne valours. *Yearly* seeing their insolencies, made no great difficultie to goe on shore at *Ozinies*, and they as little to incounter him: but marching from thence towards *Mamanahunt*, they put themselues in the same order they see vs, lead by their Captaine *Kissanacomen*, Gouernour of *Ozinies*, & so marched close along by vs, each as threatning other who should first begin. But that night we quartered against *Mamanahunt*, and they passed the Riuer. The next day we followed them; there are few places in *Virginia* had then more plaine ground together, nor more plentie of Corne, which although it was but newly gathered, yet they had hid it in the woods where we could not finde it: a good time we spent thus in arguing the cause, the Saluages without feare standing in troupes amongst vs, seeming as if their countenances had beene sufficient to dant vs: what other practises they had I know not; but to preuent the worst, our Captaine caused vs all to make ready, and vpon the word, to let flie among them, where he appointed: others also he commanded to seize on them they could for prisoners; all which being done according to our direction, the Captaine gaue the word, and wee presently discharged, where twelue lay, some dead, the rest for life sprawling on the ground, twelue more we tooke prisoners, two whereof were brothers, two of their eight Elders, the one tooke by Sergeant *Boothe*, the other by *Robert* a *Polonian*; Neere one hundred bushels of Corne we had for their ransomes, which was promised the Souldiers for a reward, but it was not performed: now *Opechankanough* had agreed with our Captaine for the subiecting of those people, that neither hee nor *Powhatan* could euer bring to their obedience, and that he should make no peace with them without his aduice: in our returne by *Ozinies* with our prisoners wee met *Opechankanough*, who with much adoe, fained with what paines hee had procured their peace, the which to requite, they called him the King of *Ozinies*, and brought him from all parts many presents of Beads, Copper, and such trash as they had; here as at many other times wee were beholding to Captaine *Henry Spilman* our Interpreter, a Gentleman had liued long time in this Countrie, and sometimes a prisoner among the Saluages, and done much good seruice, though but badly rewarded. From hence we marcht towards *James* towne, we had three

Twelue Saluages slaine, twelue prisoners taken, and peace concluded.

Boats

Boats loaded with Corne and other luggage, the one of them being more willing to be at *Iames* towne with the newes than the other, was ouerset, and eleuen men cast away with the Boat, Corne and all their prouision; notwithstanding this put all the rest of the Saluages in that feare, especially in regard of the great league we had with *Opechankanough*, that we followed our labours quietly, and in such securitie, that diuers saluages of other Nations, daily frequented vs with what prouisions they could get, and would guide our men on hunting, and oft hunt for vs themselues. Captaine *Yearly* had a Saluage or two so well trained vp to their peeces, they were as expert as any of the *English*, and one hee kept purposely to kill him fowle. There were diuers others had Saluages in like manner for their men. Thus we liued together, as if wee had beene one people, all the time Captaine *Yearley* staied with vs, but such grudges and discontents daily increased among our selues, that vpon the arriuall of Captaine *Argall*, sent by the Councell and Companie to bee our Gouernour, Captaine *Yearley* returned for *England* in the yeere 1617. *From the writings of Captaine* Nathaniel Powell, William Cantrill, *Sergeant* Boothe, Edward Gurganey. Eleuen men cast away. A bad presidene.

During this time, the Lady *Rebecca*, alias *Pocahontas*, daughter to *Powhatan*, by the diligent care of Master *Iohn Rolfe* her husband and his friends, as taught to speake such *English* as might well bee vnderstood, well instructed in Christianitie, and was become very formall and ciuill after our *English* manner; shee had also by him a childe which she loued most dearely, and the Treasurer and Company tooke order both for the maintenance of her and it, besides there were diuers persons of great ranke and qualitie had beene very kinde to her; and before she arriued at London, Captaine *Smith* to deserue her former courtesies, made her qualities knowne to the Queenes most excellent Maiestie and her Court, and writ a little booke to this effect to the Queene: An abstract whereof followeth. *Pocahontas* instructions.

To the most high and vertuous Princesse Queene Anne *of Great Brittanie*.

Most admired Queene,

THe loue I beare my God, my King and Countrie, hath so oft emboldened mee in the worst of extreme dangers, that now honestie doth constraine mee presume thus farre beyond my selfe, to present your Maiestie this short discourse: if ingratitude be a deadly poyson to all honest vertues, I must bee guiltie of that crime if I should omit any meanes to bee thankfull. So it is,

That some ten yeeres agoe being in *Virginia*, and taken prisoner by the power of *Powhatan* their chiefe King, I receiued from this great Saluage exceeding great courtesie, especially from his sonne *Nantaquaus*, the most manliest, comeliest, boldest spirit, I euer saw in a Saluage, and his sister *Pocahontas*, the Kings most deare and wel-beloued daughter, being but a childe of twelue or thirteene yeeres of age, whose compassionate pitifull heart, of my desperate estate, gaue me much cause to respect her: I being the first Christian this proud King and his grim attendants euer saw: and thus inthralled in their barbarous power, I cannot say I felt the least occasion of want that was in the power of those my mortall foes to preuent, notwithstanding al their threats. After some six weeks fatting amongst those Saluage Courtiers, at the minute of my execution, she hazarded the beating out of her owne braines to saue mine, and not onely that, but so preuailed with her father, that I was safely conducted to *Iames* towne, where I found about eight and thirtie miserable poore and sicke creatures, to keepe possession of all those large territories of *Virginia*, such was the weaknesse of this poore Commonwealth, as had the Saluages not fed vs, we directly had starued. A relation to Queene *Anne*, of *Pocahontas*.

And this reliefe, most gracious Queene, was commonly brought vs by this

Lady *Pocahontas*, notwithstanding all these passages when inconstant Fortune turned our peace to warre, this tender Virgin would still not spare to dare to visit vs, and by her our iarres haue beene oft appeased, and our wants still supplyed; were it the policie of her father thus to imploy her, or the ordinance of God thus to make her his instrument, or her extraordinarie affection to our Nation, I know not: but of this I am sure; when her father with the vtmost of his policie and power, sought to surprize mee, hauing but eighteene with mee, the darke night could not affright her from comming through the irkesome woods, and with watered eies gaue me intelligence, with her best aduice to escape his furie; which had hee knowne, hee had surely slaine her. *Iames* towne with her wild traine she as freely frequented, as her fathers habitation; and during the time of two or three yeeres, she next vnder God, was still the instrument to preserue this Colonie from death, famine and vtter confusion, which if in those times had once beene dissolued, *Virginia* might haue line as it was at our first arriuall to this day. Since then, this businesse hauing beene turned and varied by many accidents from that I left it at: it is most certaine, after a long and troublesome warre after my departure, betwixt her father and our Colonie, all which time shee was not heard of, about two yeeres after shee her selfe was taken prisoner, being so detained neere two yeeres longer, the Colonie by that meanes was relieued, peace concluded, and at last reiecting her barbarous condition, was maried to an *English* Gentleman, with whom at this present she is in *England*; the first Christian euer of that Nation, the first *Virginian* euer spake *English*, or had a childe in mariage by an *Englishman*, a matter surely, if my meaning bee truly considered and well vnderstood, worthy a Princes vnderstanding.

Thus most gracious Lady, I haue related to your Maiestie, what at your best leasure our approued Histories will account you at large, and done in the time of your Maiesties life, and howeuer this might bee presented you from a more worthy pen, it cannot from a more honest heart, as yet I neuer begged any thing of the state, or any, and it is my want of abilitie and her exceeding desert, your birth, meanes and authortie, hir birth, vertue, want and simplicitie, doth make mee thus bold, humbly to beseech your Maiestie to take this knowledge of her, though it be from one so vnworthy to be the reporter, as my selfe, her husbands estate not being able to make her fit to attend your Maiestie: the most and least I can doe, is to tell you this, because none so oft hath tried it as my selfe, and the rather being of so great a spirit, how euer her stature: if she should not be well receiued, seeing this Kingdome may rightly haue a Kingdome by her meanes; her present loue to vs and Christianitie, might turne to such scorne and furie, as to diuert all this good to the worst of euill, where finding so great a Queene should doe her some honour more than she can imagine, for being so kinde to your seruants and subiects, would so rauish her with content, as endeare her dearest bloud to effect that, your Maiestie and all the Kings honest subiects most earnestly desire: And so I humbly kisse your gracious hands.

Pocahontas meeting in *England* with Captaine *Smith*.

Being about this time preparing to set saile for *New-England*, I could not stay to doe her that seruice I desired, and she well deserued; but hearing shee was at *Branford* with diuers of my friends, I went to see her: After a modest salutation, without any word, she turned about, obscured her face, as not seeming well contented; and in that humour her husband, with diuers others, we all left her two or three houres, repenting my selfe to haue writ she could speake *English*. But not long after, she began to talke, and remembred mee well what courtesies shee had done: saying, You did promise *Powhatan* what was yours should bee his, and he the like to you; you called him father being in his land a stranger, and by the same reason so must I doe you: which though I would haue excused, I durst not allow of that title, because she was a Kings daughter; with a well set countenance she said, Were you not afraid to come into my fathers Countrie, and caused feare in him and all his people (but mee) and feare you here I should call you father; I tell

tell you then I will, and you shall call mee childe, and so I will bee for euer and euer your Countrieman. They did tell vs alwaies you were dead, and I knew no other till I came to *Plimoth*; yet *Powhatan* did command *Vttamatomakkin* to seeke you, and know the truth, because your Countriemen will lie much.

This Saluage, one of *Powhatans* Councell, being amongst them held an vnderstanding fellow; the King purposely sent him, as they say, to number the people here, and informe him well what wee were and our state. Arriuing at *Plimoth*, according to his directions, he got a long sticke, whereon by notches hee did thinke to haue kept the number of all the men hee could see, but he was quickly wearie of that taske: Comming to *London*, where by chance I met him, hauing renewed our acquaintance, where many were desirous to heare and see his behauiour, hee told me *Powhatan* did bid him to finde me out, to shew him our God, the King, Queene, and Prince, I so much had told them of: Concerning God, I told him the best I could, the King I heard he had seene, and the rest hee should see when he would; he denied euer to haue seene the King, till by circumstances he was satisfied he had: Then he replyed very sadly, You gaue *Powhatan* a white Dog, which *Powhatan* fed as himselfe, but your King gaue me nothing, and I am better than your white Dog.

Vttamacomack, obseruations of his vsage.

The small time I staid in *London*, diuers Courtiers and others, my acquaintances, hath gone with mee to see her, that generally concluded, they did thinke God had a great hand in her conuersion, and they haue seene many *English* Ladies worse fauoured, proportioned and behauioured, and as since I haue heard, it pleased both the King and Queenes Maiestie honourably to esteeme her, accompanied with that honourable Lady the Lady *De la Ware*, and that honourable Lord her husband, and diuers other persons of good qualities, both publikely at the maskes and otherwise, to her great satisfaction and content, which doubtlesse she would haue deserued, had she liued to arriue in *Virginia*.

Pocahontas her entertainment with the Queene.

The gouernment deuolued to Captaine Samuel Argall, 1617.

1617. Sir *Thomas Smith* Treasurer.

THe Treasurer, Councell and Companie, hauing well furnished Captaine *Samuel Argall*, the Lady *Pocahontas* alias *Rebecca*, with her husband and others, in the good ship called the *George*, it pleased God at *Grauesend* to take this young Lady to his mercie, where shee made not more sorrow for her vnexpected death, than ioy to the beholders, to heare and see her make so religious and godly an end. Her little childe *Thomas Rolfe* therefore was left at *Plimoth* with Sir *Lewis Stukly*, that desired the keeping of it. Captaine *Hamar* his vice-Admirall was gone before, but hee found him at *Plimoth*. In March they set saile 1617. and in May he arriued at *Iames* towne, where hee was kindly entertained by Captaine *Yearley* and his Companie in a martiall order, whose right hand file was led by an *Indian*. In *Iames* towne he found but fiue or six houses, the Church downe, the Palizado's broken, the Bridge in pieces, the Well of fresh water spoiled; the Store-house they vsed for the Church, the market-place, and streets, and all other spare places planted with Tobacco, the Saluages as frequent in their houses as themselues, whereby they were become expert in our armes, and had a great many in their custodie and possession, the Colonie dispersed all about, planting *Tobacco*. Captaine *Argall* not liking those proceedings, altered them agreeable to his owne minde, taking the best order he could for repairing those defects which did exceedingly trouble vs; we were constrained euery yeere to build and repaire our old Cottages, which were alwaies a decaying in all places of the Countrie, yea, the very Courts of Guard built by Sir *Thomas Dale*, was ready to fall, and the Palizado's not sufficient to keepe out Hogs. Their number of people were about 400. but not past 200. fit for husbandry and tillage: we found there in all one hundred twentie eight cattell, and fourescore and eight Goats, besides innumerable numbers of Swine, and good

The death of *Pocahontas*.

1000.bushels of Corne from the Saluages.

plentie of Corne in some places, yet the next yeere the Captaine sent out a Frigat and a Pinnace, that brought vs neere six hundred bushels more, which did greatly relieue the whole Colonie: For from the tenants wee seldome had aboue foure hundred bushels of rent Corne to the store, and there was not remaining of the Companies companie, past foure and fiftie men, women and Children.

1618. Sir *Thomas Smith* Treasurer.

This yeere hauing planted our fields, came a great drought, and such a cruell storme of haile, which did such spoile both to the Corne and Tobacco, that wee reaped but small profit, the Magazine that came in the *George*, being fiue moneths in her passage, proued very badly conditioned, but ere she arriued, we had gathered and made vp our Tobacco, the best at three shillings the pound, the rest at eighteene pence.

To supply vs, the Councell and Company with all possible care and diligence, furnished a good ship of some two hundred and fiftie tunne, with two hundred people and the Lord *la Ware*. They set saile in Aprill, and tooke their course by the westerne Iles, where the Gouernour of the Ile of Saint *Michael* receiued the Lord *la Ware*, and honourably feasted him, with all the content hee could giue him. Going from thence, they were long troubled with contrary winds, in which time many of them fell very sicke, thirtie died, one of which number was that most honourable Lord Gouernour the Lord *la Ware*, whose most noble and generous disposition, is well knowne to his great cost, had beene most forward in this businesse for his Countries good: Yet this tender state of *Virginia* was not growne to that maturitie, to maintaine such state and pleasure as was fit for such a personage, with so braue and great attendance: for some small number of aduentrous Gentlemen to make discoueries, and lie in Garrison, ready vpon any occasion to keepe in feare the inconstant Saluages, nothing were more requisite, but to haue more to wait & play than worke, or more commanders and officers than industrious labourers was not so necessarie: for in *Virginia*, a plaine Souldier that can vse a Pick-axe and spade, is better than fiue Knights, although they were Knights that could breake a Lance; for men of great place, not inured to those incounters; when they finde things not sutable, grow many times so discontented, they forget themselues, & oft become so carelesse, that a discontented melancholy brings them to much sorrow, and to others much miserie. At last they stood in for the coast of *New-England*, where they met a small Frenchman, rich of Beuers and other Furres. Though wee had here but small knowledge of the coast nor countrie, yet they tooke such an abundance of Fish and Fowle, and so well refreshed themselues there with wood and water, as by the helpe of God thereby, hauing beene at Sea sixteene weekes, got to *Virginia*, who without this reliefe had beene in great danger to perish. The French-men made them such a feast, with such an abundance of varietie of Fish, Fowle and Fruits, as they all admired, and little expected that wild wildernesse could affoord such wonderfull abundance of plentie. In this ship came about two hundred men, but very little prouision, and the ship called the *Treasurer* came in againe not long after with fortie passengers; the Lord *la Wares* ship lying in *Virginia* three moneths, wee victualled her with threescore bushels of Corne, and eight Hogsheads of flesh, besides other victuall she spent whilest they tarried there: this ship brought vs aduice that great multitudes were a preparing in *England* to bee sent, and relied much vpon that victuall they should finde here: whereupon our Captaine called a Councell, and writ to the Councell here in *England* the estate of the Colonie, and what a great miserie would insue, if they sent not prouision as well as people; and what they did suffer for want of skilfull husbandmen, and meanes to set their Ploughs on worke, hauing as good ground as any man can desire, and about fortie Bulls and Oxen, but they wanted men to bring them to labour, and Irons for the Ploughs, and harnesse for the Cattell. Some thirtie or fortie acres wee had sowne with one Plough, but it stood so long on the ground before it was reaped, it was most shaken, and the rest spoiled with the

The death of the Lord *la Ware*.

They are relieued in *New-England*.

Cattell,

Cattell and Rats in the Barne, but no better Corne could bee for the quantitie.

Richard Killingbeck being with the Captaine at *Kekoughtan*, desired leaue to returne to his wife at *Charles* hundred, hee went to *Iames* towne by water, there he got foure more to goe with him by land, but it proued that he intended to goe trade with the *Indies* of *Chickahamania*, where making shew of the great quantitie of trucke they had, which the Saluages perceiuing, partly for their trucke, partly for reuenge of some friends they pretended should haue beene slaine by Captaine *Yearley*, one of them with an English peece shot *Killingbeck* dead, the other Saluages assaulted the rest and slew them, stripped them, and tooke what they had: But fearing this murther would come to light, and might cause them to suffer for it, would now proceed to the perfection of villanie; for presently they robbed their Machacomocko house of the towne, stole all the *Indian* treasure thereout, and fled into the woods, as other *Indians* related. On Sunday following, one *Farfax* that dwelt a mile from the towne, going to Church, left his wife and three small children safe at home, as he thought, and a young youth: she supposing praier to be done, left the children, and went to meet her husband; presently after came three or foure of those fugitiue Saluages, entred the house, and slew a boy and three children, and also another youth that stole out of the Church in praier time, meeting them, was likewise murdered. Of this disaster the Captaine sent to *Opechankanough* for satisfaction, but he excused the matter, as altogether ignorant of it, at the same time the Saluages that were robbed were complaining to *Opechankanough*, and much feared the English would bee reuenged on them, so that *Opechankanough* sent to Captaine *Argall*, to assure him the peace should neuer be broken by him, desiring that he would not reuenge the iniurie of those fugitiues vpon the innocent people of that towne, which towne he should haue, and sent him a basket of earth, as possession giuen of it, and promised, so soone as possibly they could catch these robbers, to send him their heads for satisfaction, but he neuer performed it. *Samuel Argall, Iohn Rolfe.*

Richard Killingbeck and foure other murdered by the Saluages.

Their Church and Store-house.

Farfax, three children and two boyes also murdered.

A relation from Master Iohn Rolfe, *Iune* 15. 1618.

CONcerning the state of our new Common-wealth, it is somewhat bettered, for we haue sufficient to content our selues, though not in such abundance as is vainly reported in *England*. *Powhatan* died this last Aprill, yet the *Indians* continue in peace. *Itopatin* his second brother succeeds him, and both hee and *Opechankanough* haue confirmed our former league. On the eleuenth of May, about ten of the clocke in the night, happened a most fearefull tempest, but it continued not past halfe an houre, which powred downe hailestones eight or nine inches about, that none durst goe out of their doores, and though it tore the barke and leaues of the trees, yet wee finde not they hurt either man or beast; it fell onely about *Iames* towne, for but a mile to the East, and twentie to the West there was no haile at all. Thus in peace euery man followed his building and planting without any accidents worthy of note. Some priuate differences happened betwixt Captaine *Bruster* and Captaine *Argall*, and Captaine *Argall* and the Companie here in *England*; but of them I am not fully informed, neither are they here for any vse, and therefore vnfit to be remembred. In December one Captaine *Stallings*, an old planter in those parts, being imployed by them of the West countrie for a fishing voyage, in *New-England*, fell foule of a Frenchman whom hee tooke, leauing his owne ship to returne for *England*, himselfe with a small companie remained in the French barke, some small time after vpon the coast, and thence returned to winter in *Virginia*.

Powhatans death.

Haile-stones eight inches about.

1619. Sir *Edwin Sands* Treasurer. Master *Iohn Farer* Deputie.

The

The gouernment surrendred to Sir George Yearley.

FOr to begin with the yeere of our Lord, 1619. there arriued a little Pinnace priuatly from *England* about Easter for Captaine *Argall,* who taking order for his affaires, within foure or fiue daies returned in her, and left for his Deputy, Captaine *Nathaniel Powell.* On the eighteenth of *Aprill,* which was but ten or twelue daies after, arriued Sir *George Yearley,* by whom we vnderstood Sir *Edwin Sands* was chosen Treasurer, and Master *Iohn Farrar* his Deputy, and what great supplies was a preparing to be sent vs, which did rauish vs so much with ioy and content, we thought our selues now fully satisfied, for our long toile and labours, and as happy men as any in the world. Notwithstanding, such an accident hapned Captaine *Stallings,* the next day his ship was cast away, and he not long after slaine in a priuate quarrell. Sir *George Yearly* to beginne his gouernment, added to be of his councell, Captaine *Francis West,* Captaine *Nathaniel Powell,* Master *Iohn Pory,* Master *Iohn Rolfe,* and Master *William Wickam,* and Master *Samuel Macocke,* and propounded to haue a generall assembly with all expedition. Vpon the twelfth of this Moneth, came in a Pinnace of Captaine *Bargraues,* and on the seuenteenth Captaine *Lownes,* and one Master *Euans,* who intended to plant themselues at *Waraskoyack,* but now *Opechankanough* will not come at vs, that causes vs suspect his former promises.

Waraskoyack planted.

In May came in the *Margaret* of *Bristoll,* with foure and thirty men, all well and in health, and also many deuout gifts, and we were much troubled in examining some scandalous letters sent into *England,* to disgrace this Country with barrennesse, to discourage the aduenturers, and so bring it and vs to ruine and confusion; notwithstanding, we finde by them of best experience, an industrious man not other waies imploied, may well tend foure akers of Corne, and 1000. plants of Tobacco, and where they say an aker will yeeld but three or foure barrels, we haue ordinarily foure or fiue, but of new ground six, seuen, and eight, and a barrell of Pease and Beanes, which we esteeme as good as two of Corne, which is after thirty or forty bushels an aker, so that one man may prouide Corne for fiue, and apparell for two by the profit of his Tobacco; they say also English Wheat will yeeld but sixteene bushels an aker, and we haue reaped thirty: besides to manure the Land, no place hath more white and blew Marble than here, had we but Carpenters to build and make Carts and Ploughs, and skilfull men that know how to vse them, and traine vp our cattell to draw them, which though we indeuour to effect, yet our want of experience brings but little to perfection but planting Tobaco, and yet of that many are so couetous to haue much, they make little good; besides there are so many sofisticating Tobaco-mungers in *England,* were it neuer so bad, they would sell it for *Verinas,* and the trash that remaineth should be *Virginia,* such deuilish bad mindes we know some of our owne Country-men doe beare, not onely to the businesse, but also to our mother *England* her selfe; could they or durst they as freely defame her.

A barrell they account foure bushels.

The 25. of *Iune* came in the *Triall* with Corne and Cattell all in safety, which tooke from vs cleerely all feare of famine; then our gouernour and councell caused Burgesses to be chosen in all places, and met at a generall Assembly, where all matters were debated thought expedient for the good of the Colony, and Captaine *Ward* was sent to *Monahigan* in new *England,* to fish in May, and returned the latter end of May, but to small purpose, for they wanted Salt: the *George* also was sent to *New-found-land* with the Cape Merchant, there she bought fish, that defraied her charges, and made a good voyage in seuen weekes. About the last of August came in a dutch man of warre that sold vs twenty Negars, and *Iapazous* King of *Patawomeck,* came to *Iames* towne, to desire two ships to come trade in his Riuer, for a more plentifull yeere of Corne had not beene in a long time, yet very contagious, and by the trechery of one *Poole,* in a manner turned heathen, wee

Their time of Parlament.

were

were very iealous the Saluages would surprize vs. The Gouernours haue bounded foure Corporations; which is the Companies, the Vniuersity, the Gouernours and Gleabe land: Ensigne *Wil. Spencer*, & *Thomas Barret* a Sergeant, with some others of the ancient Planters being set free, we are the first farmers that went forth, and haue chosen places to their content, so that now knowing their owne land, they striue who should exceed in building and planting. The fourth of Nouember the *Bona noua* came in with all her people lusty and well; not long after one Master *Dirmer* sent out by some of *Plimoth* for *New-England*, arriued in a Barke of fiue tunnes, and returned the next Spring; notwithstanding the ill rumours of the vnwholsomnesse of *Iames* towne, the new commers that were planted at old *Paspaheghe*, little more then a mile from it, had their healths better then any in the Country. In December Captaine *Ward* returned from *Patawomeck*, the people there dealt falsly with him, so that hee tooke 800. bushels of Corne from them perforce. Captaine *Woddiffe* of *Bristol* came in not long after, with all his people lusty and in health, and we had two particular Gouernors sent vs, vnder the titles of Deputies to the Company, the one to haue charge of the Colledge Lands, the other of the Companies: Now you are to vnderstand, that because there haue beene many complaints against the Gouernors, Captaines, and Officers in *Virginia*, for buying and selling men and boies, or to bee set ouer from one to another for a yeerely rent, was held in *England* a thing most intolerable, or that the tenants or lawfull seruants should be put from their places, or abridged their Couenants, was so odious, that the very report thereof brought a great scandall to the generall action. The Councell in *England* did send many good and worthy instructions for the amending those abuses, and appointed a hundred men should at the Companies charge be allotted and prouided to serue and attend the Gouernour during the time of his gouernment, which number he was to make good at his departure, and leaue to his Successor in like manner, fifty to the Deputy-Gouernour of the College land, and fifty to the Deputy of the Companies land, fifty to the Treasurer, to the Secretary fiue and twenty, and more to the Marshall and Cape merchant; which they are also to leaue to their successors, and likewise to euery particular Officer such a competency, as he might liue well in his Office, without oppressing any vnder their charge, which good law I pray God it be well obserued, and then we may truly say in *Virginia*, we are the most happy people in the world. *By me* Iohn Rolfe.

Foure corporations named.

Captaine *Wards* exploit.

There went this yeere by the Companies records, 11. ships, and 1216. persons to be thus disposed on: Tenants for the Gouernors land fourescore, besides fifty sent the former spring; for the Companies land a hundred and thirty, for the College a hundred, for the Glebe land fifty, young women to make wiues ninety, seruants for publike seruice fifty, and fifty more whose labours were to bring vp thirty of the infidels children, the rest were sent to priuate Plantations.

The number of Ships and men.

Two persons vnknowne haue giuen faire Plate and Ornaments for two Communion Tables, the one at the College, the other at the Church of Mistris *Mary Robinson*, who towards the foundation gaue two hundred pound. And another vnknowne person sent to the Treasurer fiue hundred and fifty pounds, for the bringing vp of the saluage children in Christianity. Master *Nicholas Farrar* deceased, hath by his Will giuen three hundred pounds to the College, to be paid when there shall be ten young Saluages placed in it, in the meane time foure and twenty pound yeerely to bee distributed vnto three discreet and godly young men in the Colony, to bring vp three wilde young infidels in some good course of life, also there were granted eleuen Pattents, vpon condition to transport people and cattle to increase the Plantations.

Gifts giuen.

But few performe them.

A desperat Sea-fight betwixt two Spanish men of warre, and a small English ship, at the Ile of *Dominica* going to *Virginia*, by Captaine *Anthony Chester*.

1620. The Earle of Southampton Treasurer, and M. *Iohn Ferrar* Deputy.

HAuing taken our iourney towards *Virginia* in the beginning of February, a ship called the *Margaret* and *Iohn*, of one hundred and sixty tuns, eight Iron Peeces and a Falcon, with eightie Passengers besides Sailers; After many tempests and foule weather, about the foureteenth of March we were in thirteene degrees and an halfe of Northerly latitude, where we descried a ship at hull; it being but a faire gale of wind, we edged towards her to see what she was, but she presently set saile, and ran vs quickly out of sight: This made vs keepe our course for *Mettalina*, and the next day passing *Dominica*, we came to an anchor at *Guardalupo*, to take in fresh water. Six French-men there cast away sixteene moneths agoe came aboord vs; they told vs a Spanish man of Warre but seuen daies before was seeking his consort, and this was she we descried at hull. At *Meuis* we intended to refresh our selues, hauing beene eleuen weeks pestered in this vnwholsome ship; but there we found two tall ships with the *Hollanders* colours, but necessitie forcing vs on shore, we anchored faire by them, and in friendly manner sent to hale them: but seeing they were *Spaniards*, retiring to our ship, they sent such a volley of shot after vs, that shot the Boat, split the Oares, and some thorow the clothes, yet not a man hurt; and then followed with their great Ordnance, that many times ouer-racked our ship, which being so cumbred with the Passengers prouisions, our Ordnance was not well fitted, nor any thing as it should haue beene. But perceiuing what they were, we fitted our selues the best we could to preuent a mischiefe, seeing them warp themselues to windward, we thought it not good to be boorded on both sides at an anchor, we intended to set saile, but that the Vice-Admirall battered so hard our star-boord side, that we fell to our businesse, and answered their vnkindnesse with such faire shot from a Demiculuering, that shot her betweene wind and water, whereby she was glad to leaue vs and her Admirall together. Comming faire by our quarter, he tooke in his *Holland* flag, and put forth his Spanish colours, and so haled vs.

A French-man cast away at *Guardalupo*.

The *Spaniards* begin.

The Vice-Admirall shot betweene wind and water.

We quietly and quickly answered him, both what wee were, and whither bound, relating the effect of our Commission, and the cause of our comming thither for water, and not to annoy any of the King of *Spaines* Subiects, nor any. She commanded vs amaine for the King of *Spaine*, we replied with inlarging the particulars what friends both the Kings our Masters were, and as we would doe no wrong, we would take none. They commanded vs aboord to shew our Commission, which we refused, but if they would send their Boat to vs willingly they should see it. But for answer they made two great shot at vs, with a volley of small shot, which caused vs to leaue the decks; then with many ill words they laid vs aboord, which caused vs to raise our maine saile, and giue the word to our small shot which lay close and ready, that paid them in such sort, they quickly retired. The fight continued halfe an houre, as if we had beene inuironed with fire and smoke, vntill they discouered the waste of our ship naked, where they brauely boorded vs loose for loose, hasting with pikes and swords to enter, but it pleased God so to direct our Captaine, and encourage our men with valour, that our pikes being formerly placed vnder our halfe deck, and certaine shot lying close for that purpose vnder the Port holes, encountred them so rudely, that their fury was not onely rebated, but their hastinesse intercepted, and their whole company beaten backe, many of our men were hurt, but I am sure they had two for one.

The manner of their fight.

In the end they were violently repulsed, vntill they were reinforced to charge againe

againe by their commands, who standing vpon their honors, thought it a great indignity to be so affronted, which caused a second charge, and that answered with a second beating backe: whereat the Captaine grew inraged, and constrained them to come on againe afresh, which they did so effectually, that questionlesse it had wrought an alteration, if the God that tosseth Monarchies, and teareth Mountaines, had not taught vs to tosse our Pikes with prosperous euents, and powred out a volley of small shot amongst them, whereby that valiant Commander was slaine, and many of his Souldiers dropped downe likewise on the top of the hatches. This we saw with our eies, and reioyced with it at our hearts, so that we might perceiue good successe comming on, our Captaine presently tooke aduantage of their discomfiture, though with much commiseration of that resolute Captaine, and not onely plied them againe with our Ordnance, but had more shot vnder the Pikes, which was bestowed to good purpose, and amazed our enemies with the suddennesse. The Captaine slaine.

Amongst the rest, one *Lucas*, our Carpenters Mate, must not be forgotten, who perceiuing away how to annoy them; As they were thus puzled and in a confusion, drew out a Minion vnder the halfe decke, and there bent it vpon them in such a manner, that when it was fired, the cases of stones and peeces of Iron fell vpon them so thick, as cleared the decke, and slew many, and in short time we saw few assailants, but such as crept from place to place couertly from the fury of our shot, which now was thicker than theirs: for although as far as we may cōmend our enemies, they had done something worthy of commendations; yet either wanting men, or being ouertaken with the vnlooked for valour of our men, they now began to shrinke, and giue vs leaue to be wanton with our aduantage. Yet we could onely vse but foure peece of Ordnances, but they serued the turne as well as all the rest: for she was shot so oft betweene wind and water, we saw they were willing to leaue vs, but by reason she was fast in the latch of our cable, which in haste of weighing our anchor hung aloofe, she could not cleare her selfe as she wrought to doe, till one cut the Cable with an axe, and was slaine by freeing vs. Hauing beene aboord vs two houres and an halfe, seeing her selfe cleere, all the shot wee had plaied on both sides, which lasted till we were out of shot; then we discouered the Vice-Admirall comming to her assistance, who began a farre off to ply vs with their Ordnances, and put vs in minde we had another worke in hand. Whereupon we separated the dead and hurt bodies, and manned the ship with the rest, and were so well incouraged wee waifed them amaine. The *Admirall* stood aloofe off, and the other would not come within Falcon shot, where she lay battering vs till shee receiued another paiment from a Demiculuering, which made her beare with the shore for smooth water to mend her leakes. The next morning they both came vp againe with vs, as if they had determined to deuour vs at once, but it seemed it was but a brauado, though they forsooke not our quarter for a time within Musket shot; yet all the night onely they kept vs company, but made not a shot. During which time we had leasure to prouide vs better than before: but God be thanked they made onely but a shew of another assault, ere suddenly the Vice-admirall fell a starne, and the other lay shaking in the wind, and so they both left vs. The fight continued six houres, and was the more vnwelcome, because we were so ill prouided, and had no intent to fight, nor giue occasion to disturbe them. As for the losse of men, if Religion had not taught vs what by the prouidence of God is brought to passe, yet daily experience might informe vs, of the dangers of wars, and perils at sea, by stormes tempests, shipwracks, encounters with Pirats, meeting with enemies, crosse winds, long voiages, vnknowne shores, barbarous Nations, and an hundred inconueniences, of which humane pollicies are not capable, nor mens coniectures apprehensiue. We lost Doctor *Bohun*, a worthy valiant Gentleman, (a long time brought vp amongst the most learned Surgeons, and Physitions in *Netherlands*, and this his second iourney to *Virginia*:) and seuen slaine out right, two died shortly of their wounds; sixteene was shot, whose limbs

A worthy exploit of *Lucas*.

The euent of the fight.

God be thanked was recouered without maime, and now setled in *Virginia*: how many they lost we know not, but we saw a great many lie on the decks, and their skuppers runne with bloud, they were about three hundred tunnes apeece, each sixteene or twentie Brasse-peeces. Captaine *Chester*, who in this fight had behaued himselfe like a most vigilant, resolute, and a couragious souldier, as also our honest and valiant master, did still so comfort and incourage vs by all the meanes they could, at last to all our great contents we arriued in *Virginia*, and from thence returned safely to *England*.

The Names of the Aduenturers for *Virginia*, Alphabetically set downe, according to a printed *Booke, set out by the Treasurer and Councell* in this present yeere, 1620.

A

Sir William Aliffe.
Sir Roger Aston.
Sir Anthony Ashley.
Sir Iohn Akland.
Sir Anthonie Ascher.
Sir Robert Askwith.
Doctor Francis Anthony.
Charles Anthony.
Edward Allen.
Edmund Allen Esquire.
Iohn Allen.
Thomas Allen.
William Atkinson, Esquire.
Richard Ashcroft.
Nicholas Andrews.
Iohn Andrews the elder.
Iohn Andrews the younger.
James Ascough.
Giles Allington.
Morris Abbot.
Ambrose Asten.
Iames Askew.
Anthony Abdey.
Iohn Arundell, Esquire.

B

Edward, Earle of Bedford
Iames, Lord Bishop of Bathe and Wells.
Sir Francis Barrington.
Sir Morice Barkley.
Sir Iohn Benet.
Sir Thomas Beamont.
Sir Amias Bamfield.
Sir Iohn Bourcher.
Sir Edmund Bowyer.
Sir Thomas Bludder.
Sir George Bolles.
Sir Iohn Bingley.
Sir Thomas Button.
Sir Henry Beddingfield.
Companie of Barbers-Surgeons.
Companie of Bakers.
Richard Banister.
Iohn Bancks.
Miles Bancks.
Thomas Barber.
William Bonham.
Iames Bryerley.
William Barners.
Anthony Barners, Esquire.
William Brewster.
Richard Brooke.
Hugh Brooker, Esquire.
Ambrose Brewsey.
Iohn Brooke.
Matthew Bromridge.
Christopher Brooke, Esquire.
Martin Bond.
Gabriel Beadle.
Iohn Beadle.
Dauid Borne.
Edward Barnes.
Iohn Badger.
Edmund Branduell.
Robert Bowyer, Esquire.
Bobert Bateman.
Thomas Britton.
Nicholas Benson.

Edward Bishop.
Peter Burgoney.
Thomas Burgoney.
Robert Burgoney.
Christopher Baron.
Peter Benson.
Iohn Baker.
Iohn Bustoridge.
Francis Burley.
William Browne.
Robert Barker.
Samuel Burnham.
Edward Barkley.
William Bennet.
Captaine Edward Brewster.
Thomas Brocket.
Iohn Bullock.
George Bache.
Thomas Bayly.
William Barkley.
George Butler.
Timothie Bathurst.
George Burton.
Thomas Bret.
Captaine Iohn Brough.
Thomas Baker.
Iohn Blunt.
Thomas Bayly.
Richard and Edward Blunt.
Mineon Burrell.
Richard Blackmore.
William Beck.
Beniamin Brand.
Iohn Busbridge.
William Burrell.
William Barret.
Francis Baldwin.
Edward Barber.
Humphrey Basse.
Robert Bell.
Matthew Bromrick.
Iohn Beaumont.
George Barkley.
Peter Bartle.
Thomas Bretton.
Iohn Blount.
Arthur Bromfeld Esquire.
William Berbloke.
Charles Beck.

C

George, Lord Archbishop of Canterburie.
William Lord Cranborne, now Earle of Salisburie.
William, Lord Compton, now Earle of North-hampton.
William Lord Cauendish, now Earle of Deuonshire.
Richard, Earle of Clanricard.
Sir William Cauendish now Lord Cauendish.
Gray, Lord Chandos.
Sir Henry Cary.
Sir George Caluert.
Sir Lionell Cransield.
Sir Edward Cecill.
Sir Robert Cotten.
Sir Oliuer Cromwell.
Sir Anthony Cope.
Sir Walter Cope.
Sir Edward Carr.
Sir Thomas Conisbie.
Sir George Cary.
Sir Edward Conwey.
Sir Walter Chute.
Sir Edward Culpeper.
Sir Henry Cary, Captaine.
Sir William Crauen.
Sir Walter Couert.
Sir George Coppin.
Sir George Chute.
Sir Thomas Couentry.
Sir Iohn Cutts.
Lady Cary.
Company of Cloth-workers.
Citie of Chichester.
Robert Chamberlaine.
Richard Chamberlaine.
Francis Couill.
William Coyse, Esquire.
Abraham Chamberlaine.
Thomas Carpenter.
Anthony Crew.
Richard Cox.
William Crosley.
Iames Chatfeild.
Richard Caswell.
Iohn Cornelis.
Randall Carter.
Executors of Randall Carter.
William Canning.
Edward Carne, Esquire.
Thomas Cannon, Esquire.
Richard Champion.
Rawley Crashaw.
Henry Collins.
Henry Cromwell.
Iohn Cooper.
Richard Cooper.

John Casson.
Thomas Colthurst.
Allen Cotten.
Edward Cage.
Abraham Carthwright.
Robert Coppin.
Thomas Conock.
Iohn Clapham.
Thomas Church.
William Carpenter.
Laurence Campe.
James Cambell.
Christopher Clctheroe.
Matthew Cooper.
George Chamber.
Captaine Iohn Cooke.
Captaine Thomas Conwey, Esquire.
Edward Culpeper, Esquire.
Master William Crashaw.
Abraham Colmer.
Iohn Culpeper.
Edmund Colbey.
Richard Cooper.
Robert Creswell.
Iohn Cage, Esquire.
Matthew Caue.
William Crowe.
Abraham Carpenter.
Iohn Crowe.
Thomas Cordell.
Richard Connock, Esquire.
William Compton.
William Chester.
Thomas Conel.
Richard Carmarden, Esquire.
William and Paul Canning.
Henry Cromwell, Esquire.
Simon Codrington.
Clement Chichley.
James Cullemore.
William Cantrell.

D

Richard Earle of Dorset.
Edward Lord Denny.
Sir Iohn Digbie, now Lord Digbie.
Sir Iohn Doderidge.
Sir Drew Drewry the elder.
Sir Thomas Dennis.
Sir Robert Drewry.
Sir Iohn Dauers.
Sir Dudley Digs.
Sir Marmaduke Dorrel.
Sir Thomas Dale.
Sir Thomas Denton.
Companie of Drapers.
Thomas Bond, Esquire.
Dauid Bent, Esquire.
Comanie of Dyers.
Towne of Doner.
Master Richard Deane, Alderman.
Henry Dawkes.
Edward Dichfield.
William Dunne.
Iohn Dauis.
Matthew Dequester.
Philip Durdent.
Abraham Dawes.
Iohn Dike.
Thomas Draper.
Lancelot Dauis.
Rowley Dawsey.
William Dobson Esquire.
Anthony Dyot, Esquire.
Auery Dranfield.
Roger Dye.
Iohn Downes.
Iohn Drake.
Iohn Delbridge.
Beniamin Decroe.
Thomas Dyke.
Ieffery Duppa.
Daniel Darnelly.
Sara Draper.
Clement and Henry Dawkney.

E

Thomas, Earle of Exeter.
Sir Thomas Euerfield.
Sir Francis Egiock.
Sir Robert Edolph.
Iohn Eldred, Esquire.
William Euans.
Richard Euans.
Hugh Euans.
Raph Ewens, Esquire.
Iohn Elkin.
Iohn Elkin.
Robert Euelin.
Nicholas Exton.
Iohn Exton.
George Etheridge.

F

Sir Moyle Finch.
Sir Henry Fanshaw.
Sir Thomas Freake.
Sir Peter Fretchuile.

Sir William Fleetwood.
Sir Henry Fane.
Company of Fishmongers.
Iohn Fletcher.
Iohn Farmer.
Martin Freeman, Esquire.
Ralph Freeman.
William and Ralph Freeman.
Michael Fetiplace.
VVilliam Fettiplace.
Thomas Forrest.
Edward Fleetwood, Esquire.
William Felgate.
William Field.
Nicholas Ferrar.
Iohn Farrar.
Giles Francis.
Edward Fawcet.
Richard Farrington.
Iohn Francklin.
Richard Frith.
Iohn Ferne.
George Farmer.
Thomas Francis.
Iohn Fenner.
Nicholas Fuller, Esquire.
Thomas Foxall.
William Fleet.
Peter Franck, Esquire.
Richard Fishborne.
VVilliam Faldoe.
Iohn Fletcher, and Company.
VVilliam Ferrars.

G

Lady Elizabeth Gray.
Sir Iohn Gray.
Sir VVilliam Godolfine.
Sir Thomas Gates.
Sir VVilliam Gee.
Sir Richard Grobham.
Sir VVilliam Garaway.
Sir Francis Goodwin.
Sir George Goring.
Sir Thomas Grantham.
Company of Grocers.
Company of Goldsmiths.
Company of Girdlers.
Iohn Geering.
Iohn Gardiner.
Richard Gardiner.
Iohn Gilbert.
Thomas Graue.
Iohn Gray.
Nicholas Griece.
Richard Goddard.
Thomas Gipps.
Peter Gates.
Thomas Gibbs Esquire.
Laurence Greene.
William Greenwell.
Robert Garset.
Robert Gore.
Thomas Gouge.
Francis Glanuile, Esquire.

G

Henry, Earle of Huntington.
Lord Theophilus Haward, L. Walden.
Sir Iohn Harrington, L. Harington.
Sir Iohn Hollis, now Lord Haustein.
Sir Thomas Holecroft.
Sir William Harris.
Sir Thomas Haresleet.
Sir George Haiward.
Sir VVarwicke Heale.
Sir Baptist Hicks.
Sir Iohn Hanham.
Sir Thomas Horwell.
Sir Thomas Hewit.
Sir VVilliam Herrick.
Sir Eustace Hart.
Sir Pory Huntley.
Sir Arthur Harris.
Sir Edward Heron.
Sir Perseuall Hart.
Sir Ferdinando Heiborne.
Sir Lawrence Hide.
Master Hugh Hamersley, Alderman.
Master Richard Heron, Alderman.
Richard Humble, Esquire.
Master Richard Hackleuit.
Edward Harrison.
George Holeman.
Robert Hill.
Griffin Hinton.
Iohn Hawkins.
VVilliam Hancocke.
Iohn Harper.
George Hawger.
Iohn Holt.
Iohn Huntley.
Ieremy Heiden.
Ralph Hamer.
Ralph Hamer, Iunior.
Iohn Hodgeson.
Iohn Hanford.
Thomas Harris.

Richard

Richard Howell.
Thomas Henshaw.
Leonard Harwood
Tristram Hill.
Francis Haselridge.
Tobias Hinson.
Peter Heightley.
George Hawkenson.
Thomas Hackshaw.
Charles Hawkens.
Iohn Hodgis.
William Holland.
Robert Hartley.
Gregory Herst.
Thomas Hodgis.
William Hodgis.
Roger Harris.
Iohn Harris.
M. Iohn Haiward.
Iames Haiward.
Nicholas Hide, Esquire.
Iohn Hare, Esquire.
William Hackwell, Esquire.
Gressam Hoogan.
Humfrey Hanford.
William Haselden.
Nicholas Hooker.
Doctor Anthony Hunton.
Iohn Hodsale.
George Hooker.
Anthony Hinton.
Iohn Hogsell.
Thomas Hampton.
William Hicks.
William Holiland.
Ralph Harison.
Harman Harison.

I

Sir Thomas Iermyn.
Sir Robert Iohnson.
Sir Arthur Ingram.
Sir Francis Iones.
Company of Ironmongers.
Company of Inholders.
Company of Imbroyderers.
Bailiffes of Ipswich.
Henry Iackson.
Richard Ironside.
M. Robert Iohnson Alderman.
Thomas Iones.
William Iobson.
Thomas Iohnson.
Thomas Iadwine.
Iohn Iosua.
George Isam.
Philip Iacobson.
Peter Iacobson.
Thomas Iuxson Senior.
Iames Iewell.
Gabriel Iaques.
Walter Iobson.
Edward Iames.
Zachary Iones, Esquire.
Anthony Irbye, Esquire.
William I-anson.
Humfrey Iobson.

K

Sir Valentine Knightley.
Sir Robert Killegrew.
Sir Charles Kelke.
Sir Iohn Kaile.
Richard Kirrill.
Iohn Kirrill.
Raph King.
Henry Kent.
Towne of Kingslynne.
Iohn Kettleby, Esquire.
Walter Kirkham, Esquire.

L

Henry Earle of Lincolne.
Robert, L. Lisle, now Earle of Leicester.
Thomas, Lord Laware.
Sir Francis Leigh.
Sir Richard Lowlace.
Sir William Litton.
Sir Iohn Lewson.
Sir william Lower.
Sir Samuel Leonard.
Sir Samson Leonard.
Company of Lethersellers.
Thomas Laughton.
William Lewson.
Peter Latham.
Peter Van Lore.
Henry Leigh.
Thomas Leuar.
Christofer Landman.
Morris Lewellin.
Edward Lewis.
Edward Lewkin.
Peter Lodge.
Thomas Layer
Thomas Lawson.
Francis Lodge.

Iohn Langley.
Dauid Loide.
Iohn Leuitt.
Thomas Fox and Luke Lodge.
Captaine Richard Linley.
Arnold Lulls.
William Lawrence.
Iohn Landman.
Nicholas Lichfield.
Nicholas Leate.
Gedeon de Laune.

M

Philip Earle of Montgomerie.
Doctor George Mountaine, now Lord Bishop of Lincolne.
William Lord Mounteagle, now Lord Morley.
Sir Thomas Mansell.
Sir Thomas Mildmay.
Sir William Maynard.
Sir Humfrey May.
Sir Peter Manhood.
Sir Iohn Merrick.
Sir George More.
Sir Robert Mansell.
Sir Arthur Mannering.
Sir Dauid Murrey.
Sir Edward Michelborn.
Sir Thomas Middleton.
Sir Robert Miller.
Sir Caualiero Maicott.
Doctor Iames Meddus.
Richard Martin, Esquire.
Company of Mercers.
Company of Merchant Taylors.
Otho Mowdite.
Captaine Iohn Martin.
Arthur Mouse.
Adrian More.
Thomas Mountford.
Thomas Morris.
Ralph Moorton.
Francis Mapes.
Richard Maplesden.
Iames Monger.
Peter Monsell.
Robert Middleton.
Thomas Maile.
Iohn Martin.
Iosias Maude.
Richard Morton.
George Mason.
Thomas Maddock.
Richard Moore.
Nicholas Moone.
Alfonsus van Medkerk.
Captaine Henry Meoles.
Philip Mutes.
Thomas Mayall.
Humfrey Marret.
Iaruis Mundz.
Robert Mildmay.
William Millet.
Richard Morer.
Iohn Miller.
Thomas Martin.
Iohn Middleton.
Francis Middleton.

N

Dudly, Lord North.
Francis, Lord Norris.
Sir Henry Neuill of Barkshire.
Thomas Nicols.
Christopher Nicols.
VVilliam Nicols.
George Newce.
Ioseph Newberow.
Christopher Newgate.
Thomas Norincott.
Ionathan Nuttall.
Thomas Norton.

O

William Oxenbridge, Esquire.
Robert Offley.
Francis Oliuer.

P

VVilliam, Earle of Pembroke.
VVilliam, Lord Paget.
Iohn, Lord Petre.
George Percy, Esquire.
Sir Christofer Parkins.
Sir Amias Preston.
Sir Nicholas Parker.
Sir VVilliam Poole.
Sir Stephen Powell.
Sir Henry Peyton.
Sir Iames Perrot.
Sir Iohn Pettus.
Sir Robert Payne.
VVilliam Payne.
Iohn Payne.
Edward Parkins.
Edward Parkins his widow.

Adew

Aden Perkins.
Thomas Perkin.
Richard Partridge.
William Palmer.
Miles Palmer.
Robert Parkhurst.
Richard Perciuall, Esquire.
Richard Poyntell.
George Pretty.
George Pit.
Allen Percy.
Abraham Peirce.
Edmund Peirce.
Phenice Pet.
Thomas Philips.
Henry Philpot.
Master George Procter.
Robert Penington.
Peter Peate.
Iohn Prat.
William Powell.
Edmund Peashall.
Captaine William Proude.
Henry Price.
Nicholas Pewriffe.
Thomas Pelham.
Richard Piggot.
Iohn Pawlet, Esquire.
Robert Pory.
Richard Paulson.

Q

William Quicke.

R

Sir Robert Rich, now Earle of Warwicke.
Sir Thomas Row.
Sir Henry Rainsford.
Sir William Romney.
Sir Iohn Ratcliffe.
Sir Steuen Ridlesdon.
Sir William Russell.
Master Edward Rotheram, Alderman.
Robert Rich.
Tedder Roberts.
Henry Robinson.
Iohn Russell.
Richard Rogers.
Arthur Robinson.
Robert Robinson.
Millicent Rawsden.
Iohn Robinson.
George Robins.
Nichalas Rainton.
Henry Rolffe.
Iohn Reignolds.
Elias Roberts.
Henry Reignolds, Esquire.
William Roscarrocke, Esquire.
Humfrey Raymell.
Richard Robins.

S

Henry, Earle of Southampton.
Thomas Earle of Suffolke.
Edward Semer, Earle of Hartford.
Robert, Earle of Salisbury.
Mary, Countesse of Shrewsbury.
Edmund, Lord Sheffeld.
Robert, Lord Spencer.
Iohn, Lord Stanhope.
Sir Iohn Saint-Iohn.
Sir Thomas Smith.
Sir Iohn Samms.
Sir Iohn Smith.
Sir Edwin Sandys.
Sir Samuel Sandys.
Sir Steuen Some.
Sir Raph Shelton.
Sir Thomas Stewkley.
Sir William Saint-Iohn.
Sir William Smith.
Sir Richard Smith.
Sir Martin Stuteuill.
Sir Nicolas Salter.
Doctor Matthew Sutcliffe of Exeter.
Captaine Iohn Smith.
Thomas Sandys, Esquire.
Henry Sandys, Esquire.
George Sandys, Esquire.
Company of Skinners.
Company of Salters.
Company of Stationers.
Iohn Stokley.
Richard Staper.
Robert Singleton.
Thomas Shipton.
Cleophas Smith.
Richard Strongtharm.
Hildebrand Spruson.
Matthew Scriuener.
Othowell Smith.
George Scot.
Hewet Stapers.

Iames

James Swift.
Richard Stratford.
Edmund Smith.
Robert Smith.
Matthias Springham.
Richard Smith.
Edward Smith.
Ionathan Smith.
Humfrey Smith.
John Smith.
George Swinhow.
Ioseph Some.
William Sheckley.
John Southick.
Henry Shelley.
Walter Shelley.
Richard Snarsborow.
George Stone.
Hugh Shepley.
William Strachey.
Vrion Spencer.
John Scarpe.
Thomas Scott.
William Sharpe.
Steuen Sparrow.
Thomas Stokes.
Richard Shepard.
Henry Spranger.
William Stonnard.
Steuen Sad.
Iohn Stockley.
Thomas Steuens.
Matthew Shepard.
Thomas Sherwell.
William Seabright, Esquire.
Nicholas Sherwell.
Augustine Steward.
Thomas Stile.
Abraham Speckhard.
Edmund Scot.
Francis Smalman.
Gregory Sprint, Esquire.
Thomas Stacey.
William Sandbatch.
Augustine Stuard, Esquire.

T

Sir William Twisden.
Sir William Throckmorton.
Sir Nicholas Tufton.
Sir Iohn Treuer.
Sir Thomas Tracy.
George Thorpe, Esquire.
Doctor William Turner.
The Trinity house.
Richard Turner.
John Tauerner.
Daniel Tucker.
Charles Towler.
William Tayler.
Leonard Townson.
Richard Tomlins.
Francis Tate, Esquire.
Andrew Troughton.
George Tucker.
Henry Timberlake.
William Tucker.
Lewis Tite.
Robert Thornton.

V

Sir Horatio Vere.
Sir Walter Vaughan.
Henry Vincent.
Richard Venne.
Christopher Vertue.
Iohn Vassell.
Arthur Venne.

W

Henry Bishop of VVorcester
Francis West, Esquire.
Sir Ralph Winwood.
Sir Iohn Wentworth.
Sir William Waad.
Sir Robert Wroth.
Sir Percival Willoby.
Sir Charles Wilmott.
Sir Iohn Wats.
Sir Hugh Worrell.
Sir Edward Waterhouse.
Sir Thomas Wilsford.
Sir Richard Williamson.
Sir Iohn Wolstenholm.
Sir Thomas Walsingham.
Sir Thomas Watson.
Sir Thomas Wilson.
Sir Iohn Weld.
Mistris Kath. West, now Lady Conway.
Iohn Wroth, Esquire.
Captaine Maria Winckfield, Esquire.
Thomas Webb.
Rice Webb.
Edward Webb.
Sands Webb.
Felix Wilson.
Thomas White.
Richard Wiffen.

William Williamson.
Humfrey Westwood.
Hugh Williston.
Thomas Wheatley.
William Wattey.
William Webster.
Iames White.
Edmund Winne.
Iohn West.
Iohn Wright.
Edward Wooller.
Thomas Walker.
Iohn Wooller.
Iohn Westrow.
Edward Welch.
Nathaniel Waad.
Richard Widowes.
Dauid Waterhouse, Esquire.
Captaine Owen Winne.
Randall Wetwood.
George Wilmer, Esquire.
Edward Wilkes.
Leonard White.
Andrew Willmer.
Clement Willmer.
George Walker.
William Welbie.
Francis Whistler.
Thomas Wells.
Captaine Thomas Winne.
Iohn Whittingham.
Thomas Wheeler.
William Willet.
Deuereux Woogam.
Iohn Walker.
Thomas Wood.
Iohn Willet.
Nicholas Wheeler.
Thomas Wale.
William Wilston.
Iohn Waller.
William Ward.
William Willeston.
Iohn Water.
Thomas Warr, Esquire.
Dauid Wiffen.
Garret Weston.

Y

Sir George Yeardley, now Gouernour of Virginia.
William Yong.
Simon Yeomans.

Z

Edward, Lord Zouch.
Iohn Zouch, Esquire.

THat most generous and most honourable Lord, the Earle of Southhampton, being pleased to take vpon him the title of Treasurer, and Master *Iohn Farrar* his Deputy, with such instructions as were necessary, and admonitions to all Officers to take heede of extortion, ingrosing commodities, forestalling of markets, especially to haue a vigilant care, the familiarity of the Saluages liuing amongst them made them not way to betray or surprize them, for the building of Guest-houses to relieue the weake in, and that they did wonder in all this time they had made no discoueries, nor knew no more then the very place whereon they did inhabit, nor yet could euer see any returne for all this continuall charge and trouble, therefore they sent to be added to the Councell seuen Gentlemen, namely M[r]. *Thorp*, Captaine *Nuce*, M[r]. *Tracy*, Captaine *Middleton*, Captaine *Blount*, M[r]. *Iohn Pountas*, and M[r]. *Harwood*, with men, munition, and all things thought fitting, but they write from *Virginia*, many of the Ships were so pestred with diseased people, & thronged together in their passage, there was much sicknesse and a great mortality, wherfore they desired rather a few able sufficient men well prouided, then great multitudes, and because there were few accidents of note, but priuate aduertisements by letters, we will conclude this yeere, and proceed to the next. *Collected out of the Councels letters for Virginia.*

1621. The Earle of South-hampton Treasurer. Master *Iohn Farrar* Deputy.

The instructions and aduertisements for this yeere were both from *England* and *Virginia*, much like the last: only whereas before they had euer a suspicion of *Opechankanough*, and all the rest of the Saluages, they had an eye ouer him more then any, but now they all write so confidently of their assured peace with the Saluages, there is now no more feare nor danger either of their power or trechery, so that euery man planteth himselfe where he pleaseth, and followeth his businesse securely. But the time of Sir *George Yearley* being neere expired, the Councel here made

made choise of a worthy young Gentleman Sir *Francis Wyat* to succeed him, whom they forthwith furnished and prouided, as they had done his Predecessors, with all the necessary instructions all these times had acquainted them for the conuersion of the Saluages, the suppressing of planting Tobacco, and planting of Corne, not depending continually to be supplied by the Saluages, but in case of necessity to trade with them, whom long ere this, it hath beene promised and expected should haue beene fed and relieued by the English, not the English by them; and carefully to redresse all the complaints of the needlesse mortality of their people, and by all diligence seeke to send something home to satisfie the Aduenturers, that all this time had only liued vpon hopes, grew so weary and discouraged, that it must now be substance that must maintaine their proceedings, & not letters, excuses and promises; seeing they could get so much and such great estates for themselues, as to spend after the rate of 100. pounds, 2, 3, 4, 5, 6, 7, 8, 9, 10. nay some 2000. or 3000. pounds yearely, that were not worth so many pence when they went to *Virginia*, can scarce containe themselues either in diet, apparell, gaming, and all manner of such superfluity, within a lesse compasse than our curious, costly, and consuming Gallants here in *England*, which cannot possibly be there supported, but either by oppressing the Comminalty there, or deceiuing the generality here (or both.) *Extracted out of the Councels Letters for Virginia.*

The election of Sir *Francis Wyat* Gouernour for *Virginia.*

Notes worthy obseruation.

From *Virginia*, by the relations of the Chieftains there, & many I haue conferred with, that came from thence hither, I haue much admired to heare of the incredible pleasure, profit and plenty this Plantation doth abound in, and yet could neuer heare of any returne but Tobacco, but it hath oft amazed me to vnderstand how strangely the Saluages hath beene taught the vse of our armes, and imploied in hunting and fowling with our fowling peeces, and our men rooting in the ground about Tobacco like Swine; besides that, the Saluages that doe little but continually exercise their bow and arrowes, should dwell and lie so familiarly amongst our men that practised little but the Spade, being so farre asunder, and in such small parties dispersed, and neither Fort, exercise of armes vsed, Ordnances mounted, Courts of guard, nor any preparation nor prouision to preuent a forraine enemy, much more the Saluages howsoeuer; for the Saluages vncertaine conformity I doe not wonder, but for their constancy and conuersion, I am and euer haue beene of the opinion of Master *Ionas Stockam* a Minister in *Virginia*, who euen at this time, when all things were so prosperous, and the Saluages at the point of conuersion, against all their Gouernours and Councels opinions, writ to the Councell and Company in *England* to this effect.

A degression.

May 28.

WE that haue left our natiue country to soiourne in a strange land, some idle spectators, who either cowardly dare not, or couetously will not aduenture either their purses or persons in so commendable a worke; others supporting *Atlas* of this ilmost vnsupportable burdens as your selues, without whose assistance this *Virginia* Firmament (in which some) and I hope in short time will shine many more glorious Starres, though there be many Italiannated and Spaniolized Englishmen enuies our prosperities, and by all their ignominious scandals they can deuise seekes to dishearten what they can, those that are willing to further this glorious enterprize, to such I wish according to the decree of *Darius*, that whosoeuer is an enemy to our peace, and seeketh either by getting monipolicall patens, or by forging vniust tales to hinder our welfare, that his house were pulled downe, and a paire of gallowes made of the wood, and he hanged on them in the place.

Master *Stockams* relation.

As for those lasie seruants, who had rather stand all day idle, than worke, though but an houre in this Vineyard, and spend their substance riotously, than cast the superfluity of their wealth into your Treasury, I leaue them as they are to the eternall Iudge of the world. But you right worthy, that hath aduentured so freely, I will not examine, if it were for the glory of God, or your desire of gaine, which it may be you expect should flow vnto you with a full tide, for the conuersion of the Saluages: I wonder you vse not the meanes, I confesse you say well to haue them conuerted by faire meanes, but they scorne to ackowledge it, as for the gifts bestowed on them they deuoure them, and so they would the giuers if they could, and though many haue endeuoured by all the meanes they could by kindnesse to conuert them, they finde nothing from them but derision and ridiculous answers. We haue sent boies amongst them to learne their Language, but they returne worse than they went; but I am no States-man, nor loue I to meddle with any thing but my Bookes, but I can finde no probability by this course to draw them to goodnesse; I and am perswaded if *Mars* and *Minerua* goe hand in hand, they will effect more good in an houre, then those verball Mercurians in their liues, and till their Priests and Ancients haue their throats cut, there is no hope to bring them to conuersion.

The gouernment of Sir Francis Wyat.

The arriuall of Sir *Francis Wyat.*

ABout October arriued Sir *Francis Wyat*, with Master *George Sands*, appointed Treasurer, Master *Dauison* Secretary, Doctor *Pot* the Physician, and Master *Cloyburne* the Surgian, but much prouision was very badly conditioned, nay the Hogs would not eat that Corne they brought, which was a great cause of their sicknesse and mortality, and whatsoeuer is said against the *Virginia* Corne, they finde it doth better nourish than any prouision is sent thither; the Sailers still they complaine are much to blame for imbesling the prouisions sent to priuate men, killing of Swine, and disorderly trucking; for which some order would be taken.

In them nine Ships that went with Sir *Francis VVyat* not one Passenger died, at his arriuall he sent Master *Thorpe* to *Opechancanough*, whom hee found much satisfied with his comming, to confirme their leagues as he had done his Predecessors, and so contented his people should coinhabit amongst them, and hee found more motions of Religion in him than could be imagined: euery man betaking himselfe to his quarter, it was ordered, that for euery head they should plant but 1000. Plants of Tobacco, and vpon each plant nine leaues, which will be about 100. weight, the Corne being appointed but at two shillings & six pence the bushell, required such labour, it caused most men neglect it, and depend vpon trade; where were it rated at ten shillings the bushell, euery man would indeuour to haue plenty to sell to the new commers, or any that wanted, and seldome any is transported from *England*, but it standeth in as much, besides the hazard and other necessaries, the Ships might transport of that burden. The 22. of Nouember arriued Master *Gookin* out of *Ireland*, with fifty men of his owne, and thirty Passengers, exceedingly well furnished with all sorts of prouision and cattle, and planted himselfe at *Nupors-newes*: the Cotten trees in a yeere grew so thicke as ones arme, and so high as a man: here any thing that is planted doth prosper so well as in no place better. For the mortality of the people accuse not the place, for of the old Planters and the families scarce one of twenty miscarries, onely the want of necessaries are the occasions of those diseases. And so wee will conclude this yeere with the shipping and numbers sent. *Out of the Councels Letters from Virginia.*

Master *Gookins* Plantation.

The number of Ships and men

This yeere was sent one and twenty saile of Ships that imployed more than 400. sailers and 1300. men, women and children of diuers faculties, with fourescore cattle; the *Tiger* fell in the Turkes hands, yet safely escaped, and by the returne of their letters from thence, the company is assured there can bee no fitter places of Mines, Wood and Water for Iron than there; and the French men affirme no Country is more proper for Vines, Oliues, Sike, Rice and Salt, &c. of which the next yeere they promise a good quantity.

GIFTS.

GIFTS.

THe Gentlemen and Mariners that came in the *Royall Iames* from the *East-Indies*, gaue towards the building of a free Schoole 70. pound, eight shillings, and six pence; and an vnknowne person to further it, sent thirtie pounds; and another in like manner fiue & twentie pounds; another refusing to be made knowne, gaue fortie shillings yeerely for a Sermon before the *Virginia* companie: also another that would not be knowne, sent for the College at *Henrico*, many excellent good religious bookes, worth ten pound, & a most curious Map of al that coast of *America*. Master *Thomas Bargaue* their Preacher there deceased, gaue a Librarie valued at one hundred Markes: and the Inhabitants hath made a contribution of one thousand and fiue hundred pounds, to build a house for the entertaining of strangers. This yeere also there was much suing for Patents for Plantations, who promised to transport such great multitudes of people: there was much disputing concerning those diuisions, as though the whole land had beene too little for them: six and twentie obtained their desires, but as yet not past six hath sent thither a man; notwithstanding many of them would haue more, and are not well contented; whom I would intreat, and all other wranglers, to peruse this saying of honest *Claudius*.

Gifts giuen.

Patents granted.

See'st not the world of Natures worke, the fairest well, I wot,
How it, it selfe together ties, as in a true-loues knot.
Nor seest how th'Elements ayre combin'd, maintaine one constant plea,
How midst of heauen contents the Sunne, and shore containes the sea;
And how the aire both compasseth, and carrieth still earths frame,
Yet neither pressing burdens it, nor parting leaues the same.

The obseruations of Master Iohn Pory *Secretarie of* Virginia, *in his trauels.*

HAuing but ten men meanly prouided to plant the Secretaries land on the Easterne shore neere *Acomack*. Captaine *Wilcocks* plantation, the better to secure and assist each other. Sir *George Yearley* intending to visit *Smiths* Iles, fell so sicke that he could not, so that he sent me with *Estinien Moll* a French-man, to finde a conuenient place to make salt in. Not long after *Namenacus* the King of *Pawtuxunt*, came to vs to seeke for *Thomas Saluage* our Interpreter. Thus insinuating himselfe, he led vs into a thicket, where all sitting downe, he shewed vs his naked brest; asking if we saw any deformitie vpon it, we told him, No; No more, said hee, is the inside, but as sincere and pure; therefore come freely to my Countrie and welcome: which wee promised wee would within six weekes after. Hauing taken a muster of the companies tenants, I went to *Smiths* Iles, where was our Salt-house: not farre off wee found a more conuenient place, and so returned to *Iames* towne.

My iourney to the Easterne shore.

A good place to make salt in

Being furnished the second time, wee arriued at *Aquo hanock*, and conferred with *Kiptopeke* their King. Passing *Russels* Ile and *Onaucoke*, we arriued at *Pawtuxunt*: the discription of those places, you may reade in Captaine *Smiths* discoueries, therefore needlesse to bee writ againe. But here arriuing at *Attoughcomoco* the habitation of *Namenacus* and *Wamanato*, his brother, long wee staied not ere they came aboord vs with a brasse Kettle, as bright without as within, ful of boyled Oisters. Strict order was giuen none should offend vs, so that the next day I went with the two Kings a hunting, to discouer what I could in their confines. *Wamanato* brought mee first to his house, where hee shewed mee his wife and children, and many Corne-fields; and being two miles within the woods a hunting, as the younger conducted me forth, so the elder brought me home, and

The King of *Pawtxunts* entertainment.

vsed

vsed me as kindly as he could, after their manner. The next day he presented me twelue Beuer skinnes and a Canow, which I requited with such things to his content, that he promised to keepe them whilst hee liued, and burie them with him being dead. Hee much wondered at our Bible, but much more to heare it was the Law of our God, and the first Chapter of *Genesis* expounded of *Adam* and *Eue*, and simple mariage; to which he replyed, hee was like *Adam* in one thing, for he neuer had but one wife at once: but he, as all the rest, seemed more willing of other discourses they better vnderstood. The next day the two Kings with their people, came aboord vs, but brought nothing according to promise; so that Ensigne *Saluage* challenged *Namenacus* the breach of three promises, *viz.* not in giuing him a Boy, nor Corne, though they had plentie, nor *Moutapassa* fugitiue, called *Robert Marcum*, that had liued 5. yeeres amongst those northerly nations, which hee cunningly answered by excuses. *Womanato* it seemes, was guiltlesse of this falshood, because hee staied alone when the rest were gone. I asked him if he desired to bee great and rich; he answered, They were things all men aspired vnto: which I told him he should be, if he would follow my counsell, so he gaue me two tokens, which being returned by a messenger, should suffice to make him confident the messenger could not abuse vs.

Some things being stolne from vs, he tooke such order that they were presently restored, then we interchanged presents: in all things hee much admired our discretions, and gaue vs a guide that hee called brother, to conduct vs vp the Riuer: by the way we met with diuers that stil tould vs of *Marcum*: and though it was in October, we found the Countrie very hot, and their Corne gathered before ours at *Iames* towne. The next day we went to *Paccamaganant*, and they directed vs to *Assacomoco*, where their King *Cassatowap* had an old quarrell with Ensigne *Saluage*, but now seeming reconciled, went with vs, with another Werowance towards *Mattapanient*, where they perswaded vs ashore vpon the point of a thicket; but supposing it some trecherie, we returned to our boat: farre we had not gone from the shore, but a multitude of Saluages sallied out of the wood, with all the ill words and signes of hostilitie they could. When wee saw plainly their bad intent, wee set the two Werowances at libertie, that all this while had line in the Cabbin, as not taking any notice of their villanie, because we would conuert them by courtesie. Leauing them as we found them, very ciuill and subtill, wee returned the same way wee came, to the laughing Kings on the Easterne shore, who told vs plainly, *Namanicus* would also haue allured him into his Countrie, vnder colour of trade to cut his throat. Hee told vs also *Opechancanough* had imployed *Onianimo* to kill *Saluage*, because he brought the trade from him to the Easterne shore, and some disgrace hee had done his sonne, and some thirteene of his people before one hundred of those Easterlings in rescuing *Thomas Graues* whom they would haue slaine, where hee and three more did challenge the thirteene *Pamavukes* to fight, but they durst not, so that all those Easterlings so derided them, that they came there no more.

The trecherie of *Namanicus.*

This *Thomas Salnage*, it is sixteene yeeres since he went to *Virginia*, being a boy, hee was left with *Powhatan*, for *Namontacke* to learne the language, and as this Author affirmeth, with much honestie and good successe hath serued the publike without any publike recompence, yet had an arrow shot through his body in their seruice. This laughing King at *Accomack*, tels vs the land is not two daies iourny ouer in the broadest place, but in some places a man may goe in halfe a day, betwixt the Bay and the maine Ocean, where inhabit many people, so that by the narrownesse of the Land there is not many Deere, but most abundance of Fish and Fowle. *Kiptope* his brother rules as his Lieutenant, who seeing his younger brother more affected by the people than himselfe, freely resigned him the moitie of his Countrie, applying himselfe onely to husbandry and hunting, yet nothing neglected in his degree, nor is hee carelesse of any thing concernes the state, but as a vigilant and faithfull Conceller, as hee is an affectionated brother,

Thomas Saluages good seruice.

Brother, bearing the greater burden in gouernment, though the lesser honour, where cleane contrary they on the Westerne shore, the younger beares the charge, and the elder the dignitie. Those are the best husbands of any Saluages we know: for they prouide Corne to serue them all the yeare, yet spare; and the other not for halfe the yeare, yet want. They are the most ciuill and tractable people we haue met with, and by little sticks will keepe as iust an account of their promises, as by a tally. In their mariages they obserue a large distance, as well in affinitie as consanguinitie; nor doe they vse that deuillish custome in making black Boyes. There may be on this shore about two thousand people: they on the West would inuade them, but that they want Boats to crosse the Bay, and so would diuers other Nations, were they not protected by vs. A few of the Westerly Runnagados had conspired against the laughing King, but fearing their treason was discouered, fled to *Smiths* Iles, where they made a massacre of Deere and Hogges; and thence to *Rickabake*, betwixt *Cissapeack* and *Nansamund*, where they now are seated vnder the command of *Itoyatin*, and so I returned to *Iames* Towne, where I found the gouernment rendred to Sir *Francis Wyat*. In February also he trauelled to the South Riuer *Chawonock*, some sixtie miles ouer land, which he found to be a very fruitfull and pleasant Country, yeelding two haruests in a yeare, and found much of the Silke grasse formerly spoken of, was kindly vsed by the people, and so returned.

Captaine Each *sent to build a Fort to secure the Countrey.*

1622. The Earle of Southampton Treasurer, and *Nicolas Farrar* Deputy.

IT was no small content to all the Aduenturers to heare of the safe ariuall of all those ships and companies, which was thought sufficient to haue made a Plantation of themselues: and againe to second them, was sent Captaine *Each* in the *Abigale*, a ship of three or foure hundred tunnes, who hath vndertaken to make a Block-house amongst the Oyster banks, that shall secure the Riuer. The furnishing him with Instruments, cost three hundred pounds; but the whole charge and the ships returne, will be neere two thousand pounds. In her went Captaine *Barwicke* with fiue and twentie men for the building ships and Boats, and not other waies to be imploied: and also a selected number to build the *East Indie* Schoole, but as yet from *Virginia* little returnes but priuate mens Tobacco, and faire promises of plentie of Iron, Silke, Wine, and many other good and rich commodities, besides the speedy conuersion of the Saluages, that at first were much discouraged from liuing amongst them, when they were debarred the vse of their peeces; therefore it was disputed as a matter of State, whether such as would liue amongst them should vse them or not, as a bait to allure them; or at least such as should bee called to the knowledge of Christ. But because it was a great trouble for all causes to be brought to *Iames* Towne for a triall, Courts were appointed in conuenient places to releeue them: but as they can make no Lawes in *Virginia* till they be ratified here; so they thinke it but reason, none should bee inacted here without their consents, because they onely feele them, and must liue vnder them. Still they complaine for want of Corne, but what must be had by Trade, and how vnwilling any Officer when he leaueth his place, is to make good his number of men to his Successor, but many of them during their times to help themselues, vndoes the Company: for the seruants you allow them, or such as they hire, they plant on their priuate Lands, not vpon that belongeth to their office, which crop alwaies exceeds yours, besides those which are your tenants to halfes, are forced to row them vp and downe, whereby both you and they lose more then halfe. Nor are those officers the ablest or best deseruing, but make their experience vpon the companies cost, and your land lies vnmanured to any purpose, and will yeeld as little profit to your next new officers.

Fiue and twentie sent only to build Barks and Boats.

The maſſacre vpon the two and twentieth of March.

The death of *Nemattanow*, writ by M. *Wimp.*

THe Prologue to this Tragedy, is ſuppoſed was occaſioned by *Nemattanow*, otherwiſe called *Iack* of the *Feather*, becauſe hee commonly was moſt ſtrangely adorned with them; and for his courage and policy, was accounted amongſt the Saluages their chiefe Captaine, and immortall from any hurt could bee done him by the *Engliſh*. This Captaine comming to one *Morgans* houſe, knowing he had many commodities that hee deſired, perſwaded *Morgan* to goe with him to *Pamauke* to trucke, but the Saluage murdered him by the way; and after two or three daies returned againe to *Morgans* houſe, where he found two youths his Seruants, who asked for their Maſter: *Iack* replied directly he was dead; the Boyes ſuſpecting as it was, by ſeeing him weare his Cap, would haue had him to Maſter *Thorp*: But *Iack* ſo moued their patience, they ſhot him, ſo he fell to the ground, put him in a Boat to haue him before the Gouernor, then ſeuen or eight miles from them. But by the way *Iack* finding the pangs of death vpon him, deſired of the Boyes two things; the one was, that they would not make it knowne hee was ſlaine with a bullet; the other, to bury him amongſt the *Engliſh*. At the loſſe of this Saluage *Opechankanough* much grieued and repined, with great threats of reuenge; but the *Engliſh* returned him ſuch terrible anſwers, that he cunningly diſſembled his intent, with the greateſt ſignes he could of loue and peace, yet within foureteene daies after he acted what followeth.

Security a bad guard.

Sir *Francis Wyat* at his arriuall was aduertiſed, he found the Countrey ſetled in ſuch a firme peace, as moſt men there thought ſure and vnuiolable, not onely in regard of their promiſes, but of a neceſſitie. The poore weake Saluages being euery way bettered by vs, and ſafely sheltred and defended, whereby wee might freely follow our buſineſſe: and ſuch was the conceit of this conceited peace, as that there was ſeldome or neuer a ſword, and ſeldomer a peece, except for a Deere or Fowle, by which aſſurances the moſt plantations were placed ſtraglingly and ſcatteringly, as a choice veine of rich ground inuited them, and further from neighbours the better. Their houſes generally open to the Saluages, who were alwaies friendly fed at their tables, and lodged in their bed-chambers, which made the way plaine to effect their intents, and the conuerſion of the Saluages as they ſuppoſed.

Hauing occaſion to ſend to *Opechankanough* about the middle of March, hee vſed the Meſſenger well, and told him he held the peace ſo firme, the sky ſhould fall or he diſſolued it; yet ſuch was the treachery of thoſe people, when they had contriued our deſtruction, euen but two daies before the maſſacre, they guided our men with much kindneſſe thorow the woods, and one *Browne* that liued among them to learne the language, they ſent home to his Maſter; yea, they borrowed our Boats to tranſport themſelues ouer the Riuer, to conſult on the deuilliſh murder that inſued, and of our vtter extirpation, which God of his mercy (by the meanes of one of themſelues conuerted to Chriſtianitie) preuented, and as well on the Friday morning that fatall day, being the two and twentieth of March, as alſo in the euening before, as at other times they came vnarmed into our houſes, with Deere, Turkies, Fiſh, Fruits, and other prouiſions to ſell vs, yea in ſome places ſat downe at breakfaſt with our people, whom immediatly with their owne tooles they ſlew moſt barbarouſly, not ſparing either age or ſex, man woman or childe, ſo ſudden in their execution, that few or none diſcerned the weapon or blow that brought them to deſtruction: In which manner alſo they ſlew many of our people at ſeuerall works in the fields, well knowing in what places and quarters each of our men were, in regard of their familiaritie with vs, for the effecting that great maſter-peece of worke their conuerſion; and by this meanes fell that fatall morning vnder the bloudy and barbarous hands of that perfidious

The manner of the maſſacre.

fidious and inhumane people, three hundred forty seuen men, women and children, most by their owne weapons, and not being content with their liues, they fell againe vpon the dead bodies, making as well as they could a fresh murder, defacing, dragging, and mangling their dead carkases into many peeces, and carying some parts away in derision, with base and brutish triumph.

Neither yet did these beasts spare those amongst the rest well knowne vnto them, from whom they had daily receiued many benefits, but spightfully also massacred them without any remorse or pitie; being in this more fell then Lions and Dragons, as Histories record, which haue preserued their Benefactors; such is the force of good deeds, though done to cruell beasts, to take humanitie vpon them, but these miscreants put on a more vnnaturall brutishnesse then beasts, as by those instances may appeare.

Their cruelty.

That worthy religious Gentleman M. *George Thorp*, Deputie to the College lands, sometimes one of his Maiesties Pensioners, & in command one of the principall in *Virginia*; did so truly affect their conuersion, that whosoeuer vnder him did them the least displeasure, were punished seuerely. He thought nothing too deare for them, he neuer denied them any thing, in so much that when they complained that our Mastiues did feare them, he to content them in all things, caused some of them to be killed in their presence, to the great displeasure of the owners, and would haue had all the rest guelt to make them the milder, might he haue had his will. The King dwelling but in a Cottage, he built him a faire house after the English fashion, in which he tooke such pleasure, especially in the locke and key, which he so admired, as locking and vnlocking his doore a hundred times a day, he thought no deuice in the world comparable to it.

The murder of Master *Thorp*.

Thus insinuating himselfe into this Kings fauour for his religious purpose, he conferred oft with him about Religion, as many other in this former Discourse had done, and this Pagan confessed to him as he did to them, our God was better then theirs, and seemed to be much pleased with that Discourse, and of his company, and to requite all those courtesies; yet this viperous brood did, as the sequell shewed, not onely murder him, but with such spight and scorne abused his dead corps as is vnfitting to be heard with ciuill eares. One thing I cannot omit, that when this good Gentleman vpon his fatall houre, was warned by his man, who perceiuing some treachery intended by those hell-hounds, to looke to himselfe, and withall ran away for feare he should be apprehended, and so saued his owne life; yet his Master out of his good meaning was so void of suspition and full of confidence, they had slaine him, or he could or would beleeue they would hurt him. Captaine *Nathaniel Powell* one of the first Planters, a valiant Souldier, and not any in the Countrey better knowne amongst them; yet such was the error of an ouer-conceited power and prosperitie, and their simplicities, they not onely slew him and his family, but butcher-like hagled their bodies, and cut off his head, to expresse their vttermost height of cruelty. Another of the old company of Captaine *Smith*, called *Nathaniel Causie*, being cruelly wounded, and the Saluages about him, with an axe did cleaue one of their heads, whereby the rest fled and he escaped: for they hurt not any that did either fight or stand vpon their guard. In one place where there was but two men that had warning of it, they defended the house against 60. or more that assaulted it. M. *Baldwin* at *Warraskoyack*, his wife being so wounded, she lay for dead, yet by his oft discharging of his peece, saued her, his house, himselfe, & diuers others. At the same time they came to one Master *Harisons* house, neere halfe a mile from *Baldwines*, where was Master *Thomas Hamer* with six men, and eighteene or nineteene women and children. Here the Saluages with many presents and faire perswasions, fained they came for Capt. *Ralfe Hamer* to go to their King, then hunting in the woods, presently they sent to him, but he not comming as they expected, set fire of a Tobacco-house, and then came to tell them in the dwelling house of it to quench it; all the men ran towards it, but Master *Hamer* not suspecting any thing, whom the

The slaughter of Captaine *Powell*.

A Saluage slaine.

M. *Baldwines* escape.

M. *Thomas Hamer* with 22 escapeth.

the Saluages pursued, shot them full of arrowes, then beat out their braines. *Hamer* hauing finished a letter hee was a writing, followed after to see what was the matter, but quickly they shot an arrow in his back, which caused him returne and barricado vp the doores, whereupon the Saluages set fire on the house. *Harisons* Boy finding his Masters peece loaded, discharged it at randome, at which bare report the Saluages all fled, *Baldwin* still discharging his peece, and Mr *Hamer* with two and twentie persons thereby got to his house, leauing their owne burning. In like manner, they had fired Lieutenant *Basse* his house, with all the rest there about, slaine the people, and so left that Plantation.

Captaine *Ralfe Hamer* with forty escapeth.

Captaine *Hamer* all this while not knowing any thing, comming to his Brother that had sent for him to go hunt with the King, meeting the Saluages chasing some, yet escaped, retired to his new house then a building, from whence he came; there onely with spades, axes, and brickbats, he defended himselfe and his Company till the Saluages departed. Not long after, the Master from the ship had sent six Musketiers, with which he recouered their Merchants store-house, where he armed ten more, and so with thirtie more vnarmed workmen, found his Brother and the rest at *Baldwins* : Now seeing all they had was burnt and consumed, they repaired to *Iames* Towne with their best expedition ; yet not far from *Martins* hundred, where seuenty three were slaine, was a little house and a small family, that heard not of any of this till two daies after.

The Saluages attempt to surprise a ship.

All those, and many others whom they haue as maliciously murdered, sought the good of those poore brutes, that thus despising Gods mercies, must needs now as miscreants be corrected by Iustice : to which leauing them, I will knit together the thred of this discourse. At the time of the massacre, there were three or foure ships in *Iames* Riuer, and one in the next, and daily more to come in, as there did within foureteene daies after, one of which they indeuoured to haue surprised : yet were the hearts of the English euer stupid, and auerted from beleeuing any thing might weaken their hopes, to win them by kinde vsage to Christianitie. But diuers write from thence, that Almighty God hath his great worke in this Tragedy, and will thereout draw honor and glory to his name, and a more flourishing estate and safetie to themselues, and with more speed to conuert the Saluage children to himselfe, since he so miraculously hath preserued the English; there being yet, God be praised, eleuen parts of twelue remaining, whose carelesse neglect of their owne safeties, seemes to haue beene the greatest cause of their destructions : yet you see, God by a conuerted Saluage that disclosed the plot, saued the rest, and the Pinnace then in *Pamavukes* Riuer, whereof (say they) though our sinnes made vs vnworthy of so glorious a conuersion, yet his infinite wisdome can neuerthelesse bring it to passe, and in good time, by such meanes as we thinke most vnlikely : for in the deliuery of them that suruiue, no mans particular carefulnesse saued one person, but the meere goodnesse of God himselfe, freely and miraculously preseruing whom he pleased.

The Letters of Master *George Sands*, a worthy Gentleman, and many others besides them returned, brought vs this vnwelcome newes, that hath beene heard at large in publike Court, that the *Indians* and they liued as one Nation, yet by a generall combination in one day plotted to subuert the whole Colony, and at one instant, though our seuerall Plantations were one hundred and fortie miles vp on Riuer on both sides.

But for the better vnderstanding of all things, you must remember these wilde naked natiues liue not in great numbers together, but dispersed, commonly in thirtie, fortie, fiftie, or sixtie in a company. Some places haue two hundred, few places more, but many lesse ; yet they had all warning giuen them one from another in all their habitations, though farre asunder, to meet at the day and houre appointed for our destruction at al our seueral Plantations; some directed to one place, some to another, all to be done at the time appointed, which they did accordingly : Some entring their houses vnder colour of trading, so tooke their

aduantage ;

aduantage; others drawing vs abroad vnder faire pretences, and the rest suddenly falling vpon those that were at their labours.

Six of the counsell suffered vnder this treason, and the slaughter had beene vniuersall, if God had not put it into the heart of an *Indian*, who lying in the house of one *Pace*, was vrged by another *Indian* his Brother, that lay with him the night before to kill *Pace*, as he should doe *Perry* which was his friend, being so commanded from their King; telling him also how the next day the execution should be finished: *Perrys Indian* presently arose and reueales it to *Pace*, that vsed him as his sonne; and thus them that escaped was saued by this one conuerted Infidell. And though three hundred fortie seuen were slaine, yet thousands of ours were by the meanes of this alone thus preserued, for which Gods name be praised for euer and euer. Six of the Councell slaine.

Pace vpon this, securing his house, before day rowed to *Iames* Towne, and told the Gouernor of it, whereby they were preuented, and at such other Plantations as possibly intelligence could be giuen: and where they saw vs vpon our guard, at the sight of a peece they ranne away; but the rest were most slaine, their houses burnt, such Armes and Munition as they found they tooke away, and some cattell also they destroied. Since wee finde *Opechankanough* the last yeare had practised with a King on the Easterne shore, to furnish him with a kind of poison, which onely growes in his Country to poison vs. But of this bloudy acte neuer griefe and shame possessed any people more then themselues, to be thus butchered by so naked and cowardly a people, who dare not stand the presenting of a staffe in manner of a peece, nor an vncharged peece in the hands of a woman. (But I must tell those Authors, though some might be thus cowardly, there were many of them had better spirits.) How it was reuealed.

Thus haue you heard the particulars of this massacre, which in those respects some say will be good for the Plantation, because now we haue iust cause to destroy them by all meanes possible: but I thinke it had beene much better it had neuer happened, for they haue giuen vs an hundred times as iust occasions long agoe to subiect them, (and I wonder I can heare of none but Master *Stockam* and Master *Whitaker* of my opinion.) Moreouer, where before we were troubled in cleering the ground of great Timber, which was to them of small vse: now we may take their owne plaine fields and Habitations, which are the pleasantest places in the Countrey. Besides, the Deere, Turkies, and other Beasts and Fowles will exceedingly increase if we beat the Saluages out of the Countrey, for at all times of the yeare they neuer spare Male nor Female, old nor young, egges nor birds, fat nor leane, in season or out of season with them, all is one. The like they did in our Swine and Goats, for they haue vsed to kill eight in tenne more then we, or else the wood would most plentifully abound with victuall; besides it is more easie to ciuilize them by conquest then faire meanes; for the one may be made at once, but their ciuilizing will require a long time and much industry. The manner how to suppresse them is so often related and approued, I omit it here: And you haue twenty examples of the *Spaniards* how they got the *West-Indies*, and forced the treacherous and rebellious Infidels to doe all manner of drudgery worke and slauery for them, themselues liuing like Souldiers vpon the fruits of their labours. This will make vs more circumspect, and be an example to posteritie: (But I say, this might as well haue beene put in practise sixteene yeares agoe as now.) Memorandums. Captaine *Smith*.

Thus vpon this Anuill shall wee now beat our selues an Armour of proofe hereafter to defend vs against such incursions, and euer hereafter make vs more circumspect: but to helpe to repaire this losse, besides his Maiesties bounty in Armes, he gaue the Company out of the Tower, and diuers other Honorable persons haue renewed their aduentures, we must not omit the Honorable Citie of *London*, to whose endlesse praise wee may speake it, are now setting forward one hundred persons, and diuers others at their owne costs are a repairing, and all His Maiesties gift. *London* sets out 100 persons.

good men doe thinke neuer the worse of the businesse for all these disasters.

What growing state was there euer in the world which had not the like? *Rome* grew by oppression, and rose vpon the backe of her enemies: and the *Spaniards* haue had many of those counterbuffes, more than we. *Columbus*, vpon his returne from the *West-Indies* into *Spaine*, hauing left his people with the *Indies*, in peace and promise of good vsage amongst them, at his returne backe found not one of them liuing, but all treacherously slaine by the Saluages. After this againe, when the Spanish Colonies were increased to great numbers, the *Indians* from whom the *Spaniards* for trucking stuffe vsed to haue all their corne, generally conspired together to plant no more at all, intending thereby to famish them; themselues liuing in the meane time vpon Cassaua, a root to make bread, onely then knowne to themselues. This plot of theirs by the *Spaniards* ouersight, that foolishly depended vpon strangers for their bread, tooke such effect, and brought them to such misery by the rage of famine, that they spared no vncleane nor loathsome beast, no not the poisonous and hideous Serpents, but eat them vp also, deuouring one death to saue them from another; and by this meanes their whole Colony well-neere surfeted, sickned and died miserably, and when they had againe recouered this losse, by their incontinency an infinite number of them died on the *Indian* disease, we call the French Pox, which at first being a strange and an vnknowne malady, was deadly vpon whomsoeuer it lighted: then had they a little flea called *Nigua*, which got betweene the skinne and the flesh before they were aware, and there bred and multiplied, making swellings and putrifactions, to the decay and losse of many of their bodily members.

A lamentable example, too oft approued.

Againe, diuers times they were neere vndone by their ambition, faction, and malice of the Commanders. *Columbus*, to whom they were also much beholden, was sent with his Brother in chaines into *Spaine*; and some other great Commanders killed and murdered one another. *Pizzaro* was killed by *Almagros* sonne, and him *Vasco* beheaded, which *Vasco* was taken by *Blasco*, and *Blasco* was likewise taken by *Pizzaros* Brother: And thus by their couetous and spightfull quarrels, they were euer shaking the maine pillars of their Common-weale. These and many more mischiefes and calamities hapned them, more then euer did to vs, and at one time being euen at the last gaspe, had two ships not arriued with supplies as they did, they were so disheartned, they were a leauing the Countrey: yet we see for all those miseries they haue attained to their ends at last, as is manifest to all the world, both with honour, power, and wealth: and whereas before few could be hired to goe to inhabit there, now with great sute they must obtaine it; but where there was no honesty, nor equity, nor sanctitie, nor veritie, nor pietie, nor good ciuilitie in such a Countrey, certainly there can bee no stabilitie.

Note this conclusion.

Therefore let vs not be discouraged, but rather animated by those conclusions, seeing we are so well assured of the goodnesse and commodities may bee had in *Virginia*, nor is it to be much doubted there is any want of Mines of most sorts, no not of the richest, as is well knowne to some yet liuing that can make it manifest when time shall serue: and yet to thinke that gold and siluer Mines are in a country otherwise most rich and fruitfull, or the greatest wealth in a Plantation, is but a popular error, as is that opinion likewise, that the gold and siluer is now the greatest wealth of the West Indies at this present. True it is indeed, that in the first conquest the Spaniards got great and mighty store of treasure from the Natiues, which they in long space had heaped together, and in those times the Indians shewed them entire and rich Mines, which now by the relations of them that haue beene there, are exceedingly wasted, so that now the charge of getting those Metals is growne excessiue, besides the consuming the liues of many by their pestilent smoke and vapours in digging and refining them, so that all things considered, the cleere gaines of those metals, the Kings part defraied, to the Aduenturers is but small, and nothing neere so much as vulgarly is imagined; and were it not

How the *Spaniards* raise their wealth in the West Indies.

for

for other rich Commodities there that inrich them, those of the Contraction house were neuer able to subsist by the Mines onely; for the greatest part of their Commodities are partly naturall, and partly transported from other parts of the world, and planted in the *West-Indies*, as in their mighty wealth of Sugarcanes, being first transported from the Canaries; and in Ginger and other things brought out of the *East-Indies*, in their Cochanele, Indicos, Cotton, and their infinite store of Hides, Quick-siluer, Allum, Woad, Brasill woods, Dies, Paints, Tobacco, Gums, Balmes, Oiles, Medicinals and Perfumes, Sassaparilla, and many other physicall drugs: These are the meanes whereby they raise that mighty charge of drawing out their gold and siluer to the great & cleare reuenue of their King. Now seeing the most of those commodities, or as vsefull, may be had in *Virginia* by the same meanes, as I haue formerly said; let vs with all speed take the priority of time, where also may be had the priority of place, in chusing the best seats of the Country, which now by vanquishing the saluages, is like to offer a more faire and ample choice of fruitfull habitations, then hitherto our gentlenesse and faire comportments could attaine vnto.

The numbers that were slaine in those seuerall Plantations.

AT Captaine *Berkleys* Plantation, himselfe and 21. others, seated at the *Falling-Crick*, 66. miles from *Iames* City. 22

2 Master *Thomas Sheffelds* Plantation, some three miles from the *Falling-Crick*, himselfe and 12. others. 13

3 At *Henrico* Iland, about two miles from *Sheffelds* Plantation. 6

4 Slaine of the College people, twenty miles from *Henrico*. 17

5 At *Charles* City, and of Captaine *Smiths* men. 5

6 At the next adioyning Plantation. 8

7 At *William Farrars* house. 10

8 At *Brickley* hundred, fifty miles from *Charles* City, Master *Thorp* and 10

9 At *Westouer*, a mile from *Brickley*. 2

10 At Master *Iohn Wests* Plantation. 2

11 At Captaine *Nathaniel Wests* Plantation. 2

12 At Lieutenant *Gibs* his Plantation. 12

13 At *Richard Owens* house, himselfe and 6

14 At Master *Owen Macars* house, himselfe and 3

15 At *Martins* hundred, seuen miles from *Iames* City. 73

16 At another place. 7

17 At *Edward Bonits* Plantation. 50

18 At Master *Waters* his house, himselfe and 4

19 At *Apamatucks* Riuer, at Master *Perce* his Plantation, fiue miles from the College. 4

20 At Master *Macocks* Diuident, Captaine *Samuel Macock*, and 4

21 At *Flowerda* hundred, Sir *George Yearleys* Plantation. 6

22 On the other side opposite to it. 7

23 At Master *Swinhows* house, himselfe and 7

24 At Master *William Bickars* house, himselfe and 4

25 At *Weanock*, of Sir *George Yearleys* people. 21

26 At *Powel Brooke*, Captaine *Nathaniel Powel*, and 12

27 At *South-hampton* hundred. 5

28 At *Martin Brandons* hundred. 7

29 At Captaine *Henry Spilmans* house. 2

30 At Ensigne *Spences* house. 5

31 At Master *Thomas Perse* his house by *Mulbery* Ile, himselfe and 4

The whole number 347.

Men

Men in this taking bettered with affliction,
Better attend, and mind, and marke Religion,
For then true voyces issue from their hearts,
Then speake they what they thinke in inmost parts,
The truth remaines, they cast off fained Arts.

How they were reduced to fiue or six places.

THis lamentable and so vnexpected a distaster caused them all beleeue the opinion of Master *Stockam*, and draue them all to their wits end: it was twenty or thirty daies ere they could resolue what to doe, but at last it was concluded, all the petty Plantations should be abandoned, and drawne onely to make good fiue or six places, where all their labours now for the most part must redound to the Lords of those Lands where they were resident. Now for want of Boats, it was impossible vpon such a sudden to bring also their cattle, and many other things, which with much time, charge and labour they had then in possession with them; all which for the most part at their departure was burnt, ruined and destroyed by the Saluages. Only Master *Gookins* at *Nuports-newes* would not obey the Commanders command in that, though hee had scarce fiue and thirty of all sorts with him, yet he thought himselfe sufficient against what could happen, and so did to his great credit and the content of his Aduenturers. Master *Samuel Iorden* gathered together but a few of the straglers about him at Beggers-bush, where he fortified and liued in despight of the enemy. Nay, Mistrisse *Proctor*, a proper, ciuill, modest Gentlewoman did the like, till perforce the English Officers forced her and all them with her to goe with them, or they would fire her house themselues, as the Saluages did when they were gone, in whose despight they had kept it, and what they had a moneth or three weekes after the Massacre; which was to their hearts a griefe beyond comparison, to lose all they had in that manner, onely to secure others pleasures. Now here in *England* it was thought, all those remainders might presently haue beene reduced into fifties or hundreds in places most conuenient with what they had, hauing such strong houses as they reported they had, which with small labour might haue beene made inuincible Castles against all the Saluages in the Land, and then presently raised a company, as a running Armie to torment the Barbarous and secure the rest, and so haue had all that Country betwixt the Riuers of *Powhatan* and *Pamavuke* to range and sustaine them; especially all the territories of *Kecoughtan, Chiskact* and *Paspahege*, from *Ozenies* to that branch of *Pamavuke*, comming from *Youghtanund*, which strait of land is not past 4. or 5. miles, to haue made a peninsula much bigger then the Summer Iles, inuironed with the broadest parts of those two maine Riuers, which for plenty of such things as *Virgnia* affords is not to be exceeded, and were it well manured, more then sufficient for ten thousand men. This, were it well vnderstood, cannot but be thought better then to bring fiue or six hundred to lodge and liue on that, which before would not well receiue and maintaine a hundred, planting little or nothing, but spend that they haue vpon hopes out of *England*, one euill begetting another, till the disease is past cure: Therefore it is impossible but such courses must produce most fearefull miseries and extreme extremities; if it proue otherwise, I should be exceeding glad. I confesse I am somewhat too bold to censure other mens actions being not present, but they haue done as much of me; yea many here in *England* that were neuer there, & also many there that knowes little more then their Plantations, but as they are informed; and this doth touch the glory of God, the honour of my Country, and the publike good so much, for which there hath beene so many faire pretences, that I hope none will be angry for speaking my opinion, seeing the old Prouerbe doth allow losers leaue to speake; and *Du Bartas* saith,

Gookins and *Iordens* resolutions.

The opinion of Captaine *Smith*.

Euen as the wind the angry Ocean moues,
Waue hunteth Waue, and Billow Billow shoues,

So

So doe all Nations iustell each the other,
And so one people doe pursue another,
And scarce a second hath the first vnhoused,
Before a third him thence againe haue rowsed.

AMongst the multitude of these seuerall Relations, it appeares Captaine *Nuse* seeing many of the difficulties to ensue, caused as much Corne to be planted as he could at *Elizabeths* city, & though some destroyed that they had set, fearing it would serue the Saluages for Ambuscadoes, trusting to releefe by trade, or from *England*, which hath euer beene one cause of our miseries, for from *England* wee haue not had much, and for trading, euery one hath not Ships, Shalops, Interpreters, men and prouisions to performe it, and those that haue, vse them onely for their owne priuate gaine, not the publike good, so that our beginning this yeere doth cause many to distrust the euent of the next. Here wee will leaue Captaine *Nuse* for a while, lamenting the death of Captaine *Norton*, a valiant industrious Gentleman, adorned with many good qualities, besides Physicke and Chirurgery, which for the publike good he freely imparted to all *gratis*, but most bountifully to the poore; and let vs speake a little of Captaine *Croshaw* amongst the midst of those broiles in the Riuer of *Patawomeke*.

The prouidence of Captaine *Nuse*.

Being in a small Barke called the *Elizabeth*, vnder the command of Captaine *Spilman*, at *Cekacawone*, a Saluage stole aboord them, and told them of the Massacre, and that *Opechancanough* had plotted with his King and Country to betray them also, which they refused, but them of *Wighcocomoco* at the mouth of the riuer had vndertaken it; vpon this *Spilman* went thither, but the Saluages seeing his men so vigilant and well armed, they suspected themselues discouered, and to colour their guilt, the better to delude him, so contented his desire in trade, his Pinnace was neere fraught; but seeing no more to be had, *Croshaw* went to *Patawomek*, where he intended to stay and trade for himselfe, by reason of the long acquaintance he had with this King that so earnestly entreated him now to be his friend, his countenancer, his Captaine and director against the *Pazaticans*, the *Nacotchtanks*, and *Moyaons* his mortall enemies. Of this oportunity *Croshaw* was glad, as well to satisfie his owne desire in some other purpose he had, as to keepe the King as an opposite to *Opechancanough*, and adhere him vnto vs, or at least make him an instrument against our enemies; so onely *Elis Hill* stayed with him, and the Pinnace returned to *Elizabeths* City; here shall they rest also a little, till we see how this newes was entertained in *England*.

Captaine *Croshaw* his voyage to *Patawomek*.

It was no small griefe to the Councell and Company, to vnderstand of such a supposed impossible losse, as that so many should fall by the hands of men so contemptible; and yet hauing such warnings, especially by the death of *Nemattanow*, whom the Saluages did thinke was shot-free, as he had perswaded them, hauing so long escaped so many dangers without any hurt. But now to leape out of this labyrinth of melancholy, all this did not so discourage the noble aduenturers, nor diuers others still to vndertake new seuerall Plantations, but that diuers ships were dispatched away, for their supplies and assistance thought sufficient. Yet Captaine *Smith* did intreat and moue them to put in practise his old offer, seeing now it was time to vse both it and him, how slenderly heretofore both had beene regarded, and because it is not impertinent to the businesse, it is not much amisse to remember what it was.

The arriuall of this newes in *England*.

The

The proiect and offer of Captaine Iohn Smith, *to the Right* Honourable, and Right Worshipfull Company *Virginia.*

Captaine *Smiths* offer to the Company.

IF you please I may be transported with a hundred Souldiers and thirty Sailers by the next *Michaelmas,* with victuall, munition, and such necessary prouision, by Gods assistance, we would endeuour to inforce the Saluages to leaue their Country, or bring them in that feare and subiection that euery man should follow their businesse securely, whereas now halfe their times and labours are spent in watching and warding, onely to defend, but altogether vnable to suppresse the Saluages, because euery man now being for himselfe will be vnwilling to be drawne from their particular labours, to be made as pack-horses for all the rest, without any certainty of some better reward and preferment then I can vnderstand any there can or will yet giue them.

These I would imploy onely in ranging the Countries, and tormenting the Saluages, and that they should be as a running Army till this were effected, and then settle themselues in some such conuenient place, that should euer remaine a garison of that strength, ready vpon any occasion against the Saluages, or any other for the defence of the Countrey, and to see all the English well armed, and instruct them their vse. But I would haue a Barke of one hundred tunnes, and meanes to build sixe or seuen Shalops, to transport them where there should bee occasion.

Towards the charge, because it is for the generall good, and what by the massacre and other accidents, *Virginia* is disparaged, and many men and their purses much discouraged, how euer a great many doe hasten to goe, thinking to bee next heires to all the former losses, I feare they will not finde all things as they doe imagine; therefore leauing those gilded conceits, and diue into the true estate of the Colony; I thinke if his Maiestie were truly informed of their necessitie, and the benefit of this proiect, he would be pleased to giue the custome of *Virginia,* and the Planters also according to their abilities would adde thereto such a contribution, as would be fit to maintaine this garison till they be able to subsist; or cause some such other collections to be made, as may put it with all expedition in practice; otherwise it is much to be doubted, there will neither come custome, nor any thing from thence to *England* within these few yeares.

Now if this should be thought an imploiment more fit for ancient Souldiers there bred, then such new commers as may goe with me; you may please to leaue that to my discretion, to accept or refuse such voluntaries, that will hazard their fortunes in the trialls of these euents, and discharge such of my company that had rather labour the ground then subdue their enemies: what releefe I should haue from your Colony I would satisfie and spare them (when I could) the like courtesie. Notwithstanding these doubts, I hope to feede them as well as defend them, and yet discouer you more land vnknowne then they all yet know, if you will grant me such priuiledges as of necessity must be vsed.

For against any enemy we must be ready to execute the best can be deuised by your state there, but not that they shall either take away my men, or any thing else to imploy as they please by vertue of their authority, and in that I haue done somewhat for *New-England* as well as *Virginia,* so I would desire liberty and authority to make the best vse I can of my best experiences, within the limits of those two Patents, and to bring them both in one Map, and the Countries betwixt them, giuing alwaies that respect to the Gouernors and gouernment, as an Englishman doth in *Scotland,* or a Scotchman in *England,* or as the regiments in the Low-countries doe to the Gouernors of the Townes and Cities where they are billited, or in Garrison, where though they liue with them, and are as their

seruants

seruants to defend them, yet not to be disposed on at their pleasure, but as the Prince and State doth command them, and for my owne paines in particular I aske not any thing but what I can produce from the proper labour of the Saluages.

Their Answer.

Their answer.

I Cannot say, it was generally for the Company, for being published in their Court, the most that heard it liked exceeding well of the motion, and some would haue been very large Aduenturers in it, especially Sir *Iohn Brookes* and Master *Dauid Wyffin*, but there were such diuisions amongst them, I could obtaine no answer but this, the charge would be too great; their stocke was decayed, and they did thinke the Planters should doe that of themselues if I could finde meanes to effect it; they did thinke I might haue leaue of the Company, prouided they might haue halfe the pillage, but I thinke there are not many will much striue for that imploiment, for except it be a little Corne at some time of the yeere is to be had, I would not giue twenty pound for all the pillage is to be got amongst the Saluages in twenty yeeres: but because they supposed I spake only for my owne ends, it were good those vnderstand prouidents for the Companies good they so much talke of, were sent thither to make triall of their profound wisdomes and long experiences.

The manner of the Sallary.

About this time also was propounded a proposition concerning a Sallery of fiue and twenty thousand pounds to be raised out of Tobacco, as a yeerely pension to bee paid to certaine Officers for the erecting a new office, concerning the sole importation of Tobacco, besides his Maiesties custome, fraught, and all other charges. To nominate the vndertakers, fauourers and opposers, with their arguments *(pro)* and *(con)* would bee too tedious and needlesse being so publikely knowne; the which to establish, spent a good part of that yeere, and the beginning of the next. This made many thinke wonders of *Virginia*, to pay such pensions extraordinary to a few here that were neuer there, and also in what state and pompe some Chieftaines and diuers of their associates liue in *Virginia*, and yet no money to maintaine a Garrison, pay poore men their wages, nor yet fiue and twenty pence to all the Aduenturers here, and very little to the most part of the Planters there, bred such differences in opinion it was dissolued.

Captaine *Croshaw* staies at *Patawomek*, and his aduentures.

Now let vs returne to Captaine *Croshaw* at *Patawomek*, where he had not beene long ere *Opechancanough* sent two baskets of beads to this King, to kill him and his man, assuring him of the Massacre he had made, and that before the end of two Moones there should not be an Englishman in all their Countries: this fearefull message the King told this Captaine, who replied, he had seene both the cowardise and trechery of *Opechancanough* sufficiently tried by Captaine *Smith*, therefore his threats he feared not, nor for his fauour cared, but would nakedly fight with him or any of his with their owne swords; if he were slaine, he would leaue a letter for his Country men to know, the fault was his owne, not the Kings; two daies the King deliberated vpon an answer, at last told him the English were his friends, and the Saluage Emperour *Opitchapam* now called *Toyatan*, was his brother, therefore there should be no bloud shed betwixt them, so hee returned the Presents, willing the *Pamavukes* to come no more in his Country, lest the English, though against his will, should doe them any mischiefe.

The escape of *Waters* and his Wife.

Not long after, a Boat going abroad to seeke out some releefe amongst the Plantations, by *Nuports-newes* met such ill weather, though the men were saued they lost their boat, which the storme and waues cast vpon the shore of *Nandsamund*, where *Edward Waters* one of the three that first stayed in Summer Iles, and found the great peece of Amber-greece, dwelling in *Virginia* at this Massacre, hee

hee and his wife these *Nandsamunds* kept Prisoners till it chanced they found this Boat, at which purchase they so reioyced, according to their custome of triumph, with songs, dances and inuocations, they were so busied, that *Waters* and his wife found opportunity to get secretly into their Canow, and so crossed the Riuer to *Kecoughtan*, which is nine or ten miles, whereat the English no lesse wondred and reioyced, then the Saluages were madded with discontent. Thus you may see how many desperate dangers some men escape, when others die that haue all things at their pleasure.

The arriuall of Captaine *Hamar* at *Patawomek*.

All men thinking Captaine *Croshaw* dead, Captaine *Hamer* arriuing with a Ship and a Pinnace at *Patawomeke*, was kindly entertained both by him and the King; that *Don Hamar* told the King he came for Corne: the King replied hee had none, but the *Nacotchtanks* and their confederats had, which were enemies both to him and them; if they would fetch it, he would giue them 40. or 50 choise Bow-men to conduct and assist them. Those Saluages with some of the English they sent, who so well played their parts, they slew 18. of the *Nacotchtanks*, some write but 4. and some they had a long skirmish with them; where the *Patawomeks* were so eager of reuenge, they driue them not onely out of their towne, but all out of sight through the woods, thus taking what they liked, and spoiling the rest, they retired to *Patawomek*, where they left Captaine *Croshaw*, with foure men more, the rest set saile for *Iames* towne. Captaine *Croshaw* now with fiue men and himselfe found night and day so many Alarums, he retired into such a conuenient place, that with the helpe of the Saluages, hee had quickly fortified himselfe against all those wilde enemies. Captaine *Nuse* his Pinnace meeting *Hamar* by the way vnderstanding all this, came to see Captaine *Croshaw*: after their best enterchanges of courtesies, *Croshaw* writ to *Nuse* the estate of the place where he was, but vnderstanding by them the poore estate of the Colony, offered if they would send him but a bold Shallop, with men, armes and prouision for trade, the next Haruest he would prouide them Corne sufficient, but as yet it being but the latter end of Iune, there was little or none in all the Country.

Croshaws Fort and plot for trade.

Captaine *Madyson* sent to *Patawomek*.

This being made knowne to the Gouernour and the rest, they sent Captaine *Madyson* with a ship and pinnace, and some six and thirtie men: those *Croshaw* a good time taught the vse of their armes, but receiuing a letter from *Boyse* his Wife, a prisoner with nineteene more at *Pamavuke*, to vse meanes to the Gouernour for their libertie; So hee dealt with this King, hee got first two of his great men to goe with him to *Iames* towne, and eight daies after to send foure of his counsell to *Pamavuke*, there to stay till he sent one of his two to them, to perswade *Opachankanough* to send two of his with two of the *Patawomekes*, to treat about those prisoners, and the rest should remaine their hostage at *Pamavuke*; but the Commanders, at *Iames* towne, it seemes, liked not of it, and so sent the *Patawomekes* backe againe to their owne Countrie, and Captaine *Croshaw* to his owne habitation.

The industry of Captaine *Nuse*.

All this time we haue forgot Captaine *Nuse*, where we left him but newly acquainted with the Massacre, calling all his next adioyning dispersed neighbours together, he regarded not the pestring his owne house, nor any thing to releeue them, and with all speed entrenched himselfe, mounted three peece of Ordnance, so that within 14. daies, he was strong enough to defend himselfe from all the Saluages, yet when victuall grew scant, some that would forrage without order, which he punished, neere occasioned a mutiny. Notwithstanding, he behaued himselfe so fatherly and kindly to them all, they built two houses for them he daily expected from *England*, a faire Well of fresh water mantled with bricke, because the Riuer and Cricks are there brackish or salt; in all which things he plaied the Sawyer, Carpenter, Dauber, Laborer, or any thing; wherein though his courage and heart were steeled, he found his body was not made of Iron, for hee had many sicknesses, and at last a Dropsie, no lesse griefe to himselfe, then sorrow to his Wife and all vnder his gouernment. These crosses and losses were no ſmall increaſers of his malady, nor the thus abandoning our Plantations, the loſſe of our Harueſt, and alſo Tobacco which was as our money; the Vineyard our Vineyetours had brought to a good forwardneſſe, bruiſed and deſtroyed with Deere, and all things ere they came to perfection, with weeds, diſorderly perſons or wild beaſts; ſo that as we are I cannot perceiue but the next yeere will be worſe, being ſtill tormented with pride and flattery, idleneſſe and couetouſneſſe, as though they had vowed heere to keepe their Court with all the peſtilent vices in the world for their attendants, inchanted with a conceited ſtatelineſſe, euen in the very bottome of miſerable ſenſeleſneſſe.

Shortly after, Sir *George Yearly* and Captaine *William Powel*, tooke each of them a company of well diſpoſed Gentlemen and others to ſeeke their enemies. *Yearly* ranging the ſhore of *Weanock*, could ſee nothing but their old houſes which he burnt, and ſo went home: *Powel* ſearching another part, found them all fled but three he met by chance, whoſe heads hee cut off, burnt their houſes, and ſo returned; for the Saluages are ſo light and ſwift, though wee ſee them (being ſo loaded with armour) they haue much aduantage of vs though they be cowards.

Captaine *Powel* kils 3. Saluages.

I confeſſe this is true, and it may cauſe ſome ſuppoſe they are grown inuincible: but will any goe to catch a Hare with a Taber and a Pipe? for who knowes not though there be monſters both of men and beaſts, fiſh and fowle, yet the greateſt, the ſtrongeſt, the wildeſt, cruelleſt, fierceſt and cunningeſt, by reaſon, art and vigilancy, courage and induſtry hath beene ſlaine, ſubiected or made tame, and thoſe are ſtill but Saluages as they were, onely growne more bold by our owne ſimplicities, and ſtill will be worſe and worſe till they be tormented with a continuall purſuit, and not with lying incloſed within Palizados, or affrighting them out of your ſights, thinking they haue done well, can but defend themſelues: and to doe this to any purpoſe, will require both charge, patience and experience. But to their proceedings.

The opinion of Captaine *Smith*.

About the latter end of Iune, Sir *George Yearley* accompanied with the Councell, and a number of the greateſt Gallants in the Land, ſtayed three or foure daies with Captaine *Nuſe*, he making his moane to a chiefe man amongſt them for want of prouiſion for his Company, the great Commander replied hee ſhould turne them to his greene Corne, which would make them plumpe and fat: theſe fields being ſo neere the Fort, were better regarded and preſerued then the reſt, but the great mans command, as we call them, was quickly obeied, for though it was ſcarce halfe growne either to the greatneſſe or goodneſſe, they deuoured it greene though it did them ſmall good. Sir *George* with his company went to *Accomack* to his new Plantation, where he ſtaied neere ſix weekes; ſome Corne he brought home, but as he aduentured for himſelfe, he accordingly enioyed the benefit; ſome pety Magazines came this Summer, but either the reſtraint by Proclamation, or want of Boats, or both, cauſed few but the Chieftaines to be little better by them. So long as Captaine *Nuſe* had any thing we had part; but now all being ſpent, and the people forced to liue vpon Oiſters and Crabs, they became ſo faint no worke could be done; and where the Law was, no worke, no meat, now the caſe is altered, to no meat, no worke; ſome ſmall quantity of Milke and Rice the Captaine had of his owne, and that he would diſtribute *gratis* as he ſaw occaſion; I ſay *gratis*, for I know no place elſe, but it was ſold for ready paiment: thoſe eares of Corne that had eſcaped till Auguſt, though not ripe by reaſon of the late planting, the very Dogs did repaire to the Corne fields to ſeeke them as the men till they were hanged; and this I proteſt before God is true that I haue related, not to flatter *Nuſe*, nor condemne any, but all the time I haue liued in *Virginia*, I haue not ſeene nor heard that any Commander hath taken ſuch continuall paines for the publike, or done ſo little good for himſelfe, and his vertuous wife was no leſſe charitable and compaſſionate according to her power. For my owne part, although I found neither *Mulberies* planted, houſes built,

Sir *George Yearleys* iourny to *Accomack*.

Captaine *Nuſe* his miſery.

men nor victuall prouided, as the honourable Aduenturers did promise mee in *England*; yet at my owne charge, hauing made these preparations, and the silke-Wormes ready to be couered, all was lost, but my poore life and children, by the Massacre, the which as God in his mercy did preserue, I continually pray we may spend to his glory. The 9. of September, we had an alarum, and two men at their labours slaine; the Captaine, though extreme sicke, sallied forth, but the Saluages lay hid in the Corne fields all night, where they destroyed all they could, and killed two men more, much mischiefe they did to Master *Edward Hills* cattle, yet he alone defended his house though his men were sicke and could doe nothing, and this was our first assault since the Massacre.

An Alarum, foure slaine.

The kindnesse of the King of *Patawomek*.

About this time Captaine *Madyson* passed by vs, hauing taken Prisoners, the King of *Patawomek*, his sonne, and two more, and thus it happened; *Madyson* not liking so well to liue amongst the Saluages as *Croshaw* did, built him a strong house within the Fort, so that they were not so sociable as before, nor did they much like *Poole* the Interpreter; many Alarums they had, but saw no enemies: *Madyson* before his building went to *Moyaones*, where hee got prouision for a moneth, and was promised much more, so he returned to *Patawomek* and built this house, and was well vsed by the Saluages. Now by the foure great men the King sent to *Pamavuke* for the redemption of the Prisoners, *Madyson* sent them a letter, but they could neither deliuer it nor see them: so long they stayed that the King grew doubtfull of their bad vsage, that hee swore by the Skyes, if they returned not well, he would haue warres with *Opechankanough* so long as he had any thing: at this time two of *Madysons* men ranne from him, to finde them he sent Master *Iohn Vpton* and three more with an Indian guide to *Nazatica*, where they heard they were. At this place was a King beat out of his Country by the *Necosts*, enemies to the *Patawomeks*; this expulsed King though he professed much loue to the *Patawomeks*, yet hee loued not the King because he would not helpe him to reuenge his iniuries, but to our Interpreter *Poole* hee protested great loue, promising if any treason were, he would reueale it; our guide conducted this *Bandyto* with them vp to *Patawomek*, and there kept him; our Fugitiues we found the *Patawomeks* had taken and brought home, and the foure great men returned from *Pamavuke*; not long after, this expulsed King desired priuate conference with *Poole*, vrging him to sweare by his God neuer to reueale what hee would tell him, *Poole* promised he would not; then quoth this King, those great men that went to *Pamavuke*, went not as you suppose they pretended, but to contract with *Opechankanough* how to kill you all here, and these are their plots.

A Saluages policy.

First, they will procure halfe of you to goe a fishing to their furthest towne, and there set vpon them, and cut off the rest; if that faile, they will faine a place where are many strangers would trade their Furres, where they will perswade halfe of you to goe trade, and there murder you and kill them at home; and if this faile also, then they will make Alarums two nights together, to tire you out with watching, and then set vpon you, yet of all this, said he, there is none acquainted but the King and the great Coniurer.

Madison takes the King and kils 30. or 40.

This being made known to the Captain, we all stood more punctually vpon our guard, at which the Saluages wondering, desired to know the cause; we told them we expected some assault from the *Pamavukes*, whereat they seemed contented, and the next day the King went on hunting with two of our men, and the other a fishing and abroad as before, till our Shallop returned from *Iames* towne with the two Saluages, sent home with Captaine *Croshaw*: by those the Gouernour sent to *Madyson*, that this King should send him twelue of his great men; word of this was sent to the King at another towne where he was, who not comming presently with the Messenger, *Madyson* conceited hee regarded not the message, and intended as he supposed the same treason. The next morning the King comming home, being sent for, he came to the Captaine and brought him a dish of their daintiest fruit; then the Captaine fained his returne to *Iames* towne, the King

King told him he might if he would, but desired not to leaue him destitute of aid, hauing so many enemies about him; the Captaine told him he would leaue a guard, but intreated his answer concerning the twelue great men for the Gouernour; the King replied, his enemies lay so about him he could not spare them, then the Captaine desired his sonne and one other; my sonne, said the King, is gone abroad about businesse, but the other you desire you shall haue, and that other sits by him, but that man refused to goe, whereupon *Madyson* went forth and locked the doore, leauing the King, his sonne, and foure Saluages, and fiue English men in the strong house, and setting vpon the towne with the rest of his men, slew thirty or forty men, women and children; the King demanding the cause, *Poole* told him the treason, crying out to intreat the Captaine cease from such cruelty: but hauing slaine and made flye all in the towne, hee returned, taxing the poore King of treason, who denied to the death not to know of any such matter, but said, This is some plot of them that told it, onely to kill mee for being your friend. Then *Madyson* willed him, to command none of his men should shoot at him as he went aboord, which he presently did, and it was performed: so *Madyson* departed, leading the King, his sonne, and two more to his ship, promising when all his men were shipped, he should returne at libertie; notwithstanding he brought them to *Iames* towne, where they lay some daies, and after were sent home by Captaine *Hamer*, that tooke Corne for their ransome, and after set saile for New found Land. The King set at liberty.

But, alas the cause of this was onely this
They vnderstood, nor knew what was amisse.

Euer since the beginning of these Plantations, it hath beene supposed the King of *Spaine* would inuade them, or our English Papists indeuour to dissolue them. But neither all the Counsels of *Spaine*, nor Papists in the world could haue deuised a better course to bring them all to ruine, then thus to abuse their friends, nor could there euer haue beene a better plot, to haue ouerthrowne *Opechankanough* then Captaine *Chroshaws*, had it beene fully managed with expedition. But it seemes God is angry to see *Virginia* made a stage where nothing but murder and indiscretion contends for victory. A digression.

Amongst the rest of the Plantations all this Summer little was done, but securing themselues and planting Tobacco, which passes there as current Siluer, and by the oft turning and winding it, some grow rich, but many poore, notwithstanding ten or twelue ships or more hath arriued there since the massacre, although it was Christmas ere any returned, and that returne greatly reuiued all mens longing expectation here in *England*: for they brought newes, that notwithstanding their extreme sicknesse many were recouered, and finding the Saluages did not much trouble them, except it were sometimes some disorderly straglers they cut off. To lull them the better in securitie, they sought no reuenge till their Corne was ripe, then they drew together three hundred of the best Souldiers they could, that would leaue their priuate businesse, and aduenture themselues amongst the Saluages to surprize their Corne, vnder the conduct of Sir *George Yearley*, being imbarked in conuenient shipping, and all things necessary for the enterprise, they went first to *Nandsamund*, where the people set fire on their owne houses, and spoiled what they could, and then fled with what they could carry; so that the English did make no slaughter amongst them for reuenge. Their Corne fields being newly gathered, they surprized all they found, burnt the houses remained vnburnt, and so departed. Quartering about *Kecoughtan*, after the Watch was set, *Samuell Collyer* one of the most ancientest Planters, and very well acquainted with their language and habitation, humors and conditions, and Gouernor of a Towne, when the Watch was set going the round, vnfortunately by a Centinell that discharged his peece, was slaine. Their proceedings of the other plantations. 300 surpriseth *Nandsamund*. *Samuell Collyer* slaine.

Thence

They surprise *Pamavuke.*

Thence they sailed to *Pamavuke*, the chiefe seat of *Opechankanough*, the contriuer of the massacre: the Saluages seemed exceeding fearefull, promising to bring them *Sara*, and the rest of the English yet liuing, with all the Armes, and what they had to restore, much desiring peace, and to giue them any satisfaction they could. Many such deuices they fained to procrastinate the time ten or twelue daies, till they had got away their Corne from all the other places vp the Riuer, but that where the English kept their quarter: at last, when they saw all those promises were but delusions, they seised on all the Corne there was, set fire on their houses: and in following the Saluages that fled before thē, some few of those naked Deuils had that spirit, they lay in ambuscado, and as our men marched discharged some shot out of English peeces, and hurt some of them flying at their pleasures where they listed, burning their empty houses before them as they went to make themselues sport: so they escaped, and Sir *George* returned with Corne, where for our paines we had three bushels apeece, but we were enioyned before we had it, to pay ten shillings the bushell for fraught and other charges. Thus by this meanes the Saluages are like as they report, to endure no small misery this Winter, and that some of our men are returned to their former Plantations.

The opinion of Captaine *Smith.*

What other passages or impediments hapned in their proceedings, that they were not fully reuenged of the Saluages before they returned, I know not; nor could euer heare more, but that they supposed they slew two, and how it was impossible for any men to doe more then they did: yet worthy *Ferdinando Courtus* had scarce three hundred *Spaniards* to conquer the great Citie of *Mexico*, where thousands of Saluages dwelled in strong houses: but because they were a ciuilized people, had wealth, and those meere Barbarians as wilde as beasts haue nothing; I intreat your patience to tell you my opinion, which if it be Gods pleasure I shall not liue to put in practice, yet it may be hereafter vsefull for some, but howsoeuer I hope not hurtfull to any, and this it is.

How to subiect all the Saluages in Virginia.

Had these three hundred men beene at my disposing, I would haue sent first one hundred to Captaine *Rawley Chroshaw* to *Patawomek*, with some small Ordnance for the Fort, the which but with daily exercising them, would haue struck that loue and admiration into the *Patowomeks*, and terror and amazement into his enemies, which are not farre off, and most seated vpon the other side the Riuer, they would willingly haue beene friends, or haue giuen any composition they could, before they would be tormented with such a visible feare.

Now though they be generally perfidious, yet necessity constraines those to a kinde of constancy because of their enemies, and neither my selfe that first found them, Captaine *Argall*, *Chroshow*, nor *Hamar*, neuer found themselues in fifteene yeares trials: nor is it likely now they would haue so hostaged their men, suffer the building of a Fort, and their women and children amongst them, had they intended any villany; but suppose they had, who would haue desired a better aduantage then such an aduertisement, to haue prepared the Fort for such an assault, and surely it must be a poore Fort they could hurt, much more take, if there were but fiue men in it durst discharge a peece: Therefore a man not well knowing their conditions, may be as wel too iealous as too carelesse; Such another Lope Skonce would I haue had at *Onawmanient*, and one hundred men more to haue made such another at *Atquacke* vpon the Riuer of *Toppahanock*, which is not past thirteene miles distant from *Onawmanient*: each of which twelue men would keepe, as well as twelue thousand, and spare all the rest to bee imploied as there should be occasion. And all this with these numbers might easily haue beene done, if not by courtesie, yet by compulsion, especially at that time of September when all their fruits were ripe, their beasts fat, and infinite numbers of wilde Fowle began to repaire to euery creeke, that men if they would doe any thing, could not want victuall. This done, there remained yet one hundred who should haue done the like at *Ozinieke*, vpon the Riuer of *Chickahamania*, not past six miles

miles from the chiefe habitations of *Opechankanough.* These small Forts had beene cause sufficient to cause all the Inhabitants of each of those Riuers to looke to themselues. Then hauing so many Ships, Barks, and Boats in *Virginia* as there was at that present, with what facility might you haue landed two hundred and twentie men, if you had but onely fiue or six Boats in one night; forty to range the branch of *Mattapanyent*, fortie more that of *Toughtanund*, and fortie more to keepe their randiuous at *Pamavnke* it selfe. All which places lie so neere, they might heare from each other within foure or fiue houres, and not any of those small parties, if there were any valour, discretion, or industry in them, but as sufficient as foure thousand, to force them all to contribution, or take or spoile all they had. For hauing thus so many conuenient randeuous to releeue each other, though all the whole Countries had beene our enemies, where could they rest, but in the depth of Winter we might burne all the houses vpon all those Riuers in two or three daies? Then without fires they could not liue, which they could not so hide but wee should finde, and quickly so tire them with watching and warding, they would be so weary of their liues, as either fly all their Countries, or giue all they had to be released of such an hourely misery. Now if but a small number of the Saluages would assist vs, as there is no question but diuers of them would; And to suppose they could not be drawne to such faction, were to beleeue they are more vertuous then many Christians, and the best gouerned people in the world. All the *Pamavukes* might haue beene dispatched as well in a moneth as a yeare, and then to haue dealt with any other enemies at our pleasure, and yet made all this toile and danger but a recreation.

If you think this strange or impossible, 12 men with my selfe I found sufficient, to goe where I would adaies, and surprise a house with the people, if not a whole towne in a night, or incounter all the power they could make, as a whole Army, as formerly at large hath beene related: And it seemes by these small parties last amongst them, bv Captaine *Crashow, Hamar*, and *Madyson*, they are not growne to that excellency in policy and courage but they might bee encountred, and their wiues and children apprehended. I know I shall bee taxed for writing so much of my selfe, but I care not much, because the iudiciall know there are few such Souldiers as are my examples, haue writ their owne actions, nor know I who will or can tell my intents better then my selfe.

Some againe finde as much fault with the Company for medling with so many Plantations together, because they that haue many Irons in the fire some must burne; but I thinke no if they haue men enow know how to worke them, but howsoeuer, it were better some burne then haue none at all. The King of *Spaine* regards but how many powerfull Kingdomes he keepes vnder his obedience, and for the Saluage Countries he hath subiected, they are more then enow for a good Cosmographer to nominate, and is three Mole-hills so much to vs; and so many Empires so little for him? For my owne part, I cannot chuse but grieue, that the actions of an Englishman should be inferior to any, and that the command of *England* should not be as great as any Monarchy that euer was since the world began, I meane not as a Tyrant to torment all Christendome, but to suppresse her disturbers, and conquer her enemies.

For the great Romans *got into their hand*
The whole worlds compasse, both by Sea and Land,
Or any seas, or heauen, or earth extended,
And yet that Nation could not be contented.

Much about this time arriued a small Barke of *Barnestable*, which had beene at the *Summer Iles*, and in her Captaine *Nathaniel Butler*, who hauing beene Gouernor there three yeares, and his Commission expired, he tooke the opportunity of this ship to see *Virginia*: at *Iames* Towne he was kindly entertained by

The arriuall of Captaine *Butler*, & his accidents.

by Sir *Francis Wyat* the Gouernor. After he had rested there foureteene daies, he fell vp with his ship to the Riuer of *Chickahamania,* where meeting Captaine *William Powell,* ioyning together such forces as they had to the number of eighty, they set vpon the *Chickahamanians,* that fearefully fled, suffering the English to spoile all they had, not daring to resist them. Thus he returned to *James* towne, where hee staied a moneth, at *Kecoughtan* as much more, and so returned for *England.*

A strange deliuerance of Master *Argent* & others.

But riding at *Kecoughtan.* M. *Iohn Argent,* sonne to Doctor *Argent,* a young Gentleman that went with Captaine *Butler* from *England* to this place, *Michael Fuller, William Gany, Cornelius May,* and one other going ashore with some goods late in a faire euening, such a sudden gust did arise, that driue them thwart the Riuer, in that place at least three or foure miles in bredth, where the shore was so shallow at a low water, and the Boat beating vpon the Sands, they left her, wading neere halfe a mile, and oft vp to the chin: So well it hapned, Master *Argent* had put his Bandileir of powder in his hat, which next God was all their preseruations: for it being February, and the ground so cold, their bodies became so benumbed, they were not able to strike fire with a steele and a stone hee had in his pocket; the stone they lost twice, and thus those poore soules groping in the darke, it was Master *Argents* chance to finde it, and with a few withered leaues, reeds, and brush, make a small fire, being vpon the *Chisapeaks* shore, their mortall enemies, great was their feare to be discouered. The ioyfull morning appearing, they found their Boat and goods driue ashore, not farre from them, but so split shee was vnseruiceable: but so much was the frost, their clothes did freeze vpon their backs, for they durst not make any great fire to dry them, lest thereby the bloudy Saluages might discry them, so that one of them died the next day, and the next night digging a graue in the Sands with their hands, buried him. In this bodily feare they liued and fasted two daies and nights, then two of them went into the Land to seeke fresh water; the others to the Boat to get some meale and oyle, *Argent* and his Comrado found a Canow, in which they resolued to aduenture to their ship, but shee was a drift in the Riuer before they returned: thus frustrate of all hopes, Captaine *Butler* the third night ranging the shore in his Boat to seeke them, discharged his Muskets, but they supposing it some Saluages had got some English peeces, they grew more perplexed then euer, so he returned and lost his labour. The fourth day they vnloaded their Boat, and stopping her leakes with their handkerchiefes, and other rags, two rowing, and two bailing out the water; but farre they went not ere the water grew vpon them so fast, and they so tired, they thought themselues happy to be on shore againe, though they perceiued the *Indians* were not farre off by their fires. Thus at the very period of despaire, *Fuller* vndertooke to sit a stride vpon a little peece of an old Canow; so well it pleased God the wind and tide serued, by padling with his hands and feet in the water, beyond all expectation God so guided him three or foure houres vpon this boord, he arriued at their ship, where they no lesse amazed then he tired, they tooke him in. Presently as he had concluded with his Companions, he caused them discharge a peece of Ordnance if he escaped, which gaue no lesse comfort to Master *Argent* and the rest, then terror to those Planta ions that heard it, (being late) at such an vnexpected alarum: but after, with warme clothes and a little strong water, they had a little recouered him, such was his courage and care of his distressed friends, he returned that night againe with Master *Felgate* to conduct him to them, and so giuing thanks to God for so hopelesse a deliuerance, it pleased his Diuine power, both they and their prou sion came safely aboord, but *Fuller* they doubt will neuer recouer his benumbed legs and thighes.

Now before *Butlers* arriuall in *England,* many hard speeches were rumored against him for so leauing his charge, before he receiued order from the Company: Diuers againe of his Souldiers as highly commended him, for his good gouernment,

uernment, art, iudgement and industry. But to make the misery of *Virginia* appeare that it might be reformed in time, how all those Cities, Townes, Corporations, Forts, Vineyards, Nurseries of Mulberies, Glasse-houses, Iron forges, Guest-houses, Silke-wormes, Colleges, the Companies great estate, and that plenty some doe speake of here, are rather things in words and paper then in effect, with diuers reasons of the causes of those defects; if it were false, his blame nor shame could not be too much: but if there bee such defects in the gouernment, and distresse in the Colony, it is thought by many it hath beene too long concealed, and requireth rather reformation then disputation: but howeuer, it were not amisse to prouide for the worst, for the best will help it selfe. Notwithstanding, it was apprehended so hardly, and examined with that passion, that the brute thereof was spread abroad with that expedition, it did more hurt then the massacre; and the fault of all now by the vulgar rumour, must be attributed to the vnwholesomnesse of the ayre, and barrennesse of the Countrey, as though all *England* were naught, because the Fens and Marshes are vnhealthy; or barren, because some will lie vnder windowes and starue in Cheap-side, rot in Goales, die in the street, high-waies, or any where, and vse a thousand deuices to maintaine themselues in those miseries, rather then take any paines, to liue as they may by honest labour, and a great part of such like are the Planters of *Virginia*, and partly the occasion of those defailements.

In the latter end of this last yeare, or the beginning of this, Captaine *Henrie Spilman* a Gentleman, that hath liued in those Countries thirteene or fourteene yeares, one of the best Interpreters in the Land, being furnished with a Barke and six and twentie men, hee was sent to trucke in the Riuer of *Patawomek*, where he had liued a long time amongst the Saluages, whether hee presumed too much vpon his acquaintance amongst them, or they sought to be reuenged of any for the slaughter made amongst them by the English so lately, or hee sought to betray them, or they him, are all seuerall relations, but it seemes but imaginary: for then returned report they left him ashore about *Patawomek*, but the name of the place they knew not, with one and twentie men, being but fiue in the Barke, the Saluages ere they suspected any thing, boorded them with their Canowes, and entred so fast, the English were amazed, till a Sailer gaue fire to a peece of Ordnance onely at randome; at the report whereof, the Saluages leapt ouer-boord, so distracted with feare, they left their Canowes and swum a shore; and presently after they heard a great brute amongst the Saluages a shore, and saw a mans head throwne downe the banke, whereupon they weighed Anchor and returned home, but how he was surprised or slaine, is vncertaine.

1623. How Captaine *Spilman* was left in the Riuer of *Patawomek*. The Earle of Southampton Treasurer.

Thus things proceed and vary not a iot,
Whether we know them, or we know them not.

A particular of such necessaries as either priuate families, or single persons, shall haue cause to prouide to goe to Virginia, *whereby greater numbers may in part conceiue the better how to prouide for themselues.*

Apparell for one man, and so after the rate for more.

Apparell.			
A Monmoth Cap.	1 s. 10 d.	1 suit of Frize.	10 s.
3 falling bands.	1 s. 3 d.	1 suit of Cloth.	15 s.
3 shirts.	7 s. 6 d.	3 paire of Irish stockings.	4 s.
1 Waste-coat.	2 s. 2 d.	4 paire of shooes.	8 s. 8 d.
1 suit of Canuase.	7 s. 6 d.	1 paire of garters.	10 d.
		1 dozen of points.	3 d.

1 paire

1 paire of Canuas sheets. 8 s.
7 ells of Canuas to make a bed and boulster, to be filled in *Virginia*, seruing for two men. 8 s.
5 ells of course Canuas to make a bed at Sea for two men. 5 s.
1 course rug at sea for two men. 6 s.
4 l.

Victuall for a whole yeare for a man, and so after the rate for more.

8 bushels of meale. 2 l.
2 bushels of pease. 6 s.
2 bushels of Oatemeale. 9 s.
1 gallon of *Aquavita.* 2 s. 6 d.
1 gallon of oyle. 3 s. 6 d.
2 gallons of Vineger. 2 s.
3 l. 3 s.

Armes for a man, but if halfe your men be armed it is well, so all haue swords and peeces.

1 Armor compleat, light. 17 s.
1 long peece fiue foot and a halfe, neere Musket bore. 1 l. 2 s.
1 Sword. 5 s.
1 Belt. 1 s.
1 Bandilier. 1 s. 6 d.
20 pound of powder. 18 s.
60 pound of shot or Lead, Pistoll and Goose shot. 5 s.
3 l. 9 s. 6 d.

Tooles for a family of six persons, and so after the rate for more.

5 broad howes at 2 s. a peece. 10 s.
5 narrow howes at 16 d. a peece. 6 s. 8 d.
2 broad axes at 3 s. 8 d. a peece. 7 s. 4 d.
5 felling axes at 18 d. a peece. 7 s. 6 d.
2 steele handsawes at 16 d. a peece. 2 s. 8 d.
2 two handsawes at 5 s. a peece. 10 s.
1 whipsaw, set and filed, with box, file and wrest. 10 s.
2 hammers 12 d. a peece. 2 s.
3 shouels 18 d. a peece. 4 s. 6 d.
2 spades at 18 d. a peece. 3 s.
2 Augers at 6 d. peece. 1 s.
6 Chissels at 6 d. a peece. 3 s.
2 Percers stocked 4 d. a peece. 8 d.
3 Gimblets at 2 d. a peece. 6 d.
2 Hatchets at 21 d. a peece. 3 s. 6 d.
2 frowes to cleaue pale 18 d. each 3 s.
2 hand Bills 20 d. a peece. 3 s. 4 d.
1 Grindstone. 4 s.
Nailes of all sorts to the value of 2 l.
2 Pickaxes. 3 s.
6 l. 2 s. 8 d.

Houshold implements for a family and six persons, and so for more or lesse after the rate.

1 Iron pot. 7 s.
1 Kettell. 6 s.
1 large Frying pan. 2 s. 6 d.
1 Gridiron. 1 s. 6 d.
2 Skellets. 5 s.
1 Spit. 2 s.
Platters, dishes, spoones of wood. 4 s.
1 l. 8 s.

For Sugar, Spice, and Fruit, and at Sea for six men. 12 s. 6 d.
So the full charge after this rate for each person, will amount about the summe of 12 l. 10 s. 10 d.
The passage of each man is 6 l.
The fraught of these prouisions for a man, will be about halfe a tun, which is 1 l. 10 s.
So the whole charge will amount to about 20 l.

Now if the number be great, Nets, Hooks and Lines, but Cheese, Bacon, Kine and Goats must be added. And this is the vsuall proportion the *Virginia* Company doe bestow vpon their Tenents they send.

A briefe relation written by Captaine Smith *to his Maiesties Commissioners for the reformation of* Virginia, *concerning some aspersions against it.*

HOnourable Gentlemen, for so many faire and Nauigable Riuers so neere adioyning, and piercing thorow so faire a naturall Land, free from any inundations, or large Fenny vnwholsome Marshes, I haue not seene, read, nor heard of: And for the building of Cities, Townes, and Wharfage, if they will vse the meanes, where there is no more ebbe nor floud, Nature in few places affoords any so conuenient, for salt Marshes or Quagmires.

In

In this tract of *Iames* Towne Riuer I know very few; some small Marshes and Swamps there are, but more profitable then hurtfull: and I thinke there is more low Marsh ground betwixt *Eriffe* and *Chelsey*, then *Kecoughton* and the Falls, which is about one hundred and eighty miles by the course of the Riuer.

Being enioyned by our Commission not to vnplant nor wrong the Saluages, because the channell was so neere the shore, where now is *Iames* Towne, then a thicke groue of trees; wee cut them downe, where the Saluages pretending as much kindnesse as could bee, they hurt and slew one and twenty of vs in two houres: At this time our diet was for most part water and bran, and three ounces of little better stuffe in bread for fiue men a meale, and thus we liued neere three moneths: our lodgings vnder boughes of trees, the Saluages being our enemies, whom we neither knew nor vnderstood; occasions I thinke sufficient to make men sicke and die.

The causes of our first miseries.

Necessity thus did inforce me with eight or nine, to try conclusions amongst the Saluages, that we got prouision which recouered the rest being most sicke. Six weeks I was led captiue by those Barbarians, though some of my men were slaine, and the rest fled, yet it pleased God to make their great Kings daughter the means to returne me safe to *Iames* towne, and releeue our wants, and then our Common-wealth was in all eight and thirty, the remainder of one hundred and fiue.

But 38 English in all *Virginia*.

Being supplied with one hundred and twenty, with twelue men in a boat of three tuns, I spent foureteene weeks in those large waters; the contents of the way of my boat protracted by the skale of proportion, was about three thousand miles, besides the Riuer we dwell vpon, where no Christian knowne euer was, and our diet for the most part what we could finde, yet but one died.

Proofes of the healthfulnesse of the Countrey.

The Saluages being acquainted, that by command from *England* we durst not hurt them, were much imboldned; that famine and their insolencies did force me to breake our Commission and instructions, cause *Powhatan* fly his Countrey, and take the King of *Pamavnke* Prisoner; and also to keepe the King of *Paspahegh* in shackels, and put his men to double taskes in chaines, till nine and thirty of their Kings paied vs contribution, and the offending Saluages sent to *Iames* towne to punish at our owne discretions: in the two last yeares I staied there, I had not a man slaine.

How the Saluages became subiected.

All those conclusions being not able to preuent the bad euents of pride and idlenesse, hauing receiued another supply of seuentie, we were about two hundred in all, but not twentie work-men: In following the strict directions from *England* to doe that was impossible at that time; So it hapned, that neither wee nor they had any thing to eat, but what the Countrey afforded naturally; yet of eightie who liued vpon Oysters in Iune and Iuly, with a pint of corne a week for a man lying vnder trees, and 120 for the most part liuing vpon Sturgion, which was dried til we pounded it to powder for meale, yet in ten weeks but seuen died.

How we liued of the natural fruits of the Countrey.

It is true, we had of Tooles, Armes, & Munition sufficient, some *Aquavita*, Vineger, Meale, Pease, and Otemeale, but in two yeares and a halfe not sufficient for six moneths, though by the bils of loading the proportions sent vs, would well haue contented vs, notwithstanding we sent home ample proofes of Pitch, Tar, Sope Ashes, Wainskot, Clapboord, Silke grasse, Iron Ore, some Sturgion and Glasse, Saxefras, Cedar, Cypris, and blacke Walnut, crowned *Powhaton*, sought the *Monacans* Countrey, according to the instructions sent vs, but they caused vs neglect more necessary workes: they had better haue giuen for Pitch and Sope ashes one hundred pound a tun in *Denmarke*: Wee also maintained fiue or six seuerall Plantations.

Proofe of the Commodities we returned.

Iames towne being burnt, wee rebuilt it and three Forts more, besides the Church and Store-house, we had about fortie or fiftie seuerall houses to keepe vs warme and dry, inuironed with a palizado of foureteene or fifteene foot, and each as much as three or foure men could carrie. We digged a faire Well of fresh water in the Fort, where wee had three Bulwarks, foure and twentie peece of Ord-

What we built.

nance, of Culuering, Demiculuering, Sacar and Falcon, and most well mounted vpon conuenient plat-formes, planted one hundred acres of Corne. We had but six ships to transport and supply vs, and but two hundred seuenty seuen men, boies, and women, by whose labours *Virginia* being brought to this kinde of perfection, the most difficulties past, and the foundation thus laid by this small meanes; yet because we had done no more, they called in our Commission, tooke a new in their owne names, and appointed vs neere as many offices and Officers as I had Souldiers, that neither knew vs nor wee them, without our consents or knowledge; since there haue gone more then one hundred ships of other proportions, and eight or ten thousand people. Now if you please to compare what hath beene spent, sent, discouered and done this fifteene yeares, by that we did in the three first yeares, and euery Gouernor that hath beene there since, giue you but such an account as this, you may easily finde what hath beene the cause of those disasters in *Virginia*.

Then came in Captaine *Argall*, and Master *Sedan*, in a ship of Master *Cornelius*, to fish for Sturgion, who had such good prouision, we contracted with them for it, whereby we were better furnished then euer.

Not long after came in seuen ships, with about three hundred people; but rather to supplant vs then supply vs, their Admirall with their authoritie being cast away in the *Bermudas*, very angry they were we had made no better prouision for them. Seuen or eight weekes we withstood the invndations of these disorderly humors, till I was neere blowne to death with Gun-powder, which occasioned me to returne for *England*.

How I left the Country.

In the yeare 1609 about Michaelmas, I left the Countrey, as is formerly related, with three ships, seuen Boats, Commodities to trade, haruest newly gathered, eight weeks prouision of Corne and Meale, about fiue hundred persons, three hundred Muskets, shot, powder, and match, with armes for more men then we had. The Saluages their language and habitation, well knowne to two hundred expert Souldiers; Nets for fishing, tooles of all sorts, apparell to supply their wants: six Mares and a Horse, fiue or six hundred Swine, many more Powltry, what was brought or bred, but victuall there remained.

My charge.

Hauing spent some fiue yeares, and more then fiue hundred pounds in procuring the Letters Patents and setting forward, and neere as much more about *New England*, &c. Thus these nineteene yeares I haue here and there not spared any thing according to my abilitie, nor the best aduice I could, to perswade how those strange miracles of misery might haue beene preuented, which lamentable experience plainly taught me of necessity must insue, but few would beleeue me till now too deerely they haue paid for it. Wherefore hitherto I haue rather left all then vndertake impossibilities, or any more such costly taskes at such chargeable rates: for in neither of those two Countries haue I one foot of Land, nor the very house I builded, nor the ground I digged with my owne hands, nor euer any content or satisfaction at all, and though I see ordinarily those two Countries shared before me by them that neither haue them nor knowes them, but by my descriptions: Yet that doth not so much trouble me, as to heare and see those contentions and diuisions which will hazard if not ruine the prosperitie of *Virginia*, if present remedy bee not found, as they haue hindred many hundreds, who would haue beene there ere now, and makes them yet that are willing to stand in a demurre.

My reward.

For the Books and Maps I haue made, I will thanke him that will shew me so much for so little recompence, and beare with their errors till I haue done better. For the materials in them I cannot deny, but am ready to affirme them both there and here, vpon such grounds as I haue propounded, which is to haue but fifteene hundred men to subdue againe the Saluages, fortifie the Countrey, discouer that yet vnknowne, and both defend & feed their Colony, which I most humbly refer to his Maiesties most iudiciall iudgement, and the most honourable Lords of his

Priuy

Priuy Councell, you his trusty and well-beloued Commissioners, and the Honourable company of Planters and well-willers to *Virginia*, *New-England* and *Sommer-Ilands*.

Out of these Obseruations it pleased his Maiesties Commissioners for the reformation of *Virginia*, to desire my answer to *these seuen Questions.*

Quest. 1. *WHat conceiue you is the cause the Plantation hath prospered no better since you left it in so good a forwardnesse?*

Answ. Idlenesse and carelesnesse brought all I did in three yeeres in six moneths to nothing, and of fiue hundred I left, scarce threescore remained, and had Sir *Thomas Gates* not got from the *Bermudas*, I thinke they had beene all dead before they could be supplied.

Quest. 2. *What conceiue you should be the cause, though the Country be good, there comes nothing but Tobacco?*

Answ. The oft altering of Gouernours it seemes causes euery man make vse of his time, and because Corne was stinted at two shillings six pence the bushell, and Tobacco at three shillings the pound, and they value a mans labour a yeere worth fifty or threescore pound, but in Corne not worth ten pound, presuming Tobacco will furnish them with all things; now make a mans labour in Corne worth threescore pound, and in Tobacco but ten pound a man, then shall they haue Corne sufficient to entertaine all commers, and keepe their people in health to doe any thing, but till then, there will be little or nothing to any purpose.

Quest. 3. *What conceiue you to haue beene the cause of the Massacre, and had the Saluages had the vse of any peeces in your time, or when, or by whom they were taught?*

Answ. The cause of the Massacre was the want of marshall discipline, and because they would haue all the English had by destroying those they found so carelesly secure, that they were not prouided to defend themselues against any enemy, being so dispersed as they were. In my time, though Captaine *Nuport* furnished them with swords by truck, and many fugitiues did the like, and some Peeces they got accidentally, yet I got the most of them againe, and it was death to him that should shew a Saluage the vse of a Peece. Since I vnderstand they became so good shot, they were imployed for Fowlers and Huntsmen by the English.

Quest. 4. *What charge thinke you would haue setled the gouernment, both for defence and planting when you left it?*

Answ. Twenty thousand pound would haue hyred good labourers and mechanicall men, and haue furnished them with cattle and all necessaries, and 100. of them would haue done more then a thousand of those that went, though the Lord *Laware*, Sir *Ferdinando Waynman*, Sir *Thomas Gates* and Sir *Thomas Dale* were perswaded to the contrary, but when they had tried, they confessed their error.

Quest. 5. *What conceiue you would be the remedy and the charge?*

Answ. The remedy is to send Souldiers and all sorts of labourers and necessaries for them, that they may be there by next *Michaelmas*, the which to doe well will stand you in fiue thousand pound, but if his Maiesty would please to lend two of his Ships to transport them, lesse would serue, besides the benefit of his grace to the action would encourage all men.

Quest. 6. *What thinke you are the defects of the gouernment both here and there?*

Answ. The multiplicity of opinions here, and Officers there, makes such delaies by questions and formalitie, that as much time is spent in complement as in action;

on; besides, some are so desirous to imploy their ships, hauing six pounds for euery Passenger, and three pounds for euery tun of goods, at which rate a thousand ships may now better be procured then one at the first, when the common stocke defrayed all fraughts, wages, prouisions and Magazines, whereby the Ships are so pestred, as occasions much sicknesse, diseases and mortality, for though all the Passengers die they are sure of their fraught; and then all must be satisfied with Orations, disputations, excuses and hopes. As for the letters of aduice from hence, and their answers thence, they are so well written, men would beleeue there were no great doubt of the performance, and that all things were wel, to which error here they haue beene euer much subiect; and there not to beleeue, or not to releeue the true and poore estate of that Colony, whose fruits were commonly spent before they were ripe, and this losse is nothing to them here, whose great estates are not sensible of the losse of their aduentures, and so they thinke, or will not take notice; but it is so with all men: but howsoeuer they thinke or dispose of all things at their pleasure, I am sure not my selfe onely, but a thousand others haue not onely spent the most of their estates, but the most part haue lost their liues and all, onely but to make way for the triall of more new conclusions, and he that now will aduenture but twelue pounds ten shillings, shall haue better respect and as much fauour then he that sixteene yeere agoe aduentured as much, except he haue money as the other hath, but though he haue aduentured fiue hundred pound, and spent there neuer so much time, if hee haue no more and not able to begin a family of himselfe, all is lost by order of Court.

But in the beginning it was not so, all went then out of one purse, till those new deuices haue consumed both mony and purse; for at first there were but six Patentees; now more then a thousand, then but thirteene Counsailors, now not lesse then an hundred; I speake not of all, for there are some both honourable and honest, but of those Officers, which did they manage their owne estates no better then the affaires of *Virginia*, they would quickly fall to decay so well as it; but this is most euident, few Officers in *England* it hath caused to turne Banquerupts, nor for all their complaints would leaue their places, neither yet any of their Officers there, nor few of the rest but they would be at home, but fewer Aduenturers here will aduenture any more till they see the businesse better established, although there be some so wilfully improuident they care for nothing but to get thither, and then if their friends be dead, or want themselues, they die or liue but poorely for want of necessaries, and to thinke the old Planters can releeue them were too much simplicity; for who here in *England* is so charitable to feed two or three strangers, haue they neuer so much; much lesse in *Virginia* where they want for themselues. Now the generall complaint saith, that pride, couetousnesse, extortion and oppression in a few that ingrosses all, then sell all againe to the comminalty at what rate they please, yea euen men, women and children for who will giue most, occasions no small mischiefe amongst the Planters.

As for the Company, or those that doe transport them, prouided of necessaries, God forbid but they should receiue their charges againe with aduantage, or that masters there should not haue the same priuilege ouer their seruants as here, but to sell him or her for forty, fifty, or threescore pounds, whom the Company hath sent ouer for eight or ten pounds at the most, without regard how they shall be maintained with apparell, meat, drinke and lodging, is odious, and their fruits sutable, therefore such merchants it were better they were made such merchandize themselues, then suffered any longer to vse that trade, and those are defects sufficient to bring a well setled Common-wealth to misery, much more *Virginia*.

Quest. 7. *How thinke you it may be rectified?*

Answ. If his Maiestie would please to intitle it to his Crowne, and yearely that both the Gouernours here and there may giue their accounts to you, or some that are not ingaged in the businesse, that the common stocke bee not spent in maintaining

maintaining one hundred men for the Gouernour, one hundred for two Deputies, fifty for the Treasurer, fiue and twenty for the Secretary, and more for the Marshall and other Officers who were neuer there nor aduentured any thing, but onely preferred by fauour to be Lords ouer them that broke the ice and beat the path, and must teach them what to doe, if any thing happen well, it is their glory; if ill, the fault of the old directors, that in all dangers must endure the worst, yet not fiue hundred of them haue so much as one of the others; also that there bee some present course taken to maintaine a Garrison to suppresse the Saluages, till they be able to subsist, and that his Maiesty would please to remit his custome, or it is to be feared they will lose custome and all, for this cannot be done by promises, hopes, counsels and countenances, but with sufficient workmen and meanes to maintaine them, not such delinquents as here cannot be ruled by all the lawes in *England*, yet when the foundation is laid, as I haue said, and a common-wealth established, then such there may better be constrained to labour then here: but to rectifie a common-wealth with debaushed people is impossible, and no wise man would throw himselfe into such a society, that intends honestly, and knowes what he vndertakes, for there is no Country to pillage as the Romans found: all you expect from thence must be by labour.

For the gouernment I thinke there is as much adoe about it as the Kingdomes of *Scotland* and *Ireland*, men here conceiting *Virginia* as they are, erecting as many stately Offices as Officers with their attendants, as there are labourers in the Countrey, where a Constable were as good as twenty of their Captaines, and three hundred good Souldiers and labourers better then all the rest that goe onely to get the fruits of other mens labours by the title of an office. Thus they spend *Michaelmas* rent in *Mid-summer* Moone, and would gather their Haruest before they haue planted their Corne.

As for the maintenance of the Officers, the first that went neuer demanded any, but aduentured good summes, and it seemes strange to me, the fruits of all their labours, besides the expence of an hundred and fifty thousand pounds, and such multitudes of people, those collaterall Officers could not maintaine themselues so well as the old did, and hauing now such liberty to doe to the Saluages what they will, the others had not. I more then wonder they haue not fiue hundred Saluages to worke for them towards their generall maintenance, and as many more to returne some content and satisfaction to the Aduenturers, that for all their care, charge and diligence, can heare nor see nothing but miserable complaints; therefore vnder your correction to rectifie all, is with all expedition to passe the authority to them who will releeue them, lest all bee consumed ere the differences be determined. And except his Maiestie vndertake it, or by Act of Parlament some small tax may be granted throughout his Dominions, as a Penny vpon euery Poll, called a head-penny; two pence vpon euery Chimney, or some such collection might be raised, and that would be sufficient to giue a good stocke, and many seruants to sufficient men of any facultie, and transport them freely for paying onely homage to the Crowne of *England*, and such duties to the publike good as their estates increased reason should require. Were this put in practice, how many people of what quality you please, for all those disasters would yet gladly goe to spend their liues there, and by this meanes more good might be done in one yeere, then all those pety particular vndertakings will effect in twenty.

For the Patent the King may, if he please, rather take it from them that haue it, then from vs who had it first, pretending to his Maiesty what great matters they would doe, and how little we did, and for any thing I can conceiue, had we remained still as at first, it is not likely we could haue done much worse; but those oft altering of gouernments are not without much charge, hazard and losse. If I be too plaine, I humbly craue your pardon; but you requested me, therefore I doe but my duty. For the Nobility, who knowes not how freely both in their

Purses and assistances many of them haue beene to aduance it, committing the managing of the businesse to inferiour persons, amongst whom questionlesse also many haue done their vtmost best, sincerely and truly according to their conceit, opinion and vnderstanding; yet grosse errors haue beene committed, but no man liues without his fault; for my owne part, I haue so much adoe to amend my owne, I haue no leisure to looke into any mans particular, but those in generall I conceiue to be true. And so I humbly rest Yours to command, *I. S.*

The King hath pleased to take it into his consideration.

THus those discords, not being to be compounded among themselues, nor yet by the extraordinary diligences, care and paines of the noble and right worthy Commissioners, Sir *William Iones*, Sir *Nicholas Fortescue*, Sir *Francis Goston*, Sir *Richard Sutton*, Sir *Henry Bourgchier* and Sir *William Pit*; a Corante was granted against Master Deputy *Farrar*, and 20. or 30. others of that party to plead their causes before the right Honourable, the Lords of his Maiesties Priuy Councell: now notwithstanding all the Relations, Examinations, and intercepting of all Letters whatsoeuer came from thence, yet it seemes they were so farre vnsatisfied and desired to know the truth, as well for the preseruation of the Colony, as to giue content and doe all men right, they sent two Commissioners strictly to examine the true estate of the Colony. Vpon whose returne after mature deliberation, it pleased his royall Maiesty to suppresse the course of the Court at Deputy *Farrars*, and that for the present ordering the affaires of *Virginia*, vntill he should make a more full settlement thereof, the Lord Viscount *Mandeuile*, Lord President of his Maiesties Priuie Councell, and also other Priuy Councellors, with many vnderstanding Knights and Gentlemen, should euery Thursday in the afternoone meet at Sir *Thomas Smiths* in *Philpot lane*, where all men whom it should concerne may repaire, to receiue such directions and warrant for their better security, as more at large you may see in the Proclamation to that effect, vnder the great Seale of *England*, dated the 15. of Iuly, 1624. But as for the relations last returned, what numbers they are, how many Cities, Corporations, townes, and houses, cattle and horse they haue, what fortifications or discoueries they haue made, or reuenge vpon the Saluages; who are their friends or foes, or what commodities they haue more then Tobacco, & their present estate or what is presently to be put in execution, in that the Commissioners are not yet fully satisfied in the one, nor resolued in the other, at this present time when this went to the Presse, I must intreat you pardon me till I be better assured.

Thus far I haue trauelled in this Wildernesse of *Virginia*, not being ignorant for all my paines this discourse will be wrested, tossed and turned as many waies as there is leaues; that I haue writ too much of some, too little of others, and many such like obiections. To such I must answer, in the Companies name I was requested to doe it, if any haue concealed their approued experiences from my knowledge, they must excuse me: as for euery fatherles or stolne relation, or whole volumes of sofisticated rehearsals, I leaue them to the charge of them that desire them. I thanke God I neuer vndertooke any thing yet any could tax me of carelesnesse or dishonesty, and what is hee to whom I am indebted or troublesome? Ah! were these my accusers but to change cases and places with me but 2. yeeres, or till they had done but so much as I, it may be they would iudge more charitably of my imperfections. But here I must leaue all to the triall of time, both my selfe, *Virginia's* preparations, proceedings and good euents, praying to that great God the protector of all goodnesse to send them as good successe as the goodnesse of the action and Country deserueth, and my heart desireth.

FINIS.

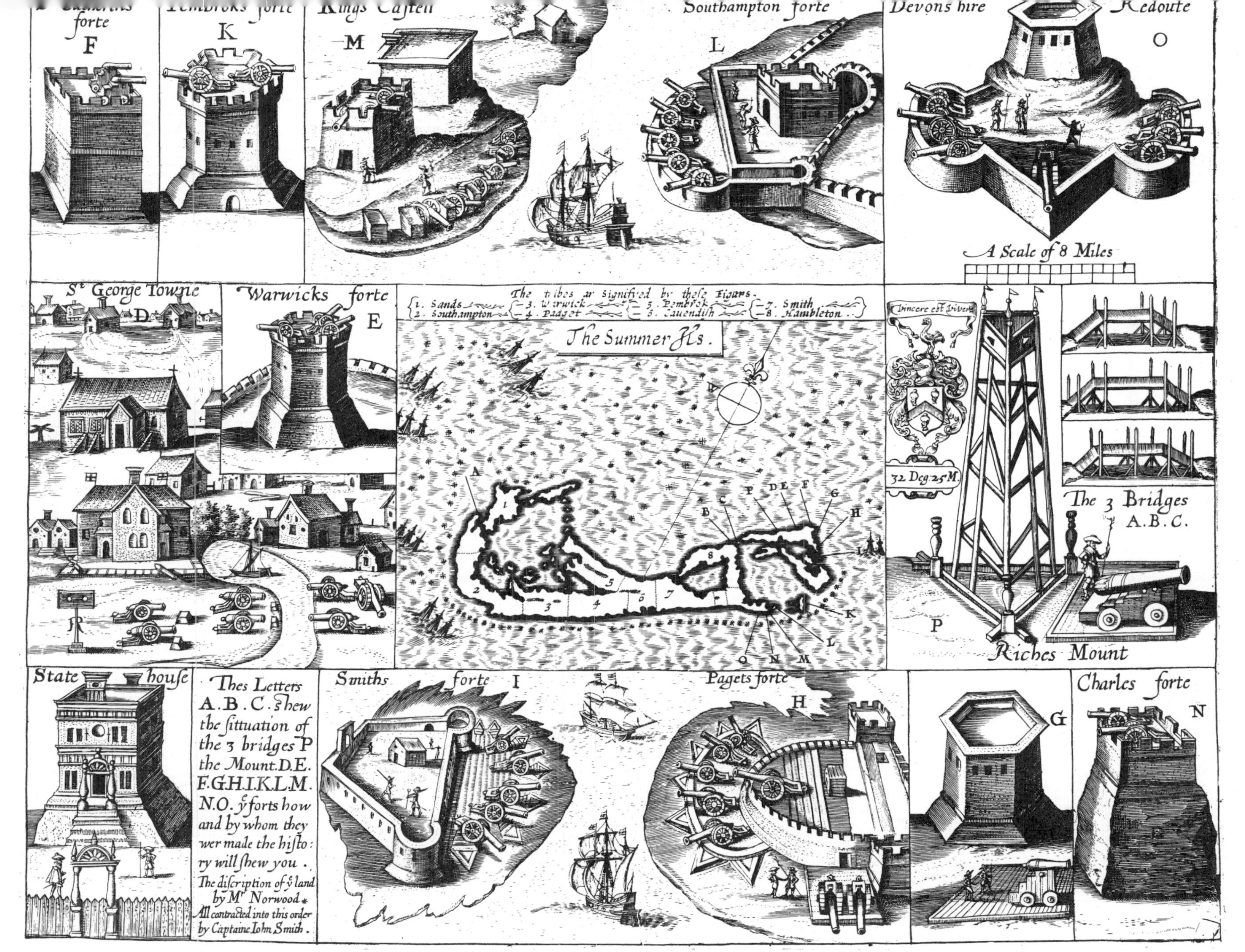
forte
F
K
Kings Castell
M
Southampton forte
L
Devons hire
Redoute
O
A Scale of 8 Miles
St George Towne
D
Warwicks forte
E
The tribes ar signifyed by these Figurs.
1. Sands
2. Southampton
3. Warwick
4. Padget
5. Pembrok
6. Cauendish
7. Smith
8. Hambleton
The Summer Ils.
Vincere est Viuere
32 Deg 25 M.
The 3 Bridges
A.B.C.
P
Riches Mount
State house
Thes Letters A.B.C. shew the situation of the 3 bridges P the Mount. D.E. F.G.H.I.K.L.M. N.O. ye forts how and by whom they wer made the histo: ry will shew you.
The discription of ye land by Mr Norwood.
All contracted into this order by Captaine Iohn Smith.
Smiths forte
I
Pagets forte
H
G
Charles forte
N

THE FIFTH BOOKE.

THE GENERALL HISTORIE OF THE BERMVDAS, now called the *Summer Iles*, from their beginning in the yeere of our Lord 1593. to this present 1624. with their proceedings, accidents and present estate.

BEfore we present you the matters of fact, it is fit to offer to your view the Stage whereon they were acted, for as Geography without History seemeth a carkasse without motion, so History without Geography, wandreth as a Vagrant without a certaine habitation. Those Ilands lie in the huge maine Ocean, and two hundred leagues from any continent, situated in 32. degrees and 25. minutes, of Northerly latitude, and distant from *England* West South-West, about 3300. miles, some twenty miles in length, and not past two miles and a halfe in breadth, enuironed with Rocks, which to the North-ward, West-ward, and South-East, extend further then they haue bin yet well discouered: by reason of those Rocks the Country is naturally very strong, for there is but two places, & scare two, vnlesse to them who know them well, where shipping may safely come in, and those now are exceeding well fortified, but within is roome to entertaine a royall Fleet: the Rocks in most places appeare at a low water, neither are they much coueréd at a high, for it ebbs and flowes not past fiue foot; the shore for most part is a Rocke, so hardened with the sunne, wind and sea, that it is not apt to be worne away with the waues, whose violence is also broke by the Rocks before they can come to the shore: it is very vneuen, distributed into hills and dales; the mold is of diuers colours, neither clay nor sand, but a meane betweene; the red which resembleth clay is the worst, the whitest resembling sand and the blackest is good, but the browne betwixt them both which they call white, because there is mingled with it a white meale is the best: vnder the mould two or three foot deep, and sometimes lesse, is a kinde of white hard substance which they call the Rocke: the trees vsually fasten their roots in it; neither is it indeed rocke or stone, or so hard, though for most part more harder then Chalke; nor so white, but pumish-like and spungy, easily receiuing and containing much water. In some places Clay is found vnder it, it seemes to be ingendred with raine water, draining through the earth, and drawing with it of his substance vnto a certaine depth where it congeales; the hardest kinde of it lies vnder the red ground like quarries, as it were thicke slates one vpon another, through which the water hath his passage, so that in such places there is scarce found any fresh water, for all or the most part of the fresh water commeth out of the Sea draining through the sand, or that substance called the Rocke, leauing the salt behinde, it becomes fresh: sometimes we digged wells of fresh water which we finde in most places, and but three or foure paces from the Sea side, some further, the most part of them would ebbe and flow as the Sea did, and be leuell or little higher then the superficies of the sea, and in some places very strange, darke and cumbersome Caues.

The description of the Iles.

The clime, temper and fertility.

The aire is most commonly cleere, very temperate, moist, with a moderate heat, very healthfull and apt for the generation and nourishing of all things, so as many things transported from hence yeeld a farre greater increase, and if it be any liuing thing it becomes fatter and better; by this meanes the country is so replenished with Hens and Turkies, within the space of three or foure yeeres, that many of them being neglected, forsake the houses and become wilde, and so liue in great abundance; the like increase there is in Hogs, tame Conies, and other Cattle according to their kindes. There seemes to be a continuall Spring, which is the cause some things come not to that maturity and perfection as were requisite; and though the trees shed their leaues, yet they are alwaies full of greene; the Corne is the same they haue in *Virginia*, and the *West-Indies*: of this and many other things without plowing or much labour, they haue two Haruests euery yeere, for they set about March, which they gather in Iuly; and againe in August, which they reape in December; and little slips of Fig-trees and Vines doe vsually beare fruit within the yeere, and sometimes in lesse; but we finde not the Grapes as yet come to any perfection; the like fertility it hath in Oranges and Limons, Pomgranates, and other things. Concerning the serenity and beauty of the skie, it may as truly be said of those Ilands as euer it was said of the Rhodes, that there is no one day throughout the 12. moneths, but that in some houre thereof, the sun lookes singularly & cleere vpon them: for the temperature it is beyond all others most admirable; no cold there is beyond an English Aprill, nor heat much greater then an ordinary Iuly in *France*, so that frost and snow is neuer seene here, nor stinking and infectious mists very seldome, by reason of the maine Ocean, there is some wind stirring that cooles the aire: the winter they haue obserues the time with ours, but the longest daies and nights are shorter then ours almost by two houres.

Trees and Fruits.

We found it at first all ouergrowne with weeds, and plants of seuerall kinds, as many tall and goodly Cedars, infinite store of Palmetoes, numbers of Mulberies, wild Oliue-trees store, with diuers others vnknowne both by name and nature, so that as yet they become lost to many vsefull imployments, which time and industry no doubt will one day discouer, and euen already certaine of the most notorious of them haue gotten them appellations from their apparent effects, as the Prickell-peare which growes like a shrub by the ground, with broad thick leaues, all ouer-armed with long and sharpe dangerous thornes, the fruit being in forme not much vnlike a small greene Peare, and on the outside of the same colour, but within bloud red, and exceeding full of iuice; with graines not much vnlike the Pomgranat, and colouring after its nature. The poysoned weed is much in shape like our English Iuy, but being but touched, causeth rednesse, itching, and lastly blisters, the which howsoeuer after a while passe away of themselues without further harme, yet because for the time they are somewhat painfull, it hath got it selfe an ill name, although questionlesse of no ill nature. Here is also frequently growing a certaine tall Plant, whose stalke being all ouer couered with a red rinde, is thereupon termed the red weed, the root whereof being soked in any liq[illegible]r, or but a small quantity of the Iuice drunke alone, procures a very forcible vomit, and yet is generally vsed by the people, and found very effectuall against the paines and distempers of the stomacke.

The Prickell Peare.

The poison weed.

The red weed.

The purging Beane.

A kinde of Wood-bind there is likewise by the Sea very commonly to bee found, which runnes vpon trees twining it selfe like a Vine: the fruit somewhat resembles a Beane, but somewhat flatter, the which any way eaten worketh excellently in the nature of a purge, and though very vehemently, yet without all perill. Contrary to this, another small tree there is, which causeth costiuenesse; there is also a certaine Plant like a bramble bush, which beares a long yellow fruit, hauing the shell very hard, and within it a hard berry, that beaten and taken inwardly purgeth gently. There is another fruit much like our Barberies, which being beaten or brused betweene the teeth, sets all the mouth on an extreme heat very terrible for the time, to auoid which they are swallowed downe whole,

The costiue tree.

Red Pepper.

and

and found of the same or better operation then the red Pepper, and thence borroweth the name. In the bottome of the Sea there is growing vpon the Rocks a large kinde of Plant in the forme of a Vine leafe, but far more spread with veines in colour of a pale red, very strangely interlaced & wouen one into another, which we call the Feather, but the vertue thereof is altogether vnknowne, but only regarded for the rarity. Now besides these naturall productions, prouidences & paines since the Plantation, haue offered diuers other seeds & plants, which the soile hath greedlily imbraced & cherished, so that at this present 1623. there are great abundance of white, red and yellow coloured Potatoes, Tobacco, Sugarcanes, Indicos, Parsnips, exceeding large Radishes, the American bread, the Cassado root, the Indian Pumpian, the Water-millon, Musk-millon, & the most delicate Pine-apples, Plantans, and Papawes, also the English Artichoke, Pease, &c. briefly whatsoeuer else may be expected for the satisfaction either of curiosity, necessity or delight.

The Sea feather. Fruits transported.

Neither hath the aire for her part been wanting with due supplies of many sorts of Fowles, as the gray and white Hearne, the gray and greene Plouer, some wilde Ducks and Malards, Coots and Red-shankes, Sea-wigions, Gray-bitterns, Cormorants, numbers of small Birds like Sparrowes and Robins, which haue lately beene destroyed by the wilde Cats, Wood-pickars, very many Crowes, which since this Plantation are kild, the rest fled or seldome seene except in the most vninhabited places, from whence they are obserued to take their flight about sun set, directing their course towards the North-west, which makes many coniecture there are some more Ilands not far off that way. Sometimes are also seene Falcons & Iar-falcons, Ospraies, a Bird like a Hobby, but because they come seldome, they are held but as passengers; but aboue all these, most deseruing obseruation and respect are those two sorts of Birds, the one for the tune of his voice, the other for the effect, called the Cahow, and Egge-bird, which on the first of May, a day constantly obserued, fall a laying infinite store of Eggs neere as big as Hens, vpon certaine small sandie baies especially in *Coupers* Ile; and although men sit downe amongst them when hundreds haue bin gathered in a morning, yet there is hath stay'd amongst them till they haue gathered as many more: they continue this course till *Midsummer*, and so tame & feareles, you must thrust them off from their Egg with your hand; then they grow so faint with laying, they suffer them to breed & take infinite numbers of their yong to eat, which are very excellent meat.

Birds. Egge-Birds.

The Cahow is a Bird of the night, for all the day she lies hid in holes in the Rocks, where they and their young are also taken with as much ease as may be, but in the night if you but whoop and hollow, they will light vpon you, that with your hands you may chuse the fat and leaue the leane; those they haue only in winter: their Eggs are as big as hens, but they are speckled, the other white. Mr. *Norwood* hath taken twenty dozen of them in three or foure houres, and since there hath beene such hauocke made of them, they were neere all destroyed, till there was a strict inhibition for their preseruation. The Tropicke bird is white, as large as a Pullet, with one onely long Feather in her taile, and is seldome seene far distant from other of the Tropicks: another small Bird there is, because she cries Pembly, so they call her so, she is seldome seene in the day but when she sings, as too oft she doth very clamorously; too true a Prophet she proues of huge winds and boysterous weather: there were a kinde of small Owles in great abundance, but they're now all slaine or fled: some tame Ducks, Geese and Pigeons there are, but the two latter prosper not.

Cahowes. The Tropicke Bird and the Pemblicos presagements.

Concerning vermine and noisome creatures, there are not many, but onely Rats and Cats, there increased since the Plantation, but how they agree together you shall heare hereafter. The Musketas and Flies are also too busie, with a certaine Indian Bug, called by the Spaniards a Cacarootch, the which creeping into Chests they eat and defile with their ill-sented dung: also the little Ants in summer time are so troublesome, they are forced to dry their figs vpon high frames, and anoint their feet with tar, wherein they sticke, else they would spoile them all

Of Vermine.

ere they could be dryed: Wormes in the earth also there are, but too many, so that to keepe them from destroying their Corne and Tobacco, they are forced to worme them euery morning, which is a great labour, else all would be destroyed. Lizards there were many and very large, but now none, and it is said they were destoyed by the Cat. Certaine Spiders also of very large size are found hanging vpon trees, but instead of being any way dangerous as in other places, they are here of a most pleasing aspect, all ouer drest, as it were with Siluer, Gold, and Pearle, and their Webs in the Summer wouen from tree to tree, are generally a perfect raw silke, and that as well in regard of substance as colour, and so strong withall, that diuers Birds bigger than Black-birds, being like Snipes, are often taken and snared in them as a Net: then what would the Silke-worme doe were shee there to feede vpon the continuall greene Mulbery?

Note.

Fishes.

But aboue all the rest of the Elements, the Sea is found most abundantly liberall: hence haue they as much excellent Fish, and as much variety as need be desired. The most of which being vnknowne to our Northerne parts, got there new names, either for their shapes or conditions; as the large Rocke-fish from his like hew, and haunting amongst the Rocks, the fat Hog-fish from his swine-like shape and snout: for this is not the old knowne Hog-fish with brussels on his backe; the delicate Amber-fish from his taste and smell, Angell-fish, Cony-fish, the small yellow taile from that naturall painting; the great Growper from his odde and strange grunting, some of them yet knowne to the *Americans*, as the Purgoose, the Cauallo, the Gar-fish, Flying-fish and Morerayes: the rest are common to other Continents; as the Whale in great numbers, the Sharke, the Pilot-fish, the Sea-Breame, the Oyster and Lobster, with diuers others; twenty Tortoises haue beene taken in a day, and some of them will affoord halfe a bushell of Egges, and suffice to feed forty men at a meale. And thus haue you briefely epitomized Mother Natures benefits to this little, yet dainty spot of earth, nether were it ingenuity to conceale wherein shee inclineth to the Stepdame, especially since the particulars are so few, as rather requisite Antidotes against idlenesse to rouse vp industry, then any great cause of much distaste, much lesse despaire: and of those to speake troth, there are onely two: *viz.* the Winds, and the Wormes, especially in the Spring and Autumne; and thus conditioned as yet we will let rest these small Ilands, in the midst of this mightie and maine Ocean, so nuironed on euery side, by infinite numbers of vncertaine scattered Rocks, lying shallowly hid vnder the surface of the water, a league, two, three, foure, or fiue, to Sea, to the which aduantages added by art, as hereafter you shall heare at large and finde described in the Map. It may well be concluded to be the most impregnable place in the world, and although the Amber Greece, Pearles, nor Tobacco, are of that quantity and certainty to be relied vpon to gaine wealth; yet by practise and experience they finde, by Silke, Saffron, Indico, Madar, Sugar-canes, Wine, Oile, and such like great profit may be expected: yet were those hopelesse in regard of their conueniency to nourish and maintaine themselues, and releeue them shall visit them with wood, water, and other necessaries, beside what an eye-sore they are already becommed to them that haue them not, and how deare and precious to them that haue them, I thinke none will deny but they are well worth the keeping: and so we will proceed to the accidents that befell the first finders; also the proceedings of the first Planters and their successors, Master *Norrod, Thomas Sparkes*, and diuers others.

The most hurtfull things in those Iles.

A briefe relation of the shipwracke of Henry May.

1593. How it is supposed they were called the *Bermud*

HOw these Iles came by the name of *Bermudas*, or the infinite number of blacke Hogs, or so fearefull to the world, that many call'd them the *Ile of Deuils*, that all men did shun as Hell and perdition, I will not expostulate, nor trouble your patiences with those vncertaine antiquities

ties further then thus; our men found diuers crosses, peeces of Spanish monies here and there. Two or three wracks also they found, by certaine inscriptions to bee some Spanish, some Dutch, some French; but the greatest rumour is, that a Spanish ship called *Bermudas* was there cast away, carrying Hogges to the West-Indies that swam a shore, and there increased: how the *Spaniards* escaped is vncertaine: but they say, from that ship those Iles were first called *Bermudas*, which till then for six thousand yeares had beene namelesse.

But the first English-man that was euer in them, was one *Henry May*, a worthy Mariner that went with Captaine *Lancaster* to the East-Indies 1591. and in their returne by the West-Indies, being in some distresse, sent this *Henry May* for England by one *Mounsier de la Barbotier*, to acquaint the Merchants with their estate. The last of Nouember, saith *May*, we departed from *Laguna* in *Hispaniola*, and the seuenteenth of December following, we were cast away vpon the North-west of the *Bermudas*; the Pilots about noone made themselues Southwards of the Iles twelue leagues, and demanded of the Captaine their Wine of hight as out of all danger, which they had: but it seemes they were either drunke, or carelesse of their charge; for through their negligences a number of good men were cast away. I being but a stranger amongst fiftie and odde French-men, it pleased God to appoint me to be one of them should be saued. In this extremity we made a raft, which we towed with our Boat, there were but six and twentie of vs saued; and I seeing scarce roome for the one halfe, durst not passe in amongst them till the Captaine called me along with him, leauing the better halfe to the seas mercy: that day we rowed till within two houres of night ere we could land, being neere dead with thirst, euery man tooke his way to seeke fresh water, at length, by searching amongst many weeds, we found some raine water, but in the maine are many faire Baies, where we had enough for digging.

Now it pleased God before our ship split we saued our Carpenters tooles, some Nailes, Sailes, and Tacklings, wherewith we went roundly to worke, and built a Barke of eighty tunnes: In stead of Pitch, we made Lime, mixed with Tortoise oyle, and as the Carpenters calked her, I and another paied the seames with this plaster, which being in Aprill, became quickly dry, and as hard as a stone.

The building and calking their Barke.

In Aprill it was so hot, we feared our water would faile, two great Chests wee made, which we calked as our ship; those we stowed on each side our maine Mast, filled them with water and thirtie liue Tortoises: wee found many Hogges, but so leane wee could not eat them; the tops of the Palmetaberries was our bread, and the iuyce we got out of the trees we cut downe our drinke, and of the leaues, which are more then an Ell long, we couered our Cabens, & made our beds, and found many of those prouisions as is related, but little foule weather. The eleuenth of May it pleased God to set vs cleere of the Ile, after wee had liued there fiue moneths: and the twentieth wee fell with Cape *Britton*, neere *New found Land*, where refreshing our selues with wood and water, and such things as we could get of the Saluages, it seemed a good Countrey, but we staied not past foure houres before we set saile for the banke of *New found land*, where wee met many ships, but not any would take in a man of vs, vntill it pleased God we met a Barke of *Fawmothe*, which receiued vs for a little time, and with her we tooke a French ship, wherein I left Captaine *de la Barbotier*, my deare friend, and all his Company: and in August arriued at *Falmouth* in this honest English Barke, 1594.

His returne for England.

Written by me Henry May.

The

The first English ship knowne to haue beene cast away vpon the Bermudas 1609. *From the relation of* M[r]. Iordan, *Master* Iohn Euens, *Master* Henry Shelly, *and diuers others.*

YOu haue heard, that when Captaine *Smith* was Gouernor of *Virginia*, there were nine ships sent with Sir *Thomas Gates*, and Sir *George Somers*, and Captaine *Nuport* with fiue hundred people, to take in the old Commission, and rectifie a new gouernment: they set saile in May, and in the height of thirty degrees of Northerly latitude, they were taken with an extreme storme, or rather a part of *Hericano*, vpon the fiue and twentieth of Iuly, which as they write, did not onely separate them from the Fleet, but with the violent working of the Seas, their ship became so shaken, torne, and leake, she receiued so much water as couered two tire of Hogsheads aboue the ballace, that they stood vp to the middles, with Buckets, Baricos, and Kettles, to baile out the water. Thus bailing and pumping three daies and three nights without intermission, and yet the water seemed rather to increase then diminish, in so much that being all vtterly spent with labour, were euen resolued without any hope to shut vp the hatches, and commit themselues to the mercy of the Sea, which is said to be mercilesse, or rather to the mercy of Almighty God, whose mercy farre exceeds all his workes; seeing no sense or hope in mans apprehension, but presently to sinke: some hauing some good and comfortable waters, fetched them and dranke one to another, as taking their last leaues vntill a more happy, and a more ioyfull meeting in a more blessed world, when it pleased God out of his most gracious and mercifull prouidence, so to direct and guide their ship for her most aduantage;

A most desperate estate by a storm.

That Sir *George Somers* all this time sitting vpon the poupe, scarce taking leisure to eat nor sleepe, couing the ship to keepe her as vpright as he could, otherwaies she must long ere that needs haue foundered, most wishedly and happily descried land; whereupon he most comfortably incouraged them to follow their worke, many of them being fast asleepe: this vnlooked for welcome newes, as if it had bin a voice from heauen, hurrieth them all aboue hatches, to looke for that they durst scarce beleeue, so that improuidently forsaking that taske which imported no lesse then their liues, they gaue so dangerous aduantage to their greedy enemy the salt water, which still entred at the large breaches of their poore wooden castle, as that in gaping after life, they had well-nigh swallowed their death. Surely it is impossible any should now be vrged to doe his best, and although they knew it, that place all men did so shun, yet they spread all the saile they could to attaine them: for not long it was before they strucke vpon a rocke, till a surge of the sea cast her from thence, and so from one to another, till most luckily at last so vpright betwixt two, as if she had beene in the stocks, till this they expected but euery blow a death: But now behold, suddenly the wind giues place to a calme, and the billowes, which each by ouertaking her, would in an instant haue shiuered her in peeces, become peaceable and still, so that with all conueniency and ease, they vnshipped all their goods, victuall, and persons into their Boats, and with extreme ioy, euen almost to amazednesse, arriued in safetie, though more then a league from the shore, without the losse of a man; yet were they in all one hundred and fiftie: yet their deliuerance was not more strange in falling so happily vpon the land, as their feeding and preseruation was beyond their hopes; for you haue heard, it hath beene to the *Spaniards* more fearefull then an Vtopian Purgatory, and to all Sea-men no lesse terrible then an inchanted den of Furies and Deuils, the most dangerous, vnfortunate, and forlorne place in the world, and they found it the richest, healthfullest and pleasantest they euer saw, as is formerly said.

The care and iudgement of Sir *George Somers.*

An euident token of Gods mercy.

Sir *George Somers* his first ranging the land.

Being thus safe on shore, they disposed themselues to search the Iles for food and

and water; others to get a shore what they could from the ship; not long Sir *George* wandred but found such a fishing, that in halfe an houre with a hooke and line, he tooke so many as sufficed the whole company; in some places they were so thicke in the Coues, and so great, they durst not goe in lest they should bite them, and these rocke fish are so great two will load a man, and fatter nor better fish cannot be. Mr. *Shelly* found a Bay neere a quarter of a mile ouer, so full of Mullets, as none of them before had euer seene or heard of the like: the next day seeking to kill them with fis-gigs, they strucke so many the water in many places was red with bloud, yet caught not one, but with a net they caught so many as they could draw a shore, with infinite number of Pilchards and diuers other sorts; great craw-fishes in a night by making a fire they haue taken in great quantity. Sir *George* had twice his hooke and line broke out of his hand, but the third time he made it so strong he caught the same fish, which had pulled him into the Sea had not his men got hold of him, whereby he had his three hookes againe were found in her belly. At their first hunting for hogs they found such abundance, they killed 32. and this hunting & fishing was appointed to Captaine *Robert Walsingham*, and Mr. *Henry Shelly* for the company in generall: they report they killed at least 500. besides Pigs, and many that were killed by diuers others; for the birds in their seasons, the facility to make their cabens of Palmeta leaues, caused many of them vtterly forget or desire euer to returne from thence, they liued in such plenty, peace and ease.

But let vs remember how the Knights began to resolue in those desperat affaires: many proiects they had, but at last it was concluded, to decke their long boat with their ship hatches; which done, with all expedition they sent Master *Rauen*, a very sufficient Mariner, with eight more in her to *Virginia*, to haue shipping from thence to fetch them away; three weekes or a moneth they expected her returne, but to this day she was neuer more heard of; all this time was spent in searching the Iles: now although God still fed them with this abundance of plenty, yet such was the malice of enuy or ambition, for all this good seruice done by *Sommers*, such a great difference fell amongst their Commanders, that they liued asunder in this distresse, rather as meere strangers then distressed friends: but necessity so commanded, patience had the victory.

What meanes they made to send to Virginia.

Two ships at this time by those seuerall parties were a building; in the meane time two children were borne, the Boy was called *Bermudas*, the Girle *Bermuda*, and amongst all those sorrowes they had a merry English mariage; the forme of those Iles you may see at large in the Map of Mr. *Norwood*, where you may plainly see no place knowne hath better walls, nor a broader ditch. But hauing finished and rigged their two new Cedar ships with such prouisions they saued from the Sea-aduenturer they left amongst the Rocks, they called the one the *Patience*, the other the *Deliuerance*; they vsed Lime and Oile, as *May* did for Pitch and Tar. Sir *George Summers* had in his Barke no Iron at all but one bolt in her Keele; now hauing made their prouisions of victuall and all things ready, they set saile the tenth of May 1610. onely leauing two men behinde them, called *Christopher Carter* and *Edward Waters*, that for their offences, or the suspition they had of their iudgements, fled into the woods, and there rather desired to end their daies then stand to their trials and the euent of Iustice; for one of their consorts was shot to death, and *Waters* being tied to a tree also to be executed, had by chance a Knife about him, and so secretly cut the Rope, he ran into the woods where they could not finde him. There were two Saluages also sent from *Virginia* by Captain *Smith*, the one called *Namuntack*, the other *Matchumps*, but some such differences fell betweene them, that *Matchumps* slew *Namuntack*, and hauing made a hole to bury him, because it was too short, he cut of his legs and laid them by him, which murder he concealed till he was in *Virginia*.

A mariage, and two children borne.

The foure and twentieth of the same moneth they arriued in *Virginia* at *James towne*, where they found but threescore persons, as you may reade at large in the History of *Virginia*, of the fiue hundred left by Captaine *Smith*, also of the arriuall

Their arriuall in Virginia.

of

of the Lord *Laware*, that met them thus bound for *England*, returned them backe, and vnderstanding what plenty there was of hogs and other good things in the *Bermudas*, was desirous to send thither to supply his necessary occasions; whereupon Sir *George Summers*, the best acquainted with the place, whose noble minde euer regarded a generall good more then his owne ends, though aboue threescore yeeres of age, and had meanes in *England* sutable to his ranke, offered himselfe by Gods helpe to performe this dangerous voyage againe for the *Bermudas*, which was kindly accepted, so vpon the 19. of Iune, he imbarked in his Cedar ship, about the burthen of thirty tunnes, and so set saile.

Sir *George Summers* his returne to the *Bermudas*.

Much foule and crosse weather he had, and was forced to the North parts of *Virginia*, where refreshing himselfe vpon this vnknowne coast, he could not bee diuerted from the search of the *Bermudas*, where at last with his company he safely arriued: but such was his diligence with his extraordinary care, paines and industry to dispatch his businesse, and the strength of his body not answering the euer memorable courage of his minde, hauing liued so long in such honourable seruices, the most part of his well beloued and vertuous life, God and nature here determined, should euer remaine a perpetuall memory of his much bewailed sorrow for his death: finding his time but short, after he had taken the best course he could to settle his estate, like a valiant Captaine he exhorted them with all diligence to be constant to those Plantations, and with all expedition to returne to *Virginia*. In that very place which we now call Saint *Georges* towne, this noble Knight died, whereof the place taketh the name. But his men, as men amazed, seeing the death of him who was euen as the life of them all, embalmed his body and set saile for *England*, being the first that euer went to seeke those Ilands, which haue beene euer since called *Summers* Iles, in honour of his worthy memory, leauing three men behind them, that voluntarily stayed, whose names were *Christopher Carter*, *Edward Waters*, there formerly left as is said, and *Edward Chard*. This Cedar ship at last with his dead body arriued at *Whit-Church* in *Dorsetshire*, where by his friends he was honourably buried, with many vollies of shot, and the rites of a Souldier, and vpon his tombe was bestowed this Epitaph.

His Epitaph.

Hei mihi Virginia quod tam cito præterit Æstas,
Autumnus sequitur, sæuiet inde & hiems;
At ver perpetuum nascetur, & Anglia læta,
Decerpit flores florida terra tuas.

In English thus:

Alas Virginia's Summer so soone past,
Autumne succeeds and stormy Winters blast,
Yet Englands *ioyfull Spring with ioyfull showers,*
O Florida, *shall bring thy sweetest flowers.*

The proceedings of the three men.

THe honour of this resolution belongs principally to *Carter*, for through his importunity, not to leaue such a place abandoned, *Chard* & *Waters* were moued to stay with him, and the rest promised with all the speed they could againe to reuisit them. But the ship once out of sight, those three Lords, the sole inhabitants of all those Ilands, began to erect their little common wealth for a while with brotherly regency, repairing the ground, planting Corne, and such seeds and fruits as they had, building a house, &c. Then making priuy search amongst the creuises and corners of those craggy Rocks, what this maine Ocean since the worlds creation had throwne amongst them, at last they chanced vpon the greatest peece of Amber-greece was euer seene or heard of in one lumpe, being in weight fourescore pound, besides diuers other small peeces.

A peece of Amber-greece of 80. pound weight.

But now being rich, they grew so proud and abitious, contempt tooke such place,

place, they fell out for superiority, though but three forlorne men, more then three thousand miles from their natiue Country, and but small hope euer to see it againe. Notwithstanding, they sometimes fell from words to blowes about meere trifles: in one of which fights, one of them was bitten with his owne dog, as if the dumbe beast would reproue them of their folly; at last *Chard* and *Waters*, the two greater spirits, must try it out in the field, but *Carter* wisely stole away their weapons, affecting rather to liue amongst his enemies, then by being rid of them liue alone; and thus those miserable men liued full two yeeres, so that all their clothes were neere worne cleane from their backs, and their hopes of any forraine releefe as naked as their bodies. At last they began to recouer their wits, yet in a fashion perhaps would haue cost them dearer then when they were mad; for concluding a tripartite peace of their Matachin warre, they resolued to frame as good a Boat as they could, and therein to make a desperate attempt for *Virginia*, or *New found Land*; but no sooner were they entred into that resolution, but they descried a saile standing in for the shore, though they neither knew what she was, nor what she would, they were so ouer-ioyed, with all possible speed they went to meet her, and according to their hearts desire she proued an English-man, whom they safely conducted into their harbour.

Now you are to vnderstand, that Captaine *Matthew Somers*, Nephew and heire to Sir *George*, that returned with his dead body, though both he and his Company did their vtmost in relating all those passages to their Countrey-men and aduenturers, their relations were beleeued but as trauellers tales, till it came to be apprehended by some of the *Virginia* Company, how beneficiall it might be, and helpfull to the Plantation in *Virginia*, so that some one hundred and twentie of them bought the pretended right of all the Company, and had sent this ship to make a triall; but first they had obtained Letters Patents of the Kings most excellent Maiestie. Sir *Thomas Smith* was elected Treasurer and Gouernor heere, and Master *Richard More* to be Gouernor of the Iles and Colony there. How they were supplied. 1611.

The first beginning of a Colonie in the Somer Iles, vnder the command of Master Richard More, *extracted out of a plot of Master* Richard Norwood *Surueior, and the relations of diuers others.*

MAster *More* thus finding those three men not onely well and lusty, but well stored with diuers sorts of prouisions, as an Acre of Corne ready to be gathered, numbers of Pumpions and Indian Beanes, many Tortoises ready taken, good store of hogs flesh salted, and made in flitches of Bacon, were very good, and so presently landed his goods and sixty persons towards the beginning of Iuly 1612. vpon the South side of *Smiths* Ile. The arriuall of Master *More*. 1612. Sir *Thomas Smith* Treasurer.

Not long after his arriuall, *More* hauing some priuate intelligence of this Amber-greece, tooke first *Chard* in examination, he being one of the three the most masterfull spirit, what Amber-greece, Pearle, Treasure, or other Commodities they had found. *Chard* no lesse witty then resolute, directly answered; Not any thing at all but the fruits of the Ile, what his fellowes had done he knew not, but if they had, he doubted not but to finde it out, and then hee should know it certainly. This he spake onely to win time to sweare his Consorts to secrecy, and he would finde the meanes how they should all returne in that ship with it all for *England*, otherwise they should be deceiued of all. Till this was effected they thought euery houre an age; now for the better conueiance of it aboord, they acquainted it to Captaine *Dauis*, master of the ship, and one Master *Edwin Kendall*, that for their secrecy and transportation should participate with them: Without further ceremony the match was accepted, and absolutely concluded, the plot laid, time and place set downe to haue it aboord. But *Carter*, were it for feare the Gouernor at last should know of it, to whom so oft they had denied it, or that the Their differences about the Amber-greece.

rest should deceiue him, is vncertaine; but most certaine it is, he reuealed all the plot to Master *More*: To get so much wealth he knew would please them in *England*, though it did displease all his Company, and to lose such a prize he would not for hazarding a mutiny. So first hee reuealed himselfe to *Kendall* in faire tearmes, reprouing his dishonesty, but not being answered according to his expectation, he committed both *Chard* and him to person. The next Sabboath day *Dauis* comming on shore, *More* also taxed with very hard language and many threats, to lay him fast also if he mended not his manners; *Dauis* for the present replied little, but went with him to the place of praier: but in the midst of diuine seruice he goeth away, commanding all his Sea-men to follow him presently aboord, where he encourageth them to stand to him like men, and hee would free the Prisoners, haue all the Amber-greece for themselues, and so be gone.

Chard in danger of hanging.

The Gouernor hearing of this resolution, prepares with his company to repulse force with force, so that a generall expectance of a ciuill vnciuill warre possessed euery man; but this threatning gust passed ouer more calmlier then was expected; for *Dauis* hauing better aduised with himselfe, repented his rashnesse, and desired a reconcilement with the Gouernor. Peace thus concluded, *Kendall* was set at libertie, but *Chard* was condemned, and vpon the ladder to be hanged for his obstinacy; yet vpon better consideration *More* repriued him, but kept him a prisoner all the time he staied in the Country, which was generally thought a very bad reward for his great desert, and that there was more of this Amber-greece imbeziled, then would haue contented all the finders, that neuer had any consideration at all. The greatest part though *More* thus recouered, yet *Dauis* and *Kendall* had so much, either by the ignorance or conniuency of the Gouernors, that arriuing in *England*, they prepared themselues for a new voiage; at last they two falling out, the Company hauing notice thereof, so tormented them both, they gaue ouer their voiage, and durst not be seene a long time after.

Master *Mores* industry in fortifying and planting.

The Gouernor thus rid of the ship and those discontents, remoued his seat from *Smiths* Ile to Saint *Georges*, after he had fitted vp some small Cabbens of Palmata leaues for his wife and family, in that valley where now stands their prime towne called *S. Georges*, hee began to apply himselfe to fortifie the Countrey, and training his men in the exercise of armes. For although he was but a Carpenter, he was an excellent Artist, a good Gunner, very witty and industrious: he built and laid the foundation of eight or nine Forts, called the *Kings* Castle, *Charles* Fort, *Pembrookes* Fort, *Smiths* Fort, *Pagits* Fort, *Gates* Fort, *Warwicks* Castle, Saint *Katharines* Fort, &c. mounting in them all the Ordnance he had, preparing the ground to build Houses, plant Corne, and such Fruits as they had.

A contention of the Minister against the Gouernor.

Being thus busied, and as the necessitie of the time required, keeping his men somewhat hard at worke, Master *Keath* his Minister, were it by the secret prouocation of some drones, that grew weary of their taskes, or his affection to popularity is not certaine: But he begins to tax the Gouernor in the Pulpit, hee did grinde the faces of the poore, oppressing his Christian brethren with *Pharoahs* taxes. *More* finding this in short time, might breed ill bloud, called the Company together and also the Minister, vrging them plainly, to tell him wherein he had deserued those hard accusations: whereupon, with an vniuersall cry they affirmed the contrary, so that *Keath* downe of his knees to aske him forgiuenesse. But Master *More* kindly tooke him vp, willing him to kneele to God, and hereafter be more modest and charitable in his speeches; notwithstanding two other discontents so vpbraided *More* with that doctrine, and stood to maintaine it, he impaneled a Iury, with a great deale of seeming much adoe he would hang them being condemned, one of them with the very feare, fell into a dead Palsie; so that the other was set at libertie, and proued after a very good labourer.

Many conclusions he tried about the *Sea-venture*, the wracke of Sir *George Somers*,

mers, but he got onely for his paines but two peece of Ordnance. Hauing framed a Church of timber, it was blowne downe by a tempest, so that he built another in a more closer place with Palmeta leaues.

Two peeces weighed out of the *Sea Aduenture*.

Before this yeere was expired, the aduenterers sent them an *aduiso* with thirtie Passengers and good prouisions, to prepare with all expedition for their defence against the *Spaniard*, whom they vnderstood ere long would visit them: This occasioned him to keepe all his men together in that Ile so hard at worke, that wanting libertie to goe abroad for food, liuing onely on that they had, and expected daily to receiue from *England*, they were so ouer-toiled, many fell sicke, but none died. Very earnest this ship was to haue all the Amber-greece, which M. *More* perceiuing, was the chiefest cause of their comming, and that it was the onely loadstone to draw from *England* still more supplies; for all the expresse command sent from the Company, he returned this ship but with the one third part; so from thence she went to *Virginia*, and not long after arriued safely in *England*.

The first supply.

1613. The second supply. Sir *Thomas Smith* Treasurer.

But before her returne the Company sent the *Martha* with sixtie Passengers more; they arriued in Iune with one Master *Bartlet* to suruey the Iland, and the estate of the Colonie, with expresse command for all the Amber-greece: but *More* perceiuing him not as he would haue him, and that the Company began to mistrust him, would send no more but another third part, wherewith they returned, leauing a French-man to make triall of the Mulberies for Silke, but he did not bring any thing to perfection; excusing himselfe, they were not the right Mulberies he expected. About this time they were in hope of a small crop of Tobacco, but it was most spoiled for want of knowledge to vse it. Now in *England* Master *More* became amongst the Merchants maruelous distastfull, for the detaining so long the Amber-greece; which delaies they so much abhorred, they forthwith dispatched the *Elizabeth* the second time and forty Passengers, much rebuking *More* for so long detaining the Amber-greece: for the which, hauing now no more colourable excuses, he deliuered it, wherewith the ship went to *Virginia*, & thence home. In this ship was brought the first Potato roots, which flourished exceedingly for a time, till by negligence they were almost lost (all but two cast-away roots) that so wonderfully haue increased, they are a maine releefe to all the Inhabitants. This ship was not long gone but there came two Spanish ships, sounding with their Boat, which attempted to come in: but from the Kings Castle Master *More* made but two shot, which caused them presently depart. Marke here the handy-worke of the diuine prouidence, for they had but three quarters of a barrell of powder, and but one shot more, and the powder by carelesnesse was tumbled downe vnder the mussels of the two peeces, were discharged, yet not touched with fire when they were discharged.

A strange increase of Potatoes.

The attempt of two Spanish ships.

This feare thus past, appeares another much worse, which was the extremity of famine; in this extemity God sent Captaine *Daniel Elfrid* with a caruell of meale which a little relieued them, but brought withall so many Rats, that within two yeeres after neere ruined all; now though *Elfrid* had deceiued his friend *Fisher* of this Caruell in the *West-Indies*, they reuenged *Fishers* iniury, for *Elfrid* had his passage for *England*, and they made vse of all he had. Some two moneths after, came in the *Blessing* with an hundred Passengers; and two daies after the *Starre* with a hundred and fourescore more, amongst which were many Gentlemen, as Master *Lower* for Marshall, Master *Barret*, Master *Felgate*, and diuers others; but very vnproper for what they vndertooke. Within foureteene daies after came in the *Margaret* and two Frygats, and in them one hundred and threescore Passengers; also Master *Bartlet* came now expresly to diuide the Country into Tribes, and the Tribes into shares. But Master *More* finding no mention made of any part for himselfe nor all them with him, as he was promised in *England*, by no meanes would admit of any diuision, nor suffer his men from finishing their fortifications, which was so necessary, it was his maine ambition to see that accomplished; but such vnkindnesse grew betwixt this Master *Bartlet* and the Gouernour, that the rude multitude with all the disdaine they could deuise caused *Bartlet* returne for *England* as he came. About this time *William Millington* was drawne into the Sea by a fish, but neuer after euer seene.

1614. A great famine and mortalitie. Sir *Thomas Smith* Treasurer.

The neglect of this diuision was very hardly conceited in *England*, so that Master *More* grew more and more in dislike with the company; notwithstanding he followed the building of these Forts so earnestly, neglecting planting of Corne, till their store was neere all consumed, whereby they became so feeble and weake, some would not, others could not goe abroad to seeke releefe, but starued in their houses, and many that went abroad, through weaknesse were subiect to be suddenly surprized with a disease called the Feauges, which was neither paine nor sicknesse, but as it were the highest degree of weaknesse, depriuing them of power and ability from the execution of any bodily exercises, whether it were working, walking, or what else: being thus taken, if any presently gaue them food, many times they straight recouered, yet some after a little rest would bee able to walke, but if they found not present succour, died.

A strange being of Rauens.

About this time or immediatly before, came in a company of Rauens, which continued amongst them all the time of this mortality and then departed, which for any thing knowne, neither before nor since were euer seene or heard of: this with diuers other reasons caused Master *More* to goe out to Sea, to see if he could discouer any other Ilands, but he went not farre ere ill weather forced him backe, and it were a noble aduenture of him would vndertake to make more perfect all the dangers are about the *Summer Iles*.

All workes abandoned to get onely victuals.

Thus famine and misery caused Gouernour *More* leaue all his workes, and send them abroad to get what they could; one hundred and fifty of the most weake and sicke he sent to *Coupers* Ile, where were such infinite numbers of the Birds called Cahowes, which were so fearelesse they might take so many as they would, and that admired abundance of fish, that the extremity of their hunger, and their gluttony was such, those heauenly blessings they so consumed and wasted by carelesnesse and surfetting, many of them died vpon those silly Birds that offered themselues to the slaughter, which the Gouernour vnderstanding, caused them for change of aire to be remoued to *Port-royall*, and a Company of Fishers with a Boat to releeue them with fish, but the Gange grew so lazie the poore weaklings still died; they that remained killed the Cattle they found in the Ile, faining the heat caused them to runne into the Sea and so were drowned; so that the Gouernour sent againe for them home, but some obtained leaue still to liue abroad; one amongst the rest hid himselfe in the Woods, and liued onely on Wilkes and land Crabs, fat and lusty many moneths, but most of them being at Saint *Georges*, ordinarily was taken one hundred and fifty or two hundred great fishes daily for their food; for want of hookes and lines, the Smith made hookes of old swords, and lines of old ropes, but finding all those poore Engines also decay, they sent one of the two Frigats last left with them for *England*, to tell them of this misery. All which was now attributed to Master *Mores* peruersnesse, who at first when he got the Amber-Greece had not such a generall applause, but now all the worst could possibly be suggested was too good for him; yet not knowing for the present how to send a better, they let him continue still, though his time was neere expired, and with all speed sent the *Welcome* fraught with prouision, where shee well arriued, and proued her selfe as welcome in deed as in name; for all those extremities, Master *Lewes Hues* writeth, not one of all those threescore that first beganne this Plantation was dead, which shewes it was not impossible, but industry might haue preuented a great part of the others sluggish carelesnesse.

A supply, and M. *Mores* returne.

This ship much refreshed this miserable Colony, but Master *More* seeing they sent not for him, his time being now expired, vnderstanding how badly they reputed him in *England*, and that his imploiment now was more for their owne ends then any good for himselfe, resolued directly to returne with this ship. Hauing setled all things in the best order he could, left the gouernment to the charge

of

of the counsell of six to succeed each other monethly, till they had further directions from *England*; whose names were Captaine *Miles Kendall*, Captaine *Iohn Mansfield*, *Thomas Knight*, *Charles Caldycot*, *Edward Waters*, and *Christopher Carter*, with twelue others for their assistances. *More* thus taking leaue of those Ilands, arriued in *England*, much wrangling they had, but at last they confirmed him according to promise eight shares of Land, and so he was dismissed of his charge, with shew of fauour and much friendship.

The rule of the six Gouernors.

THE first thing they did was casting of lots, who should rule first, which lot lighted vpon Master *Caldicot*. This last supply somewhat abated the extremitie of their miseries, and the better in that their fortifications being finished, they had the more leasure to goe abroad with that meanes was brought to that purpose to fish. *Chard* as you haue heard, whom all this while *More* had kept Prisoner, they set at libertie: now by reason of their former miseries, little or nothing could be done; yet this Gouernor hauing thus concluded his moneth, and prepared a Frigot and two and thirtie men, hee imbarked himselfe with two other of his fellow counsellers; namely, *Knight* and *Waters* for the West-Indies, to get Fruits and Plants, Goats, young Cattle, and such like. But this poore vessell, whether through ill weather, or want of Mariners, or both, in stead of the *Indies* fell with the *Canaries*, where taking a poore *Portugall*, the which they manned with ten of their owne people, as soone after separated from her in a storme, & the next day was taken by a French Pickaroune, so that the Frigot out of hope of her prize, makes a second time for the West-Indies, where she no sooner arriued, but foundred in the sea; but the men in their Boat recouered a desolate Ile, where after some few moneths stay, an English Pyrat tooke them in, and some of them at last got for *England*, and some few yeares after returned to the *Somer Iles*.

1615. Sir *Thomas Smith* Treasurer.

Captaine Iohn Mansfield *his moneth.*

THE Frigot thus gone, Captaine *Mansfield* succeeded. Then was contriued a petition, as from the generalitie, vnto the triumuirat Gouernors; wherein they supplicated, that by no meanes they should resigne the gouernment to any should come from *England*, vpon what tearmes soeuer, vntill six moneths after the returne of their ship sent to the West-Indies: about this vnwarrantable action, Master *Lewes Hues* their Preacher was so violent in suppressing it, that such discontents grew betwixt the Gouernors and him, and diuisions among the Company, he was arraigned, condemned, and imprisoned, but not long detained before released. Then the matter fell so hotly againe to be disputed betwixt him and one Master *Keath* a Scotch-man, that professed schollership, that made all the people in a great combustion: much adoe there was, till at last as they sate in the Church and ready to proceed to a iudiciary course against Master *Hues*; suddenly such an extreme gust of wind and weather so ruffled in the trees and Church, some cried out, A miracle; others, it was but an accident common in those Iles, but the noise was so terrible it dissolued the assembly: notwithstanding, Master *Hues* was againe imprisoned, and as suddenly discharged; but those factions were so confused, and their relations so variable, that such vnnecessary circumstances were better omitted then any more disputed.

This mans moneth thus ended, begins Master *Carter*, which was altogether spent in quietnesse, and then Captaine *Miles Kendall* had the rule, whose moneth was also as quietly spent as his Predecessors. Then Captaine *Mansfield* begins his second moneth, when the ship called the *Edwin* arriued with good supplies. About this time diuers Boats going to sea were lost, and some men drowned; and many

Master *Carter*. Captaine *Kendall* Capt. *Mansfield*.

many of the Company repaired to Master *Hues*, that there might bee a Councell according to Master *Mores* order of six Gouernours, and twelue Assistants, whereupon grew as many more such silly brawles as before, which at last concluded with as simple a reconciliation. In the *interim* happened to a certaine number of priuate persons as miserable and lamentable an accident, as euer was read or heard of, and thus it was:

A wonderfull accident.

In the month of March, a time most subiect of all others to such tempests; on a Friday there went seuen men in a boat of two or three tunnes to fish. The morning being faire, so eager they were of their iourney, some went fasting: neither carried they either meat or drinke with them, but a few Palmeta berries, but being at their fishing place some foure leagues from the shoare, such a tempest arose, they were quickly driuen from the sight of land in an ouergrowne Sea, despairing of all hope, onely committing themselues to Gods mercy, let the boat driue which way shee would. On Sunday the storme being somewhat abated, they hoysed saile as they thought towards the Island. In the euening it grew starke calme; so that being too weake to vse their oares, they lay a drift that night. The next morning *Andrew Hilliard*, for now all his companions were past strength either to helpe him or themselues: before a small gale of wind spred his saile againe. On Tuesday one died, whom they threw ouer board. On Wednesday three. And on Thursday at night the sixt. All these but the last were buried by *Hilliard* in the Sea, for so weake hee was growne hee could not turne him ouer as the rest, whereupon hee stripped him, ripping his belly with his knife, throwing his bowels into the water, hee spread his body abroad tilted open with a sticke, and so lets it lie as a cisterne to receiue some lucky raine-water, and this God sent him presently after, so that in one small shoure hee recouered about foure spoonefuls of raine water to his vnspeakeable refreshment; he also preserued neere halfe a pint of blood in a shooe, which he did sparingly drinke of to moist his mouth: two seuerall daies he fed on his flesh, to the quantity of a pound, on the eleuenth day from his losing the sight of land, two flying fishes fals in his boat, whose warme iucie blood hee sucked to his great comfort. But within an houre after to his greater comfort you will not doubt, he once againe descried the land, and within foure houres after was cast vpon a rocke neere to Port royall, where his boat was presently split in pieces, but himselfe, though extreamly weake, made shift to clamber vp so steepe and high a rocke, as would haue troubled the ablest man in the Ile to haue done that by day hee did by night.

Being thus astride on a rocke, the tumbling Sea had gotten such possession in his braines, that a good while it was before his giddy head would suffer him to venture vpon the forsaking it: towards the morning he craules a shore, and then to his accomplished ioy descernes where hee is, and trauels halfe a day without any refreshment then water, whereof wisely and temperately he stinted himselfe, otherwise certainely hee had drunke his last. In which case hee attaines a friends house: where at the first they tooke him for a ghost, but at last acknowledged and receiued him with ioy, his story after some houres of recouery of strength to tell it, heard out with admiration: he was not long after conueyed to the towne, where he receiued his former health, and was liuing in the yeere 1622.

Treasure found in the *Summer Iles*.

The next newes that happened in this time of ease, was, that a merry fellow hauing found some few Dollars against the Flemish wracke, the bruit went currant the treasure was found, and they all made men. Much adoe there was to preuent the purloining of it, before they had it: vvhere after they had tyred themselues vvith searching, that they found, amounted not to aboue twenty pounds starling, vvhich is not vnlike but to be the remainder of some greater store, washed from some wracke not farre from the shore.

A new Gouernor chosen.

The company by the *Edwin* receiuing newes of the reuels vvere kept in *Sommer Iles*, resolued to make choice of a new Gouernour, called Master *Daniel Tucker*, that a long time had bin a planter in *Virginia* in the gouernment of Captaine *Smith*.

Smith. All things being furnished for his voyage; hee set saile in the *George*, consorted with the *Edwin*, with many passengers, which being discouered by them in those Iles, they supposed them the Frigot sent to the West Indies; but when they vnderstood what they were, much preparation they made to resist the new Gouernour. Many great ostentations appeared on both sides, but when the *quondam* Gouernour did see his men for most part forsake him; all was very well and quietly compounded, and with much kindnesse receiued and welcomed a shore, where his Commission was no sooner read, then they accepted and acknowledged him for their Gouernour.

The Gouernment of Captaine Daniel Tuckar.

ABout the mistd of May arriued this Gouernor, where finding the Inhabitants both abhorring all exacted labour, as also in a manner disdaining and grudging much to be commanded by him; it could not but passionate any man liuing. But at last according to the *Virginia* order, hee set euery one was with him at Saint *Georges*, to his taske, to cleere grounds, fell trees, set corne, square timber, plant vines and other fruits brought out of *England*. These by their taske Masters by breake a day repaired to the wharfe, from thence to be imployed to the place of their imployment, till nine of the clocke, and then in the after-noone from three till Sunne-set. Beside meat, drinke and cloaths, they had for a time a certaine kinde of brasse money with a hogge on the one side, in memory of the abundance of hogges was found at their first landing. 1616. Sir *Thomas Smith* Treasurer.

This course thus squared, imitating diuers orders vsed in *Virginia*, by Sir *Tho. Dale*: he began by them to looke into his instructions giuen by the Company. Whereupon by one Mr. *Richard Norwood* a Suruayor, sent ouer for that purpose, in the time of Master *Moore*, hee began to lay out the eight tribes in the maine, which were to consist of fifty shares to a tribe; and twenty fiue acers to euery share. He also began to plant some Colony men, on some of the especiall shares. He swore also certaine of the chiefe men of euery tribe to bee Bailiffes thereof; and appointed as many men as hee was able for all supplied shares. The goods landed in the store houses hee sent from thence, and dispersed it to his workemen in generall: some Boats also began to be builded; but the pinace called the *Thomas* suspected might make an escape, was laid vp in a docke, were shee yet remaineth. Captaine *Tuckars* proceedings.

In the beginning of the second moneth of his gouernment, he directed warrants to all the Bailiffes, for the holding of a generall Assise at Saint *Georges*, and appointed Master *Stokes* Lieutenant of the Kings Castle at the Gurnets head. The *Edwin* came with him he sent to the West Indies by directions from *England*, to trade with the natiues, for cattell, corne, plants, and other commodities. A course of great importance, which had it been pursued, would certainly haue produced more hopefull effects for the good of the Colony, then all the supplies and *Magazines* from *England* hath or will in a long time. A Barke sent to the West Indies.

Presently after her departure began the Assises, executed by his Deputy. The chiefe matter handled was the hanging one *Iohn Wood* a French man, for speaking many distastefull and mutinous speeches against the Gouernour, to shew the rest by that example, the power of his authority, which after with his owne hands he so oft executed with a bastinado amongst the poorer sort; many tearmed it a cruelty, not much lesse then tyranny: but the sequell is more then strange. The Assises.

So it was that fiue of them, seeing by no meanes they could get passage for *England*, resolued to vndergoe all hazards but they would make an escape from such seruitude. The chiefe mariner and plotter of this businesse, was *Richard Sanders* and his confederates, *William Goodwin* a ship Carpenter, *Thomas Harison* a Ioyner, *Iames Barker* a Gentleman, and *Henry Puet*. These repairing to the Gouernour, and with pleasing insinuations told him, if hee would allow them but things The strange aduenture of fiue men in a boat.

things necessary, they would build him a boat of two or three tunnes, with a close decke, should goe a fishing all weathers. The Gouernour halfe proud that hee had brought his men to so good a passe, as he conceiued, to offer themselues to so necessary a worke; instantly with all willingnesse furnished them with all things they could desire, and many faire promises to incourage them to performe it with all expedition. Hauing made choise of a place most fit from molestation, they went forward with that expedition, that in a short time shee was brought to perfection. By this time, the ship that brought the Gouernour, being ready to depart, hee sends a lusty gange to goe fetch his new boat to carry him aboard, but arriuing at the place where she was built, they could heare no more of her, but she was gone the last euening to Sea, to try how shee would saile. Much search and dispute was where this boat should be: but at last they found diuers letters in the cabbins, to this effect, directed to the Gouernour, and other their friends: that their hard and bad vsage was so intolerable, and their hope so small euer againe to see their Countrey, or be deliuered from such seruitude, they did rather chuse to put themselues to that desperate hazard to goe for *England*, in which if they miscaried, as it was much to be mistrusted, their liues and bloods should be required at their hands was the cause. A compasse Diall *Barker* had borrowed of Master *Hues*, to whom he writ that as hee had oft perswaded them to patience, and that God would pay them though none did: hee must now bee contented with the losse of his Diall, with his owne doctrine. Such leasure they found to bee merry when in the eye of reason they were marching into a most certaine ruine. The Gouernour being thus satisfied of their escape, extreamly threatned them no lesse then a hanging, but the stormes of the Ocean they now more feared then him; good prouision by bartering they had got from the ship, where *Goodwin* in a brauado told the Mariners, though he could not be permitted to goe with them, yet peraduenture hee might be in *England* before them, whereat the Master and his Mate laughed merrily. But hauing beene now vnder saile three weekes, the winds so fauoured them, they felt nothing of what they had cause to feare: then a blustering gale blowing in their teeth, put them to much extremity for diuers dayes, then becomming more gentle away they past prosperously some eight or ten dayes more, till meeting a French Piccaroune of whom they desired succour, hee like himselfe tooke from them what hee liked, leauing them not so much as a crosse-staffe to obserue withall, and so cast them off: their course still they continued till their victuall began to fall to the lowest ebbe; and the very knees of their small vessell were halfe hewed away for fire wood. At last to their infinit ioy they arriued in *Ireland*, where the Earle of *Tomund* honorably entertained them, and caused the boat to be hung vp for a Monument, and well she might, for shee had sailed more then 3300. miles by a right line thorow the maine Sea, without any sight of land, and I thinke since God made the world, the like nauigation was neuer done, nor heard of. This fortunate *Sanders* going to the *East Indies*, in the rifling some ships there tooke, it was his chance to buy an old chest, for three or foure shillings, but because it wanted a key hee repented his bargaine, and would gladly haue sold it againe for lesse. A certaine time it lay tossed to and fro as a thing hee little regarded, but at last hauing little to doe, hee broke it open, where he found a thousand pounds starling, or so much gold as bought him in *England* a good estate, which leauing with his wife he returned againe to the *East Indies*.

Plants from the West Indies.

The *George* setting saile three dayes after this escape, the Gouernour seazed and confiscated all that those fugitiues left behinde them. Within a weeke after returned the *Edwin* from the *West Indies*, furnished with figges, pynes, sugar-canes, plantaines, papanes and diuers other plants, which were presently replanted, and since increased into greater numbers, also an *Indian* and a *Negar*, and so much *ligna vita* as defrayed all the charge. The Gouernor thus busied amongst his plants, making hedges of Figtrees, and Pomgranets, and seuerall diuisions by

palizadoes

Palizadoes for the defence of their guarding and keeping their cattell, for in such husbandry qualities he well deserued great commendations. The Adventurers to supply him sent with all speed they could the *Hopewell*, a small Barke, but an excellent sailer, and in her one Captaine *Powell* an excellent Mariner, and well acquainted in the Indies where he was to goe trade, after he had landed his passengers in the Summer Iles: but in his iourney at the Westerne Iles meeting a *Brasile* man, hee liked the suger and passengers so well, hee mand the Caruill with his owne men, and continued his course, but bethinking himselfe how this would be entertained at the Summer Iles, hee found such doubts, hee went directly for the West Indies to take time to resolue what to doe: arriuing there hee met a French rouer, one euery way as cunning as himselfe, but much more trecherous. A great league of kindnesse is soone made betweene them, vpon confidence whereof, *Powell* and some of the chiefe with him being inuited aboord him, is easily entised, and in the midst of their cups both hee and his company treacherously made prisoners; and thus was forced to giue him their prise, or hang at the yards arme with all his company. Hauing set them a shore, away goes the French man; *Powels* ship being but hard by, presently fetcht them all a boord, but finding his victuall neere spent, and no hope at all to recouer his prize, set his Portugales on shore, and set saile for the Summer Iles; where safely arriuing, hee declared the whole passage to the Gouernour, lest some other in telling might make it worse, of which the Gouernour seemed well enough to approue. The exploits of Captain *Powell*.

This Gouernour still spent his time in good husbandry, although some of the snarling sort here in *England*, whom nothing will please, writ to him hee was fitter to be a Gardiner then a Gouernour: some time he spent in digging of a great pond, but that worke proued altogether vnprofitable: about that time was held the second Assise. The greatest matter passed, was a Proclamatiō against the spoile of Cahowes, but it came too late, for they were most destroyed before: a platforme hee caused to be erected by *Pagits* Fort, where a good Fort were very necessary. Captaine *Powell* not hauing performed his seruice in the West Indies, he conditioned with the Company, is sent thither againe by this Gouernour, and thirteene or fourteene of his best men, furnished with all things necessary. In the meane time the Company vnderstanding, that in Ianuary, February and March, there are many Whales, for which fishing they sent the Neptune, a tall ship well prouided with euery thing fitting for that purpose. But before she arriued, Captaine *Tuckar*, who had brought also with him most prouisions for that imploiment, sent three good Shalops to try what could be done, but whether it was the swiftnes of the Whale in swimming, or the condition of the place, certaine it is for all their labour and hazard, they could kill none, though they strucke many. The second Assise.

To begin his second yeere, he called the third Assise, where diuers were punished as their faults deserued: three were condemned to die; two were repriued, but the third was hanged: the next day there was also a leuy for the repairing two Forts; but that labour tooke not such effect as was intended, for want of good directions. 1617. The third Assise. Sir *Thomas Smith* Treasurer.

But the great God of heauen being angry at somewhat happened in those proceedings, caused such an increase of silly rats, in the space of two yeeres so to abound, before they regarded them, that they filled not onely those places where they were first landed, but swimming from place to place, spread themselues into all parts of the Countrey, insomuch that there was no Iland but it was pestered with them; and some fishes haue beene taken with rats in their bellies, which they caught in swimming from Ile to Ile: their nests they had almost in euery tree, and in most places their burrowes in the ground like conies: they spared not the fruits of the plants, or trees, nor the very plants themselues, but ate them vp. When they had set their corne, the rats would come by troupes in the night and scratch it out of the ground. If by diligent watch any escaped till it came to earing, it should then very hardly escape them: and they became noysome euen to the very persons of men. They vsed all the diligence they could for the destroying of The countrey neere deuoured with rats.

them, nourishing cats both wilde and tame, for that purpose; they vsed ratsbane, and many times set fire on the woods, that oft ran halfe a mile before it was extinct; euery man was enioyned to set twelue traps, and some of their owne accord haue set neere an hundred, which they euer visited twice or thrice in a night; they also trained vp their dogges to hunt them, wherein they became so expert, that a good dog in two or three houres would kil forty or fifty. Many other deuices they vsed to destroy them, but could not preuaile, finding them still increasing against them: nay they so deuoured the fruits of the earth, that they were destitute of bread for a yeere or two; so that when they had it afterwards, they were so wained from it, they easily neglected to eat it with their meat. Besides they endeuoured so much for the planting Tobacco for present gaine, that they neglected many things might more haue preuailed for their good, which caused amongst them much weaknesse and mortality, since the beginning of this vermine.

A strange confusion of rats.

At last it pleased God, but by what meanes it is not well knowne, to take them away; in so much that the wilde cats and many dogs which liued on them, were famished, and many of them leauing the woods, came downe to their houses, and to such places where they vse to garbish their fish, and became tame. Some haue attributed the destruction of them the to encrease of wild cats, but that is not likely they should be so suddenly encreased rather at that time, then foure yeeres before; and the chiefe occasion of this supposition was, because they saw some companies of them leaue the woods, and flew themselues for want of food. Others by the coldnesse of winter, which notwithstanding is neuer so great there, as with vs in March, except it be in the wind; besides the rats wanted not the fethers of young birds and chickins, which they daily killed, and Palmeta mosse to build themselues warme nests out of the wind, as vsually they did; neither doth it appeare that the cold was so mortall to them, seeing they would ordinarily swimme from place to place, and bee very fat euen in the midst of winter. It remaineth then, that as God doth sometimes effect his will without subordinate and secondary causes, so wee need not doubt, but that in the speedy encrease of this vermine; as also by the preseruation of so many of them by such weake meanes as they then enioyed, and especially in the so sudden remouall of this great annoyance, there was ioyned with and besides the ordinary and manifest meanes, a more mediate and secret worke of God.

About this time *Henry Long*, with seuen others in an extreame storme were cast away, but three of them escaped. One of them being asked what hee thought in the worst of that extremity, answered, he thought nothing but gallowes claime thy right, and it seemes God well heard his prayer, and rewarded his ingratitude; for he was hanged within halfe a yeere after. In that March also fiue men went to Sea, but as yet was neuer heard of, and three more drowned in a boat. By *Helliards* house grew a very faire Cedar, which by a thunder clap was rent almost to small shiuers, and a man stood by him, and *Samuel Tanton* most fearfully blasted, yet neither they, the house, nor a little childe, yet a paire of racks in the house was all torne to fitters. The *Neptune* not long after arriuing to fish for whale, her fortune proued no better then the Gouernours, yet some are of opinion, profit might be made by them.

The returne of M. *Powel* from the Indies.

In May they discried foure saile, so that manning all their Forts, they stood two daies in Armes, expecting what they were; at last they found it Master *Powell* returned from the West-Indies in the *Hopewell*, where missing such trade as he expected, these three Frigots comming in his way, he could not chuse but take them; Meale, Hides and Munition was their lading: Faire weather the Gouernor made with *Powell*, till he had got all the goods into his owne possession, and then called *Powell* to a strict account for doing such an vnwarrantable act; much adoe then was betwixt the taker and receiuer; but *Powell* was glad to be excused to answer it in *England*, leauing all hee had taken behinde him in the Iles: The *Neptune* also returned with him, but noble *Powell* lost all his pay and pillage for this

this yeeres worke. For which the Company sent for to *Tucker*, so that he also lost his part as well as *Powell*: Notwithstanding, the Gouernour by this meanes being strong in shipping, fitted the Caruill with twelue men, vnder the command of *Edward Waters* formerly spoken of, and sent them to *Virginia* about such businesse as hee had conceiued. Arriuing there, they obtained some goates, and and hogs, & what they could spare, and so returned for the *Summer Iles*; but whether they could not finde the Iles for want of skill, or beaten off by ill weather, or the ill will they bare the Gouernor, it matters not much: but they bare vp again for *Virginia*, where they all remained, and would returne no more to *Summer Iles*.

The Gouernour thinking to make some vse of the hides, set some that professed themselues Tanners, to make tryall of their skill; but they lost their labours and spoiled the hides. Also he called another Assise cōcerning a poore fellow called *Gabriel*, for concealing some speeches M. *Pollard* and M. *Rich* should vse, tending to the dis-reputation of the Gouernour, and his iniustice and cruelties; which being brought within the compasse of sedition and mutiny, though a yeere agoe; many were called in question about it, although euery one ordinarily had spoke as much. Yet *Gabriel* for example sake was condemned to bee hanged, and was vpon the ladder, but reprieued. The other two M. *Pollard*, and M. *Rich* were imprisoned, but vpon better consideration, the fact appeared so small and ridiculous, vpon their submission they were pardoned, and restored to their places.

A supposed mutiny by M. *Pollard*, and M. *Rich*.

The diuision of the Summer Iles into Tribes, by Master Richard Norwood, *Surueyor*.

1618. The diuision of the Iles into Tribes. Sir *Thomas Smith* Treasurer.

According to the directions of the Councell and Company, as they had determined by lot, M. *Norwood* tooke a plot of the Ile, and diuided it with as much faithfulnes as he could, assigning to euery Aduenturer his share or proportion, as namely, to lay out a large proportion, to bee called the generall land, and imployed for publike vses, as for the maintenance of the Gouernour, Ministers, Commanders of Forts, souldiers, and such like: and to this end was assigned S. *Georges* Iland, S. *Dauids* Iland, *Longbridge* Iland, *Smiths* Iland, *Coopers* Iland, *Cony* Iland, *Nonesuch* Iland, part of the maine, and sundry other small Iles. The rest was to be diuided into eight parts, each part to be called a tribe, and to haue his denomination of some principall person that was Aduenturer therein: and accordingly the first Tribe to bee Eastward, was then called *Bedfords* Tribe, now *Hamiltons*: the second, *Smiths*: Tribe the third, *Cavendish*, now *Devonshires*: the fourth, *Pembrooks*: the fift, *Pagits*: the sixt, *Mansils*, now *Warwicks*: the seuenth, *Southhampton*: the eighth, *Sands*: in the honours of the Right honorable the Marquis *Hamilton*, Sir *Thomas Smith*, the Earle of *Deuonshire*, the Earle of *Pembrooke*, the *Lord Pagit*, the Earle of *Warwicke*, the Earle of *Southhampton*, and Sir *Edwin Sands*. Againe each of those Tribes were to bee diuided into fifty parts, called shares; and euery Aduenturer to haue his shares in these tribes as was determined, by casting lots in *England*, the manner of it appeares by the *Map*, and more largely by his Booke of the Suruay of the Countrey, which is in the Records of the Colony. And then began this which was before as you haue heard, but as an vnsetled and confused Chaos, to receiue a disposition, forme, and order, and become indeed a Plantation.

The names of the Aduenturers, and their ſhares in *euery Tribe, according to the ſuruey, and the beſt information* yet aſcertained, of any of their alterations.

Hamiltons Tribe.

	Share.
Iames L. Marquis Hamil.	6
Sir Edward Harwood.	4
M. *Iohn Delbridge.*	3
M. *Iohn Dike.*	3
M. *Ellis Roberts.*	2
M. *Robert Phips.*	1
M. *Ralph King.*	1
M. *Quicks aſſignes.*	2
M. *William Cannig.*	4
M. *William Cannig.*	1
M. *William Web.*	1
M. *Iohn Bernards aſſignes.*	2
M. *Elias Roberts Iun.*	1
M. *Iohn Gearing.*	2
M. *Cleophas Smith.*	2
Robert Earle of Warwick.	4
M. *Thomas Couell.*	3
M. *Greenwels aſſignes.*	1
M. *Cley.*	1
M. *Powlſon.*	2
M. *Iohn Dike.*	1.$\frac{1}{2}$
Cōmon land for conuenlency.	25
M. *Iohn Dike.*	1.$\frac{1}{2}$
M. *George Thorps aſſignes.*	1

2. Smiths Tribe.

Sir Dudley Digs aſſignes.	2
M. *Richard Edwards.*	2
M. *William Pane.*	4
M. *Robert Smith.*	2
M. *George Barkley aſſignes.*	5
Sir Samuel Sands.	1
M. *Anthony Penniſtone.*	4
Sir Edwin Sands.	5
Sir Thomas Smith.	5
M. *Richard More.*	4
M. *Ad. Brumfield*	2
M *Rob. Iohnſon Alderman.*	5
M. *Iohn Wroth.*	3
M. *George Smith.*	4

3. Deuonſhire Tribe.

	Shares.
M. *Anth. Peniſtone.*	2
M. *Iohn Dike.*	1
M. *Iohn Dike.*	1
M. *Iohn Bernards heires.*	2
Robert Earle of Warwick.	2
M. *Francis Weſt.*	2
Will. Lord Cavendiſh.	5
Will. Earle of Deuonſhire.	5
M. *Edw. Luckin.*	5
M. *Edw. Ditchfield.*	1
M. *Edw. Ditchfield.*	4
M. *Will. Nicols.*	2
M. *Edw. Ditchfield.*	1
M. *Iohn Fletcher.*	2
M. *Gedion Delawne.*	2
M. *Anth. Penniſtone.*	3
M. *Beſt.*	2
M. *Edw. Luckin.*	2
M. *Richard Rogers.*	2
M. *Will. Palmer.*	4

4. Pembrookes Tribe.

M. *George Smith.*	4
Gleab land.	2
M. *Nicholas Hide.*	1
Sir Lawrence Hide.	1
M. *Thomas Iudwyn.*	2
Will. Earle of Pemb.	10
M. *Richard Edwards.*	1
M. *Harding.*	1
M. *Rich. Edwards.*	1
M. *Elias Roberts.*	1
M. *Rich. Edwards.*	1
M. *Iacobſons aſſignes.*	1
M. *Iohn Farrar.*	1
M. *Nicholas Farrar.*	1
M. *Nicholas. Farrar.*	1
M. *Will. Canning.*	2
M. *Richard Martin.*	2
M. *Moris Abbot.*	2
M. *Rich. Caſwell.*	1
M. *Rich. Caſwell.*	2
M. *VVill. Caſwell.*	1
M. *Rich. Edwards.*	2
M. *Rich. Caſwell.*	1
M. *Rich. Edwards.*	1
M. *George Sands aſſignes.*	2
M. *Will. Paine.*	2

5. Pagits Tribe.

	Shares.
M. *Iohn Chamberlaine.*	5
M. *Tho. Ayres, and* M. *Rich. Wiſeman.*	4
M. *Rich. Wiſeman*	1
Will. Lord Pagit.	10
M. *Will. Palmer.*	4
M. *Bagnell.*	5
M. *Iohn Bale.*	1
M. *Wheatley.*	4
M. *Chriſtop. Barron.*	4
M. *Iohn Wodall.*	1
M. *Iohn Wodall.*	1
M. *Lewis.*	2
M. *Owen Arthors aſſignes.*	2
M. *George Etheridge.*	4
	2
Sir VVill. VVade.	1
M. *Iohn Bernards heires.*	1

6. Warwicks Tribe.

M. *VVheatley.*	2
Cap. Daniel Tuckar.	2
M. *Will. Felgate.*	1
Rob. Earle of Warwicke.	5
M. *George Smith.*	5
M. *Sam. Tickner.*	2
M. *Francis Mevell.*	1
M. *Sephen Sparrow.*	1
M. *Ioſeph Man.*	5
Cap. Daniel Tuckar.	2
M. *Elias More.*	1
Doctor. Anth. Hunton	2
M. *Francis Moverill.*	1
M. *Rich. Poulſon*	1
M. *Math. Shephard.*	1
M. *George Tuckar.*	10
M. *Ch. Clitheroe.*	1
M. *George Swinow.*	2
M. *Rich. Tomlings.*	1
M. *Francis Meverill.*	1
M. *Iohn Waters.*	2
M. *Martin Bond.*	2

7. Southamptons Tribe.

Cap. Dan. Tuckar.	4
M. *Iohn Britton.*	1
M. *Rich. Chamberland.*	3
M. *Leon. Harwods aſſignes.*	1
M. *Iohn Banks.*	1
Sir Nathanael Rich.	12
Rob. Earle of VVarwicke.	3

	Shares.
M. Richard More.	6
M. George Scot. / *M. Edward Scot.* / *M. Antho. Abdy.*	6
Hen. Earle of Southampton.	4
M. And. Broumfield.	2
M. Henry Timbed.	2
Sir Tho. Hewet.	2
M. Perce.	1
Sir Ralph Winwood.	2

8. Sandys Tribe.

	Shares.
M. George Barcklies heires.	5
Sir Edwin Sands.	5
M. Ierom Hidon.	10
M. Tho. Millin and / *M. Iohn Cuffe.*	2
M. Robert Chamberlaine.	2
M. Abr. Chamberlaine.	1

	Shares.
M. George Smith.	2
M. Robert Gore.	3
Sir Edw. Sackvile.	1
Sir Iohn Dauers.	1
M. Robert Gore.	2
M. Iohn Delbridge.	1
M. Iohn VVroth.	1
M. Iohn VVests heires.	4
M. Richard Chamberlaine.	10

Touching the common ground in each Tribe, as also the ouer-plus, you may finde that at large in the Booke of Surueyes amongst their Records.

Now though the Countrey was small, yet they could not conueniently haue beene disposed and well setled, without a true description and a suruey of it; and againe, euery man being setled where he might constantly abide, they knew their businesse, and fitted their houshold accordingly: then they built no more Cabbens, but substantiall houses, they cleered their grounds, and planted not onely such things as would yeeld them their fruits in a few moneths, but also such as would affoord them profit within a few yeares, so that in a short time the Countrey began to aspire, and neerely approach vnto that happinesse and prosperitie, wherein now it flourisheth, &c.

The first Magazin. 1618.

But to follow the History; vpon the best plot of ground could be found, the Gouernor preuailed so much with the generalitie, they built a faire house of Cedar, which being done, he appropriated it to himselfe, which occasioned exceeding much distaste. About this time arriued the *Diana* with a good supply of men and prouision, and the first Magazin euer seene in those Iles; which course is not so much commended here, as cursed and abhorred by reason of enhansements of all the Inhabitants there; six or seuen weeks this ship staied, then hauing towards her fraught thirtie thousand weight of Tobacco; which prouing good, and comming to a lucky Market, gaue great encouragement to the Aduenturers to goe lustily forward in their Plantation, and without such successe, there is nothing but grudging and repining. But about the appropriation of this new built house, many bad discontents grew betwixt the oppressed Colony and the Gouernor, especially betwixt him and the Minister, and *Lewes*, who would neither be feared with threats nor imprisonment, that their malice continued till they met in *England*, of which the Minister made the cause so plaine, hee very well and honestly it seemes, discharged himselfe.

Two exploits of desperate Fugitiues.

Now in those times of these endlesse vnciuill broiles, two desperate men and a proper Gentlewoman got into a Boat, and thinking to make an escape to *Virginia*, as appeared by some Letters they left behinde them were neuer more heard on. The very next moneth after the like was attempted by six others, so desirous they were to be rid of their seruitude; but their plot being discouered by one of their societie, they were apprehended, arraigned, and condemned to be hanged: the next day being led with halters about their neckes to the place of execution, one was hanged, and the rest repriued.

The arriuall of the *Blessing*.

The *Diana* arriuing well in *England*, for all the infinite numbers of complaints, the Tobacco did helpe to sweeten all manner of grieuances, yet it bred a distaste in the opinions of so many, they began to thinke of another Gouernor; but for that time it was so qualified by diuers of his friends, they dispatched away the *Blessing*, which arriued in the *Somer Iles*. Though their generall Letter was faire and courteous to the Gouernor, yet by the report of the Passengers and diuers particular letters from his friends, it was assured him his cruelty and couetousnesse, for all his paines and industry was much disliked, nor was he like to enioy his house,

house,and that land he had planted for himselfe, by the extreme oppression of the Comminalty. This caused so many ielousies to arise in his conceit, that at last he fully resolued to returne by this ship, that no sooner set saile from *England*, then they proceeded to the nomination of a new Gouernor. Many were presented according to the affections of those that were to giue in their voices, but it chiefely rested betwixt one Captaine *Southwell*, and one Mr *Nathaniel Butler*, where wee will leaue them a while to the consideration of the Court and Company. Now Captaine *Tuckar* hauing instituted Captaine *Kendall* one of the six Gouernors before spoken of for his substitute, returned with this ship directly for *England*, as well to excuse himselfe of those obiections he suspected, as to get assured him the house and land he had alotted for himselfe, lest it might otherwise be disposed of in his absence.

Collected out of their Records by N. B. *and the relations of M.* Pollard, *and diuers others.*

The Gouernment of Captaine Miles Kendall, *Deputy for Captaine* Tuckar.

The arriuall of two ships.

THE vnexpected returne of Captaine *Tuckar*, caused a demurre in the election of the new Gouernor; some perswading these oft changes were so troublesome, dangerous, and chargeable, it were best to continue Captaine *Kendall*; others againe stood for Captaine *Tuckar*, but during the time of these opinions, the *Gilliflower* was dispatched with a supply. Now I should haue remembred, *Tuckar* was no sooner out of the harbour, but he met Master *Elfred* in a ship called the *Treasurer*, sent from *Virginia* to trade: by her he writ to his Deputy Master *Kendall*, to haue a care of all things, and beware of too much acquaintance with this ship, which hee suspected was bound for the West-Indies. Notwithstanding, *Elfred* receiued what kindnesse the Ile could afford; he promised to reuisit them at his returne; this done, because they would not be gouernlesse when his Deputiship was expired, there was a generall assembly, and by that Election *Kendall* was confirmed to succeed still Gouernor. Now they began to apply themselues to the finishing some plat-forme about *Smiths* Fort, and laying the foundation of a Church to be built of Cedar, till the *Gillyflower* arriued with some priuate letters to *Kendall*, how he was elected Gouernor of those Iles for three yeeres. During her stay they held their Assises, where for some few suspected facts three were condemned, and the better to terrifie the rest, led to the place of execution, but reprieued; diuers of the rest had their faults pardoned, and the *Gilliflower* set saile for *New found land*.

Captaine Butler chosen Gouernor.

The loue and kindnesse, honesty and industry of this Captaine *Kendall*, hath beene very much commended; by others, somewhat disliked: but an Angell in those imploiments cannot please all men, yet this consideration bred much ill bloud as well here as there, so that the Company directly concluded, Captaine *Butler* should with what expedition they could, goe to be their Gouernor: In the *Interim* they tooke the opportunitie of a ship, called the *Sea-flower*, bound for *Virginia*, and by her sent a Preacher and his Family, with diuers Passengers, and newes of a new Gouernor. This bred a great distaste amongst many, that still they should haue new officers and strangers for their Gouernors they neuer heard of, and themselues still kept there whether they would or no, without any preferment, no nor scarce any of them their inhabiting, to haue any land at all of their owne, but liue all as tenants, or as other mens poore seruants.

About this time came in Captaine *Kerby* with a small Barke from the West-Indies, who hauing refreshed himselfe, was very kindly vsed by the Gouernor

and

and so departed. Not long after a Dutch Frigot was cast away vpon the Westerne shore, yet by the helpe of the English they saued the men, though the ship perished amongst the Rocks. A little after one Ensigne *Wood* being about the loading of a peece, by thrusting a pike into the concauitie, grating vpon the shot, or somewhat about the powder, strucke fire within her and so discharged, but wounded him cruelly and blew him into the Sea, though hee was got out by some that stood by him, yet hee died of those wounds. Within two or three daies after, Captaine *Elfred* now comes in a second time: but of that we shall say more in the gouernment of Captaine *Butler*, who presently after arriued with a good supply, and was kindly entertained by Captaine *Kendall* and all the Colony.

From a relation of Tho. Sparks, *and diuers others.*

The Gouernment of Captaine Nathaniel Butler.

Captaine *Butler* being arriued the twentieth of October, 1619. some mutterings there was how to maintaine their election of Captaine *Kendall*, but better remembring themselues, that conceit quickly dissolued. The next day, *Kendall*, the Ministers, and the Counsell went aboord to salute the new Gouernor, where after they had dined with the best entertainment he could giue them; they saw the Redout belonging to the Kings Castle by a mischance on fire, whither he repaired with all the meanes he could to quench it; but all the platforme and cariages were consumed before their faces, and they could not helpe it. Two daies after he went vp to the Towne, had his Commission publikely read, made a short speech to the Company, and so tooke vpon him the gouernment. Then presently he began to repaire the most necessary defects. The next moneth came in the *Garland*, sent from *England* six or seuen weekes before him; so that being seuenteene weeks in her voyage, it was so tedious and grieuous to diuers of the Fresh-water Passengers, that such a sicknesse bred amongst them, many died as well Sailers as Passengers. Hauing taken the best order he could for their releefe, passed through all the Tribes, and held his first Assise in Captaine *Tuckars* house at the ouer-plus. Towards the last of this moneth of Nouemb. there arose a most terrible storme or *Hericano*, that blew vp many great trees by the roots, the *Warwick* that brought the Gouernor was cast away, but the *Garland* rid by her, saued her selfe by cutting downe her Masts; and not long after a second storme, no lesse violent then the first, wherein the Mount which was a frame of wood built by Master *Moore* for a Watch-tower to looke out to Sea, was blowne vp by the roots, and all that Winter crop of corne blasted: And thus was the new Gouernor welcomed. A plat-forme burnt, and much hurt by a *Hericano*. *1619.*

With the beginning of the new yeere he began his first peece of fortification, vpon a Rocke which flankers the Kings Castle, and finding the ship called the *Treasurer* starke rotten and vnseruiceable, hee tooke nine peeces of Ordinance from her to serue other vses. The *Garland* for want of meanes, could not make her voiage to *Virginia* as she was appointed; wherefore he entertained her to returne to *England*, with all the Tabacco they had in the Ile. It was Ianuary before she departed, in which time shee failed not much to haue beene twice cast away. But those strange and vnauoidable mischances, rather seemed to quicken the Gouernors industry then to dull it. Hauing finished the Church begun by Captaine *Kendall*, with an infinite toile and labour he got three peeces out of the wracke *VVarwicke*. Hauing an excellent Dutch Carpinter he entertained of them that were cast away in the Dutch Frigot, he imploied him in building of Boats, whereof they were in exceeding great want. In February they discouered a tall ship beating too and againe, as it seemed by her working, being ignorant of the Coast; some thought her a *Spaniard* to view their Forts, which stand most to The refortifying the Kings Castle.

that

that part she so neerely approached; some, English; but the most, some Dutch man of Warre: The wind blew so high, they durst not send out a Boat, though they much doubted she would be foule of their Rocks, but at last she bore vp romny for the Sea, and we heard of her no more. That euening, a lucky fellow it should seeme he was, that found a peece of Amber-greece of eight ounces, as he had twice before, which bringing to the Gouernor, he had ready money for the one halfe, after three pound an ounce, according to their order of Court, to encourage others to looke out for more, and preuent the mischiefe insueth by concealing of it.

Amber-greece found.

The arriuall of two Dutch Frigots.

Within a few daies after, they descried two Frigots that came close to the shore, and sent a Letter to the Gouernor, writ in *Italian*, that they were *Hollanders* had beene in the West-Indies, and desired but to arriue, refresh themselues with wood and water, and so be gone. The Gouernor forthwith sent them to vnderstand, that being there vnder his Maiestie of *England* to command those Iles, he was to carrie himselfe a friend to his friends, and an enemy to his enemies; if therefore he could shew a lawfull Commission for his being honestly and nobly emploied, he and his should be kindly welcome, otherwise they were to aduenture at their perills. But his Commission was so good, he staied there two moneths, and was so well fitted with Oile & Bacon, they were all glad and happy of this Dutch Captaine *Scoutans* arriuall, with many thanks to their old friend Captaine *Powell* that had conducted him thither: the Colony being exceedingly in great want and distresse, bought the most part of it at reasonable rates, so Captaine *Scoutan* returned to the West-Indies, and Captaine *Powell* for his part in the Low-Countries. Whilest these things were in action, the Aduenturers in *England* made many a long looke for their ships; at last the *Garland* brought them all the newes, but the Tobacco was so spoiled either in the leaking ship, or the making vp, it caused a great suspicion there could none was good come from those Iles; where (were they but perfit in the cure) questionlesse it would be much better then a great quantitie of that they sell for *Verinas*, and many a thousand of it in *London* hath beene bought and sold by that title.

The differences betwixt the Ministers.

The Gouernor being cleere of those distractions, falls vpon the restoring of the burnt Redoubt, where he cuts out a large new plat-forme, and mounts seuen great peece of Ordnance vpon new cariages of Cedar. Now amongst all those troubles, it was not the least to bring the two Ministers to subscribe to the Booke of Common Praier, which all the Bishops in *England* could not doe. Finding it high time to attempt some conformitie, bethought himselfe of the Liturgie of *Garnsey* and *Iarse*, wherein all those particulars they so much stumbled at, were omitted. No sooner was this propounded, but it was gladly imbraced by them both, whereupon the Gouernor translated it *verbatim* out of French into English, and caused the eldest Minister vpon Easter day to begin the vse thereof at *S. Georges* towne, where himselfe, most of the Councell, Officers and Auditorie receiued the Sacrament: the which forme they continued during the time of his gouernment.

The rebuilding the Mount.

Much about this time, in such a faire morning, that had inuited many Boats farre out to the Sea to fish, did rise such a *Hericano* that much indangered them all, so that one of them with two Boies were driuen to Sea and neuer more heard of. The Ministers thus agreed, a Proclamation was published for keeping of the Sabbath, and all the defectiue cariages he endeuoured to haue renewed, builded a small Boat of Cedar onely to goe with Ores, to be ready vpon any occasion to discouer any shipping, and tooke order euery Fort should haue the like: Also caused numbers of Cedars to be brought from diuers places in flotes, to rebuild the Mount, which with an vnspeakable toile, was raised seuen foot higher then before, and a Falcon mounted at the foot, to be alwaies discharged for a warning to all the Forts vpon the discouery of any shipping, and this he called Rich Mount. This exceeding toile and labour, hauing no Cattle but onely mens

strengths

strengths, caused many petitions to the Gouernour, that all those generall works might cease till they had reaped their haruests, in that they were in great distresse for victuall; which hee so well answered, their owne shames did cause them desist from that importunity, and voluntarily performe as much as hee required.

Finding accidentally a little crosse erected in a by place, amongst a many of bushes, vnderstanding there was buried the heart and intrailes of Sir *George Summers*, hee resolued to haue a better memory for so worthy a Souldier, then that. So finding also a great Marble stone brought out of *England*, hee caused it by Masons to bee wrought handsomely and laid ouer the place, which hee inuironed with a square wall of hewen stone, Tombe like; wherein hee caused to bee grauen this *Epitaph* he had composed, and fixed it vpon the Marble stone; and thus it was, The Tombe of Sir *George Summers*.

In the yeere 1 6 1 1,
Noble Sir George Summers *went hence to heauen;*
Whose well tri'd worth that held him still imploid,
Gaue him the knowledge of the world so wide.
Hence 't was by heauens decree, that to this place
He brought new guests, and name to mutuall grace.
At last his soule and body being to part,
He here bequeath'd his entrails and his heart.

Vpon the sixt of Iune began the second Assise, that reduced them to the direct forme vsed in *England*. For besides the Gouernour and Councell, they haue the Bailiffes of the Tribes, in nature of the Deputy Lieutenants of the shires in *England*, for to them are all precepts and warrants directed, and accordingly answered and respected; they performe also the duties of Iustices of Peace, within their limits. The subordinate Officers to these in euery tribe, are the Constables, Head-borowes, and Church-wardens; these are the triers of the Tobacco, which if they allow not to be marchantable, is burnt: and these are the executioners of their ciuill and politicke causes. Their manner of lawes reformed.

For points of warre and martiall affaires, they haue the Gouernour for Lieutenant generall, the Sergeant maior, Master of Ordinance, Captaines of Companies, Captaines of Forts, with their seuerall officers, to traine and exercise those numbers vnder their charge, in martiall discipline. Martiall Officers.

Concerning their Courts for decision of right and iustice, the first, though last in constitution, is their generall assembly; allowed by the state in *England*, in the nature of a Parliament, consisting of about forty persons; *viz.* the Gouernour, the Counsell, the Bailiffes of the tribes, and two Burgesses of each tribe chosen by voyces in the tribe, besides such of the Clergie as the Gouernour thinkes most fit, to be held once a yeere, as you shal heare more thereof hereafter. The next Court is the Assise or Iayles of deliuerie, held twice euery yeere, in Christmas, and Whitson weeke, for all criminall offenders, and ciuill causes betwixt party and party; as actions of debt, trespasse, battery, slander, and the like: and these are determined by a Iury of twelue men, and aboue them is also a grand Iury to examine matters of greater consequence. The last day of the Assise might also well be held a Court, for hearing the trangressions in matters of contempt, mis-behauiour towards any Magistrate, riots, seditious speakers, contemners of warrants, and such like: there are also as occasion shall require, many matters heard by the Gouernor, or his Officers, and oft iustice done in seuerall places, but those are but as daies of hearing, and as preparatiues against their Courts, &c. Ciuill Officers and Courts.

At this last Assize eighteene were arrained for criminall causes, a number very extraordinary considering the place; but now occasioned by reason of the hard yeere, and the store of ill chosen new commers; of these, some were censured to the whipping post, some burned in the hand, but two were condemned to die, yet the one was reprieued, the other hanged; this done, euery man returned to his home: many trials they made againe about the Warwicke, but to small pur- The second Assise.

pose, her Ordnance being lashed so fast they could not be vnloosed, till the ropes and decks were rotten, yet some few buttes of beare being flotie they got, which though it had lien six moneths vnder water was very good, notwithstanding the next yeere they recouered fiue peeces of Ordnance.

A generall assemblie in manner a Parliament.

Vpon the first of August, according to the Companies instructions from *England*, began the generall assembly at the towne of Saint *George*, which was the first these Iles euer had; consisting as is said, of the Gouernour, Councell, Bailiffes, and Burgesses, and a Secretarie to whom all bils were presented, and by him openly read in the house, also a Clerke to record the Acts, being thirty two in all; fifteene of which being sent into *England*, were by a generall consent receiued and enacted, the titles whereof are these following: as for all the reasons for them, they would be too tedious to recite.

Their Acts.

The first was against the vniust sale and letting of apprentises and other seruants, and this was especially for the righting the vndertakers in *England*. The second, concerning the disposing of aged, diseased, and impotent persons, for it being considered how carelesse many are in preferring their friends, or sending sometimes any they can procure to goe, such vnseruiceable people should be returned back at their charge that sent them, rather then be burdensome to the poore Inhabitants in the Iles. The third, the necessary manning the Kings Castle, being the key of the Ile, that a garison of twelue able men should bee there alwaies resident: and 3000. eares of corne, and 1000. pounds of Tobacco payed them by the generality yeerely, as a pension. The fourth, against the making vnmarchantable Tobacco, and Officers sworne to make true trials, & burne that was naught. The fift, inioyned the erection of certaine publike bridges, and the maintenance of them. The sixt, for a continuall supply of victuall for all the Forts, to bee preserued, till some great occasion to vse it. The seuenth was, for two fixed dayes euery yeere for the Assises. The eight, commands the making of high-waies, and prohibiting the passage ouer mens grounds and planted fields, as well to preuent the spoyling of gardens, as conueniencie to answer any alarum. The ninth, for the preseruing young tortoises and birds, that were carelesly destroyed. The tenth, prouided against vagabonds, & prohibited the entertainement of other mens seruants. The eleuenth, compelled the setting of a due quantity of corne for euery family. The twelfth, the care corne being set, enioyned the keeping vp of their poultry till it was past their reaches. The thirteenth, for the preseruation of sufficient fences, & against the felling of marked trees appointed for bounds. The fourteenth, granted to a leuy for a thousand pound weight of Tobacco, towards the payment of publike workes, as the bridges and the mount. The fifteenth, for the enioyning an acknowledgement and acception of all resident Gouernours, and the warranting him to continue, though his time be expired, till the arriuall of a legitimate successor from *England*, to preuent all vnmeet and presumptuous elections, besides it was desired by petition in *England*, the new Gouernous should liue two months as a priuate man after his arriuall, if his predecessor did stay so long, the better to learne and obserue his course. And these are the contents of those fifteene Acts, applied as you may perceiue: which the lawes of *England* could not take notice of, because euery climate hath somewhat to it selfe in that kinde in particular; for otherwise as it is conceiued, it had beene a high impudency and presumption to haue medled with them, or indeed with any such as these lawes, that had with such great iudgement and iustice alwaies prouided for.

The arriuall of the *Magazin* ship.

No sooner was this businesse ouer, but the *Magazin* ship is discouered, and that night came into the Harbour, but in a very weake and sickly case, hauing cast ouer board twenty or thirty of her people, and so violent was the infection, that the most part of the sailers, as well as passengers, were so sicke, or dismaid, or both, that the Master confessed, had they stayed at the Sea but a weeke longer, they had all perished. There arriued with this ship diuers Gentlemen of good fashion, with their wiues and families; but many of them crasie by the tediousnesse of the voyage:

age: howsoeuer most of them, by the excellent salubrity of the aire, then which the world hath not a better, soone after recouered; yet some there were that died presently after they got ashore, it being certainly the quality of the place, either to kill, or cure quickly, as the bodies are more or lesse corrupted. By this ship the Company sent a supply of ten persons for the generality, but of such bad condition that it seemed they had picked the Males out of *Newgate*, the Females from *Bridewell*: As the Gouernour found it his best course, to grant out the women to such as were so greedy of wiues, and would needs haue them for better for worse; and the men hee placed in the Kings Castle for souldiers. But this bad, weake, sickly supply being dispersed for their best reliefe, by the much imployment of his boats in remoouing them, many of his owne men became infected, so that for some weekes, they were not able to doe him any seruice at all. Strict instructions also they brought for the planting of Sugar canes, for which the Iland being rockie and dry, is so vnproper, that few as yet haue beene seene to prosper: yet there are others hold the contrary opinion, that there is raine so ordinarily, the Iles are so moist, as produceth all their plants in such infinit abundance: there is no great reason to suspect this, were it rightly vsed, more then the rest. Seuenty thousand weight of Tobacco being prepared towards her fraught, shee returned for *England*. No sooner was shee gone then came in another, sent by the Company and generalty, well conditioned, but shee failed not much to haue beene cast away amongst those dangerous & terrible rocks; by her came also expresse command, they should entertaine no other ships, then were directly sent from the Company: this caused much grudging, and indeed a generall distraction and exclamation among the Inhabitants, to be thus constrained to buy what they wanted, and sell what they had at what price the *Magazin* pleased, and to debarre true men from comming to them for trade or reliefe, that were daily receiued in all the harbours in *England*. So long this ship stayed going for fraught and wages, the Master not caring how long he lay at that rate in a good harbour, the Gouernour was ready to send her away by Proclamation. Thus ended the first yeere of the gouernment of C. *Butler*.

70000. weight of Tobacco.

With the first of the second yeere were held the Assises, where all the Bailiffes were fined for not giuing a beginning to the building of the bridges; there was also an order to restraine the excessiue wages all handicrafts men would haue: and that the Church-wardens should meet twice a yeere, to haue all their presentments made perfect against the Assises. The Assises done, all the ablest men were trained in their armes, and then departed to their owne homes. The towne thus cleered, he made certaine new carriages for some demy Culuerings, and a large new storehouse of Cedar for the yeerely *Magazines* goods; finished *Warwicks* Fort begun by Master *More*, and made a new platforme at *Pagits* Fort, also a faire house of lime and stone for the Townes-house. The three bridges appointed by the generall assembly, was followed with such diligence, though they were more then an hundred, or an hundred and twenty foot in length, hauing the foundation and arches in the Sea, were raised and accomplished, so that man or beast with facility might passe them.

1620. The building of three bridges and other works.

At Whitsonday was held the fourth generall Assise at Saint *Georges*, where were tryed twenty seuerall causes; foure or fiue were whipped or burnt in the hand, for breaking of houses: also an order was made, that the party cast in the triall of any cause, should pay to euery of the Iurours foure pence: moreouer, that not past ten leaues at the most should grow vpon a plant of Tobacco, and that also in the making it vp, a distinction should diligently be obserued of two kinds, a better and a worse: then they built a strong stone house for the Captaine of the Kings Castle and *corps du guard*; and repaired what defects they could finde in the platformes and carriages.

The generall Assises, and the proceedings.

Captaine *Powell* so oft mentioned, hauing beene in the West-Indies for the States of *Holland*, came to an anchor within shot of their Ordnance, desiring admittance for wood and water, of which hee had great need, but the Gouernor would not permit him, so he weighed and departed, whereat the company were so madded, it was not possible to constraine them to cease their exclamations against the Companies inhibition, till they were weary with exclaming: But still for their better defence, not thinking themselues sufficiently secure, hauing finished two new plat-formes more, arriued the Magazin ship, but her Master was dead, and many of the Passengers, the rest for most part very sicke; and withall, a strange and wonderfull report of much complaint made against the Gouernor to the Company in *England*, by some of them returned in the last yeeres shipping: but it was eight daies before she could get in by reason of ill weather, being forced againe to Sea; so that time, they kept euery night continually great fires, she might see the Ile as well by night as day; but at last she arriued, and he plainly vnderstood, he had more cause a great deale to looke for misconstruction of all his seruice then an acknowledgment, much lesse a recompence any better then his predecessors; but it is no new thing to requite the best desert with the most vildest of ingratitude.

A strange deliuerance of a Spanish wracke.

The very next daies night after the arriuall of the Magazins ship, newes was brought the Gouernor by a dismaied Messenger from *Sands* his Tribe, that one hundred *Spaniards* were landed in that part, and diuers ships discouered at Sea, whereupon he presently manned the Forts, and instantly made thitherward in person with twentie men, determining as he found cause to draw together more strength by the way. Being got thither by the breake of the next day, in stead of an enemy which he expected, he met onely with a company of poore distressed *Portugals* and *Spaniards*, who in their passage from *Carthagena* in the *West-Indies*, in consort with the Spanish fleet of Plait; by the same storme that had indangered the Magazin ship, lost theirs vpon those terrible Rocks, being to the number of seuenty persons, were strangely preserued; and the manner was thus.

About Sunne-set their ship beating amongst the Rocks, some twenty of the Sailers got into the Boat with what treasure they could, leauing the Captaine, the Master, and all the rest to the mercy of the Sea. But a Boy not past fourteene yeares of age that leaped after to haue got into the Boat, missing that hope, it pleased God he got vpon a Chest a drift by him, whereon they report he continued two daies, and was driuen neere to the cleane contrary part of the Ile, where he was taken vp neere dead, yet well recouered. All this night the ship sticking fast, the poore distressed in her the next day spying land, made a raft, and were those gaue the alarum first a shore about three of the clocke in the after noone. The morning after, about seuen of the clocke came in the Boat to a place called *Mangroue Bay*; and the same day their Carpenter was driuen a shore vpon a Planke neere *Hog Bay*. There was a Gentlewoman that had stood wet vp to the middle vpon the raft from the ship to the shore, being big with childe; and although this was vpon the thirteenth of September, she tooke no hurt, and was safely deliuered of a Boy within three daies after. The best comfort could be giuen them in those extremities they had, although some of the baser sort had beene rifling some of them before the Gouernors arriuall: Also the Spanish Captaine and the chiefe with him, much complained of the treachery of his men to leaue him in that manner, yet had conueyed with them the most of the money they could come by, which he easily missed; whereupon hee suddenly caused all them he accused, to be searched, and recouered to the value of one hundred and fortie pounds starling, which he deliuered into the Captaines hands, to be imploied in a generall purse towards their generall charge: during their stay in the Iles, some of the better sort, nine or ten weeks dieted at his owne table, the rest were billited amongst the Inhabitants at foure shillings the weeke, till they found shipping for their passage, for which they paied no more then the English paied themselues; and for the passage of diuers of them, the Gouernor was glad to stand bound to the Master; some others that were not able to procure such friendship, were so constrained to stay in the Iles, till by their labours they had got

so

so much as would transport them; and thus they were preserued, releeued, and deliuered.

In the moneth insuing arriued the second ship, and she also had lost her Master, and diuers of her Passengers; in her came two *Virginian* Women to be married to some would haue them, that after they were conuerted and had children, they might be sent to their Countrey and kindred to ciuilize them. Towards the end of this moneth came in the third ship with a small Magazin, hauing sold what she could, caried the rest to *Virginia*, and neuer did any of those Passengers complaine either of their good diet, or too good vsage at sea; but the cleane contrary still occasioned many of those extremities. The fift of Nouember the damnable plot of the powder treason was solemnized, with Praiers, Sermons, and a great Feast, whereto the Gouernor inuited the chiefe of the *Spaniards*, where drinking the Kings health, it was honored with a quicke volly of small shot, which was answered from the Forts with the great Ordnance, and then againe concluded with a second volley of small shot; neither was the afternoone without musicke and dancing, and at night many huge bone-fires of sweet wood.

How they solemnized the powder treason, and the arriuall of two ships.

The *Spaniards* to expresse their thankfulnesse at their departure, made a deed of gift to the Gouernor of whatsoeuer he could recouer of the wracked ship; but the ships as they went out came so dangerously vpon a Rock, that the poore *Spaniards* were so dismaied, swearing this place was ominous vnto them, especially the women, that desired rather to goe a shore and die howsoeuer, than aduenture any further in such a Labyrinth of dangers, but at last she got cleere without danger, and well to *England*; the other went to *Virginia*, wherein the Gouernor sent two great Chests filled with all such kinds and sorts of Fruits and Plants as their Ilands had; as Figs, Pomgranats, Oranges, Lemons, Sugar-canes, Plantanes, Potatoes, Papawes, Cassado roots, red Pepper, the Prickell Peare, and the like. The ships thus dispatched, hee goeth into the maine, and so out to sea to the Spanish wracke. He had beene there before presently after her ruine, for neuer had ship a more sudden death, being now split in peeces all vnder water. He found small hope to recouer any thing, saue a Cable and an Anchor, and two good Sacars; but the wind was so high hee was forced to returne, being ten miles from the shore, onely with three Murderers, which were knowne to be the same Captaine *Kendall* had sold to Captaine *Kerby*, whose ship was taken by two men of warre of *Carthagena*, the most of his men slaine or hanged, and he being wounded, died in the woods. Now their Pilot being at this seruice, got thus those three Murderers to their ship, and their ship thus to the *Bermudas*, as the *Spaniards* remaining related to the Gouernor and others.

The Spaniards returne, and in danger againe.

1621.

Three English Murderers found in the Spanish wracke.

Hauing raised three small Bulwarkes at *Southhamptons* Fort, with two Curtaines, and two Rauilings, which indeed is onely the true absolute peece of fortification in the Iles; Christmas being come, and the prefixed day of the Assise; diuers were whipped and burnt in the hand, onely three young boyes for stealing were condemned, and at the very point of hanging repriued. The Gouernour then sent his Lieutenant all ouer the maine to distribute Armes to those were found most fit to vse them, & to giue order for their randezuous, which were hanged vp in the Church. About this time it chanced a pretty secret to be discouered to preserue their corne from the fly, or weauell, which did in a manner as much hurt as the rats. For the yeere before hauing made a Proclamation that all Corne should be gathered by a certaine day, because many lazy persons ranne so after the ships to get Beere and *Aquavita*, for which they will giue any thing they haue, much had beene lost for want of gathering. This yeare hauing a very faire crop, some of the Inhabitants, none of the best husbands, hastily gathered it for feare of the penaltie, threw it in great heaps into their houses vnhusked, and so let it lie foure or fiue moneths, which was thought would haue spoiled it: where the good husbands husked it, and with much labour hung it vp, where the Flies did so blow on it, they increased to so many Weauels, they generally

Their Assises, and other passages.

complai-

complained of great losse; but those good fellowes that neuer cared but from hand to mouth, made their boasts, that not a graine of theirs had beene touched nor hurt, there being no better way to preserue it then by letting it lie in it's huske, and spare an infinite labour formerly had beene vsed. There were also very luckily about this time found out diuers places of fresh water, of which many of the Forts were very destitute, and the Church-wardens and Side-men were very busie in correcting the prophaners of the Sabbath, Drunkards, Gamesters, and such like. There came also from *Virginia* a small Barke with many thanks for the presents sent them; much Aquauitæ, Oile, Sacke and Bricks they brought in exchange of more Fruits and Plants, Ducks, Turkies and Limestone, of which she had plenty, and so returned. During the aboad of the stay of this ship, the mariage of one of the *Virginia* maides was consummated with a husband fit for her, attended with more then one hundred guests, and all the dainties for their dinner could be prouided; they made also another triall to fish for Whales, but it tooke no more effect then the former: this was done by the Master of the *Virginia* ship that professed much skill that way, but hauing fraughted his ship with Limestone, with 20000. weight of Potatoes, and such things as he desired, returned for *Virginia*.

A strange Sodomy.

Aprill and May were spent in building a strong new Prison, and perfecting some of the Fortifications, and by the labour of twenty men in fourteene daies was got from the Spanish wracke foure excellent good Sacres, and mounted them at the Forts. Then began the generall Assize, where not fewer then fi[illegible], ciuill, or rather vnciuill actions were handled, and twenty criminall prisoners brought to the bar; such a multitude of such vild people were sent to this Plantation, that he thought himselfe happy his time was so neere expired: three of the foulest acts were these: the first for the rape of a married woman, which was acquitted by a senselesse Iury; the second for buggering a Sow, and the third for Sodomy with a boy, for which they were hanged; during the time of the imprisonment of this Buggerer of the Sow, a Dung-hill Cocke belonging to the same man did continually haunt a Pigge of his also, and to the wonder of all them that saw it who were many, did so frequently tread the Pigge as if it had beene one of his Hens, that the Pigge languished and died within a while after, and then the Cocke resorted to the very same Sow (that this fellow was accused for) in the very same manner; and as an addition to all this, about the same time two Chickens were hatched, the one whereof had two heads, the other crowed very loud and lustily within twelue houres after it was out of the shell. A desperate fellow being to bee arraigned for stealing a Turky, rather then he would endure his triall, secretly conueighed himselfe to Sea in a little Boat, and neuer since was euer heard of, nor is he euer like to be, without an exceeding wonder, little lesse then a miracle. In Iune they made another triall about the Spanish wracke, and recouered another Sacre and a Murderer, also he caused to be hewed out of the maine Rocke a paire of large staires for the conuenient landing of goods and passengers, a worke much to the beauty and benefit of the towne. With twenty chosen men, and two excellent Divers, the Gouernour went himselfe to the wracke *Warwick*, but they could recouer but one Murderer, from thence he went to the *Sea-aduenture*, the wracke of Sir *George Summers*, the hull though two or three fathomes in the water, they found vnperished and with much a doe weighed a Sacre, her sheat Anchor, diuers barres of Iron and pigs of Lead, which stood the Plantation in very great stead. Towards the end of Iuly he went to seeke for a wracke they reported lay vnder water with her hatches spiked vp, but they could not finde her, but from the Spanish wracke lay there by they weighed three faire Sacres more, and so returned through the Tribes to Saint *Georges*: some were also imployed to seeke out beds of Oisters for Pearle, some they found, some seed Pearle they got, but out of one little shell aboue all the rest they got about 120. small Pearle, but somewhat defectiue in their colour.

More trialls about the wracks.

The time of Captain *Butlers* gouernment drawing neere an end, the Colony presented vnto him diuers grieuances, to intreat him to remember to the Lords and Company in *England* at his returne: also they appointed two to be ioyned with him, with letters of credence to solicit in their behalfe those grieuances following: First, they were defrauded of the food of their soules: for being not fewer then one thousand and fiue hundred people, dispersed in length twenty miles, they had at that present but one Minister, nor neuer had but two, and they so shortned of their promises, that but onely for meere pity they would haue forsaken them. Secondly, neglected in the safety of their liues by wants of all sorts of munition. Thirdly, they had beene censured contrary to his Maiesties Lawes, and not allowed them the benefit of their booke as they are in *England*, but by Captaine *Butler*. Fourthly, they were frustrated of many of their couenants, and most extremely pinched and vndone by the extortion of the Magazine, for although their Tobacco was stinted but at two shillings sixpence the pound, yet they pitched their commodities at what rate they pleased. Fifthly, their fatherlesse children are left in little better condition then slaues, for if their Parents die in debt, their children are made as bondmen till the debt be discharged: these things being perfected, there grew a great question of one *Heriot* for plotting of factions and abusing the Gouernour, fot which he was condemned to lose his eares, yet he was vsed so fauourably he lost but the part of one in all.

The Planters complaints.

By this time it being growne past the wonted season of the comming in of ships from *England*, after a generall longing and expectation, especially of the Gouernour, whose Commission being neere vpon expiration, gaue him cause to wish for a meane of deliuerance from so troublesome and thanklesse an imploiment as he had hitherto found it; a saile is discouered, and long it was not before shee arriued in the Kings Castle-Harbour: this Barke was set out by two or three priuate men of the Company, and hauing landed her supplies, was to goe for *Virginia*; by her the Gouernour receiued certaine aduertisements of the carriage and behauiour of the Spaniards, which he had relieued as you haue heard the yeere before; that quite contrary both to his merit, their vow, and his owne expectation, they made clamours against him, the which being seconded by the Spanish Ambassadour, caused the State to fall in examination about it; whereupon hauing fully cleared their ingratefulnesse and impudency, and being assured of the choice of a successor that was to be expected within fiue or six weekes; hee was desirous to take the opportunity of this Barke, and to visit the Colony in *Virginia* in his returne for *England*: leauing the gouernment to Captaine *Felgat*, Captaine *Stokes*, Master *Lewis Hewes*, Master *Nedom* and Master *Ginner*, but now his time being fully expired, and the fortifications finished, *viz.* The *Kings Castle* wherein were mounted vpon sufficient Platformes sixteene peece of Ordnances: In *Charles* Fort two; In *Southampton* Fort fiue, betwixt which and the Castle passeth the Chanell into the Harbour, secured by three and twenty peeces of good artillery to play vpon it. In *Cowpers* Ile is *Pembrocks* Fort, where is two Peeces. The Chanell of Saint *George* is guarded by *Smiths* Fort, and *Pagits* Fort, in which is eleuen peece of Ordnance. Saint *George* towne is halfe a league within the Harbour, commanded by *Warwicks* Fort, where are three great Peeces, and on the Wharfe before the Gouernours house eight more, besides the warning Peece by the mount, and three in Saint *Katharines*; so that in all there are ten Forresses and two and fifty peeces of Ordnance sufficient and seruiceable: their formes and situations you may see more plainlier described in the Map; and to defend those, he left one thousand fiue hundred persons with neere a hundred boats, and the Ile well replenished with store of such fruits, prouisions and Poultry, as is formerly related; yet for so departing and other occasions, much difference hath beene betwixt him and some of the Company, as any of his Predecessors, which I rather wish were reconciled, then to be a reporter of such vnprofitable dissentions.

The returne of Captaine *Butler*.

For

For

Till trechery and faction, and auarice be gone,
Till enuy and ambition, and backbiting be none,
Till periury and idlenesse, and iniury be out,
And truly till that villany the worst of all that rout;
Unlesse those vises banisht be, what euer Forts you haue,
A hundred walls together put will not haue power to saue.

Master Iohn Barnard *sent to be Gouernour.*

1622. The Lord *Cauendish* Treasurer. Master *Nicholas Farrar* Deputy.

TO supply this place was sent by the noble aduenturers *Iohn Bernard*, a Gentleman both of good meanes and quality, who arriued within eight daies after *Butlers* departure with two ships, and about one hundred and forty passengers with armes and all sorts of munition and other prouisions sufficient. During the time of his life which was but six weekes in reforming all things he found defectiue, he shewed himselfe so iudiciall and industrious as gaue great satisfaction, and did generally promise vice was in great danger to be suppressed, and vertue and the Plantation much aduanced; but so it hapned that both he and his wife died in such short time they were both buried in one day and one graue, and Master *Iohn Harrison* chosen Gouernour till further order came from *England*.

What hapned in the gouernment of Master Iohn Harrison.

1623. Sir *Edward Sackuil* Treasurer. Master *Gabriel Barber* Deputy.

THey are still much troubled with a great short worme that deuours their Plants in the night, but all the day they lie hid in the ground, and though early in the morning they kill so many, they would thinke there were no more, yet the next morning you shall finde as many. The Caterpillers to their fruits are also as pernicious, and the land Crabs in some places are as thicke in their Borowes as Conies in a Warren, and doe much hurt; besides all this, there hapned this yeere a very heauy disaster, for a ship wherein there had beene much swearing and blaspheming vsed all the voyage, and landed what she had to leaue in those Iles, iouially froliking in their Cups and Tobacco, by accident fired the Powder, that at the very instant blew vp the great Cabin, and some one way and some another, it is a wonder to thinke how they could bee so blowne out of the gun-roome into the Sea, where some were taken vp liuing, so pitifully burned, their liues were worse then so many deaths, some died, some liued, but eighteene were lost at this fatall blast, the ship also immediatly sunke with threescore barrels of meale sent for *Virginia*, and all the other prouision in her was thus lost.

Note.

Now to consider how the Spaniards, French, and Dutch, haue beene lost and preserued in those inuincible Iles, yet neuer regarded them but as monuments of miseries, though at this present they all desire them; How Sir *Thomas Gates*, and Sir *George Summers* being ready to sinke in the sea were saued, what an incredible abundance of victuall they found, how it was first planted by the English, the strange increase of Rats, and their sudden departure, the fiue men came from *England* in a boat, the escape of *Hilliard*, and the rest of those accidents there hapned, a man would thinke it a tabernacle of miracles, and the worlds wonder, that from such a Paradise of admiration who would thinke should spring such wonders of afflictions as are onely fit to be sacrificed vpon the highest altars of sorrow, thus to be set vpon the highest Pinacles of content, and presently throwne downe to the lowest degree of extremity, as you see haue beene the yeerely succeedings of those Plantations; the which to ouercome, as it is an incomparable honour, so it can be no dishonour if a man doe miscarry by vnfortunate accidents in such honourable actions, the which renowne and vertue to attaine hath

caused

caused so many attempts by diuers Nations besides ours, euen to passe through the very amazement of aduentures. Vpon the relation of this newes the Company hath sent one Captaine *Woodhouse*, a Gentleman of good repute and great experience in the warres, and no lesse prouident then industrious and valiant: then returned report, all goeth well there. It is too true, in the absence of the noble Treasurer, Sir *Edward Sackvill*, now Earle of *Dorset*, there haue beene such complaints betwixt the Planters and the Company, that by command the Lords appointed Sir *Thomas Smith* againe Treasurer, that since then according to their order of Court he is also elected, where now we must leaue them all to their good fortune and successe, till we heare further of their fortunate proceedings.

1624. Sir *Thomas Smith* Treasurer, and Master *Edwards* Deputy.

FINIS.

To his friend Captaine *Smith*, vpon his *description of* New-England.

Sir; your Relations I haue read: which shew,
Ther's reason I should honour them *and* you:
And if their meaning I haue vnderstood,
I dare to censure thus: Your Proiect's *good;*
And may (if follow'd) doubtlesse quit the paine,
With honour, pleasure and a trebble gaine;
Beside the benefit that shall arise
To make more happy our Posterities.
For would we daigne to spare, though 'twere no more
Then what ore-fils, and surfets vs in store,
To order Nature's *fruitfulnesse a while*
In that rude Garden, *you* New-England *stile;*
With present good, ther's hope in after-daies
Thence to repaire what Time *and* Pride *decaies*
In this rich Kingdome. And the spacious West
Being still more with English *bloud possest,*
The proud Iberians *shall not rule those Seas,*
To checke our ships from sailing where they please;
Nor future times make any forraine power
Become so great to force a bound to Our.
Much good my minde foretels would follow hence
With little labour, and with lesse expence.
Thriue therefore thy Designe, *who ere enuy:*
England *may ioy in* England's *Colony,*
Virginia *seeke her Virgin sisters good,*
Be blessed in such happy neighbourhood:
Or, whatsoere Fate pleaseth to permit,
Be thou still honour'd for first mouing it.

George Wither, *e societate Lincol.*

To that worthy and generous Gentleman, *my very good friend, Captaine* Smith.

May Fate thy Proiect prosper, that thy name
May be eternized with liuing fame:
Though foule Detraction Honour would peruert,
And Enuie euer waits vpon desert:

In spight of Pelias, *when his hate lies cold,*
Returne as Iason *with a fleece of gold.*
Then after-ages shall record thy praise,
That a New-England *to this Ile didst raise:*
And when thou di'st (as all that liue must die)
Thy fame liue here; thou, with Eternity.

R. Gunnell.

To his worthy Captaine, the Author.

OFt thou hast led, when I brought vp the Rere
In bloudy wars, where thousands haue beene slaine.
Then giue me leaue in this some part to beare;
And as thy seruant, here to reade my name.
Tis true, long time thou hast my Captaine beene
In the fierce warres of Transiluania:
Long ere that thou America *hadst seene,*
Or led wast captiu'd in Virginia;
Thou that to passe the worlds foure parts dost deeme
No more, then t'were to goe to bed, or drinke,
And all thou yet hast done, thou dost esteeme
As nothing. This doth cause me thinke
That thou I'aue seene so oft approu'd in dangers,
(And thrice captiu'd, thy valour still hath freed)
Art yet preserued, to conuert those strangers:
By God thy guide I trust it is decreed.
For me: I not commend but much admire
Thy England yet vnknowne to passers by-her.
For it will praise it selfe in spight of me;
Thou it, it thou, to all posterity.

Your true friend and souldier, *Ed. Robinson.*

To my honest Captaine, the Author.

MAlignant Times! What can be said or done,
But shall be censur'd and traduc't by some!
This worthy Worke, which thou hast bought so deare,
Ne thou, nor it, Detractors need to feare.
Thy words by deeds so long thou hast approu'd,
Of thousands know thee not thou art belou'd.
And this great Plot will make thee ten times more
Knowne and belou'd, than ere thou wert before.
I neuer knew a Warrier yet, but thee,
From wine, Tobacco, debts, dice, oaths, so free.
I call thee Warrier: *and I make the bolder;*
For, many a Captaine *now, was neuer Souldier.*
Some such may swell at this: but (to their praise)
When they haue done like thee, my Muse shall raise
Their due deserts to Worthies yet to come,
To liue like thine (admir'd) till day of Doome.

Your true friend, sometimes your souldier, *Tho. Carlton.*

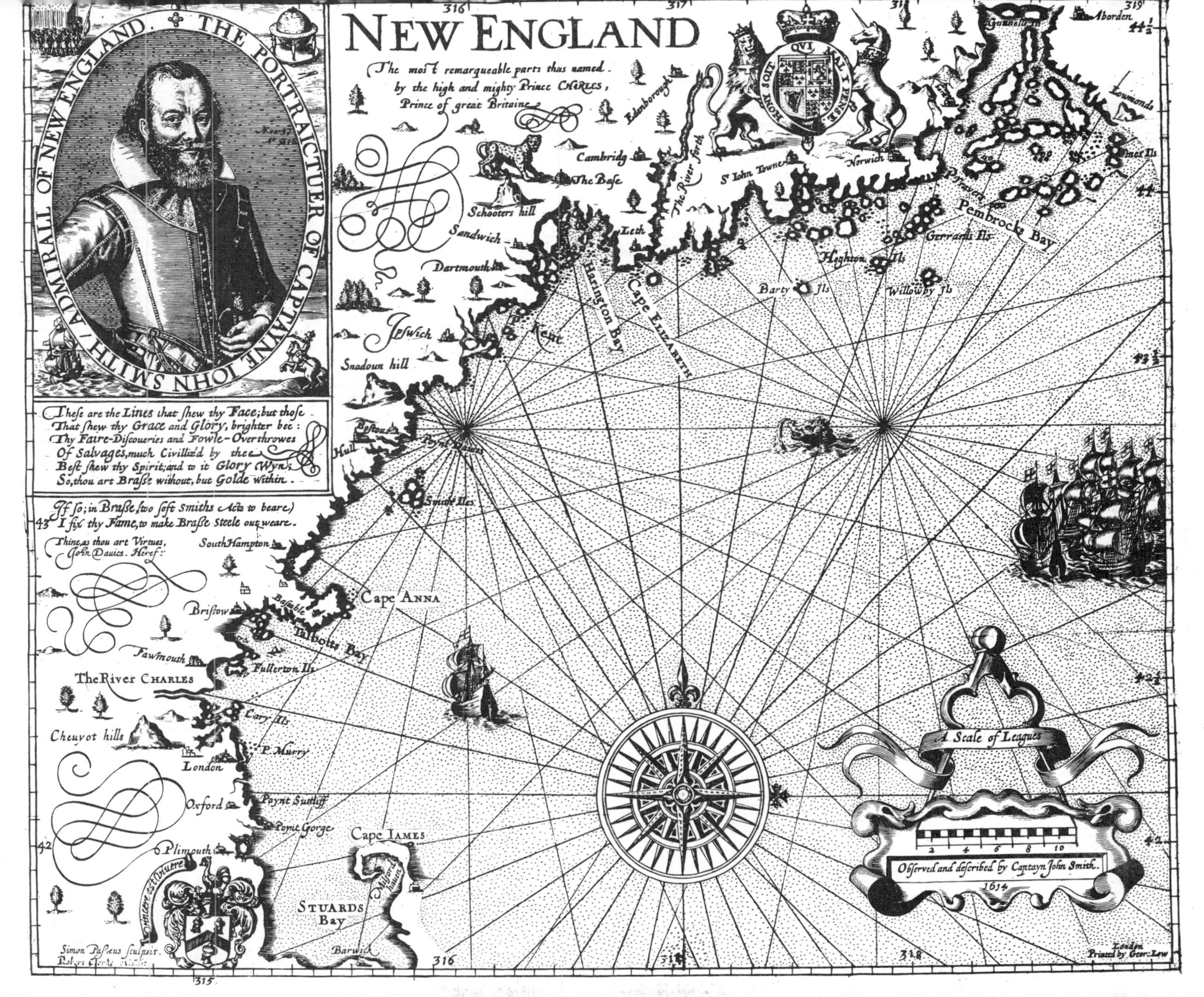

NEW ENGLAND
The most remarqueable parts thus named by the high and mighty Prince CHARLES, Prince of great Britaine
THE PORTRAICTUER OF CAPTAYNE IOHN SMITH, ADMIRALL OF NEW ENGLAND
These are the Lines that shew thy Face; but those
That shew thy Grace and Glory, brighter bee:
Thy Faire-Discoueries and Fowle-Overthrowes
Of Salvages, much Civilliz'd by thee
Best shew thy Spirit; and to it Glory (Wyn)
So, thou art Brasse without, but Golde within.
If so; in Brasse, (too soft Smiths Acts to beare)
I fix thy Fame, to make Brasse Steele out weare.
Thine, as thou art Virtues, John Dauies. Heref:
HONY SOIT QVI MAL Y PENSE
Edenborough
Cambridg
The Base
The River Forth
St John Towne
Norwich
Schooters hill
Sandwich
Leth
Dartmouth
Harington Bay
Cape ELIZABETH
Pembrock Bay
Gerrards Ils
Heghton Ils
Barty Ils
Willowby Ils
Aborden
Lowmonds
Ipswich
Kent
Snadoun hill
Hull
Poynt Dauies
Smiths Iles
SouthHampton
Cape ANNA
Bristow
Talbotts Bay
Fawmouth
Fullerton Ils
The River CHARLES
Cary Ils
Cheuyot hills
P. Murry
London
Oxford
Poynt Suttliff
Poynt Gorge
Cape IAMES
Plimouth
STUARDS Bay
Barwick
Vincere est Viuere
A Scale of Leagues
2 4 6 8 10
Observed and described by Captayn John Smith. 1614
Simon Passeus sculpsit.
London Printed by Geor: Low
316
317
318
319
315
44½
44
43½
43
42½
42

THE SIXTH BOOKE.

THE GENERALL HISTORIE OF NEW-ENGLAND.

Concerning this History you are to vnderstand the Letters-Patents granted by his Maiesty in 1606. for the limitation of *Virginia*, did extend from 34. to 44. which was diuided in two parts; namely, the first Colony and the second: the first was to the honourable City of London, and such as would aduenture with them to discouer and take their choice where they would, betwixt the degrees of 34. and 41. The second was appropriated to the Cities of *Bristol*, *Exeter* and *Plimoth*, &c. and the West parts of *England*, and all those that would aduenture and ioine with them, and they might make their choise any where betwixt the degrees of 38. and 44. prouided there should bee at least 100. miles distance betwixt these 2. Colonies, each of which had lawes, priuileges and authoritie, for the gouernment and aduancing their seuerall Plantations alike. Now this part of *America* hath formerly beene called *Norumbega*, *Virginia*, *Nuskoncus*, *Penaquida*, *Cannada*, and such other names as those that ranged the Coast pleased. But because it was so mountainous, rocky and full of Iles, few haue aduentured much to trouble it, but as is formerly related; notwithstanding, that honourable Patron of vertue, Sir *Iohn Popham*, Lord chiefe Iustice of *England*, in the yeere 1606. procured meanes and men to possesse it, and sent Captaine *George Popham* for President, Captaine *Rawley Gilbert* for Admirall, Captaine *Edward Harlow* master of the Ordnance, Captaine *Robert Dauis* Sargeant-Maior, Captaine *Elis Best* Marshall, Master *Seaman* Secretary, Captaine *Iames Dauis* to be Captaine of the Fort, Master *Gome Carew* chiefe Searcher: all those were of the Councell, who with some hundred more were to stay in the Country: they set saile from *Plimoth* the last of May, and fell with *Monahigan* the eleuenth of August. At *Sagadahock* 9. or 10. leagues southward, they planted themselues at the mouth of a faire nauigable Riuer, but the coast all thereabouts most extreme stony and rocky: that extreme frozen Winter was so cold they could not range nor search the Country, and their prouision so small, they were glad to send all but 45. of their company backe againe: their noble President Captaine *Popham* died, and not long after arriued two ships well prouided of all necessaries to supply them, and some small time after another, by whom vnderstanding of the

Sir *Francis Popham* Treasurer.

death of the Lord chiefe Iustice, and also of Sir *Iohn Gilbert*, whose lands there the President *Rawley Gilbert* was to possesse according to the aduenturers directions, finding nothing but extreme extremities, they all returned for *England* in the yeere 1608. and thus this Plantation was begunne and ended in one yeere, and the Country esteemed as a cold, barren, mountainous, rocky Desart.

Notwithstanding, the right Honourable *Henry* Earle of South-hampton and those of the Ile of *Wight*, imploied Captaine *Edward Harlow* to discouer an Ile supposed about Cape *Cod*, but they found their plots had much abused them, for falling with *Monahigan*, they found onely Cape *Cod* no Ile but the maine, there they detained three Saluages aboord them, called *Pechmo*, *Monopet* and *Pekenimne*, but *Pechmo* leapt ouer board, and got away; and not long after with his consorts cut their Boat from their sterne, got her on shore, and so filled her with sand, and guarded her with Bowes and Arrowes the English lost her: not farre from thence they had three men sorely wounded with Arrowes. Anchoring at the Ile of *Nohono*, the Saluages in their Canowes assaulted the Ship till the English Guns made them retire, yet here they tooke *Sakaweston*, that after he had liued many yeeres in *England* went a Souldier to the warres of *Bohemia*. At *Capawe* they tooke *Coneconam* and *Epenow*, but the people at *Agawom* vsed them kindly, so with fiue Saluages they returned for *England*, yet Sir *Francis Popham* sent diuers times one Captaine *Williams* to *Monahigan* onely to trade and make core fish, but for any Plantations there was no more speeches. For all this, as I liked *Virginia* well, though not their proceedings, so I desired also to see this country, and spend some time in trying what I could finde for all those ill rumors and disasters. *From the relations of Captaine* Edward Harlow *and diuers others.*

My first voyage to *New England.* 1614.

In the month of Aprill 1614. at the charge of Capt. *Marmaduke Roydon*, Capt. *George Langam*, Mr. *Iohn Buley* and Mr. *William Skelton*, with two ships from *London*, I chanced to arriue at *Monahigan* an Ile of *America*, in 43½. of Northerly latitude: our plot was there to take Whales, for which we had one *Samuel Cramton* and diuers others expert in that faculty, & also to make trialls of a Mine of gold & copper; if those failed, Fish and Furs were then our refuge to make our selues sauers howsoeuer: we found this Whale-fishing a costly conclusion, we saw many and spent much time in chasing them, but could not kill any. They being a kinde of *Iubartes*, and not the Whale that yeelds Fins and Oile as we expected; for our gold it was rather the Masters deuice to get a voyage that proiected it, then any knowledge he had at all of any such matter; Fish and Furs were now our guard, & by our late arriuall and long lingring about the Whale, the prime of both those seasons were past ere wee perceiued it, wee thinking that their seasons serued at all times, but we found it otherwise, for by the middest of *Iune* the fishing failed, yet in *Iuly* and *August* some were taken, but not sufficient to defray so great a charge as our stay required: of dry fish we made about forty thousand, of Cor-fish about seuen thousand. Whilest the Sailers fished, my selfe with eight others of them might best bee spared, ranging the Coast in a small Boat, we got for trifles neere eleuen thousand Beuer skinnes, one hundred Martins, as many Otters, and the most of them within the distance of twenty leagues: we ranged the Coast both East and West much further, but Eastward our commodities were not esteemed, they were so neere the French who afforded them better, with whom the Saluages had such commerce that only by trade they made exceeding great voyages, though they were without the limits of our precincts; during the time we tried those conclusions, not knowing the coast, nor Saluages habitations: with these Furres, the traine Oile and Cor-fish, I returned for *England* in the Barke, where within six moneths after our departure from the Downes, wee safely arriued backe; the best of this fish was sold for 5. li. the hundred, the rest by ill vsage betwixt three pounds and 50. shillings. The other ship stayed to fit her selfe for Spaine with the dry fish which was sold at *Maligo* at forty Rialls the Quintall, each hundred weighing two quintals and a halfe. But one *Thomas Hunt* the

The cōmodities I got amounted to 1500. pounds.

The trechery of Master *Hunt*.

the Master of this ship (when I was gone) thinking to preuent that intent I had to make there a Plantation, thereby to keepe this abounding Countrey still in obscuritie, that onely he and some few Merchants more might enioy wholly the benefit of the Trade, and profit of this Countrey, betraied foure and twenty of those poore Saluages aboord his ship, and most dishonestly and inhumanely for their kinde vsage of me and all our men, caried them with him to *Maligo*, and there for a little priuate gaine sold those silly Saluages for Rials of eight; but this vilde act kept him euer after from any more imploiment to those parts. Now because at this time I had taken a draught of the Coast, and called it *New England*, yet so long he and his Consorts drowned that name with the Eccho of *Cannaday*, and some other ships from other parts also, that vpon this good returne the next yeere went thither, that at last I presented this Discourse with the Map, to our most gracious Prince *Charles*, humbly intreating his Highnesse hee would please to change their barbarous names for such English, as posteritie might say Prince *Charles* was their God-father; which for your better vnderstanding both of this Discourse and the Map, peruse this Schedule, which will plainly shew you the correspondency of the old names to the new, as his Highnesse named them.

How Prince *Charles* called the most remarkable places in *New England*.

The old names.	The new names.	The old names.	The new names.
Cape *Cod*.	Cape *Iames*.	*Babanna*.	*Dartmouth*.
The Harbor at Cape *Cod*.	*Milforth* hauen.	A good Harbor within that Bay.	*Sandwich*.
Chawum.	*Barwick*.	*Ancocisco's* Mount.	*Shuters* hill.
Accomack.	*Plimoth*.	*Ancocisco*.	The *Base*.
Sagoquas.	*Oxford*.	*Anmoughcawgen*.	*Cambridge*.
Massachusets Mount.	*Cheuit* hills.	*Kenebecka*.	*Edenborow*.
Massachusits Riuer.	*Charles* Riuer.	*Sagadahock*.	*Leth*.
Totan.	*Famouth*.	*Pemmayquid*.	*S. Iohns* towne.
A great Bay by Cape *Anne*.	*Bristow*.	*Segocket*.	*Norwich*.
Cape *Tragabigsanda*.	Cape *Anne*.	*Mecadacut*.	*Dunbarton*.
Naembeck.	*Bastable*.	*Pennobscot*.	*Aberden*.
Aggawom.	*Southampton*.	*Nusket*.	*Low mounds*.
Smiths Iles.	*Smiths* Iles.	Those being omitted I named my selfe.	
Passataquack.	*Hull*.		
Accominticus.	*Boston*.	*Monahigan*.	*Barties* Iles.
Sassanows Mount.	*Snowdon* hill.	*Matinack*.	*Willowbies* Iles.
Sowocatuck.	*Ipswich*.	*Metinacus*.	*Haughtons* Iles.

The rest of the names in the Map, are places that had no names we did know.

Aspersions against *New England*.

But to continue the History succeedingly as neere with the day and yeere as may bee. Returning in the Barke as is said; it was my ill chance to put in at *Plimoth*, where imparting those my purposes to diuers I thought my friends, whom as I supposed were interested in the dead Patent of this vnregarded Countrey, I was so encouraged and assured to haue the managing their authoritie in those parts during my life, and such large promises, that I ingaged my selfe to vndertake it for them. Arriuing at *London*, though some malicious persons suggested there was no such matter to be had in that so bad abandoned Country, for if there had, other could haue found it so well as I; therefore it was to be suspected I had robbed the French men in *New France* or *Cannada*, and the Merchants set me forth seemed not to regard it, yet I found so many promised me such assistance, that I entertained *Michael Cooper* the Master of the Barke, that returned with me and others of the Company: how he dealt with others, or others with him, I know not; but my publike proceeding gaue such encouragement, that it became so well apprehended by some few of the *Virginia* Company, as those proiects

for

for fishing onely was so well liked, they furnished *Couper* with foure good ships to Sea, before they at *Plimoth* had made any prouision at all for me; but onely a small Barke set out by them of the Ile of *Wight*. Some of *Plimoth*, and diuers Gentlemen of the West Countrey, a little before I returned from *New England*, in search for a Mine of Gold about an Ile called *Capawuck*, South-wards from the Shoules of Cape *Iames*, as they were informed by a Saluage called *Epenew*; that hauing deluded thē as it seems thus to get home, seeing they kept him as a prisoner in his owne Countrey, and before his friends, being a man of so great a stature, he was shewed vp and downe *London* for money as a wonder, and it seemes of no lesse courage and authoritie, then of wit, strength, and proportion: for so well he had contriued his businesse, as many reported he intended to haue surprised the ship; but seeing it could not be effected to his liking, before them all he leaped ouer-boord. Many shot they made at him, thinking they had slaine him, but so resolute they were to recouer his body, the master of the ship was wounded, and many of his company; And thus they lost him, & not knowing more what to do, returned againe to *England* with nothing, which so had discouraged all your West Countrey men, they neither regarded much their promises, and as little either me or the Countrey, till they saw the *London* ships gone and me in *Plimoth* according to my promise, as hereafter shall be related.

Captaine *Hobson* his voiage to *Capawuk*.

The Londoners send foure good ships to New *England*.

I must confesse I was beholden to the setters forth of the foure ships that went with *Couper*, in that they offered me that imploiment if I would accept it; and I finde still my refusall incurred some of their displeasures, whose loue and fauour I exceedingly desired; and though they doe censure me opposite to their proceedings, they shall yet still in all my words and deeds finde, it is their error, not my fault that occasions their dislike: for hauing ingaged my selfe in this businesse to the West Countrey, I had beene very dishonest to haue broke my promise, nor will I spend more time in discouery or fishing, till I may goe with a Company for a Plantation; for I know my grounds, yet euery one to whom I tell them, or that reads this Booke, cannot put it in practise, though it may helpe any that hath seene or not seene to know much of those parts: And though they endeuour to worke me out of my owne designes, I will not much enuy their fortunes: but I would be sorry their intruding ignorance should by their defailments bring those certainties to doubtfulnesse. So that the businesse prosper I haue my desire, be it by whomsoeuer that are true subiects to our King and Countrey: the good of my Countrey is that I seeke, and there is more then enough for all, if they could be contented.

The situation of New England.

New England is that part of *America* in the Ocean Sea, opposite to *Noua Albion* in the South Sea, discouered by the most memorable Sir *Francis Drake* in his Voyage about the world, in regard whereof this is stiled *New England*, being in the same latitude *New France* of it is Northwards, Southwards is *Virginia*, and all the adioyning continent with new *Granado*, new *Spaine*, new *Andolosia*, and the *West-Indies*. Now because I haue beene so oft asked such strange questions of the goodnesse and greatnesse of those spatious Tracts of Land, how they can be thus long vnknowne, or not possessed by the *Spaniards*, and many such like demands; I intreat your pardons if I chance to be too plaine or tedious in relating my knowledge for plaine mens satisfaction.

Notes of *Florida*.

Florida is the next adioyning to the *Indies*, which vnprosperously was attempted to be planted by the French, a Countrey farre bigger then *England*, *Scotland*, *France* and *Ireland*, yet little knowne to any Christian, but by the wonderfull endeuours of *Ferdinando de Soto*, a valiant *Spaniard*, whose writings in this age is the best guide knowne to search those parts.

Notes of *Virginia*.

Virginia is no Ile as many doe imagine, but part of the Continent adioyning to *Florida*, whose bounds may be stretched to the magnitude thereof, without offence to any Christian Inhabitant, for from the degrees of thirtie to forty eight, his Maiesty hath now enlarged his Letters Patents. The Coast extending Southwest

west and North-east about sixteene or seuenteene hundred miles, but to follow it aboord the shore may well be three thousand miles at the least: of which twentie miles is the most giues entrance into the Bay of *Chisapeacke*, where is the London Plantation, within which is a Countrey, as you may perceiue by the Map, of that little I discouered, may well suffice three hundred thousand people to inhabit: but of it, and the discoueries of Sir *Ralph Laine* and Master *Heriot*, Captaine *Gosnold*, and Captaine *Waymouth*, they haue writ so largely, that posteritie may be bettered by the fruits of their labours. But for diuers others that haue ranged those parts since, especially this Countrey now called *New England*, within a kenning sometimes of the shore; some touching in one place, some in another; I must intreat them pardon me for omitting them, or if I offend in saying, that their true descriptions were concealed, or neuer were well obserued, or died with the Authors, so that the Coast is yet still but euen as a Coast vnknowne and vndiscouered. I haue had six or seuen seuerall plots of those Northerne parts, so vnlike each to other, or resemblance of the Country, as they did me no more good then so much waste paper, though they cost me more, it may bee it was not my chance to see the best; but lest others may be deceiued as I was, or through dangerous ignorance hazard themselues as I did, I haue drawne a Map from point to point, Ile to Ile, and Harbour to Harbour, with the Soundings, Sands, Rocks, and Land-markes, as I passed close aboord the shore in a little Boat; although there bee many things to bee obserued, which the haste of other affaires did cause me to omit: for being sent more to get present Commodities, then knowledge of any discoueries for any future good, I had not power to search as I would; yet it will serue to direct any shall goe that waies to safe Harbours and the Saluages habitations: what Merchandize and Commodities for their labours they may finde, this following discourse shall plainly demonstrate.

Obseruations for presumptuous ignorant directors.

Thus you may see of these three thousand miles, more then halfe is yet vnknowne to any purpose, no not so much as the borders of the Sea are yet certainly discouered: as for the goodnesse and true substance of the Land, we are for most part yet altogether ignorant of them, vnlesse it be those parts about the Bay of *Chisapeack* and *Sagadahock*, but onely here and there where we haue touched or seene a little, the edges of those large Dominions which doe stretch themselues into the maine, God doth know how many thousand miles, whereof we can yet no more iudge, then a stranger that saileth betwixt *England* and *France*, can describe the harbours and dangers by landing here or there in some Riuer or Bay, tell thereby the goodnesse and substance of *Spaine, Italy, Germany, Bohemia, Hungaria*, and the rest; nay, there are many haue liued fortie yeeres in London, and yet haue scarce beene ten miles out of the Citie: so are there many haue beene in *Virginia* many yeeres, and in *New England* many times, that doe know little more then the place they doe inhabit, or the Port where they fished, and when they come home, they will vndertake they know all *Virginia* and *New England*, as if they were but two Parishes or little Ilands. By this you may perceiue how much they erre, that thinke euery one that hath beene in *Virginia* or *New England*, vnderstandeth or knoweth what either of them are; Or that the Spaniards know one halfe quarter of those large Territories they possesse, no not so much as the true circumference of *Terra incognita*, whose large Dominions may equalize the goodnesse and greatnesse of *America* for any thing yet knowne. It is strange with what small power he doth range in the *East-Indies*, and few will vnderstand the truth of his strength in *America*: where hauing so much to keepe with such a pampered force, they need not greatly feare his fury in *Sommer Iles, Virginia*, or *New England*, beyond whose bounds *America* doth stretch many thousand miles. Into the frozen parts whereof, one Master *Hutson* an English Mariner, did make the greatest discouerie of any Christian I know, where hee vnfortunately was left by his cowardly Company, for his exceeding deserts, to end and die a most miserable death.

For

For *Affrica*, had not the industrious *Portugals* ranged her vnknowne parts, who would haue sought for wealth amongst those fried Regions of blacke brutish *Negars*, where notwithstanding all their wealth and admirable aduentures and endeuours more then one hundred and fortie yeeres, they know not one third part of those blacke habitations. But it is not a worke for euery one to manage such an affaire, as make a discouery and plant a Colony, it requires all the best parts of art, iudgement, courage, honesty, constancy, diligence, and industry, to doe but neere well; some are more proper for one thing then another, and therein best to be imploied: and nothing breeds more confusion then misplacing and misimploying men in their vndertakings. *Columbus*, *Courtes*, *Pitzara*, *Zoto*, *Magilanus*, and the rest serued more then a Prentiship, to learne how to begin their most memorable attempts in the *West-Indies*, which to the wonder of all ages successefully they effected, when many hundreds of others farre aboue them in the worlds opinion, being instructed but by relation, came to shame and confusion in actions of small moment, who doubtlesse in other matters were both wise, discreet, generous and couragious. I say not this to detract any thing from their incomparable merits, but to answer those questionlesse questions, that keepe vs backe from imitating the worthinesse of their braue spirits, that aduanced themselues from poore Souldiers to great Captaines, their posterity to great Lords, their King to be one of the greatest Potentates on earth, and the fruits of their labours his greatest power, glory, and renowne.

The Description of New England.

THat part we call *New England*, is betwixt the degrees of fortie one and fortie fiue, the very meane betwixt the North pole and the line; but that part this Discourse speaketh of, stretcheth but from *Penobscot* to Cape *Cod*, some seuentie fiue leagues by a right line distant each from other; within which bounds I haue seene at least fortie seuerall habitations vpon the Sea Coast, and sounded about fiue and twentie excellent good Harbours, in many whereof there is anchorage for fiue hundred saile of ships of any burden; in some of them for one thousand, and more then two hundred Iles ouer-growne with good Timber of diuers sorts of wood, which doe make so many Harbours, as required a longer time then I had to be well obserued.

The principall Countries or gouernments.

The principall habitation Northward we were at, was *Pennobscot*: Southward along the Coast and vp the Riuers, we found *Mecadacut*, *Segocket*, *Pemaquid*, *Nuscoucus*, *Sagadahock*, *Aumoughcowgen*, and *Kenebeke*; and to those Countries belong the people of *Segotago*, *Paghhuntanuck*, *Pocopassum*, *Taughtanakagnet*, *Warbigganus*, *Nassaque*, *Masherosqueck*, *Wawrigweck*, *Moshoquen*, *Wakcogo*, *Pasharanack*, &c. To these are alied in confederacy, the Countries of *Ancocisco*, *Accomynticus*, *Passataquack*, *Aggawom*, and *Naemkeck*: All these for any thing I could perceiue, differ little in language, fashion, or gouernment, though most of them be Lords of themselues, yet they hold the *Bashabes* of *Penobscot*, the chiefe and greatest amongst them.

The next I can remember by name, are *Mattahunts*, two pleasant Iles of Groues, Gardens, and Corne fields a league in the Sea from the maine: Then *Totant*, *Massachuset*, *Topent*, *Secassaw*, *Totheet*, *Nasnocomacack*, *Accomack*, *Chawum*, *Patuxet*, *Massasoyts*, *Pakanokick*: then Cape *Cod*, by which is *Pawmet* and the Ile *Nawset*, of the language and aliance of them of *Chawum*; the others are called *Massachusets*, and differ somewhat in language, custome, and condition: for their Trade and Merchandize, to each of their principall families or habitations, they haue diuers Townes and people belonging, and by their relations and descriptions, more then twentie seuerall habitations and riuers that stretch themselues farre into the Countrey, euen to the Borders of diuers great Lakes, where they kill and take most of their Otters, from *Pennobscot* to *Sagadahoc*. This Coast

is

is mountainous, and Iles of huge Rockes, but ouer-growne for most part, with most sorts of excellent good woods, for building Houses, Boats, Barks or Ships, with an incredible abundance of most sorts of Fish, much Fowle, and sundry sorts of good Fruits for mans vse.

Betwixt *Sagadahock* & *Sowocatuck*, there is but two or three Sandy Bayes, but betwixt that and Cape *Iames* very many: especially the Coast of the *Massachusets* is so indifferently mixed with high Clay or Sandy clifts in one place, and the tracts of large long ledges of diuers sorts, and Quaries of stones in other places, so strangely diuided with tinctured veines of diuers colours: as Free-stone for building, Slate for tyling, smooth stone to make Furnasses and Forges for Glasse and Iron, and Iron Ore sufficient conueniently to melt in them; but the most part so resembleth the Coast of *Deuonshire*, I thinke most of the clifts would make such Lime-stone: if they bee not of these qualities, they are so like they may deceiue a better iudgement then mine: all which are so neere adioyning to those other aduantages I obserued in these parts, that if the Ore proue as good Iron and Steele in those parts as I know it is within the bounds of the Countrey, I dare ingage my head (hauing but men skilfull to worke the Simples there growing) to haue all things belonging to the building and rigging of ships of any proportion and good Merchandise for their fraught, within a square of ten or foureteene leagues, and it were no hard matter to proue it within a lesse limitation.

A proofe of an excellent clime.

And surely by reason of those sandy clifts, and clifts of rocks, both which we saw so planted with Gardens and Corne fields, and so well inhabited with a goodly, strong, and well proportioned people, besides the greatnesse of the Timber growing on them, the greatnesse of the Fish, and the moderate temper of the aire (for of fiue and forty not a man was sicke, but two that were many yeares diseased before they went, notwithstanding our bad lodging and accidentall diet) who can but approue this a most excellent place, both for health and fertilitie; and of all the foure parts of the world I haue yet seene not inhabited, could I haue but meanes to transport a Colony, I would rather liue here then any where, and if it did not maintaine it selfe, were we but once indifferently well fitted, let vs starue.

Staple Commodities present.

The maine staple from hence to bee extracted for the present, to produce the rest, is Fish, which howbeit may seeme a meane and a base Commoditie; yet who will but truly take the paines and consider the sequell, I thinke will allow it well worth the labour. It is strange to see, what great aduentures the hopes of setting forth men of warre to rob the industrious innocent would procure, or such massie promises in grosse, though more are choaked then well fed with such hastie hopes. But who doth not know that the poore *Hollanders* chiefely by fishing at a great charge and labour in all weathers in the open Sea, are made a people so hardy and industrious, and by the venting this poore Commoditie to the Easterlings for as meane, which is Wood, Flax, Pitch, Tarre, Rozen, Cordage, and such like; which they exchange againe to the *French, Spaniards, Portugals*, and *English*, &c. for what they want, are made so mighty, strong, and rich, as no state but *Venice* of twice their magnitude is so well furnished, with so many faire Cities, goodly Townes, strong Fortresses, and that abundance of shipping, and all sorts of Merchandize, as well of Gold, Siluer, Pearles, Diamonds, precious Stones, Silkes, Veluets, and Cloth of Gold; as Fish, Pitch, Wood, or such grosse Commodities? What voiages and discoueries, East and West, North and South, yea about the world, make they? What an Army by Sea and Land haue they long maintained, in despight of one of the greatest Princes of the world, and neuer could the *Spaniard* with all his Mines of Gold and Siluer, pay his debts, his friends, and Army, halfe so truly as the *Hollanders* still haue done by this contemptible Trade of Fish. Diuers (I know) may alleage many other assistances; but this is the chiefest Mine, and

Obseruations of the *Hollanders*.

the Sea the source of those siluer streames of all their vertue, which hath made them now the very miracle of industry; the onely paterne of perfection for these affaires: and the benefit of fishing is that *Primum Mobile* that turnes all their spheares to this height, of plentie, strength, honor, and exceeding great admiration.

Note. Herring, Cod, and Ling, is that triplicitie, that makes their wealth and shippings multiplicitie such as it is: and from which (few would thinke it) they should draw so many millions yeerely as they doe, as more in particular in the trials of *New England* you may see; and such an incredible number of ships, that breeds them so many Sailers, Mariners, Souldiers, and Merchants, neuer to be wrought out of that Trade, and fit for any other. I will not deny but others may gaine as well as they that will vse it, though not so certainly, nor so much in quantitie, for want of experience: and this Herring they take vpon the Coast of *England* and *Scotland*, their Cod and Ling vpon the Coast of *Izeland*, and in the North seas, if wee consider what gaines the *Hamburgans*, the *Biskinners*, and *French* make by fishing; nay, but how many thousands this fiftie or sixty yeeres haue beene maintained by *New found land*, where they take nothing but small Cod, whereof the greatest they make Cor-fish, and the rest is hard dried, which we call Poore-Iohn, would amaze a man with wonder. If then from all those parts such paines is taken for this poore gaines of Fish, especially by the *Hollanders*, that hath but little of their owne, for building of ships and setting them to sea; but at the second, third, fourth, or fift hand, drawne from so many parts of the world ere they come together to be vsed in those voiages: If these (I say) can gaine, why should we more doubt then they; but doe much better, that may haue most of all those things at our doores for taking and making, and here are no hard Landlords to racke vs with high rents, or extorting fines, nor tedious pleas in Law to consume vs with their many yeeres disputation for Iustice; no multitudes to occasion such impediments to good orders as in popular States: so freely hath God and his Maiestie bestowed those blessings, on them will attempt to obtaine them, as here euery man may be master of his owne labour and land, or the greatest part (if his Maiesties royall meaning be not abused) and if he

Note. haue nothing but his hands, he may set vp his Trade; and by industry quickly grow rich, spending but halfe that time well, which in *England* we abuse in idlenesse, worse, or as ill. Here is ground as good as any lieth in the height of forty one, forty two, forty three, &c. which is as temperate, and as fruitfull as any other parallel in the world.

Examples of the Altitude comparatiuely. As for example, on this side the line, West of it in the South Sea, is *Noua Albion*, discouered as is said by Sir *Francis Drake*: East from it is the most temperate part of *Portugall*, the ancient Kingdomes of *Galizia*, *Bisky*, *Nauarre*, *Aragon*, *Cattilonia*, *Castillia* the old, and the most moderatest of *Castillia* the new, & *Valen-*

In *Spaine*. *tia*, which is the greatest part of *Spaine*; which if the Histories be true, in the *Romans* time abounded no lesse with gold & siluer Mines, then now the *West-Indies*, the *Romans* then vsing the *Spaniards* to worke in those Mines, as now the *Spani-*

In *France*. *ards* doe the *Indians*. In *France* the Prouinces of *Gascony*, *Langadocke*, *Auignon*, *Prouince*, *Dolphine*, *Pyamont*, and *Turyne*, are in the same parallel, which are the best and richest parts of *France*. In *Italy* the Prouinces of *Genua*, *Lumbardy*, and *Verona*, with a great part of the most famous state of *Venice*, the Dukedomes of *Bononia*, *Mantua*, *Ferrara*, *Rauenna*, *Bolognia*, *Florence*, *Pisa*, *Sienna*, *Vrbine*, *Ancona*, and the ancient Citie and Countrey of *Rome*, with a great part of the Kingdome of *Naples*. In *Slauonia*, *Istria*, and *Dalmatia*, with the King-

In *Greece*. domes of *Albania*. In *Grecia* those famous Kingdomes of *Macedonia*, *Bullulgaria*, *Thessalia*, *Thracia*, or *Romania*, where is seated the most pleasant and plentifull Citie in *Europe*, *Constantinople*.

In *Asia*. In *Asia* in the same latitude, are the temperatest parts of *Natolia*, *Armenia*, *Persia*,

Persia, and *China*; besides diuers other large Countries and Kingdomes in those most milde and temperate Regions of *Asia*. Southward in the same height is the richest of Gold Mines, *Chily*, and *Baldinia*, and the mouth of the great Riuer of *Plate*, &c. for all the rest of the world in that height is yet vnknowne. Besides these reasons, mine owne eies that haue seene a great part of those Cities and their Kingdomes (as well as it) can finde no aduantage they haue in Nature but this, they are beautified by the long labour and diligence of industrious people and art; This is onely as God made it when hee created the world: Therefore I conclude, if the heart and intrailes of those Regions were sought, if their Land were cultured, planted, and manured by men of industry, iudgement, and experience; what hope is there, or what need they doubt, hauing the aduantages of the Sea, but it might equalize any of these famous Kingdomes in all commodities, pleasures, and conditions, seeing euen the very hedges doe naturally affoord vs such plentie, as no ship need returne away emptie, and onely vse but the season of the Sea. Fish will returne an honest gaine, besides all other aduantages, her treasures hauing yet neuer beene opened, nor her originals wasted, consumed, nor abused.

Beyond the line.

And whereas it is said the *Hollanders* serue the Easterlings themselues, and other parts that want with Herring, Ling, and wet Cod: The Easterlings, a great part of *Europe*, with Sturgion and Cauiare, as the Blacke Sea doth *Grecia*, *Podolia*, *Sagonia*, *Natolia*, and the *Hellespont*. Cape *Blanke*, *Spaine*, *Portugall*, and the *Leuant*, with Mulit and Puttargo. *New found land*, the most part of the chiefe Southerne Ports in *Europe*, with a thin Poore-Iohn, which hath beene so long, so much ouer-laied with Fishers, as the fishing decaieth, so that many oft times are constrained to returne with a small fraught. *Norway* and *Poland* affoords Pitch and Tarre, Masts and Yards. *Sweathland* and *Russia*, Iron and Ropes. *France* and *Spaine*, Canuase, Wine, Steele, Iron, and Oile. *Italy* and *Greece*, Silkes and Fruits. I dare boldly say, because I haue seene naturally growing or breeding in those parts, the same materials that all these are made of, they may as well bee had here, or the most part of them within the distance of seuentie leagues for some few ages, as from all those parts, vsing but the same meanes to haue them that they doe; but surely in *Virginia*, their most tender and daintiest fruits or commodities, would be as perfit as theirs, by reason of the heat, if not in *New England*, and with all those aduantages.

The particular staple commodities that may be had by industry.

First, the ground is so fertill, that questionlesse it is capable of producing any Graine, Fruits, or Seeds, you will sow or plant, growing in the Regions aforenamed: But it may be not to that perfection of delicacy, because the Summer is not so hot, and the Winter is more cold in those parts we haue yet tried neere the Sea side, then wee finde in the same height in *Europe* or *Asia*: yet I made a Garden vpon the top of a Rocky Ile in three and forty degrees and an halfe, foure leagues from the maine in May, that grew so well, as it serued vs for Sallets in Iune and Iuly. All sorts of Cattle may here be bred and fed in the Iles or Peninsulaes securely for nothing. In the *Interim*, till they increase (if need be) obseruing the seasons, I durst vndertake to haue Corne enough from the Saluages for three hundred men, for a few trifles; and if they should be vntowards, as it is most certaine they will, thirtie or fortie good men will be sufficient to bring them all in subiection, and make this prouision, if they vnderstand what to doe; two hundred whereof may eight or nine moneths in the yeere be imploied in helping the Fisher-men, till the rest prouide other necessaries, fit to furnish vs with other Commodities.

The nature of the ground approued.

In March, Aprill, May, and halfe Iune, heere is Cod in abundance; In May, Iune, Iuly, and August, Mullit and Sturgion, whose Roes doe make Cauiare and Puttargo; Herring, if any desire them: I haue taken many out of the bellies of Cods, some in nets; but the Saluages compare the store in the Sea with the haires of their heads: and surely there are an incredible abundance vpon this Coast.

The seasons for fishing approued.

In the end of August, September, October, and Nouember, you may haue Cod againe to make Core-fish or Poore-Iohn: Hake you may haue when the Cod failes in Summer, if you will fish in the night, which is better then Cod. Now each hundred you take here, is as good as two or three hundred in *New found Land*; so that halfe the labour in hooking, splitting and touring, is saued: And you may haue your fish at what market you will, before they haue any in *New found land*, where their fishing is chiefely but in Iune and Iuly, where it is here in March, Aprill, May, September, October and Nouember, as is said; so that by reason of this Plantation, the Merchants may haue their fraught both out and home, which yeelds an aduantage worth consideration. Your Core-fish you may in like manner transport as you see cause, to serue the Ports in *Portugall*, as *Lisbone, Auera, Porta* Port, and diuers others, (or what market you please) before your Ilanders returne. They being tied to the season in the open Sea, and you hauing a double season, and fishing before your doores, may euery night sleep quietly ashore with good cheere, and what fires you will, or when you please with your wiues and family: they onely and their ships in the maine Ocean, that must carie and containe all they vse, besides their fraught. The Mullits here are in that abundance, you may take them with nets sometimes by hundreds, where at Cape *Blanke* they hooke them; yet those are but a foot and a halfe in length; these two, three, or foure, as oft I haue measured, which makes me suspect they are some other kinde of fish, though they seeme the same, both in fashion and goodnesse. Much Salmon some haue found vp the Riuers as they haue passed, and here the aire is so temperate, as all these at any time may be preserued. Now, young Boies and Girles Saluages, or any other bee they neuer such idlers, may turne, carie or returne a fish, without either shame or any great paine: He is very idle that is past twelue yeeres of age and cannot doe so much, and she is very old that cannot spin a threed to make Engins to catch a fish.

Imploiment for poore people and fatherlesse children.

The facilitie of the Plantation.

For their transportation, the ships that goe there to fish may transport the first: who for their passage will spare the charge of double manning their ships, which they must do in *New found land* to get their fraught; but one third part of that company are onely proper to serue a stage, carie a Barrow, and turne Poore-Iohn; notwithstanding, they must haue meat, drinke, clothes, & passage so well as the rest. Now all I desire is but this, That those that voluntarily will send shipping, should make here the best choice they can, or accept such as shall bee presented them to serue them at that rate: and their ships returning leaue such with me, with the value of that they should receiue comming home, in such prouisions and necessarie tooles, armes, bedding, apparell, salt, nets, hookes, lines, and such like, as they spare of the remainings; who till the next returne may keepe their Boats, and doe them many other profitable offices. Prouided, I haue men of abilitie to teach them their functions, and a company fit for Souldiers to be ready vpon any occasion, because of the abuses that haue beene offered the poore Saluages, and the libertie that both French and English, or any that will, haue to deale with them as they please; whose disorders will be hard to reforme, and the longer the worse: Now such order with facilitie might be taken, with euery Port, Towne, or Citie, with free power to conuert the benefit of their fraughts to what aduantage they please, and increase their numbers as they see occasion, who euer as they are able to subsist of themselues, may begin the new Townes in *New England*, in memory of their old: which freedome being confined but to the necessitie of the generall good, the euent (with Gods helpe) might produce an honest, a noble, and a profitable emulation.

Present Commodities.

Salt vpon Salt may assuredly be made, if not at the first in ponds, yet till they be prouided this may be vsed: then the ships may transport Kine, Horse, Goats, course Cloth, and such Commodities as we want; by whose arriuall may be made that prouision of fish to fraught the ships that they stay not; and then if the Sailers goe for wages it matters not, it is hard if this returne defray not the charge: but

Kermes. Musquasses. Beuers. Mines.

but care must be had they arriue in the Spring, or else that prouision be made for them against winter. Of certaine red berries called Kermes, which is worth ten shillings the pound, but of these haue beene sold for thirty or forty shillings the pound, may yeerely be gathered a good quantity. Of the Muskrat may be well raised gaines worth their labour, that will endeuour to make triall of their goodnesse. Of Beuers, Otters and Martins, blacke Foxes, and Furres of price, may yeerely be had six or seuen thousand, and if the trade of the French were preuented, many more: 25000. this yeere were brought from those northerne parts into *France*, of which trade we may haue as good part as the *French* if we take good courses. Of Mines of Gold and Siluer, Copper, and probabilities of Lead, Crystall and Allum, I could say much if relations were good assurances; it is true indeed, I made many trialls according to the instructions I had, which doth perswade me I need not despaire but that there are metals in the Country; but I am no Alcumist, nor will promise more then I know: which is, who will vndertake the rectifying of an iron Forge, if those that buy meat and drinke, coles, ore, and all necessaries at a deare rate, gaine, where all these things are to be had for taking vp, in my opinion cannot lose.

Woods.

Of woods, seeing there is such plenty of all sorts, if those that build ships and boats, buy wood at so great a price, as it is in *England, Spaine, France* and *Holland*, and all other prouisions for the nourishment of mans life, liue well by their trade; when labour is all required to take these necessaries without any other tax, what hazard will be here but to doe much better, and what commodity in Europe doth more decay then wood? for the goodnesse of the ground, let vs take it fertill or barren, or as it is, seeing it is certaine it beares fruits to nourish and feed man & beast as well as *England*, and the Sea those seuerall sorts of fishes I haue related: thus seeing all good things for mans sustenance may with this facility be had by a little extraordinary labour, till that transported be increased, & all necessaries for shipping onely for labour, to which may added the assistance of the Saluages which may easily be had, if they be discreetly handled in their kinds, towards fishing, planting, and destroying woods, what gaines might be raised if this were followed (when there is but once men to fill your store houses dwelling there, you may serue all Europe better and farre cheaper then can the Iland Fishers, or the Hollanders, Cape-blanke, or *Newfound land*, who must be at much more charge then you) may easily be coniectured by this example.

An example of the gaines vpon euery yeere or six moneths returne.

Two thousand will fit out a ship of 200. tunnes, & one of 100. tuns, if of the dry fish they both make fraught, that of 200. and goe for *Spaine*, sell it but at ten shillings a quintall, but commonly it giues fifteene or twenty, especially when it commeth first, which amounts to 3. or 4000. pound, but say but ten, which is the lowest, allowing the rest for waste, it amounts at that rate to 2000. which is the whole charge of your two ships and the equipage, then the returne of the mony and the fraught of the ship for the vintage or any other voyage is cleere gaine, with your ship of one hundred tunnes of traine Oile and Cor-fish, besides the Beuers and other commodities, and that you may haue at home within six moneths if God please to send but an ordinary passage; then sauing halfe this charge by the not staying of your ships, your victuall, ouerplus of men and wages, with her fraught thither with necessaries for the Planters, the Salt being there made, as also may the nets and lines within a short time; if nothing may be expected but this, it might in time equalize your Hollanders gaines, if not exceede them, hauing their fraughts alwaies ready against the arriuall of the ships, this would so increase our shipping and sailers, and so incourage and imploy a great part of our Idlers and others that want imployment fitting their qualities at home, where they shame to doe that they would doe abroad, that could they but once taste the sweet fruits of their owne labours, doubtlesse many thousands would be aduised by good discipline to take more pleasure in honest industry, then in their humors of dissolute idlenesse.

But

A description of the Countrey in particular, and their situations.

But to returne a little more to the particulars of this Countrey, which I intermingle thus with my projects and reasons, not being so sufficiently yet acquainted in those parts, to write fully the estate of the Sea, the Aire, the Land, the Fruits, their Rocks, the People, the Gouernment, Religion, Territories, Limitations, Friends and Foes: But as I gathered from their niggardly relations in a broken language, during the time I ranged those Countries, &c. the most Northerne part I was at, was the Bay of *Pennobscot*, which is East and West, North and South, more then ten leagues: but such were my occasions, I was constrained to be satisfied of them I found in the Bay, that the Riuer ranne farre vp into the Land, and was well inhabited with many people, but they were from their habitations, either fishing amongst the Iles, or hunting the Lakes and Woods for Deere and Beuers: the Bay is full of great Iles of one, two, six or eight miles in length, which diuides it into many faire and excellent good Harbours. On the East of it are the *Tarrentines*, their mortall enemies, where inhabit the French, as they report, that liue with those people as one Nation or Family: And Northwest of *Pennobscot* is *Mecaddacut*, at the foot of a high Mountaine, a kinde of fortresse against the *Tarrentines*, adioyning to the high Mountaines of *Pennobscot*, against whose feet doth beat the Sea; but ouer all the Land, Iles, or other impediments, you may well see them foureteene or eighteene leagues from their situation. *Segocket* is the next, then *Nuskoucus*, *Pemmaquid*, and *Sagadahock*: vp this Riuer, where was the Westerne Plantation, are *Aumoughcawgen*, *Kinnebeke*, and diuers others, where are planted some Corne fields. Along this Riuer thirtie or fortie miles, I saw nothing but great high cliffs of barren Rocks ouergrowne with Wood, but where the Saluages dwell there the ground is excellent salt, and fertill. Westward of this Riuer is the Country of *Aucocisco*, in the bottome of a large deepe Bay, full of many great Iles, which diuides it into many good Harbours. *Sawocotuck* is the next, in the edge of a large Sandy Bay, which hath many Rockes and Iles, but few good Harbours, but for Barkes I yet know; but all this Coast to *Pennobscot*, and as farre as I could see Eastward of it is nothing, but such high craggy clifty Rockes and stony Iles, that I wonder such great Trees could grow vpon so hard foundations. It is a Countrey rather to affright then delight one, and how to describe a more plaine spectacle of desolation, or more barren, I know not, yet are those rocky Iles so furnished with good Woods, Springs, Fruits, Fish and Fowle, and the Sea the strangest Fish-pond I euer saw, that it makes me thinke, though the coast be rocky and thus affrightable, the Vallies and Plaines and interior parts may well notwithstanding be very fertill. But there is no Country so fertill hath not some part barren, and *New-England* is great enough to make many Kingdomes and Countries, were it all inhabited. As you passe the coast still westward, *Accominticus* and *Passataquack* are two conuenient Harbours for small Barkes; and a good Country within their craggy clifts. *Augoan* is the next: this place might content a right curious judgement, but there are many sands at the entrance of the Harbour, and the worst is, it is imbayed too farre from the deepe Sea; here are many rising hils, and on their tops and descents are many corne fields and delightfull groues: On the East is an Ile of two or three leagues in length, the one halfe plaine marish ground, fit for pasture or salt Ponds, with many faire high groues of Mulbery trees and Gardens; there is also Okes, Pines, Walnuts, and other wood to make this place an excellent habitation, being a good and safe Harbour.

Naiemkeck, though it be more rocky ground, for *Augoan* is sandy, not much inferiour neither for the harbour, nor any thing I could perceiue but the multitude of people: from hence doth stretch into the Sea the faire headland *Tragabigzanda*, now called Cape *An*, fronted with the three Iles wee called the three Turkes heads; to the north of this doth enter a great Bay, where we found some habitations and Corne fields, they report a faire Riuer and at least 30. habitations

ons doth possesse this Country. But because the French had got their trade, I had no leisure to discouer it: the Iles of *Mattahunts* are on the west side of this Bay, where are many Iles and some Rocks that appeare a great height aboue the water like the Pyramides in Ægypt, and amongst them many good Harbours, and then the country of the *Massachusits*, which is the Paradice of all those parts, for here are many Iles planted with Corne, Groues, Mulberies, saluage Gardens and good Harbours, the Coast is for the most part high clayie sandy clifts, the sea Coast as you passe shewes you all along large Corne fields, and great troupes of well proportioned people: but the French hauing remained here neere six weekes, left nothing for vs to take occasion to examine the Inhabitants relations, *viz.* if there be three thousand people vpon those Iles, and that the Riuer doth pierce many daies iourney the entrailes of that Country: we found the people in those parts very kinde, but in their fury no lesse valiant, for vpon a quarrell we fought with forty or fifty of them, till they had spent all their Arrowes, and then we tooke six or seuen of their Canowes, which towards the euening they ransomed for Beuer skinnes, and at *Quonahassit* falling out there but with one of them, he with three others crossed the Harbour in a Canow to certaine rockes whereby wee must passe, and there let flie their Arrowes for our shot, till we were out of danger, yet one of them was slaine, and another shot through his thigh. An Indian slaine, another shot.

Then come you to *Accomacke* an excellent good Harbour, good land, and no want of any thing but industrious people: after much kindnesse, wee fought also with them, though some were hurt, some slaine, yet within an houre after they became friends. *Cape Cod* is the next presents it selfe, which is onely a headland of high hils, ouer-growne with shrubby Pines, hurts and such trash, but an excellent harbour for all weathers. This Cape is made by the maine Sea on the one side, and a great Bay on the other in forme of a Sickell, on it doth inhabit the people of *Pawmet*, and in the bottome of the Bay them of *Chawum*: towards the South and South-west of this Cape, is found a long and dangerous shoule of rocks and sand, but so farre as I incercled it, I found thirty fathome water and a strong currant, which makes mee thinke there is a chanell about this Shoule, where is the best and greatest fish to be had winter and summer in all the Country; but the Saluages say there is no Chanell, but that the Shoales beginne from the maine at *Pawmet* to the Ile of *Nawset*, and so extends beyond their knowledge into the Sea. The next to this is *Capawucke*, and those abounding Countries of Copper, Corne, People and Mineralls, which I went to discouer this last yeere, but because I miscarried by the way I will leaue them till God please I haue better acquaintance with them.

The *Massachusets* they report sometimes haue warres with the *Bashabes* of *Pennobscot*, & are not alwaies friends with them of *Chawum* and their alliance, but now they are all friends, and haue each trade with other so farre as they haue society on each others frontiers, for they make no such voyages as from *Pennobscot* to *Cape Cod*, seldome to *Massachset*. In the North as I haue said they haue begun to plant Corne, whereof the south part hath such plenty as they haue what they will from them of the North, and in the Winter much more plenty of fish and fowle, but both Winter & Summer hath it in one part or other all the yeere, being the meane and most indifferent temper betwixt heat and cold, of all the Regions betwixt the Line and the Pole, but the Furs Northward are much better, and in much more plenty then Southward.

The remarkablest Iles and Mountaines for land Markes are these: the highest Ile is *Sorico* in the Bay of *Pennobscot*, but the three Iles, and the Iles of *Matinack* are much further in the Sea: *Metynacus* is also three plaine Iles, but many great Rocks: *Monahigan* is a round high Ile, and close by it *Monanis*, betwixt which is a small Harbour where we rid; in *Damerils* Iles is such another, *Sagadahocke* is knowne by *Satquin*, and foure or fiue Iles in their mouth. *Smiths* Iles are a heape The land Markes.

together

gether, none neere them against *Accomintycus*: the three *Turkes heads*, are three Iles, seene farre to Sea-ward in regard of the Head-land. The chiefe Head-lands, are onely Cape *Tragabigzanda*, and Cape *Cod*, now called Cape *Iames*, and Cape *Anne*.

The chiefe Mountaines, them of *Pennobscot*, the twinkling Mountaine of *Acocisco*, the great Mountaine of *Sassanow*, and the high Mountaine of *Massachuset*. Each of which you shall finde in the Map, their places, forme, and altitudes. The waters are most pure, proceeding from the intrailes of rocky Mountaines: the Herbs and Fruits are of many sorts and kinds, as Alkermes, Currans, Mulberries, Vines, Respises, Gooseberies, Plums, Wall-nuts, Chesse-nuts, Small-nuts, Pumpions, Gourds, Strawberies, Beanes, Pease, and Maize; a kinde or two of Flax, wherewith they make Nets, Lines, and Ropes, both small and great, very strong for their quantities.

Herbs and Fruits

Woods. Oake is the chiefe wood, of which there is great difference, in regard of the soyle where it groweth, Firre, Pine, Wall-nut, Chesse-nut, Birtch, Ash, Elme, Cipris, Cedar, Mulbery, Plum tree, Hazell, Saxefras, and many other sorts.

Birds. Eagles, Grips, diuers sorts of Hawkes, Craines, Geese, Brants, Cormorants, Ducks, Cranes, Swannes, Sheldrakes, Teale, Meawes, Gulls, Turkies, Diue-doppers, and many other sorts whose names I know not.

Fishes. Whales, Grompus, Porkpisces, Turbut, Sturgion, Cod, Hake, Haddocke, Cole, Cuske or small Ling, Sharke, Mackarell, Herring, Mullit, Base, Pinnacks, Cunners, Pearch, Eeles, Crabs, Lobsters, Mustels, Wilks, Oisters, Clamps, Periwinkels, and diuers others, &c.

Beasts. Moos, a beast bigger than a Stag, Deare red and fallow, Beuers, Wolues, Foxes both blacke and other, Aroughcunds, wilde Cats, Beares, Otters, Martins, Fitches, Musquassus, and diuers other sorts of Vermin whose names I know not: all these and diuers other good things doe here for want of vse still increase and decrease with little diminution, whereby they grow to that abundance, you shall scarce finde any bay, shallow shore or Coue of sand, where you may not take many clamps or Lobsters, or both at your pleasure, and in many places load your Boat if you please, nor Iles where you finde not Fruits, Birds, Crabs, and Mustels, or all of them; for taking at a low water Cod, Cuske, Hollibut, Scate, Turbut, Mackarell, or such like are taken plentifully in diuers sandy Bayes, store of Mullit, Bases, and diuers other sorts of such excellent fish as many as their Net can hold: no Riuer where there is not plenty of Sturgion, or Salmon, or both, all which are to be had in abundance obseruing but their seasons: but if a man will goe at Christmas to gather Cherries in Kent, though there be plenty in Summer, he may be deceiued; so here these plenties haue each their seasons, as I haue expressed; we for the most part had little but bread and Vinegar, and though the most part of Iuly when the fishing decayed, they wrought all day, lay abroad in the Iles all night, and liued on what they found, yet were not sicke: But I would wish none long put himselfe to such plunges, except necessity constraine it: yet worthy is that person to starue that here cannot liue, if he haue sense, strength and health, for there is no such penury of these blessings in any place but that one hundred men may in two or three houres make their prouisions for a day, and he that hath experience to manage these affaires, with forty or thirty honest industrious men, might well vndertake (if they dwell in these parts) to subiect the Saluages, and feed daily two or three hundred men, with as good Corne, Fish, and Flesh as the earth hath of those kinds, and yet make that labour but their pleasure; prouided that they haue Engines that be proper for their purposes. Who can desire more content that hath small meanes, or but onely his merit to aduance his fortunes, then to tread and plant that ground he hath purchased by the hazard of his life; if hee haue but the taste of vertue and magnanimity, what to such a minde can bee more pleasant then planting and building a foundation for his posterity, got from the rude earth by Gods blessing and his owne

A note for men that haue great spirits and small meanes.

owne industry without preiudice to any, if hee haue any graine of faith or zeale in Religion, what can he doe lesse hurtfull to any, or more agreeable to God, then to seeke to conuert those poore Saluages to know Christ and humanity, whose labours with discretion will triple requite thy charge and paine; what so truly sutes with honour and honesty, as the discouering things vnknowne, erecting Townes, peopling Countries, informing the ignorant, reforming things vniust, teaching vertue and gaine to our natiue mother Country; a Kingdome to attend her, finde imploiment for those that are idle, because they know not what to doe: so farre from wronging any, as to cause posterity to remember thee, and remembring thee, euer honour that remembrance with praise. Consider what were the beginnings and endings of the Monarchies of the Chaldeans, the Syrians, the Grecians and Romans, but this one rule; what was it they would not doe for the good of their common weale, or their mother City? For example: *Rome*, what made her such a Monarchesse, but onely the aduentures of her youth, not in riots at home, but in dangers abroad, and the iustice and iudgement out of their experiences when they grew aged; what was their ruine and hurt but this, the excesse of idlenesse, the fondnesse of parents, the want of experience in Maiestrates, the admiration of their vndeserued honours, the contempt of true merit, their vniust iealousies, their politike incredulities, their hypocriticall seeming goodnesse and their deeds of secret lewdnesse; finally in fine, growing onely formall temporists, all that their Predecessors got in many yeeres they lost in a few daies: those by their paines and vertues became Lords of the world, they by their ease and vices became slaues to their seruants; this is the difference betwixt the vse of armes in the field, and on the monuments of stones, the golden age and the leaden age, prosperity and misery, iustice and corruption, substance and shadowes, words and deeds, experience and imagination, making common weales, and marring common weales, the fruits of vertue, and the conclusions of vice.

Then who would liue at home idly, or thinke in himselfe any worth to liue, onely to eat, drinke and sleepe, and so die; or by consuming that carelesly, his friends got worthily, or by vsing that miserably that maintained vertue honestly, or for being descended nobly, and pine with the vaine vaunt of great kindred in penury, or to maintaine a silly shew of brauery, toile out thy heart, soule and time basely; by shifts, tricks, Cards and Dice, or by relating newes of other mens actions, sharke here and there for a dinner or supper, deceiue thy friends by faire promises and dissimulation, in borrowing where thou neuer meanest to pay, offend the Lawes, surfet with excesse, burthen thy Countrie, abuse thy selfe, despaire in want, and then cousen thy Kindred, yea euen thy owne brother, and wish thy Parents death (I will not say damnation) to haue their estates, though thou seest what honours and rewards the world yet hath for them, that will seeke them and worthily deserue them.

I would bee sorry to offend, or that any should mistake my honest meaning; for I wish good to all, hurt to none: but rich men for the most part are growne to that dotage through their pride in their wealth, as though there were no accident could end it or their life.

And what hellish care doe such take to make it their owne misery and their Countries spoile, especially when there is most need of their imploiment, drawing by all manner of inuentions from the Prince and his honest Subiects, euen the vitall spirits of their powers and estates: as if their baggs or brags were so powerfull a defence, the malicious could not assault them, when they are the onely bait to cause vs not onely to bee assaulted, but betrayed and murthered in our owne security ere wee will perceiue it.

Imploiments for Labourers.

For Labourers, if those that sow Hempe, Rape, Turnups, Parsnips, Carrats, Cabidge, and such like; giue twentie, thirtie, fortie, fiftie shillings yeerely for an Acre of Land, and meat, drinke, and wages to vse it, and yet grow rich: when better, or at least as good ground may bee had and cost nothing but labour; it seemes strange to me any such should grow poore.

My purpose is not to perswade children from their parents, men from their wiues, nor seruants from their masters; onely such as with free consent may bee spared: but that each Parish, or Village, in Citie, or Countrey, that will but apparell their fatherlesse children of thirteene or fourteene yeeres of age, or young maried people that haue small wealth to liue on, here by their labour may liue exceeding well. Prouided alwaies, that first there be a sufficient power to command them, houses to receiue them, meanes to defend them, and meet prouisions for thẽ, for any place may be ouer-laine: and it is most necessary to haue a fortresse (ere this grow to practise) and sufficient masters, of all necessarie, mecanicall qualities, to take ten or twelue of them for Apprentises; the Master by this may quickly grow rich, these may learne their trades themselues to doe the like, to a generall and an incredible benefit for King and Countrey, Master and Seruant.

Examples of the *Spaniards*.

It would be a History of a large volume, to recite the aduentures of the *Spaniards* and *Portugals*, their affronts and defeats, their dangers and miseries; which with such incomparable honor, and constant resolution, so farre beyond beleefe, they haue attempted and indured in their discoueries and plantations, as may well condemne vs of too much imbecillitie, sloth, and negligence; yet the Authors of these new inuentions were held as ridiculous for a long time, as now are others that doe but seeke to imitate their vnparalleld vertues, and though we see daily their mountaines of wealth (sprung from the Plants of their generous indeuours) yet is our sensualitie and vntowardnesse such, & so great, that we either ignorantly beleeue nothing, or so curiously contest, to preuent we know not what future euents; that we either so neglect, or oppresse and discourage the present, as wee spoile all in the making, crop all in the blooming; and building vpon faire Sand rather then vpon rough Rocks, iudge that we know not, gouerne that wee haue not, feare that which is not; and for feare some should doe too well, force such against their wils to be idle, or as ill. And who is hee hath iudgement, courage, and any industry or quality with vnderstanding, will leaue his Country, his hopes at home, his certaine estate, his friends, pleasures, libertie, and the preferment sweet *England* doth affoord to all degrees, were it not to aduance his fortunes by enioying his deserts, whose prosperitie once appearing, will encourage others: but it must be cherished as a childe, till it be able to goe and vnderstand it selfe, and not corrected nor oppressed aboue it strength, ere it know wherefore. A childe can neither performe the office nor deeds of a man of strength, nor endure that affliction he is able: nor can an Apprentise at the first performe the part of a Master, and if twentie yeeres be required to make a childe a man, seuen yeeres limited an Apprentise for his trade: if scarce an age be sufficient to make a wise man a States-man, and commonly a man dies ere he hath learned to be discreet; if perfection be so hard to be obtained, as of necessitie there must be Practice as well as Theoricke: Let no man then condemne this paradox opinion, to say that halfe seuen yeres is scarce sufficient for a good capacitie to learne in these affaires how to carrie himselfe. And who euer shall try in these remote places the erecting of a Colony, shall finde at the end of seuen yeeres occasion enough to vse all his discretion: and in the *Interim*, all the content, rewards, gaines, and hopes, will be necessarily required, to be giuen to the beginning, till it be able to creepe, to stand, and goe, and to encourage desert by all possible meanes; yet time enough to keepe it from running, for there is no feare it will grow too fast, or euer to any thing, except libertie, profit, honor, and prosperitie there found, more binde the Planters of those affaires in deuotion to effect it; then bondage, violence, tyrannie, ingratitude, and such double dealing, as bindes free men to become slaues,

The causes of our defailments.

and

and honest men turne knaues; which hath euer beene the ruine of the most popular Common-weales, and is very vnlikely euer well to begin anew.

Who seeth not what is the greatest good of the *Spaniard*, but these new conclusions in searching those vnknowne parts of this vnknowne world; by which meanes he diues euen into the very secrets of all his neighbours, and the most part of the world; and when the *Portugals* and *Spaniards* had found the *East* and *West-Indies*, how many did condemne themselues, that did not accept of that honest offer of Noble *Columbus*; who vpon our neglect brought them to it, perswading our selues the world had no such places as they had found: and yet euer since we finde, they still (from time to time) haue found new Lands, new Nations, and Trades, and still daily doe finde, both in *Asia*, *Affrica*, *Terra incognita*, and *America*, so that there is neither Souldier nor Mechanicke, from the Lord to the Begger, but those parts affoords them all imploiment, & discharges their natiue soile of so many thousands of all sorts, that else by their sloth, pride, and imperfections, would long ere this haue troubled their neighbours, or haue eaten the pride of *Spaine* it selfe.

The blisse of *Spaine*.

Now hee knowes little that knowes not *England* may well spare many more people then *Spaine*, and is as well able to furnish them with all manner of necessaries; and seeing for all they haue, they cease not still to search for that they haue not, and know not; it is strange we should be so dull, as not maintaine that which we haue, and pursue that we know: Surely, I am sure many would take it ill, to be abridged of the titles and honors of their predecessors; when if but truly they would iudge themselues, looke how inferior they are to their Noble Vertues; so much they are vnworthy of their honors and liuings, which neuer were ordained for shewes and shadowes, to maintaine idlenesse and vice, but to make them mordable to abound in honor, by Heroicall deeds of action, iudgement, pietie, and vertue. What was it both in their purse and person they would not doe, for the good of their Common-wealth, which might moue them presently to set out their spare children in these generous designes; Religion aboue all things should moue vs, especially the Clergie, if we are religious, to shew our faith by our works, in conuerting those poore Saluages to the knowledge of God, seeing what paines the *Spaniards* takes to bring them to their adultered faith. Honor might moue the Gentry, the valiant, and industrious; and the hope and assurance of wealth, all, if we were that we would seeme, and be accounted; or be we so farre inferior to other Nations, or our spirits so farre deiected from our ancient predecessors, or our mindes so vpon spoile, piracy, and such villany, as to serue the *Portugall*, *Spaniard*, *Dutch*, *French*, or *Turke*, (as to the cost of *Europe* too many doe) rather then our God, our King, our Country, and our selues; excusing our idlenesse and our base complaints by want of imploiment, when here is such choice of all sorts, and for all degrees, in the planting and discouering these North parts of *America*.

My second voyage to New England.

IN the yeere of our Lord 1615. I was imploied by many my friends of *London*, and Sir *Ferdinando Gorges*, a noble Knight, and a great fauourer of those actions, who perswaded the reuerend Deane of *Exeter* Doctor *Sutliffe*, and diuers Merchants of the West, to entertaine this Plantation. Much labour I had taken to bring the *Londoners* and them to ioyne together, because the *Londoners* haue most Money, and the Westerne men are most proper for fishing; and it is neere as much trouble, but much more danger, to saile from *London* to *Plimoth*, then from *Plimoth* to *New England*, so that halfe the voiage would thus be saued, yet by no meanes I could preuaile, so desirous they were both to be Lords of this fishing. Now to make my words more apparant by my deeds, to begin a Plantation

My second Voiage to *New England*. 1615.

tion for a more ample triall of those conclusions, I was to haue staied there but with sixteene men, whose names were;

Tho. Dirmer. *Edw. Stallings.* *Daniel Cage.* *Francis Abbot.*	Gent.	*Iohn Gosling.* *William Ingram.* *Dauid Cooper.* *Iohn Partridge.*	Sould.	*Thomas Digby.* *Daniel Baker.* *Adam Smith.* *Tho. Watson.*	*Walter Chisell.* *Robert Miller.* And two Boyes	were to learne to be Sailers.

I confesse I could haue wished them as many thousands, had all other prouisions beene in like proportion; nor would I haue had so few, could I haue had means for more; yet would God haue pleased we had safely arriued, I doubted not but to haue performed more then I promised, and that many thousands ere this would haue bin there ere now. The maine assistance next God I had to this small number, was my acquaintance amongst the Saluages, especially with *Dohoday*, one of their greatest Lords, who had liued long in *England*, and another called *Tantum*, I caried with mee from *England*, and set on shore at Cape *Cod*; by the meanes of this proud Saluage, I did not doubt but quickly to haue got that credit amongst the rest of the Saluages and their alliance, to haue had as many of them as I desired in any designe I intended, and that trade also they had by such a kinde of exchange of their Countrey Commodities, which both with ease and securitie might then haue beene vsed with him and diuers others: I had concluded to inhabit and defend them against the *Tarentines*, with a better power then the *French* did them; whose tyrannie did inforce them to embrace my offer with no small deuotion: and though many may think me more bold then wise, in regard of their power, dexteritie, treachery, and inconstancy, hauing so desperately assaulted, and betraied many others; I say but this (because with so many, I haue many times done much more in *Virginia* then I intended here, when I wanted that experience *Virginia* taught mee) that to me it seemes no more danger then ordinary: and though I know my selfe the meanest of many thousands, whose apprehensiue inspection can pierce beyond the bounds of my abilities, into the hidden things of Nature, Art, and Reason: yet I intreat such, giue mee leaue to excuse my selfe of so much imbecillitie, as to say, that in these eighteene yeeres which I haue beene conuersant with these affaires, I haue not learned, there is a great difference betwixt the directions and iudgement of experimentall knowledge, and the superficiall coniecture of variable relation: wherein rumour, humour, or misprision haue such power, that oft times one is enough to beguile twentie, but twentie not sufficient to keepe one from being deceiued. Therefore I know no reason but to beleeue my owne eies before any mans imagination, that is but wrested from the conceits of my owne proiects and endeuours, but I honor with all affection, the counsell and instructions of iudiciall directions, or any other honest aduertisement, so farre to obserue, as they tie me, not to the crueltie of vnknowne euents. These are the inducements that thus drew me to neglect all other imploiments, and spend my time and best abilities in these aduentures, wherein though I haue had many discouragements, by the ingratitude of some, the malicious slanders of others, the falsenesse of friends, the treachery of cowards, and slownesse of Aduenturers.

The ground and plot for our plantation.

The meanes vsed to preuent it and me.

Now you are to remember, as I returned first from *New England* at *Plimoth*, I was promised foure good ships ready prepared to my hand the next Christmas, and what conditions and content I would desire, to put this businesse in practise, and arriuing at *London*, foure more were offered me with the like courtesie. But to ioyne the *Londoners* & them in one, was most impossible; so that in Ianuary with two hundred pound in Chash for aduenture, and six Gentlemen well furnished, I went from *London* to the foure ships were promised me at *Plimoth*, but I found no such matter: and the most of those that had made such great promises, by the bad returne of the ship went for Gold, and their priuate emulations, were extinct and qualified. Notwithstanding at last, with a labyrinth of trouble, though the

How I set saile and returned.

greatest of the burden lay on me, and a few of my particular friends, I was furnished with a ship of two hundred tunnes, and another of fiftie: But ere I had sailed one hundred and twentie leagues, she brake all her Masts, pumping each watch fiue or six thousand strokes; onely her spret-saile remained to spoone before the winde, till we had re-accommodated a Iury-mast to returne for *Plimoth*, or founder in the Seas.

My reimbarkement, encounter with Pirats, and imprisonment by the French.

My Vice-Admirall being lost, not knowing of this, proceeded her voyage; now with the remainder of those prouisions, I got out againe in a small Barke of sixtie tuns with thirty men: for this of two hundred, and prouision for seuentie, which were the sixteene before named, and fourteene other Sailers for the ship; with those I set saile againe the foure and twentieth of Iune, where what befell me (because my actions and writings are so publike to the world) enuy still seeking to scandalize my endeuours, and seeing no power but death can stop the chat of ill tongues, nor imagination of mens minds, lest my owne relations of those hard euents might by some constructors bee made doubtfull, I haue thought it best to insert the examinations of those proceedings, taken by Sir *Lewis Stukeley*, a worthy Knight, and Vice-Admirall of *Deuonshire*, which was as followeth.

The Examination of Daniel Baker, *late Steward to Captaine* Iohn Smith, *in the returne of* Plimoth, *taken before Sir* Lewis Stukeley *Knight, the eighth of December,* 1615.

THE effect in briefe was this: being chased by one *Fry* an English Pirat, *Edward Chambers* the Master, *Iohn Minter* his Mate, *Thomas Digby* the Pylot, and diuers others importuned him to yeeld; much swaggering wee had with them, more then the Pirats, who agreed vpon such faire conditions as we desired, which if they broke, he vowed to sinke rather then be abused. Strange they thought it, that a Barke of threescore tuns with foure guns should stand vpon such termes, they being eightie expert Sea-men, in an excellent ship of one hundred and fortie tuns, and thirty six cast Peeces and Murderers: But when they knew our Captaine, so many of them had beene his Souldiers, and they but lately runne from *Tunis*, where they had stolne this ship, wanted victuall, and in combustion amongst themselues, would haue yeelded all to his protection, or wafted vs any whither: but those mutinies occasioned vs to reiect their offer, which afterward we all repented. For at *Fiall* we met two French Pirats, the one of two hundred tuns, the other thirty: no disgrace would cause our mutiners fight, till the Captaine offered to blow vp the ship rather then yeeld, till hee had spent all his powder: so that together by the eares we went, and at last got cleere of them for all their shot. At *Flowers* we were againe chased with foure French men of warre, the *Admirall* one hundred and fortie tuns, and ninety men well armed; the rest good ships, and as well prouided: much parly we had, but vowing they were *Rochilers*, and had a Commission from the King onely to secure true men, and take *Portugals*, *Spaniards*, and Pirats, and as they requested, our Captaine went to shew his Commission, which was vnder the broad Seale, but neither it nor their vowes they so much respected, but they kept him, rifled our ship, manned her with French men, and dispersed vs amongst their Fleet: within fiue or six daies they were increased to eight or nine saile. At last they surrendred vs our ship, and most of our prouisions, the defects they promised the next day to supply, and did. Notwithstanding, there was no way but our mutiners would for *England*, though we were as neere *New England*, till the major part resolued with our Captaine to proceed. But the *Admirall* sending his Boat for our Captaine, they espying a Saile, presently gaue chase, whereby our mutiners finding an opportunitie in the night ran away, and thus left our Captaine in his Cap, Bretches, and Wast-coat, alone among the French men: his clothes, armes, and what he had, our mutiners shared among them, and with a false excuse, faining for

for feare lest he should turne man of warre, they returned for *Plimoth*: fifteene of vs being Land-men, not knowing what they did. *Daniel Cage, Edward Stalings, Walter Chisell, David Cooper, Robert Miller*, and *Iohn Partridge*, vpon oath affirmes this for truth before the Vice-Admirall.

A double treachery.

Now the cause why the French detained mee againe, was the suspition this *Chambers* and *Minter* gaue them, that I would reuenge my selfe vpon the *Banke*, or in *New found land*, of all the French I could there encounter, and how I would haue fired the ship, had they not ouer-perswaded me: and that if I had but againe my Armes, I would rather sinke by them, then they should haue from me but the value of a Bisket; and many other such like tales to catch but opportunitie in this manner to leaue me, and thus they returned to *Plimoth*, and perforce with the French men I thus proceeded. Being a fleet of eight or nine saile, we watched for the *West-Indies* fleet, till ill weather separated vs from the other eight: still wee spent our time about the Iles of the *Assores*, where to keepe my perplexed thoughts from too much meditation of my miserable estate, I writ this Discourse, thinking to haue sent it to you of his Maiesties Councell by some ship or other, for I saw their purpose was to take all they could. At last we were chased by one Captaine *Barra*, an English Pirat in a small ship, with some twelue Peece of Ordnance, about thirty men, and neere all starued. They sought by courtesie releefe of vs, who gaue them such faire promises, as at last they betraied Captaine *Wollistone* his Lieutenant, and foure or fiue of his men aboord vs, and then prouided to take the rest perforce. Now my part was to be prisoner in the Gun-roome, and not to speake to any of them vpon my life, yet had *Barra* knowledge what I was. Then *Barra* perceiuing well those French intents, made ready to fight, and *Wollistone* as resolutely regarded not their threats, which caused vs demurre vpon the matter longer some sixteene houres, and then returned them againe Captaine *Wollistone* and all their Prisoners, and some victuall also vpon a small composition: But whilest we were bartering thus with them; a Caruill before our faces got vnder the Castle of *Gratiosa*, from whence they beat vs with their Ordnance.

A fleet of nine French men of war, and fights with the Spaniard.

A prise of Fish.

The next wee tooke was a small English man of *Poole* from *New found land*: the great Cabben at this present was my prison, from whence I could see them pillage these poore men of all that they had, and halfe their fish: when hee was gone, they sold his poore clothes at the maine Mast by an out-cry, which scarce gaue each man seuen pence a peece.

A Scotch prise.

Not long after we tooke a *Scot* fraught from Saint *Michaels* to *Bristow*, he had better fortune then the other; for hauing but taken a Boats loading of Sugar, Marmelade, Suckets, and such like, we descried foure saile, after whom we stood, who forling their maine Sailes attended vs to fight, but our French spirits were content onely to perceiue they were English red Crosses. Within a very small time after wee chased 4. Spanish ships that came from the *Indies*, we fought with them foure or fiue houres, tore their sailes and sides with many a shot betwixt wind and weather, yet not daring to boord them, lost them, for which all the Sailers euer after hated the Captaine as a professed coward.

A prise worth 36000 crownes.

A poore Caruill of *Brasile* was the next wee chased; and after a small fight, thirteene or foureteene of her men being wounded, which was the better halfe, we tooke her with three hundred and seuenty chests of Sugar, one hundred hides, and thirty thousand Rialls of eight.

The next was a ship of *Holland*, which had lost her Consorts in the Streights of *Magilans*, going for the South sea, she was put roomy, she also these French men with faire promises, cunningly betraied to come aboord them to shew their Commission, and so made prise of all: the most of the *Dutch-men* we tooke aboord the *Admirall*, and manned her with *French-men*, that within two or three nights after ran away with her for *France*, the wounded *Spaniards* we set on shore on the Ile of *Tercera*, the rest we kept to saile the Caruill.

A prise worth 200000 crownes.

Within a day or two after, we met a *West-Indies* man of warre, of one hundred and

and sixtie tuns, a fore noone wee fought with her, and then tooke her with one thousand one hundred Hides, fiftie Chests of Cutchanele, foureteene Coffers of wedges of Siluer, eight thousand Rialls of eight, and six Coffers of the King of *Spaines* Treasure, besides the good pillage and rich Coffers of many rich Passengers.

Two moneths they kept me in this manner to manage their fights against the *Spaniards*, and bee a Prisoner when they tooke any English. Now though the Captaine had oft broke his promise, which was to put me on shore the Iles, or the next ship he tooke; yet at the last he was contented I should goe in the Caruill of Sugar for *France*, himselfe seeming as resolued to keepe the Seas, but the next morning we all set saile for *France*, and that night we were separated from the *Admirall* and the rich prise by a storme. Within two daies after wee were hailed by two *West-Indies* men: but when they saw vs waife them for the King of *France*, they gaue vs their broad sides, shot thorow our maine Mast, and so left vs. Hauing liued now this Summer amongst those French men of warre, with much adoe we arriued at the *Gulion*, not farre from *Rotchell*: where in stead of the great promises they alwaies fed me with, of double satisfaction and full content, and tenne thousand Crownes was generally concluded I should haue; they kept me fiue or six daies Prisoner in the Caruill, accusing me to be he that burnt their Colony in *New France*; to force me to giue them a discharge before the Iudge of the Admiraltie, and stand to their courtesies for satisfaction, or lie in prison, or a worse mischiefe: Indeed this was in the time of combustion, that the Prince of *Cundy* was with his Army in the field, and euery poore Lord, or men in authoritie, as little Kings of themselues: For this iniury was done me by them that set out this voyage (not by the Sailers) for they were cheated of all as well as I, by a few Officers aboord, and the owners on shore.

My escape from the French men.

But to preuent this choise, in the end of such a storme that beat them all vnder hatches, I watched my opportunitie to get a shore in their Boat, whereinto in the darke night I secretly got, and with a halfe Pike that lay by me, put a drift for *Rat* Ile: but the currant was so strong, and the Sea so great, I went a drift to Sea, till it pleased God the wind so turned with the tide, that although I was all this fearefull night of gusts and raine in the Sea the space of twelue houres, when many ships were driuen ashore, and diuers split: (and being with skulling and bayling the water tired, I expected each minute would sinke me) at last I arriued in an Oazy Ile by *Charowne*, where certaine Fowlers found me neere drowned, and halfe dead, with water, cold, and hunger. My Boat I pawned to finde meanes to get to *Rotchell*; where I vnderstood our man of war & the rich prize, wherein was the Cap. called *Mounsieur Poyrune*, and the thirtie thousand Rialls of eight we tooke in the Caruill, was split, the Captaine drowned and halfe his Company the same night, within six or seuen leagues of that place; from whence I escaped in the little Boat by the mercy of God, far beyond all mens reason or my expectation, arriuing at *Rotchell*: vpon my complaint to the Iudge of the Admiraltie, I found many good words and faire promises, and ere long many of them that escaped drowning, told me the newes they heard of my owne death: These I arresting, their seuerall examinations did so confirme my complaint, it was held proofe sufficient. All which being performed according to their order of justice, from vnder the Iudges hand, I presented it to Sir *Thomas Edmonds*, then Ambassadour at *Burdeaux*, where it was my chance to see the arriuall of the Kings great mariage brought from *Spaine*.

What law I had.

Here it was my good fortune to meet my old friend Master *Crampton*, that no lesse grieued at my losse, then willingly to his power did supply my wants, and I must confesse, I was more beholden to the French men that escaped drowning in the man of warre, Madam *Chanoyes* at *Rotchell*, and the Lawyers of *Burdeaux*, then all the rest of my Country-men I met in *France*. Of the wracke of the

 rich

rich prise, some three thousand six hundred crownes worth of goods came ashore, and was saued with the Caruill, which I did my best to arrest: the Iudge promised I should haue Iustice, what will be the conclusion as yet I know not. But vnder the couler to take Pirats and the *West-Indie* men (because the *Spaniards* will not suffer the French to trade in the *West-Indies*) any goods from thence, though they take them vpon the Coast of *Spaine* are lawfull prize, or from any of his Teritories out of the limits of *Europe*: and as they betraied me, though I had the broad-seale, so did they rob and pillage twentie saile of English men more, besides them I knew not of the same yeere.

My returne for England.

Leauing thus my businesse in *France* I returned to *Plimoth*, to finde them had thus buried me amongst the French; and not onely buried me, but with so much infamy as such treacherous cowards could suggest to excuse their villanies. The Chiefetaines of this mutiny that I could finde, I laid by the heeles, the rest like themselues confessed the truth, as you haue heard. Now how I haue or could preuent these accidents, hauing no more meanes, I rest at your censures; but to proceed to the matter; yet must I sigh and say, How oft hath Fortune in the world (thinke I) brought slauery, freedome, and turned all diuersly. *Newfoundland* I haue heard at the first, was held as desperate a fishing as this I proiect for *New England*. *Placentia*, and the *Banke* neare also as doubtfull to the French: But for all the disasters hapned me, the businesse is the same it was, and the fiue ships went from *London*, whereof one was reported more then three hundred tunnes, found fish so much, that neither *Izeland* man, nor *Newfoundland* man I could heare of hath bin there, will go any more to either place, if they may go thither. So

The successe of my Vice-Admirall.

that vpon the good returne of my *Vice-Admirall*, this yeere are gone 4 or 5 saile from *Plimoth*, and from *London* as many, only to make voyages of profit: whereas if all the English had bin there till my returne, put all their returnes together, they would scarce make one a sauour of neere a dozen I could nominate, except one sent by Sir *Francis Popam*; though there be fish sufficient, as I am perswaded, to fraught yeerely foure or fiue hundred Saile, or as many as will goe. For this fishing stretcheth along the Sea Coast from Cape *Iames* to *Newfoundland*, which is seuen or eight hundred miles at the least, and hath his course in the deepes, and by the shore, all the yere long, keeping their hants and feedings, as the beasts of the field, and the birds of the aire. But all men are not such as they should be, that haue vndertaken those voyages: All the *Romans* were not *Scipioes*, nor *Carthagenians Hanibals*, nor all the *Genweses Columbusses*, nor all the *Spaniards Courtesos*: had they diued no deeper in the secrets of their discoueries then we, or stopped at such doubts and poore accidentall chances, they had neuer beene remembred as they are, yet had they no such certainties to begin as we.

But to conclude, *Adam* and *Eue* did first begin this innocent worke to plant the earth to remaine to posterity, but not without labour, trouble, and industry. *Noe* and his family began againe the second Plantation; and their seed as it still increased, hath still planted new Countries, and one Countrey another, and so the world to that estate it is: but not without much hazard, trauell, mortalities, discontents, and many disasters. Had those worthy Fathers, and their memorable off-spring, not beene more diligent for vs now in these ages, then we are to plant that yet is vnplanted for the after liuers. Had the seed of *Abraham*, our Sauiour Christ, and his Apostles, exposed themselues to no more dangers to teach the Gospell then we, euen wee our selues had at this present beene as saluage, and as miserable as the most barbarous Saluage, yet vnciuilized. The *Hebrewes* and *Lacedemonians*, the *Gothes*, the *Grecians*, the *Romanes*, and the rest, what was it they would not vndertake to inlarge their Teritories, enrich their subiects, resist their enemies. Those that were the founders of those great Monarchies and their vertues, were no siluered idle golden Pharises, but industrious Iron steeled Publicans: They regarded more prouisions and necessaries for

for their people, then Iewels, riches, ease, or delight for themselues; Riches were their Seruants, not their Masters. They ruled (as Fathers, not as Tirants) their people as Children, not as Slaues; there was no disaster could discourage them; and let none thinke they incountred not with all manner of incumbrances. And what hath euer beene the worke of the greatest Princes of the Earth, but planting of Countries, and ciuilizing barbarous and inhumane Nations to ciuilitie and humanitie, whose eternall actions fills our Histories.

Lastly, the *Portugals* and *Spaniards*, whose euer-liuing actions before our eies will testifie with them our idlenesse, and ingratitude to all posterities, and the neglect of our duties, in our pietie and religion. We owe our God, our King and Countrey, and want of Charitie to those poore Saluages, whose Countrey wee challenge, vse and possesse; except wee be but made to vse, and marre what our fore-fathers made, or but onely tell what they did, or esteeme our selues too good to take the like paines. Was it vertue in them to prouide that doth maintaine vs, and basenesse in vs to doe the like for others? Surely no. Then seeing we are not borne for our selues, but each to help other, and our abilities are much alike at the houre of our birth, and the minute of our death: seeing our good deeds or our bad by faith in Christs merits, is all we haue, to carie our soules to heauen or hell. Seeing honor is our liues ambition, and our ambition after death to haue an honorable memory of our life: and seeing by no meanes we would be abated of the dignities and glories of our predecessors, let vs imitate their vertues to be worthily their successors: to conclude with *Lucretius*,

Its want of reason, or its reasons want
Which doubts the minde and iudgement, so doth dant,
That those beginnings makes men not to grant.

Iohn Smith writ this with his owne hand.

Here followeth a briefe Discourse of the trials of New England, *with certaine Obseruations of the* Hollanders *vse and gaine by fishing, and the present estate of that happy Plantation, begun but by sixtie weake men, in the yeere of our Lord 1620. and how to build a fleet of good ships to make a little Nauy Royall, by the former Author.*

HE saith, that it is more then foure and forty yeeres agoe, and it is more then fortie yeeres agoe since he writ it; that the Herring Busses out of the Low Countries vnder the King of *Spaine*, were fiue hundred, besides one hundred French men, and three or foure hundred saile of *Flemings*. The Coast of *Wales* and *Lancashire* was vsed by 300 Saile of Strangers. *Ireland* at *Beltamore*, fraughted yeerely three hundred saile of *Spaniards*, where King *Edward* the sixt intended to haue made a strong Castle, because of the straight to haue tribute for fishing. *Black Rocke* was yerely fished by three or foure hundred saile of *Spaniards*, *Portugals*, and *Biskiners*. M. Dee his report.

The *Hollanders* raise yeerely by Herring, Cod, and Ling, thirty thousand pounds: English and French, by Salt-fish, Poore-Iohn, Salmons, and Pilchards, three hundred thousand pounds: *Hambrough* and the Sound, for Sturgion, Lobsters and Eeles, one hundred thousand pounds: Cape *Blanke* for Tunny and Mullit, by the *Biskiners* and *Spaniards*, thirty thousand pounds. The benefit of fishing, as Mr *Gentleman* and others report.

That the Duke of *Medina* receiueth yeerely tribute of the Fishers, for Tunny, Mullit, and Porgos, more then ten thousand pounds. *Lubecke* hath seuen hundred The Records of *Holland* and other learned obseruers

dred ships; *Hambrough* six hundred; *Emden* lately a Fisher towne, one thousand foure hundred, whose customes by fishing hath made them so powerfull as they be. *Holland* and *Zeland* not much greater then *Yorkeshire*, hath thirty walled Townes, foure hundred Villages, and twenty thousand saile of Ships and Hoies; three thousand six hundred are Fisher-men, whereof one hundred are Doggers, seuen hundred Pinkes and Well-Boats, seuen hundred Fraud-boats, Britters, and Tode-boats, with thirteene hundred Busses, besides three hundred that yeerely fish about *Yarmouth*, where they sell their fish for Gold: and fifteene yeeres agoe they had more then an hundred and sixteene thousand Sea-faring men.

These fishing ships doe take yeerely two hundred thousand last of fish, twelue barrels to a last, which amounts to 300000. pounds by the fisher mens price, that 14. yeeres agoe did pay for their tenths three hundred thousand pound, which venting in *Pumerland, Sprussia, Denmarke, Lefeland, Russia, Swethland, Germany, Netherlands, England*, or else where,&c. makes their returnes in a yeere about threescore and ten hundred thousand pounds, which is seuen millions; and yet in *Holland* there is neither matter to build ships nor merchandize to set them forth, yet by their industry they as much increase as other nations decay; but leauing these vncertainties as they are, of this I am certaine.

That the coast of *England, Scotland* and *Ireland*, the North Sea with *Island* and the *Sound, Newfound-land* and Cape *Blanke*, doe serue all Europe, as well the land townes as ports, and all the Christian shipping, with these sorts of staple fish, which is transported from whence it is taken many a thousand mile, *viz.* Herring, salt Fish, Poore-Iohn, Sturgion, Mullit, Tunny, Porgos, Cauiare, Buttargo.

Now seeing all these sorts of fish, or the most part of them may be had in a land more fertill, temperate and plentifull of all necessaries, for the building of ships, boats and houses, and the nourishment of man, the seasons are so proper, and the fishings so neere the habitations we may there make, that *New-England* hath much aduantage of the most of those parts, to serue all Europe farre cheaper then they can, who at home haue neither wood, salt, nor food, but at great rates, at Sea nothing but what they carry in their ships, an hundred or two hundred leagues from the habitation. But *New-Englands* fishings is neere land, where is helpe of Wood, Water, Fruits, Fowles, Corne or other refreshings needfull, and the *Terceras, Mederas, Canaries, Spaine, Portugall, Prouances, Sauoy, Sicillia*, and all *Italy*, as conuenient markets for our dry fish, greene fish, Sturgion, Mullit, Cauiare and Buttargo, as *Norway, Swethland, Littuania* or *Germany* for their Herring, which is heare also in abundance for taking; they returning but Wood, Pitch, Tar, Sope-ashes, Cordage, Flax, Wax, and such like commodities; wee Wines, Oiles, Sugars, Silkes, and such merchandize as the Straits offoord, whereby our profit may equalize theirs, besides the increase of shipping and Marriners: and for proofe hereof,

1614. In the yeere of our Lord 1614. you haue read how I went from *London*: also the
1615. next yeere 1615. how foure good ships went from *London*, and I with two more
1616. from *Plimoth*, with all our accidents, successes and returnes: in the yeere 1616. ere I returned from *France*, the Londoners for all their losse by the Turkes, sent foure ships more; foure more also went from *Plimoth*; after I returned from
1617. *France*, I was perswaded againe to goe to *Plimoth* with diuers of my friends with one hundred pound for our aduentures besides our charges, but wee found all things as vntoward as before, and all their great promises nothing but aire: yet to prepare the voyage against the next yeere, hauing acquainted a great part of the Nobility with it, and ashamed to see the Prince his Highnesse till I had done some what worthy his Princely view; I spent that Summer in visiting the Cities and Townes of *Bristoll, Exeter, Bastable, Bodnam, Perin, Foy, Milborow, Saltash, Dartmouth, Absom, Tattnesse*, and the most of the Gentry in *Cornewall* and *Deuonshire*, giuing them Bookes and Maps, shewing how in six moneths the most of those

My sute to the Country.

those ships had made their voyages, and some in lesse, and with what good successe; by which incitation they seemed so well contented, as they promised twenty saile of ships should goe with mee next yeere, and in regard of my paines, charge, and former losses, the westerne Commissioners in behalfe of themselues and the rest of the Company, and them hereafter that should be ioyned to them, contracted with me by articles indented vnder our hands, to be Admirall of that Country during my life, and in the renewing of their Letters-Patents so to be nominated. Halfe the fruits of our endeuours to be theirs, the rest our owne; being thus ingaged, now the businesse is made plaine and likely to prosper, some of them would not onely forget me and their promises, but also obscure me, as if I had neuer beene acquainted in the businesse, but I am not the first they haue deceiued.

There was foure good ships prepared at *Plimoth*, but by reason of their disagreement, the season so wasted, as onely two went forward, the one being of two hundred tunnes, returned well fraught to *Plimoth*, and her men in health, within fiue moneths; the other of fourescore tunnes went for bilbow with drie fish and made a good returne. In this voyage *Edward Rowcroft*, alias *Stallings*, a valiant Souldier, that had beene with me in *Virginia*, and was with me also when I was betrayed by the French, was sent againe in those ships, and hauing some wrong offered him there by a French man, he tooke him, and as he writ to me, went with him to *Virginia* with fish, to trade with them for such commodities as they might spare: he had not past ten or twelue men, and knew both those countries well, yet he promised me the next spring to meet me in *New-England*, but the ship and he both perished in *Virginia*. 1618.

This yeere againe, diuers ships intending to goe from *Plimoth*, so disagreed, there went but one of two hundred tunnes, who stayed in the Country about six weeks, which with eight and thirty men and boies had her fraught, which she sold at the first penny for 2100. besides the Furres: so that euery poore Sailer that had but a single share had his charges and sixteene pound ten shillings for his seuen moneths worke. Master *Thomas Dirmire* an vnderstanding and industrious Gentleman, that was also with me amongst the French men, hauing liued about a yeere in *Newfoundland*, returning to *Plimoth*, went for *New-England* in this ship, so much approued of this Country, that he staied there with fiue or six men in a little Boat, finding two or three French men amongst the Saluages who had lost their ship, augmented his company, with whom he ranged the Coast to *Virginia*, where he was kindly welcommed and well refreshed, thence returned to *New-England* againe, where hauing beene a yeere, in his backe returne to *Virginia* he was so wounded by the Saluages, he died vpon it; let not men attribute these their great aduentures, and vntimely deaths to vnfortunatenesse, but rather wonder how God did so long preserue them with so small meanes to doe so much, leauing the fruits of their labours to be an incouragement to those our poore vndertakings, and as warnings for vs not to vndertake such great workes with such small meanes, and this for aduantage as they writ vnto me, that God had laid this Country open for vs, and slaine the most part of the inhabitants by ciuill warres and a mortall disease, for where I had seene one hundred or two hundred Saluages, there is scarce ten to be found, and yet not any one of them touched with any sicknesse but one poore French man that died; 1619.

They say this plague vpon them thus sore fell,
It was because they pleas'd not Tantum *well.*

From the West Country to make triall this yeere onely to fish, is gone six or seuen saile, three of which I am certainly informed made so good a voyage, that euery Sailer that had a single share had twenty pound for his seuen moneths work, which is more then in twenty moneths he should haue gotten, had he gone 1620.

for

for wages any where. Now although these former ships haue not made such good voiages as they expected, by sending opinionated vnskilfull men, that had not experienced diligence to saue that they tooke, nor take that there was, which now patience and practice hath brought to a reasonable kinde of perfection; in despight of all detractors and calumniations the Country yet hath satisfied all, the defect hath beene in their vsing or abusing it, not in it selfe nor me: But,

Adue desert, for fortune makes prouision
For Knaues and Fooles, and men of base condition.

My sute to the Citie.

Now all these proofes and this relation I now called *New-Englands* triall. I caused two or three thousand of them to be printed, one thousand with a great many Maps both of *Virginia* and *New-England*, I presented to thirty of the chiefe Companies in *London* at their Halls, desiring either generally or particularly (them that would) to imbrace it, and by the vse of a stocke of fiue thousand pound, to ease them of the superfluity of the most of their companies that had but strength and health to labour; neere a yeere I spent to vnderstand their resolutions, which was to me a greater toile and torment, then to haue beene in *New-England* about my businesse but with bread and water, and what I could get there by my labour; but in conclusion, seeing nothing would be effected, I was contented as well with this losse of time and charge as all the rest.

A Plantation in New-England.

1620.

VPon these inducements some few well disposed Gentlemen, and Merchants of *London* and other places, prouided two ships, the one of a hundred and threescore tunnes, the other of threescore and ten, they left the Coast of *England* the two and thirtieth of August, with about a hundred and twenty persons, but the next day the lesser ship sprung a leake, that forced their returne to *Plimoth*, where discharging her and twenty passengers; with the greater ship and one hundred passengers besides Sailers, they set saile againe the sixt of September, and the ninth of Nouember fell with Cape *Iames*, but being pestred nine weekes in this leaking vnwholsome ship, lying wet in their Cabins, most of them grew very weake and weary of the Sea; then for want of experience, ranging two and againe six weekes before they found a place they liked to dwell on, forced to lie on the bare ground without couerture, forty of them died, and threescore were left in very weake estate at the ships comming away, about the fifth of Aprill following, and arriued in *England* the sixth of May. Though the Harbour be good, the shore is so shallow, they were forced to wade a great way vp to the knees in water, & vsed that that did them much hurt; & little fish they found but Whailes, and a great kinde of Mustell so fat, that few did eat of them that were not sicke: these miseries occasioned some discord, and gaue some appearance of faction, but all was so reconciled, that they vnited themselues by common consent vnder their hands, to a kinde of combination of a body politike, by vertue whereof to inact and constitute lawes and ordinances, and Officers from time to time, as should bee thought most conuenient for their generall good.

Their first iourny by land.

Sixteene or seuenteene daies they could doe little for want of their Shallop which was amending, yet Captaine *Miles Standish*, vnto whom was ioyned in Councell, *William Bradfor*, *Stephen Hopkins* and *Edward Tilly*, went well armed a shore, and by that time they had gone a mile, met fiue or six Indians that fled into the Woods: we traced them by the footing eight or ten miles, then the night approaching we made a fire, by which we lay that night, and the next morning followed the Saluages by their tract, thinking to finde their habitations, but by the

the way we found a Deere amongst many faire springs of water, where we refreshed our selues; then we went a shore and made a fire, that they at the ship might perceiue where we were, and so marched to a place where we supposed was a Riuer; by the way we saw many Vines, Saxefras, haunts of Deere & Fowle, and some fifty Acres of plaine ground had beene planted by the Indians, where were some of their graues; from thence we followed a path that brought vs through three or foure fields that had bin planted that yeere; in one graue we digged, we found a basket or two of Indian Corne, so much as we could carry we tooke with vs, the rest we buried as we found it, and so proceeded to the place we intended, but we found it not such a Harbour as we expected; and so we returned, till the night caused vs take vp our lodging vnder a tree, where it rained six or seuen houres: the next morning as we wandred, we passed by a tree, where a young sprig was bowed downe ouer a bough, and some Acornes strewed vnder it, which was one of their Gins to a catch a Deere, and as we were looking at it, *Bradford* was suddenly caught by the leg in a noosed Rope, made as artificially as ours; as we passed we see a lease of Bucks, sprung some Partriges, and great flocks of wilde Geese and Ducks, and so we returned well wearied to our ship.

Their first iourny by Shallop.

Master *Iones* our Master with foure and thirty men, also went vp and downe in the frost and snow, two or three daies in the extremity of the cold, but could finde no harbour; only among the old graues we got some ten bushels of Corne, some Beanes, and a bottle of Oile; and had we not thus haply found it, we had had no Corne for seede, so that place we euer called *Corne-hill*; the next day Master *Iones* with the Corne and our weakest men returned to the Ship, but eighteene of vs quartered there that night, and in the morning following the paths, wee found in the Snow in a field a greater hill or graue then the rest, digging it wee found first a Mat, vnder that a boord three quarters long, painted and carued with three Tyns at the top like a Croner, betweene the Mats also were Bowles, Traies and Dishes and such trash, at length we found a faire new Mat, and vnder that two bundles, the one biggar the other lesse; in the greater wee found a great quantity of fine red powder like a kinde of imbalmement, and yeelded a strong but no offensiue smell, with the bones and skull of a man that had fine yellow haire still on it, and some of the flesh vnconsumed, a Knife, a Packneedle, and two or three old Iron things was bound vp in a Sailers canuase Cassocke, also a paire of cloth Breeches; in the lesse bundle we found likewise of the same powder, and the bones and head of a little childe; about the legs and other parts of it was bound strings and braslets of white beades, there was also a little Bow, and some other odde knacks, the prettiest we tooke, and couered againe the corps as they were: not farre from thence were two of their houses, where were a great deale of their miserable houshold stuffe, which we left as wee found, and so returned to our Boat, and lay aboord that night.

Accidents.

Many arguments we had to make here our Plantation or not; in the *Intrim*, Mistris *White* was brought to bed of a young sonne, which was called *Perigrine*: and a Sailer shooting at a Whale, his peece flew in peeces stocke and all, yet he had no hurt. A foolish boy discharging his fathers peece hard by halfe a barrell of Powder, and many people by it, it pleased God it escaped firing, so that no hurt was done.

Their second iourney by water to finde a place to plant in.

But to make a more certaine discouery where to seat our selues, Captaine *Standish*, Master *Caruer*, *William Branford*, *Edward Winsloe*, *Iohn Tilly*, *Edward Tilly*, with diuers others to the number of seuenteene, vpon the sixt of December set saile, and hauing sailed six or seuen leagues, we espied eight or ten Saluages about a dead Grampus: still following the shore we found two or three more cast vp by the ill weather, many we see in the water, therefore we called it *Grampus Bay*: Ships may ride well in it, but all the shore is very shallow flats of sand; at last seuen or eight of vs went a shore, many fields we saw where the Saluages had inhabited, and a buriall place incompassed with a Palizado, so we returned to our Shallop.

lop, in the night we heard a hideous cry and howling of Wolues and Foxes; in the morning as we were ready to goe into our Shallop, one of our men being in the woods, came running crying, Indians, Indians, and with all their Arrowes flying amongst vs, some of our men being in the boat, and their Armes a shore, so well it chanced, Captaine *Standish* with two or three more discharged their peeces till the rest were ready, one Saluage more stout then the rest kept vnder a tree, till he had shot three or foure Arrowes, and endured three or foure Musket shot, but at last they all fled, this was about breake of day in the morning when they saw vs, and we not them.

Their first fight with the Saluages.

The description of their place to plant in.

Hauing the wind faire, we sailed along the coast 8. or 10. leagues, thinking to haue got to a Harbour where one of our company had beene, within 8. leagues of Cape *Cod*, for neither cricke nor Harbour in this bay we could finde, and the wind so increased, our Rudder broke, and our Mast flew ouer-boord, that we were in danger to be cast away, but at last it pleased God we were in a harbor we knew not, thinking it one we were acquainted with, this we found to be an Ile where we rid that night, and hauing well viewed the land about it, and sounded the Bay to be a good Harbour for our ship, compassed with good land, and in it two faire Iles, where there is in their seasons innumerable store of all sorts of fish and fowle, good water, much plaine land, which hath beene planted; with this newes we returned to our ship, and with the next faire wind brought her thither, being but within the sight of Cape *Cod*; in the meane time *Goodwife Alderton* was deliuered of a sonne, but dead borne. Vpon the 28. of December, so many as could went to worke vpon the hill, where we purposed to build our Platforme for our ordnance, which doth command all the Plaine and the Bay, and from whence wee may see far into the Sea, and be easily impailed, so in the afternoone we went to measure out the grounds, and diuided our company into 19. families, alotting to euery person halfe a poule in bredth and three in length, and so we cast lots where euery man should lie, which we staked out, thinking this proportion enough at the first to impale for lodgings and gardens.

Another Boy borne in *New-England.*

Their first Plantation.

Two faire Lakes.

Francis Billington from the top of a tree seeing a great water some three miles from vs in the land, went with the Masters Mate, and found it two great Lakes of fresh water, the bigger fiue or six miles in circuit, and an Ile in it of a Cables length square; the other three miles in compasse, full of fish and fowle, and two brooks issuing from it, which will be an excellent helpe in time for vs, where they saw seuen or eight Indian houses, but no people. Foure being sent a mile or two from our plantation, two of them stragling into the woods was lost, for comming to a Lake of water they found a great Deere, hauing a mastiue Bitch and a Spanell with them, they followed so farre they could not finde the way backe, that afternoone it rained, and did freeze and snow at night; their apparell was very thin, and had no weapons but two sickles, nor any victuals, nor could they finde any of the Saluages habitations; when the night came they were much perplexed that they had no other bed then the earth, nor couerture then the skies, but that they heard, as they thought, two Lions roaring a long time together very nigh them, so not knowing what to doe, they resolued to climbe vp into a tree, though that would be an intollerable cold lodging, expecting their cōming they stood at the trees root, and the bitch they held fast by the necke, for shee would haue beene gone to the Lions or what they were, that as it chanced came not nigh them, so they watched the tree that extreme cold night, and in the morning trauelling againe, passing by many lakes, brooks and woods, and in one place where the Saluages had burnt 4. or 5. miles in length, which is a fine champion Country, in the afternoone they discouered the two Iles in their Bay, and so that night neere famished they got to their Plantation, from whence they had sent out men euery way to seeke them; that night the house they had built and thatched, where lay their armes, bedding, powder, &c. tooke fire and was burnt, the Coast is so shoule, the ship rides more then a mile from the Fort, but God be thanked no man was hurt though much was burnt.

Two men lost themselues in the woods.

All

All this time we could not haue conference with a Saluage, though we had many times seene them and had many alarums, so that we drew a Councell, and appointed Captaine *Standish* to haue the command of all martiall actions, but euen in the time of consultation the Saluages gaue an alarum: the next day also as wee were agreeing vpon his orders, came a tall Saluage boldly amongst vs, not fearing any thing, and kindly bad vs welcome in English; he was a *Sagamo*, towards the North, where the ships vse to fish, and did know the names of most of the Masters that vsed thither: such victuall as we had we gaue him, being the first Saluage we yet could speake with, he told vs this place where we were was called *Patuxet*, and that all the people three or foure yeeres agoe there died on the plague: in a day or two we could not be rid of him, then he returned to the *Massasoyts* from whence he came, where is some sixty people, but the *Nawsits* are 100. strong, which were they encountred our people at the first. Two daies after this *Samoset*, for so was his name, came againe, and brought fiue or six of the *Massasoyts* with him, with certaine skinnes, and certaine tooles they had got that we had left in the woods at their alarums: much friendship they promised, and so departed, but *Samoset* would not leaue vs, but fained himselfe sicke, yet at last he went to entreat the Saluages come againe to confirme a peace: now the third time, as we were consulting of our Marshall orders, two Saluages appeared, but when we went to them they vanished: not long after came *Samoset*, & *Squanto*, a natiue of *Patuxet* where we dwell, and one of them carried into *Spaine* by *Hunt*, thence brought into *England*, where a good time he liued; and now here signified vnto vs, their great *Sachem* of *Massasoyt*, with *Quadaquina* his brother, and all their men, was there by to see vs: not willing to send our Gouernour, we sent *Edward Wollislo* with presents to them both, to know their minds, making him to vnderstand by his Interpreters how King *Iames* did salute him and was his friend; after a little conference with twenty of his men, he came ouer the brooke to our Plantation, where we set him vpon a rug, and then brought our Gouernour to him with Drums and Trnmpets; where after some circumstances, for they vse few complements, we treated of peace with them to this effect.

Their first conference with a Saluage.

The second conference.

That neither he nor any of his should iniury or doe hurt to any of vs; if they did, he should send vs the offender, that we might punish him, and wee would doe the like to him: if any did vniustly warre against him, we would aid him, as he should vs against our enemies, and to send to his neighbour confederats to certifie them of this, that they might likewise be comprised in these conditions, that when any of them came to vs, they should leaue their Bow and Arrowes behinde them, as we would our peeces when we came to them, all which the King seemed to like well of, and was applauded of his followers, in his person hee is a very lusty man, in his best yeeres, an able body, graue of countenance, and spare of speech: in his attire little differing from the rest; after all was done, the Gouernour conducted him to the brooke, but kept our hostage till our messengers returned: in like manner we vsed *Quaddaquina*, so all departed good friends.

Their conditions of peace.

Two of his people would haue staied with vs, but wee would not permit them, onely *Samoset* and *Squanto* wee entertained kindly; as yet wee haue found they intend to keepe promise, for they haue not hurt our men they haue found stragling in the Woods, and are afraid of their powerfull Aduersaries the *Narrohiggansets*, against whom hee hopes to make vse of our helpe. The next day *Squanto* went a fishing for Eeles, and in an houre he did tread as many out of the Ose with his feet as he could lift with his hand, not hauing any other instrument.

But that we might know their habitations so well as they ours, *Stephen Hopkins* and *Edward Winslo* had *Squantum* for their guide and Interpreter; to *Packanoki*, the habitation of the King of *Massasoyt*, with a red horsemans coat for a present, to entreat him by reason we had not victuall to entertaine them

A iourney to Pakanoki.

 as

as we would, he would defend his people so much from visiting vs; and if hee did send, he should alwaies send with the Messenger a copper Chaine they gaue him, that they might know he came from him, and also giue them some of his Corne for seede: that night they lodged at *Namascet*, some fifteene miles off: by the way we found ten or twelue women and children that still would pester vs till we were weary of them, perceiuing it is the manner of them, where victuall is to bee gotten with most ease, there they will liue; but on that Riuer of *Namaschet* haue beene many habitations of the Saluages that are dead, and the land lies waste, and the Riuer abounding with great plenty of fish, and hath beene much frequented by the French.

A great courage of two old Saluages.

The next day trauelling with six or seuen Indians, where we were to wade ouer the Riuer, did dwell onely two old men of that Nation then liuing, that thinking vs enemies, sought the best aduantage they could to fight with vs, with a wonderfull shew of courage, but when they knew vs their friends they kindly welcommed vs; after we came to a towne of the *Massasoits*, but at *Pakanoki* the King was not: towards night he arriued and was very proud, both of our message and presents, making a great oration to all his people, Was not he *Massasoit*, Commander of the country about him, was not such a towne his, and the people of it, and 20. townes more he named was his? and should they not bring their skins to vs? to which they answered, they were his and they would; victual they had none, nor any lodging, but a poore planke or two, a foot high from the ground, wheron his wife and he lay at the one end, we at the other, but a thin Mat vpon them, two more of his chiefe men pressed by and vpon vs, so that we were worse weary of our lodging then of our iourney. Although there is such plenty of fish and fowle and wild beasts, yet are they so lasie they will not take paines to catch it till meere hunger constraine them, for in two or three daies we had scarce a meales meat, whereby we were so faint, we were glad to be at home: besides what for the fleas, and their howling and singing in the night in their houses, and the *Musketas* without doores, our heads were as light for want of sleepe, as our bellies empty for want of meat. The next voiage we made was in a Shallop with ten men to *Nawsit*, sixteene miles from vs, to fetch a Boy was lost in the Woods we heard was there, whom *Aspinet* their King had bedecked like a saluage, but very kindly he brought him to vs, and so returned well to *Patuyet*.

How the King vsed them.

A voyage to *Nawsit*.

1621. Immediatly after the arriuall of the last ship, they sent another of fiue and fifty tuns to supply them; with seuen and thirty persons they set saile in the beginning of Iuly, but being crossed by westernly winds, it was the end of August ere they could passe *Plimoth*, and arriued in *New-England* at *New-Plimoth*, now so called the 11. of *Nouember*, where they found all the people they left so ill, lusty and well for all their pouerties, except six that died: a moneth they stayed ere they returned to *England*, loaded with Clap-boord, Wainscot and Wallnut, with about three hogs-heads of Beuer skinnes the 13. of December: and drawing neere our coast was set on by a French man set out by the Marquesse of *Cera*, Gouernour of Ile *Deu*, where they kept the ship, imprisoned the Master and company, tooke from them to the value of 500. pound, and after 14. daies sent them home with a poore supply of victuall, their owne being deuoured by the Marquesse and his hungry seruants.

Now you are to vnderstand this 37. brought nothing, but relied wholly on vs to make vs more miserable then before, which the *Sachem Couanacus* no sooner vnderstood, but sent to *Tusquantum* our Interpreter, a bundle of new arrowes in a Snakes skinne; *Tusquantum* being absent, the Messenger departed, but when we vnderstood it was a direct challenge, we returned the skin full of powder and shot, with an absolute defiance, which caused vs finish our fortification with all expedition. Now betwixt our two Saluages, *Tusquantum* and *Hobbamock*, grew such great emulation, we had much adoe to know which best to trust. In a iourney we vndertooke, in our way we met a Saluage of *Tusquantums*, that had cut his face

fresh

fresh bleeding, to assure vs *Massasoyt* our supposed friend, had drawne his forces to *Packanokick* to assault vs. *Hobomak* as confidently assured vs it was false, and sent his wife as an espy to see; but when she perceiued all was well, shee told the King *Massasoyt* how *Tusquantum* had abused him, diuers Saluages also hee had caused to beleeue we would destroy them, but he would doe his best to appease vs; this he did onely to make his Country-men beleeue what great power hee had with vs to get bribes on both sides, to make peace or warre when he would, and the more to possesse them with feare, he perswaded many we had buried the plague in our store house, which wee could send when we listed whither wee would, but at last all his knauery being discouered, *Massasowat* sent his knife with Messengers for his head or him, being his subiect; with much adoe we appeased the angry King and the rest of the Saluages, and freely forgaue *Tusquantum*, because he speaking our language we could not well be without him.

A iourney to the Towne of Namaschet, *in defence of the King of* Massasoyt, *against the* Narrohigganses, *and the supposed death of* Squantum.

A Great difference there was betwixt the *Narrohigganses* and the *Massasoytes*, that had alwaies a iealousie; *Coubatant* one of their petty *Sachems* was too conuersant with the *Narrohigganses*, this *Coubatant* liued much at *Namaschet*, and much stormed at our peace with his King and others; also at *Squantum*, and *Tokamahamon*, and *Hobomak* our friends, and chiefe occasioners of our peace, for which he sought to murther *Hobomak*; yet *Tokamahamon* went to him vpon a rumour he had taken *Masasoyt* prisoner, or forced him from his Country, but the other two would not, but in priuat to see if they could heare what was become of their King; lodging at *Namaschet* they were discouered to *Coubatant*, who surprized the house and tooke *Squantum*, saying, if hee were dead the English had lost their tongue; *Hobomak* seeing that, and *Coubatant* held a knife at his brest, being a strong lusty fellow, brake from them and came to *New-Plimoth*, full of sorrow for *Squantum*, whom he thought was slaine.

The next day we sent ten men with him armed to be reuenged of *Coubatant*, who conducted vs neere *Namaschet*, where we rested and refreshed our selues til midnight, and then we beset the house as we had resolued; those that entred the house demanded for *Coubatant*, but the Saluages were halfe dead with feare, we charged them not to stirre, for we came to hurt none but *Coubatant*, for killing *Squantum*, some of them seeking to escape was wounded, but at last perceiuing our ends, they told vs *Coubatant* was gone and all his men, and *Squantum* was yet liuing, & in the towne; in this hurly burly we discharged two peeces at randome, which much terrified all the inhabitants except *Squantum* and *Tokamahamon*, who though they knew not the end of our coming, yet assured themselues of our honesties, that we would not hurt them; the women and children hung about *Hobomak*, calling him friend, and when they saw we would hurt no women, the young youths cryed we are women; to be short, we kept them all, and whilest we were searching the house for *Coubatant*, *Hobomak* had got to the top, and called *Squantum* & *Tokamahamon*, which came vnto vs accompanied with others, some armed, others naked, those that had bowes we tooke them from them, promising them againe when it was day: the house wee tooke for our quarter that night and discharged the prisoners, and the next morning went to breakfast to *Squantums* house; thither came all them that loued vs to welcome vs, but all *Coubatants* faction was fled, then we made them plainly know the cause of our comming, & if their King *Massasoyt* were not well, we would be reuenged vpon the *Narrohigganses*, or any that should doe iniury to *Hobomak*, *Squantum*, or any of their friends; as for those were wounded we were sorry for it, and offered our Surgion should heale them, of this offer a man and a woman accepted, that went

They surprise the Saluages.

home with vs, accompanied with *Squantum*, and many other knowne friends, that offered vs all the kindnesse they could.

From the West of *England* there is gone ten or twelue ships to fish, which were all well fraughted: those that came first at Bilbow, made seuenteene pound a single share, besides Beuers, Otters, and Martins skinnes; but some of the rest that came to the same ports, that were all ready furnished, so glutted the market, that the price was abated, yet all returned so well contented, that they are a preparing to goe againe.

1622. There is gone from the West Countrey onely to fish, fiue and thirtie ships, and about the last of Aprill two more from *London*; the one of one hundred tunnes, the other of thirtie, with some sixtie Passengers to supply the Plantation. Now though the *Turke* and *French* hath beene somewhat too busie in taking our ships, would all the Christian Princes be truly at vnitie, as his Royall Maiestie our Soueraigne King *Iames* desireth, seuentie Saile of good ships were sufficient to fire the most of his Coasts in the Leuant, and make such a guard in the Straights of *Hellespont*, as would make the great *Turke* himselfe more affraid in *Constantinople*, then the smallest Red-Crosse that crosses the Seas would be, either of any French *Pickaroun*, or the Pirats of *Algere*.

An abstract of diuers Relations sent from the Colony in New England, *Iuly* 16. 1622.

Notes and obseruations.

SInce the massacre in *Virginia*, though the *Indians* continue their wonted friendship, yet wee are more wary of them then before; for their hands hath beene imbrued in much English bloud, onely by too much confidence, but not by force, and we haue had small supplies of any thing but men. Here I must intreat a little your fauours to digresse, they did not kill the English in *Virginia*, because they were Christians: but for their weapons and Copper, which were rare noueltie; but now they feare we may beat them out of their dens, which Lions and Tigers will not admit but by force. But must this be an argument for an English man, and discourage any in *Virginia* or *New England*: No, for I haue tried them both, as you may reade at large in the Historie of *Virginia*; notwithstanding since I came from thence, the Honourable Company hath beene humble suiters to his Maiestie, to get vagabonds and condemned men to goe thither; nay, so the businesse hath beene so abused, that so much scorned was the name of *Virginia*, some did chuse to be hanged ere they would goe thither, and were: Yet for all the worst of spight, detraction, and discouragement, and this lamentable massacre, there is more honest men now suiters to goe, then euer hath beene constrained knaues. And it is not vnknowne to most men of vnderstanding, how happy many of those Collumners hath thought themselues that they might be admitted; and yet pay for their passage to goe now to *Virginia*, and I feare mee there goeth too many of those, that hath shifted heere till they could no longer; and they will vse that qualitie there till they hazard all.

To range this Countrey of *New England* in like manner, I had but eight, as is said, and amongst their bruit conditions, I met many of their silly encounters, and I giue God thankes, without any hurt at all to me, or any with mee. When your West-Countrey men were so wounded and tormented with the Saluages, though they had all the Politicke directions that had beene gathered from all the secret informations could be heard of, yet they found little, and returned with nothing. I speak not this out of vaine-glory, as it may be some gleaners, or some who were neuer there may censure me; but to let all men be assured by those examples, what those Saluages are, that thus strangely doe murder and betray our Countrymen: but to the purpose;

The *Paragon* with thirtie seuen men sent to releeue them, miscaried twice vpon

our

our English Coast, whereby they failed of their supplies. It is true, there hath beene taken one thousand Bases at a draught; and in one night twelue Hogsheads of Herrings: but when they wanted all necessaries both for fishing and sustinance, but what they could get with their naked industry, they indured most extreme wants, hauing beene now neere two yeeres without any supply to any purpose, it is a wonder how they should subsist, much lesse so to resist the Saluages, fortifie themselues, plant sixtie acres of Corne, besides their Gardens that were well replenished with many vsuall fruits. But in the beginning of Iuly came in two ships of Master *Westons*, though we much wanted our selues, yet we releeued them what we could: And to requite vs, they destroied our Corne and Fruits then planted, and did what they could to haue done the like to vs. At last they were transported to *Wichagušcusset* at the *Massachusets*, where they abused the Saluages worse then vs. We hauing neither Trade, nor scarce any thing remaining, God sent in one Master *Iones*, and a ship of *Westons* had beene at *Monahigan* amongst the Fisher-men, that for Beuer skinnes and such Merchandize as wee had, very well refreshed vs, though at deere rates. *Weston* left also his men a small Barke, and much good prouision, and so set saile for *England*. Then wee ioyned with them to trade to the Southward of Cape *Cod*, twice or thrice wee were forced to returne; first by the death of their Gouernor; then the sicknesse of Captaine *Standish*. At last our Gouernor Master *Bradford* vndertooke it himselfe to haue found the passage betwixt the Shoules and the Maine, then *Tusquantum* our Pilot died, so that we returned to the *Massachusets*, where we found the trade spoiled, and nothing but complaints betwixt the Saluages and the English. At *Nawset* we were kindly vsed and had good trade, though we lost our Barge, the Saluages carefully kept both her wracke, and some ten Hosheads of Corne three moneths, and so we returned some by land, some in the ship.

They liued two yeeres without supply.

Westons Plantation.

The death of *Tusquantum*.

Captaine *Standish* being recouered, went to fetch them both, and traded at *Namasket* and *Monomete*, where the people had the plague, a place much frequented with *Dutch* and *French*. Here the *Sachem* put a man to death for killing his fellow at play, wherein they are so violent, they will play their coats from their backs, and also their wiues, though many miles from them. But our prouision decaying, *Standish* is sent to *Mattachist*, where they pretended their wonted loue; yet it plainly appeared they intended to kill him. Escaping thence, wee went to *Monomete*, where we found nothing but bad countenances. Heare one *Wittuwamat* a notable villaine, would boast how many French and English hee had slaine: This Champion presenting a Dagger to the *Sachem Canacum* he had got from the English, occasioned vs to vnderstand how they had contriued to murder all the English in the Land, but hauing such a faire opportunitie, they would begin heere with vs. Their scornfull vsage made the Captaine so passionate to appease his anger and choler, their intent made many faire excuses for satisfaction: *Scar* a lusty Saluage, alwaies seeming the most to effect vs, bestowed on vs the best presents he had without any recompence, saying; Hee was rich enough to bestow such fauours on his friends, yet had vndertaken to kill the Captaine himselfe, but our vigilencies so preuented the aduantage they expected, we safely returned, little suspecting in him any such treachery.

Tusquantum at his death desired the English to pray he might go dwell with the English mens God, for theirs was a good God.

They contriue to murder all the English.

During this time a *Dutch* ship was driuen a shore at *Massasowat*, whose King lay very sicke, now because it is a generall custome then for all their friends to visit them: Master *Winslow*, and Master *Hamden*, with *Habamok* for their guide, were sent with such Cordialls as they had to salute him; by the way they so oft heard the King was dead, *Habamok* would breake forth in those words, My louing *Sachem*, my louing *Sachem*, many haue I knowne, but neuer any like thee, nor shall euer see the like amongst the Saluages; for he was no lier, nor bloudy and cruell like other *Indians*, in anger soone reclaimed, he would be ruled by reason, not scorning the aduice of meane men, and gouerned his men better with a few strokes, then others with many: truly louing where he loued, yea he feared wee had

The sicknesse of King *Massasowat*.

had not a faithfull friend left amongst all his Countrey-men, shewing how oft he had restrained their malice, much more with much passion he spoke to this purpose, till at last we arriued where we found the *Dutchmen* but newly gone, and the house so full we could hardly get in. By their charmes they distempered vs that were well, much more him that was sicke, women rubbing him to keepe heat in him; but their charmes ended, vnderstanding of vs, though he had lost his sight, his vnderstanding failed not; but taking *Winslow* by the hand, said, Art thou *Winslow*, Oh *Winslow*, I shall neuer see thee againe! *Hobamock* telling him what restauratiues they had brought, he desired to taste them, with much adoe they got a little Confexion of many comfortable Conserues into his mouth, as it desolued he swallowed it, then desoluing more of it in water, they scraped his tongue, which was al furred & swolne, and washed his mouth, and then gaue him more of it to eat, and in his drinke, that wrought such an alteration in him in two or three houres, his eies opened to our great contents; with this and such brothes as they there prouided for him, it pleased God he recouered: and thus the manner of his sicknesse and cure caused no small admiration amongst them.

His cure by the English.

The Kings thankfulnesse.

During the time of their stay to see his recouery, they had sent to *New Plimoth* for diuers good things for him, which he tooke so kindly, that he fully reuealed all the former conspiracies against vs, to which he had oft beene moued; and how that all the people of *Powmet*, *Nawset*, *Succpnet*, *Mattachist*, *Manamet*, *Augawam*, and *Capawac*, were ioyned to murder vs; therefore as we respected our liues, kill them of *Massachuset* that were the authors; for take away the principals and the plot wil cease, thus taking our leaues, & arriuing at our fort, we found our braue liberall friend of *Pamet* drawing *Standish* to their Ambuscados, which being thus discouered, we sent him away, as though he knew nor suspected any thing. Them at the *Massachusets*, some were so vilde they serued the Saluages for victuall, the rest sent vs word the Saluages were so insolent, they would assault them though against their Commission, so fearefull they were to breake their Commission, so much time was spent in consultations, they all were famished, till *Wassapinewat* againe came and told them the day of their execution was at hand.

A bad example.

Captaine *Standish* sent to suppresse the Saluages.

Then they appointed *Standish* with eight chosen men, vnder colour of Trade to catch them in their owne trap at *Massachuset*, & acquaint it with the English in the Towne, where arriuing he found none in the Barke, and most of the rest without Armes, or scarce clothes, wandering abroad, all so sencelesly secure, he more then wondered they were not all slaine, with much adoe he got the most of them to their Towne. The Saluages suspecting their plots discouered, *Pecksnot* a great man, and of as great a spirit, came to *Habamak*, who was then amongst them, saying; Tell *Standish* we know he is come to kill vs, but let him begin when he dare. Not long after many would come to the Fort and whet their Kniues before him, with many brauing speeches. One amongst the rest was by *Wittawamat* bragging he had a Knife, that on the handle had the picture of a womans face, but at home I haue one hath killed both French & English, and that hath a mans face on it, and by and by these two must marrie: but this here, by and by shall see, and by and by eat, but not speake; Also *Pecksnot* being of a greater stature then the Captaine, told him, though he were a great Captaine he was but a little man, and I though no *Sachem*, yet I am of great strength and courage. These things *Standish* bare patiently for the present; but the next day seeing he could not get many of them together, but these two Roarers, and two more being in a conuenient roome, and his company about him, *Standish* seased on *Pecksnots* Knife then hanging about his necke, wherewith he slew him, and the rest slew *Wittuwamat* and the other Saluage, but the youth they tooke, who being Brother to *Wittuwamat*, and as villanous as himselfe, was hanged. It is incredible how many wounds they indured, catching at their weapons without any feare or bruit, till the last gasp. *Habamack* stood by all this time very silent, but all ended, he said, Yesterday *Pecksnot* bragged of his strength and stature, but I see you are big enough to lay him on the ground.

Two desperate Saluages slaine.

The

The Towne he left to the guard of *Westons* people: three Saluages more were slaine; vpon which rumour they all fled from their houses. The next day they met with a file of Saluages that let fly their Arrowes, shot for shot till *Hobamack* shewed himselfe, and then they fled. For all this, a Saluage Boy to shew his innocency, came boldly vnto vs and told vs: Had the English Fugitiues but finished the three Canowes they were a making, to haue taken the ship, they would haue done as much to all the English, which was onely the cause they had forborne so long. But now consulting and considering their estates, those that went in the Pinnace to *Barty* Iles to get passage for *England*, the rest to *New Plimoth*, where they were kindly entertained. The *Sachem Obtakeest*, & *Powas*, and diuers other were guilty, the three fugitiues in their fury there slew; but not long after so distracted were those poore scattered people, they left their habitations, liuing in swamps, where with cold and infinite diseases they endured much mortalitie, suing for peace, and crying the God of *England* is angry with them. Thus you see where God pleases, as some flourish, others perish. The Saluages ouercommed.

Now on all hands they prepare their ground, and about the middest of Aprill, in a faire season they begin to plant till the latter end of May; but so God pleased, that in six weekes after the latter setting there scarce fell any raine; so that the stalke was first set, began to eare ere it came to halfe growth, and the last not like to yeeld any thing at all. Our Beanes also seemed so withered, we iudged all vtterly dead, that now all our hopes were ouerthrowne, and our ioy turned into mourning. And more to our sorrow, we heard of the twice returne of the *Paragon*, that now the third time was sent vs three moneths agoe, but no newes of her: onely the signes of a wracke we saw on the Coast which wee iudged her. This caused not euery of vs to enter into a priuate consideration betwixt God and our consciences, but most solemnly to humble our selues before the Lord by fasting and praying, to releeue our deiected spirits by the comforts of his mercy. In the morning when wee assembled all together, the skies were as cleere, and the drought as like to continue as euer; yet our exercise continued eight or nine houres. Before our departure, the skies were all ouer-cast, and on the next morning distilled such soft, sweet, moderate showers, continuing foureteene daies, mixed with such seasonable weather, as it was hard to say, whether our withered Corne, or drooping affections were most quickned and reuiued; such was the bounty and mercy of God. Of this the *Indians* by the meanes of *Hobamock* tooke notice, who seeing vs vse this exercise in the midst of the weeke, said; It was but three daies since Sunday, and desired to know the reason; which when hee vnderstood, he and all of them admired the goodnesse of God towards vs, shewing the difference betwixt their coniurations and our praiers, and what stormes and dangers they oft receiue thereby. To expresse our thankfulnesse, wee assembled together another day, as before, and either the next morning, or not long after, came in two ships to supply vs, and all their Passengers well except one, and he presently recouered. For vs, notwithstanding all these wants, there was not a sicke person amongst vs. The greater ship we returned fraught; the other wee sent to the Southward, to trade vnder the command of Captaine *Altom*. So that God be thanked, we desire nothing, but what we will returne Commodities to the value. 1623. An extreme drought. A wonderfull blessing & signe of Gods loue.

Thus all men finde our great God he,
That neuer wanted nature,
To teach his truth, that onely he
Of euery thing is Author.

For this yeere from *England* is gone about fortie saile of ships, only to fish, and as I am informed, haue made a farre better voyage then euer. Forty saile sent to fish.

Now some new great obseruers will haue this an Iland, because I haue writ it is the

the Continent: others report, that the people are so bruit, they haue no religion, wherein surely they are deceiued; for my part, I neuer heard of any Nation in the world which had not a Religion, deare, bowes and arrowes. They beleeue as doe the *Virginians*, of many diuine powers, yet of one aboue all the rest, as the Southerne *Virginians* call their chiefe God *Kewassa*, and that wee now inhabit *Oke*, but both their Kings *Werowance*. The *Masachusets* call their great God *Kiehtan*, and their Kings there abouts *Sachems*: The *Penobscotes* their greatest power *Tantum*, and their Kings *Sagomos*. Those where is this Plantation, say *Kiehtan* made all the other Gods: also one man and one woman, and of them all mankinde, but how they became so dispersed they know not. They say, at first there was no King but *Kiehtan* that dwelleth farre westerly aboue the heauens, whither all good men goe when they die, and haue plentie of all things. The bad men goe thither also and knocke at the doore, but he bids them goe wander in endlesse want and miserie, for they shall not stay there. They neuer saw *Kiehtan*, but they hold it a great charge and dutie, that one age teach another; and to him they make feasts, and cry and sing for plentie and victorie, or any thing is good. They haue another Power they call *Hobamock*, which wee conceiue the Deuill, and vpon him they call to cure their wounds and diseases: when they are curable he perswades them he sent them, because they haue displeased him; but if they be mortall, then he saith, *Kiehtan* sent them, which makes them neuer call on him in their sicknesse. They say this *Hobamock* appeares to them somtimes like a Man, a Deere, or an Eagle, but most commonly like a Snake; not to all, but only to their *Powahs* to cure diseases, and *Vndeses*, which is one of the chiefe next the King, and so bold in the warres, that they thinke no weapon can kill them: and those are such as coniure in *Virginia*, and cause the people to doe what they list.

Their Religion.

Their Gouernment.

For their Gouernment: euery *Sachem* is not a King, but their great *Sachems* haue diuers *Sachems* vnder their protection, paying them tribute, and dare make no warres without his knowledge; but euery *Sachem* taketh care for the Widowes, Orphans, the aged and maimed, nor will they take any to first wife, but them in birth equall to themselues, although they haue many inferior Wiues and Concubins that attend on the principall; from whom he neuer parteth, but any of the rest when they list, they inherit by succession, and euery one knowes their owne bounds. To his men, hee giueth them land, also bounded, and what Deere they kill in that circuit, he hath the fore-part; but if in the water, onely the skin: But they account none a man, till hee hath done some notable exploit: the men are most imploied in hunting, the women in slauery; the younger obey the elders: their names are variable; they haue harlots and honest women: the harlots neuer marrie, or elsea re widowes. They vse diuorcement, and the King commonly punisheth all offenders himselfe: when a maid is maried, she cutteth her haire, and keepes her head couered till it be growne againe. Their arts, games, musicke, attire, burials, and such like, differ very little from the *Virginians*, onely for their Chronicles they make holes in the ground, as the others set vp great stones. Out of the Relations of Master *Edward Winslow*.

An answer to Obiections.

Now I know the common question is, For all those miseries, where is the wealth they haue got, or the Gold or Siluer Mines? To such greedy vnworthy minds I say once againe: The Sea is better then the richest Mine knowne, and of all the fishing ships that went well prouided, there is no complaint of losse nor misery, but rather an admiration of wealth, profit, and health. As for the land were it neuer so good, in two yeeres so few of such small experience liuing without supplies so well, and in health, it was an extraordinary blessing from God. But that with such small meanes they should subsist, and doe so much, to any vnderstanding judgement is a wonder. Notwithstanding, the vaine expectation of present gaine in some, ambition in others, that to be great would haue all else slaues, and the carelesnesse in prouiding supplies, hath caused those defailements in all those Plantations, and how euer some bad conditions will extoll the actions of any Nation but their owne: yet if we may giue credit to the *Spaniards*, *Portugals*, and *French* writings, they indured as many miseries, and yet not in twenty yeeres effected so much, nay scarce in fortie.

Thus you may see plainly the yeerely successe from *New England* by *Virginia*, which hath beene so costly to this Kingdome, and so deare to me, which either to see perish, or but bleed; Pardon me though it passionate me beyond the bounds of modesty, to haue beene sufficiently able to fore-see their miseries, and had neither power nor meanes to preuent it. By that acquaintance I haue with them, I call them my children, for they haue beene my Wife, my Hawks, Hounds, my Cards, my Dice, and in totall, my best content, as indifferent to my heart, as my left hand to my right. And notwithstanding, all those miracles of disasters haue crossed both them and me, yet were there not an Englishman remaining, as God bethanked notwithstanding the massacre there are some thousands; I would yet begin againe with as small meanes as I did at first, not that I haue any secret encouragement (I protest) more then lamentable experience; for all their discoueries I haue yet heard of, are but Pigs of my owne Sow, nor more strange to me, then to heare one tell me hee hath gone from *Billingsgate* and discouered *Grauesend*, *Tilbury*, *Quinborow*, *Lee*, and *Margit*, which to those did neuer heare of them, though they dwell in *England*, might bee made some rare secrets and great Countries vnknowne, except some few Relations of Master *Dirmer*. In *England*, some are held great trauellers that haue seene *Venice*, and *Rome*, *Madrill*, *Toledo*, *Siuill*, *Algere*, *Prague*, or *Ragousa*, *Constantinople*, or *Ierusalem*, and the Piramides of *Egypt*; that thinke it nothing to goe to *Summer Iles*, or *Virginia*, which is as far as any of them; and I hope in time will proue a more profitable and a more laudable iourney: as for the danger, you see our Ladies and Gentlewomen account it nothing now to goe thither; and therefore I hope all good men will better apprehend it, and not suffer them to languish in despaire, whom God so wonderfully and oft hath preserued.

The ordinary voyage to goe to *Virginia* or *New-England*.

What here I haue writ by Relation, if it be not right I humbly intreat your pardons, but I haue not spared any diligence to learne the truth of them that haue beene actors, or sharers in those voyages; In some particulars they might deceiue mee, but in the substance they could not: for few could tell me any thing, except where they fished. But seeing all those haue liued there, doe confirme more then I haue writ, I doubt not but all those testimonies with these new begun examples of Plantation, will moue both Citie and Country, freely to aduenture with me more then promises.

But because some Fortune-tellers say, I am vnfortunate; had they spent their time as I haue done, they would rather beleeue in God then their calculations, and peraduenture haue giuen as bad an account of their actions, and therefore I intreat leaue to answer those obiecters, that thinke it strange, if this be true, I haue made no more vse of it, rest so long without imploiment, nor haue no more reward nor preferment: To which I say;

The obiections against me.

I thinke it more strange they should tax me, before they haue tried as much as I haue, both by land and sea, as well in *Asia* and *Affrica*, as *Europe* and *America*, where my Commanders were actors or spectators, they alwaies so freely rewarded me, I neuer needed bee importunate, or could I euer learne to beg: What there I got, I haue spent; yet in *Virginia* I staied, till I left fiue hundred behinde me better prouided then euer I was, from which blessed Virgin (ere I returned) sprung the fortunate habitation of *Summer Iles*.

My answer.

This Virgins Sister, now called *New England*, at my humble sute, by our most gracious Prince *Charles*, hath beene neere as chargeable to me and my friends: for all which, although I neuer got shilling but it cost mee a pound, yet I would thinke my selfe happy could I see their prosperities.

But if it yet trouble a multitude to proceed vpon these certainties, what thinke you I vndertooke when nothing was knowne but that there was a vast land? I

Considerations.

neuer had power and meanes to doe any thing, though more hath beene spent in formall delaies then would haue done the businesse, but in such a penurious and miserable manner, as if I had gone a begging to build an Vniuersitie: where had men beene as forward to aduenture their purses, and performe the conditions they promised mee, as to crop the fruits of my labours, thousands ere this had beene bettered by these designes. Thus betwixt the spur of desire and the bridle of reason, I am neere ridden to death in a ring of despaire; the reines are in your hands, therefore I intreat you ease me, and those that thinke I am either idle or vnfortunate, may see the cause and know: vnlesse I did see better dealing, I haue had warning enough not to be so forward againe at euery motion vpon their promises, vnlesse I intended nothing but to carie newes; for now they dare aduenture a ship, that when I went first would not aduenture a groat, so they may be at home againe by Michaelmas, which makes me remember and say with Master *Hackluit*; Oh incredulitie the wit of fooles, that slouingly doe spit at all things faire, a sluggards Cradle, a Cowards Castle, how easie it is to be an Infidell. But to the matter: By this all men may perceiue, the ordinary performance of this voyage in fiue or six moneths, the plentie of fish is most certainly approued; and it is certaine, from *Cannada* and *New England*, within these six yeeres hath come neere twenty thousand Beuer skinnes: Now had each of these ships transported but some small quantitie of the most increasing Beasts, Fowles, Fruits, Plants, and Seeds, as I proiected; by this time their increase might haue beene sufficient for more then one thousand men: But the desire of present gaine (in many) is so violent, and the endeuours of many vndertakers so negligent, euery one so regarding their priuate gaine, that it is hard to effect any publike good, and impossible to bring them into a body, rule, or order, vnlesse both honesty, as well as authoritie and money, assist experience. But your home-bred ingrossing Proiecters will at last finde, there is a great difference betwixt saying and doing, or those that thinke their directions can be as soone and easily performed, as they can conceit them; or that their conceits are the fittest things to bee put in practise, or their countenances maintaine Plantations. But to conclude, the fishing will goe forward whether you plant it or no; whereby a Colony may be then transported with no great charge, that in short time might prouide such fraughts, to buy on vs there dwelling, as I would hope no ship should goe or come emptie from *New England*.

The charge. The charge of this is onely Salt, Nets, Hookes, Lines, Kniues, Irish-rugges, course cloth, Beads, Glasse, and such trash, onely for fishing and trade with the Saluages, besides our owne necessarie prouisions, whose endeuours would quickly defray all this charge, and the Saluages did intreat me to inhabit where I would. Now all those ships till these last two yeeres, haue beene fishing within a square of two or three leagues, and scarce any one yet will goe any further in the Port they fish in, where questionlesse fiue hundred may haue their fraught as well as elsewhere, and be in the market ere others can haue the fish in their ships, because *New Englands* fishing begins in February, in *Newfoundland* not till the midst of May; the progression hereof tends much to the aduancement of *Virginia* and *Summer Iles*, whose empty ships may take in their fraughts there, and would be also in time of need a good friend to the Inhabitants of *Newfoundland*.

The order of the westerne men. The returnes made by the Westerne men, are commonly diuided in three parts; one for the owner of the ship; another for the Master and his Company; the third for the victualers, which course being still permitted, will be no hinderance to the Plantation as yet goe there neuer so many, but a meanes of transporting that yeerely for little or nothing, which otherwise wil cost many hundreds of pounds. The gaines. If a ship can gaine twenty, thirty, fifty in the hundred; nay three hundred for one hundred in seuen or ten moneths, as you see they haue done, spending twice so much time in comming and going as in staying there: were I there planted, seeing the variety of the fishings serue the most part of the yeere, and with a little labour we might make all the Salt we need vse, as is formerly said, and can

conceiue

conceiue no reason to distrust of good successe by Gods assistance; besides for the building of ships, no place hath more conuenient Harbours, ebbe, nor floud, nor better timber; and no Commoditie in *Europe* doth more decay then wood.

Master Dee *his opinion for the building of ships.*

MAster *Dee* recordeth in his Brittish Monarchy, that King *Edgar* had a Nauy of foure thousand saile, with which he yeerely made his progresse, about this famous Monarchy of *Great Britaine*, largely declaring the benefit thereof; whereupon hee proiected to our most memorable Queene *Elizabeth*, the erecting of a Fleet of sixty Saile, he called a little Nauy Royall: imitating that admired *Pericles* Prince of *Athens*, that could neuer secure that tormented estate, vntill he was Lord and Captaine of the Sea. At this none need wonder, for who knowes not her Royall Maiestie during her life, by the incredible aduentures of her Royall Nauy, and valiant Souldiers and Sea-men, notwithstanding all treacheries at home, the protecting and defending *France* and *Holland*, and reconquering *Ireland*; yet all the world by Sea and Land both feared or loued, and admired good Queene *Elizabeth*. Both to maintaine and increase that incomparable honour (God be thanked) to her incomparable Successor, our most Royall Lord and Soueraigne King *Iames*, this great Philosopher hath left this to his Maiestie and his Kingdomes consideration: that if the tenths of the earth be proper to God, it is also due by Sea. The Kings high waies are common to passe, but not to dig for Mines or any thing: So *Englands* Coasts are free to passe but not to fish, but by his Maiesties Prerogatiue.

The effects of shipping.

His Maiesty of *Spaine* permits none to passe the Popes order, for the East and West Indies but by his permission, or at their perils; if all that world be so iustly theirs, it is no iniustice for *England* to make as much vse of her owne shores as strangers doe, that pay to their owne Lords the tenth, and not to the owner of those liberties any thing to speake of, whose subiects may neither take nor sell any in their Teritories: which small tribute would maintaine this little Nauy Royall, and not cost his Maiesty a peny, and yet maintaine peace with all Forrainers, and allow them more courtesie then any Nation in the world affords to *England*. It were a shame to alleage, that *Holland* is more worthy to enioy our fishing as Lords thereof, because they haue more skill to handle it then we, as they can our wooll and vndressed Cloth, notwithstanding all their warres and troublesome disorders.

The Popes order for the East and West Indies.

To get money to build this Nauy, he saith, who would not spare the one hundreth penny of his rents, and the fiue hundreth penny of his goods; each seruant that taketh forty shillings wages, foure pence; and euery forrainer of seuen yeeres of age foure pence, for seuen yeeres; not any of these but they will spend three times so much in pride, wantonnesse, or some superfluitie: And doe any men loue the securitie of their estates, that of themselues would not bee humble suters to his Maiesty to doe this of free will as a voluntary beneuolence, or but the one halfe of this (or some such other course as I haue prounded to diuers of the Companies) free from any constraint, tax, lottery, or imposition; so it may be as honestly and truly imploied, as it is proiected, the poorest Mechanicke in this King would gaine by it. Then you might build ships of any proportion and numbers you please, fiue times cheaper then you can doe here, and haue good merchandize for their fraught in this vnknowne Land, to the aduancement of Gods glory, his Church and Gospel, and the strengthning and releefe of a great part of Christendome without hurt to any, to the terror of Pirats, the amazement of enemies, the assistance of friends, the securing Merchants, and so much increase of Nauigation, to make *Englands* trade and shipping as much as any Nations in the world, besides a hundred other benefits, to the generall good of all true subiects, & would cause thousands yet vnborne to blesse the time, and all them that first put it in practise.

How to get money to build this little Nauy.

Contention for *New-Englands* goods, not her good.

Now lest it should be obscured as it hath beene to priuat ends, or so weakely vndertaken by our ouerweening incredulity, that strangers may possesse it whilest we contend for *New-Englands* goods, but not *Englands* good; I haue presented it as I haue said, to the Prince and Nobility, the Gentry and Commonalty, hoping at last it will moue the whole land to know it and consider of it; since I can finde them wood and halfe victuall, with the foresaid aduantages: were this Country planted, with what facility they may build and maintaine this little Nauy Royall, both with honour, profit and content, and inhabit as good a Country as any in the world within that paralell, which with my life and what I haue, I will endeuour to effect, if God please and you permit. But no man will goe from hence to haue lesse freedome there then here, nor aduenture all they haue to prepare the way for them will scarce thanke them for it; and it is too well knowne there haue beene so many vndertakers of Patents, and such sharing of them, as hath bred no lesse discouragement then wonder, to heare such great promises and so little performance; in the *Interim*, you see the French and Dutch already frequent it, and God forbid they in *Virginia*, or any of his Maiesties subiects, should not haue as free liberty as they. To conclude, were it not for Master *Cherley* and a few priuate aduenturers with them, what haue we there for all these inducements? As for them whom pride or couetousnesse lulleth asleepe in a Cradle of slothfull carelesnesse, would they but consider how all the great Monarchies of the earth haue beene brought to confusion, or but remember the late lamentable experiences of *Constantinople*, and how many Cities, Townes and Prouinces, in the faire rich Kingdoms of *Hungaria*, *Transiluania*, *Wallachia* & *Moldauia*, and how many thousands of Princes, Earles, Barons, Knights, Merchants, and others, haue in one day lost goods, liues and honours, or sold for slaues like beasts in a market place, their wiues, children and seruants slaine, or wandring they knew not whither, dying or liuing in all extremities of extreme miseries and calamities, surely they would not onely doe this, but giue all they haue to enioy peace and liberty at home, or but aduenture their persons abroad; to preuent the conclusions of a conquering Foe, who commonly assaulteth and best preuaileth where he findeth wealth and plenty, most armed with ignorance and security.

The necessity of martiall power.

Though the true condition of warre is onely to suppresse the proud and defend the innocent, as did that most generous Prince *Sigismundus*, Prince of those Countries, against them whom vnder the colour of iustice and piety, to maintaine their superfluity of ambitious pride, thought all the world too little to maintaine their vice, and vndoe them, or keepe them from ability to doe any thing, that would not admire and adore their honours, fortunes, couetousnesse, falshood, bribery, cruelty, extortion, and ingratitude, which is worse then cowardize or ignorance, and all manner of vildnesse, cleane contrary to all honour, vertue, and noblenesse. Iohn Smith *writ this with his owne hand.*

Here follow certaine notes and obseruations of Captaine *Charles Whitbourne* concerning *New-found land*, which although euery master trained vp in fishing, can make their proportions of necessaries according to their custome, yet it is not much amisse here to insert them, that euery one which desires the good of those actions know them also. Besides in his Booke intituled, *A discouery of New-found land, and the commodities thereof*, you shall finde many excellent good aduertisements for a Plantation; and how that most yeeres this Coast hath beene frequented with 250. saile of his Maiesties subiects, which supposing but 60. tunnes a peece, one with another, they amount to 15000. tunnes, and allowing 25. men and boies to euery Barke, they will make 5000. persons, whose labours returne yeerely to about 135000. pound sterling, besides the great numbers of Brewers, Bakers, Coupers, Ship-Carpenters, Net-makers, Rope-makers, Hooke-makers, and the most of all other mecanicall trades in *England*.

The

The charge of setting forth a ship of 100. tuns with 40. persons, both to make a fishing voyage, and increase the Plantation.

	l. s. d.
INprimis, 10000. *weight of Bisket at 15. s. a 100. weight.*	82. 10.
26 Tun of Beere and Sider at 53. s. 4. d. a Tun.	69. 7.
2 Hogsheads of English Beefe.	10.
2 Hogsheads of Irish Beefe.	5.
10 Fat Hogs salted with Salt and Caske.	10. 10.
30 Bushels of Pease.	6.
2 Ferkins of Butter.	3.
200 Waight of Cheese.	2. 10.
1 Bushell of Mustard-seed.	6.
1 Hogshead of Vinegar.	1. 5.
Wood to dresse meat withall.	1.
1 Great Copper Kettle.	2.
2 Small Kettles.	2.
2 Frying-Pans.	3. 4.
Platters, Ladles and Cans.	1.
a paire of Bellowes for the Cooke.	2. 6.
Taps, Boriers and Funnels.	2.
Locks for the Bread roomes.	2. 6.
100 weight of Candles.	2. 10.
150 quarters of Salt at 2. s. the Bushell.	10. 4.
Mats & dinnage to lie vnder it.	2. 10.
Salt Shouels.	10
Particulars for the 40. persons to keepe 8. fishing boats at Sea, with 3. men in euery boat, imploies 24. and 500. foot of Elme boords of an inch thicke, 8. s. each one.	2.
2000 Nailes for the 8. Boats, at 13. s. 4. d. a 1000.	1. 6. 8.
4000 Nailes at 6. s. 8. d. 1000.	1. 6. 8.
2000 Nailes at 5. d. 100.	8.
500 weight of pitch at 8. s. 100.	2.
2000 of good orlop nailes.	2. 5.
More for other small necessaries.	3.
A barrell of Tar.	10.
200 weight of black Ocome.	1.
Thrums for pitch Maps.	1. 6.
Bolls, Buckets and Pumps.	1.
2 brazen Crocks.	2.
Canuas to make Boat sailes & small ropes, at 25. s. for each saile,	12. 10.
10 rode Ropes which containe 600. weight at 30 s. the 100.	10.
12 dozen of fishing lines.	6.
24 dozen of fishing hookes.	2.
for Squid line.	3.
For Pots and liuer maunds.	18.
Iron works for the boats ruthers.	2.
10 Kipnet Irons.	10.
Twine to make kipnets and gagging hooks.	6.
10 good Nets at 26. s. a net.	13.
2 Saynes, a great and a lesse.	12.
200 weight of Sow-lead.	1.
2 couple of ropes for the Saynes.	1.
Dry-fats to keepe them in.	6.
Twine for store.	5.
Flaskets and bread Baskets.	15.
For haire cloth.	10.
3. Tuns of vinegar caske for water.	1. 6. 8.
1 donzen of Deale Bourds.	10.
2 Barrels of Oatmeale.	1. 6.
100 weight of Spikes.	2. 5.
2 good Axes, 4. hand Hatchets, 4. Drawers, 2. drawing Irons.	16.
3 yards of wollencloth for cuffs.	10.
8 yards of good Cannasse.	10.
A Grind-stone or two.	6.
2000 of poore Iohn to spend in going.	6. 10.
1 Hogshead of Aquauitæ.	4.
4 arme Sawes. 4. Handsawes, 4. thwart Sawes, 3. Augers, 2. Crowes of Iron, 3. Sledges. 4. shod Shouels, 2. Pickaxes, 4. Matocks, and 4. Hammers.	5.
The totall summe is	420. 11. 0.

All these prouisions the Master or Purser is to be accountable what is spent and what is left, with those which shall continue there to plant, and of the 40. thus prouided for the voyage, ten may well be spared to leaue behind them, with 500. weight of Bisket, 5. hogsheads of Sider or beere, halfe a hogshead of Beefe, 4. sides of dry Bakon, 4. bushell of Pease, halfe a ferkin of Butter, halfe 100. weight of Cheese, a pecke of Mustard-seed, a barrell of Vinegar, 12. pound of Candles, 2. pecks of Oa meale, halfe a hogshead of Aquauitæ, 2. copper Kettles, 1. brasse Crock, 1. Frying-pan, a Grindstone, and all the Hatchets, Woodhooks, Sawes, Augers, &c. and all other iron tooles, with the 8. Boats and their implements, and

and spare salt, and what else they vse not in a readinesse from yeere to yeere, and in the meane time serued them to helpe to build their houses, cleanse land, and further their fishing whilst the ships are wanting.

By his estimation and calculation these 8. Boats with 22. men in a Summer doe vsually kill 25000. fish for euery Boat, which may amount to 200000. allowing 120. fishes to the 100. sometimes they haue taken aboue 35000. for a Boat, so that they load not onely their owne ship, but prouide great quantities for sacks, or other spare ships which come thither onely to buy the ouerplus: if such ships come not, they giue ouer taking any more, when sometimes there hath beene great abundance, because there is no fit houses to lay them in till another yeere, now most of those sacks goeth empty thither, which might as well transport mens prouision and cattle at an easie rate as nothing, either to *New-England* or *New-found land*, but either to transport them for nothing or pay any great matter for their liberty to fish, will hardly effect so much as freedome as yet; nor can this be put in practice as before I said, till there be a power there well planted and setled to entertaine and defend them, assist and releeue them as occasion shall require, otherwaies those small diuisions will effect little, but such miserable conclutions as both the French and we too long haue tried to our costs. Now commonly 200000. fish will load a ship of 100. tunnes in *New-found land*, but halfe so many will neere doe it in *New-England*, which carried to *Toloune* or *Merselus*, where the custome is small, and the Kintall lesse then 90. English pounds weight, and the prise when least, 12. shillings the Kintall, which at that rate amounts to 1320.ℓ. starling; and the ship may either there be discharged or imployed as hath beene said to refraught for *England*, so that the next yeere she may be ready to goe her fishing voyage againe, at a farre cheaper rate then before.

To this adde but 12. tuns of traine oile, which deliuered in *New-found land*, is 10.ℓ. the tun, makes 120.ℓ. then it is hard if there be not 10000. of Cor-fish, which also sold there at 5.ℓ. the 1000. makes 50.ℓ. which brought to *England*, in somes places yeelds neere halfe so much more; but if at *Merselus* it be sold for 16.s. the Kentall, as commonly it is, and much dearer, it amounts to 1760.ℓ. and if the Boats follow the fishing till the 15. of October, they may take 80000. more, which with their traine in *New-found land* at 4.ℓ. the 1000. will amount to 320.ℓ. which added to 1320.ℓ. with 120.ℓ. for Oile, and 10000. of Cor-fish 50.ℓ. and the ouerplus at *Merselus*, which will be 440.ℓ. make the totall 2250.ℓ. which diuided in three parts according to their custome, the Victualer hath for the former particulars, amounting to 420.ℓ. 751.ℓ. so all the charge defraied, hee gaines 331.ℓ. 11.s. then for the fraught of the ship there is 751.ℓ. and so much for the Master and his company, which comparing with the voiages hath beene made to *New-England*, you may easily finde which is the better though both bee good.

The facility of the fishing lately obserued.

But now experience hath taught them at *New-Plimoth*, that in Aprill there is a fish much like a Herring that comes vp into the small Brookes to spawne, and where the water is not knee deepe, they will presse vp through your hands, yea though you beat at them with Cudgels, and in such abundance as is incredible, which they take with that facility they manure their land with them when they haue occasion; after those the Cod also presseth in such plenty, euen into the very Harbours, they haue caught some in their armes, and hooke them so fast, three men oft loadeth a Boat of two tuns in two houres, where before they vsed most to fish in deepe water.

The present estate of New-Plimoth.

AT *New-Plimoth* there is about 180 persons, some cattell and goats, but many swine and poultry, 32 dwelling houses, whereof 7 were burnt the last winter, and the value of fiue hundred pounds in other goods; the Towne is impailed about halfe a mile compasse. In the towne vpon a high Mount they haue a Fort well built with wood, lome, and stone, where is planted their Ordnance: Also a faire Watch-tower, partly framed for the Sentinell, the place it seemes is healthfull, for in these last three yeeres, notwithstanding their great want of most necessaries, there hath not one died of the first planters, they haue made a saltworke, and with that salt preserue the fish they take, and this yeare hath fraughted a ship of 180. tunnes. The Gouernour is one Mr. *William Bradford*, their Captaine *Miles Standish*, a bred Souldier in *Holland*; the chiefe men for their assistance is Master *Isaak Alderton*, and diuers others as occasion serueth; their Preachers are Master *William Bruster* and Master *Iohn Layford*.

The present estate of the plantation at New-Plimoth.

1624.

The most of them liue together as one family or houshold, yet euery man followeth his trade and profession both by sea and land, and all for a generall stocke, out of which they haue all their maintenance, vntill there be a diuident betwixt the Planters and the Aduenturers. Those Planters are not seruants to the Aduenturers here, but haue onely councells of directions from them, but no iniunctions or command, and all the masters of families are partners in land or whatsoeuer, setting their labours against the stocke, till certaine yeeres be expired for the diuision: they haue young men and boies for their Apprentises and seruants, and some of them speciall families, as Ship-carpenters, Salt-makers, Fish-masters, yet as seruants vpon great wages. The Aduenturers which raised the stocke to begin and supply this Plantation were about 70. some Gentlemen, some Merchants, some handy-crafts men, some aduenturing great summes, some small, as their estates and affection serued. The generall stocke already imploied is about 7000.P. by reason of which charge and many crosses, many of them would aduenture no more, but others that knowes, so great a designe cannot bee effected without both charge, losse and crosses, are resolued to goe forward with it to their powers; which deserue no small commendations and encouragement. These dwell most about *London*, they are not a corporation, but knit together by a voluntary combination in a society without constraint or penalty, aiming to doe good & to plant Religion; they haue a President & Treasurer, euery yeere newly chosen by the most voices, who ordereth the affaires of their Courts and meetings, and with the assent of the most of them, vndertaketh all ordinary businesses, but in more weighty affaires, the assent of the whole Company is required. There hath beene a fishing this yeere vpon the Coast about 50. English ships: and by Cape *Anne*, there is a Plantation a beginning by the Dorchester men, which they hold of those of *New-Plimoth*, who also by them haue set vp a fishing worke; some talke there is some other pretended Plantations, all whose good proceedings the eternal God protect and preserue. And these haue beene the true proceedings and accidents in those Plantations.

Their order of gouernment.

Now to make a particular relation of all the acts and orders in the Courts belonging vnto them, of the anihilating old Patents and procuring new; with the charge, paines and arguments, the reasons of such changes, all the treaties, consultations, orations, and dissentions about the sharing and diuiding those large territories, confirming of Counsailers, electing all sorts of Officers, directions, Letters of aduice, and their answers, disputations about the Magazines and Impositions, suters for Patents, positions for Freedomes, and confirmations with complaints of iniuries here, and also the mutinies, examinations, arraignements, executions, and the cause of the so oft reuolt of the Saluages at large, as many

would

would haue had, and it may be some doe expect it would make more quarrels then any of them would willingly answer, & such a volume as would tire any wise man but to read the contents; for my owne part I rather feare the vnpartiall Reader wil thinke this rather more tedious then necessary: but he that would be a practitioner in those affaires, I hope will allow them not only needfull but expedient: but how euer, if you please to beare with those errors I haue committed, if God please I liue, my care and paines shall endeuour to be thankfull: if I die, accept my good will: If any desire to be further satisfied, what defect is found in this, they shall finde supplied in me, that thus freely haue throwne my selfe with my mite into the Treasury of my Countries good, not doubting but God will stirre vp some noble spirits to consider and examine if worthy *Columbus* could giue the Spaniards any such certainties for his designe, when Queene *Isabel* of *Spaine* set him forth with 15. saile, and though I promise no Mines of gold, yet the warlike Hollanders let vs imitate but not hate, whose wealth and strength are good testimonies of their treasury gotten by fishing; and *New-England* hath yeelded already by generall computation one hundred thousand pounds at the least. Therefore honourable and worthy Country men, let not the meannesse of the word fish distaste you, for it will afford as good gold as the Mines of *Guiana* or *Potassie*, with lesse hazard and charge, and more certainty and facility. *I. S.*

FINIS.

Errata.

PAg. 1. line 7. for *Quineth* reade *Gwineth*. pag. 153. li. 5. reade *from the company. and* li. 20. for 25000. *pounds* reade 2500. *pounds*. pag. 164. li. 53. for 1500. *men*, reade 150. *men*. pag. 168. li. 11: for *Goston* reade *Gofton*. and *Coranto Quowarranto*, and li. 13 reade before the Iudges in Westminster hall, *for the Lords of his Maiesties Priuy Counsell*. There are many other errors, which being but small I intreat the courteous reader to correct as he findeth them.